MAJ. GEN. LLOYD B. RAMSEY
UNITED STATES ARMY RETIRED

A MEMOIR

Maj. Gen. Lloyd B. Ramsey
U.S. Army Retired

MAJ. GEN. LLOYD B. RAMSEY
U.S. ARMY RETIRED

Copyright © 2006 Maj. Gen. Lloyd B. Ramsey, Ret.

ISBN 0-9786523-0-4
ISBN 987-0-9786523-0-2

No part of this book may be reproduced in any form without written authorization from the author or publisher.

Published by
Clinton County Historical Society
P.O. Box 177
Albany, Kentucky 42602
(606) 387-6021

First Edition Published 2006

Jacket design by Heather Allison Brent

Printed in the United States of America
by: Litho Printers & Bindery
Cassville, Mo 65625

TABLE OF CONTENTS

Foreword...3

Introduction..5

Things that I remember in my early days............................6

Chapter 1: Birth to High School, 1918-1932......................9

Chapter 2: High School, 1932-1936..................................29

Chapter 3: College Period, 1936-1940...............................57

Chapter 4: Entered Army – WWII, 1941-1943................103

Chapter 5: WWII, 1943-1945..131

Chapter 6: Germany – Fort Benning, Georgia..................180

Chapter 7: 1946-1957..210

Chapter 8: 1957-1968..232

Chapter 9: Vietnam, 1968-1970..261

Chapter 10: 1970-1974..298

Chapter 11: Retirement, 1974-2000..................................337

Acknowledgments...375

FOREWORD

There are many biographies and memoirs that cover certain periods of one's life. This Memoir covers the first 84 years of Major General Lloyd B. Ramsey's life. It starts at a time when there were no televisions, radios, telephones, very little electricity, or running water outside of the cities. As General Ramsey grew up, he became president of his junior and senior classes as well as captain of his football team in high school. At the University of Kentucky, he was captain of the freshman football team, captain and coach of the swimming team, vice president of his fraternity, and Cadet Colonel of the ROTC Cadet Corps.

During 34 years in the United States Army, some of his assignments were aide de camp to General Alexander, British, Deputy Commanding General to General Eisenhower, and commander of the forces in the field. He visited many times with Generals Eisenhower, Patton, Bradley, Montgomery (British), and many others. He met King George VI and spent some time with Prime Minister Winston Churchill when he visited General Alexander. Later he commanded an Infantry Battalion in combat for about ten months. He was wounded five times.

After the war, one of General Ramsey's assignments was the Army Senior Liaison Officer to the United States Senate. In this position, he often was called to see Senator Jack Kennedy and Senator Lyndon B. Johnson. He became acquainted with Vice President Richard Nixon and later worked with the House and saw much of Congressman Gerald Ford.

In Vietnam, General Ramsey commanded the Americal Division. When he took command, Major Colin Powell was one of his staff officers. Later he selected a battalion commander – Norman Schwarzkopf – from a group of names. They were both very fine officers. One day, in rainy and cloudy weather, his command helicopter crashed in the jungle and he, the crew, and passengers, were missing for 18 hours. Of the eight people in the helicopter, two were killed and all the others injured. General Ramsey's injuries consisted of five crushed vertebrae and a badly injured left arm. He recovered well from these injuries.

This book warrants the serious attention of anyone who seeks to know how some World War II men were brought up and how they fought in WWII. It also covers many of General Ramsey's actions in Vietnam, plus many of his actions in peacetime.

E. W. WILLIAMSON
Major General, US Army Retired
Arlington, Virginia

INTRODUCTION

This Memoir is dedicated to my late wife Glenda who passed away October 20, 2000. She was my lovely, beautiful, adorable wife, my lover, my best friend, my most loyal supporter, and, after I retired in 1974, my constant companion. She was the wonderful mother of our three outstanding children, the grandmother of our five grandchildren, and the great-grandmother of our two great-grandchildren.

The Memoir is notes in my life, or things that I remember during my lifetime up to November 2000. I have put them together for the benefit of my children, my grandchildren, and other family members or relatives, and for friends who may be interested in my life.

Many of these events are described from memory and may not be correct, especially places, dates, and, in some cases, names. Most of the notes on military events, places, and dates are from histories and should be correct. However, some of my descriptions of the events are based on my memory and should be judged accordingly.

I have not received permission to use anything that I have copied from histories, other books, magazines, newspapers (including pictures), except the book *Combat Medic*, which I have Isadore Valenti's permission to use. When I have quoted from a document, I have given the document credit. I have also published a list of acknowledgments.

My thanks to J. Calvin Liggan for his assistance in keeping my computer going and for helping me with word processing and to Donald E. Prescott for spending many hours editing parts of this manuscript. I have added and revised a number of pages since Don did the editing.

THINGS THAT I REMEMBER IN MY EARLY DAYS

I remember that the horse, horse and buggy, and horse and wagon were the primary means of transportation. If you were going any distance, the train was the way to go. In the cities, you would ride the trolley cars. Very few people had electricity; they depended on kerosene lamps for lighting. Those who had enough money would buy gasoline lamps, which were much brighter than kerosene lamps.

Few people had running water. They got their water from springs, wells, or cisterns. A cistern was a holding tank, and rainwater from the roof of the house was directed into it. Water was cranked up from it by putting tin cups on chains and cranking them up. Since there was no running water, bathroom facilities were sparse. To relieve yourself you had to go to the "outhouse," which was always a good distance from the house for health reasons. The outhouse was a small wooden building with holes for two people cut in the seat. Underneath was a deep trench. The outhouse had no heat or water. Many times, the only toilet paper available was an old Sears and Roebuck catalog. I used the outhouse many times in freezing weather and it was most uncomfortable.

For those that were ill, or the weather was too bad to go to the outhouse, there was a "slop jar" (other names were used) in every bedroom that could be used. A slop jar was about the size of a five-gallon bucket, except that it was a few inches taller. It was covered with enamel and the top edge was curved outward so that you could sit on it. After you used the slop jar, you would pour some water in it and then put the lid on it. The next day you would carry it by its handle and dump the contents into the outhouse. You would then take the slop jar to the house and clean it with boiling water.

Taking a bath was a chore. The houses that had a bathroom had a bathtub. If you did not have a bathroom and tub, you would bathe in a large washtub. You boiled water on the coal stove and carried it to the bathroom. You already had buckets of cold water there so that you could get the water at the right temperature. Those who did not have a bathroom had to find a private place for their washtub bath.

There were no such things as radios or televisions. We received our news from the newspapers and magazines. If you went to a movie, there was no sound; we only had silent pictures and the movie was in black and white. When the actors said something, their words were printed across the bottom of the screen.

CHAPTER 1

BIRTH TO HIGH SCHOOL, 1918 – 1932

1918 – 1921: Birth and Place

I was born on May 29, 1918, on East Mount Vernon Street, Somerset, Kentucky, about one or two blocks from the city limits. The house in which I was born was in the front yard of the home of my grandparent, Napolean L. Barnett. Grandfather had deeded this plot of ground to my mother and father by a hand-written document. My father was William Harold Ramsey, born June 11, 1890. Dad was known to everyone as "Bill." My mother was Mary Ella Barnett Ramsey, born April 22, 1892. My mother was known to everyone as "Mimi." She had dropped her maiden name of Barnett and went by Mary Ella Ramsey.

I am not sure we had electricity and indoor plumbing at this house. I remember that my grandparents did not have indoor plumbing. I remember the well in their backyard where they would pump their water. I can also remember when they got indoor plumbing. I can picture my grandmother doing her laundry in a large black metal tub in the backyard over an open fire. She would give me the job of stirring the clothes in the tub with a long wooden stick. She also used soap that was made at home from the fat of hogs which they had killed for meat.

How I Got the Nickname "Feller"

I was the youngest of three boys, and my dad always referred to me as the "Little Feller." My brothers dropped the word "Little" and started calling me "Feller." Many of my close friends did not know that my real name was Lloyd. The nickname "Feller" stuck with me through college and in the Army until I reached the rank of Colonel on January 31, 1955. The people that I met after that in the Army and civilian life called me Lloyd.

1921: Move to Stanford Pike

In 1921, we moved to a house on Stanford Pike, about one-half mile from the northern city limits of Somerset. This house had no electricity, no running water, and no indoor plumbing. We had a cistern on the back porch. I can remember when my father had an electric wire run from the city to our house. Soon thereafter he had a one-inch water line run to our house and we had indoor plumbing. At the end of this chapter, there is a picture of me sitting on the front porch (Inclusion #1).

1918 –1924: Ice Delivery

During the period of 1918-1924, we either had no electricity, or if we did, we had no electric refrigerator. In those days, there were no electric refrigerators. I am not sure that they had been invented. A horse and wagon would come by the house each day to deliver ice. In order to save time and lots of walking for the iceman, you would put a card in your window that told how much ice you wanted. The ice card was square, about 10" x 10", and on each edge was listed 25–75 –100. The edge that you put at the top meant that you wanted that many pounds. If you did not want ice that day, you did not put a card in the window.

The ice came in 100-pound blocks. The blocks of ice were about two feet high, two feet wide, and about eight inches thick. The blocks were slightly sawed on each side in such a way that the driver, using an ice pick, could split the block into two 50-pound blocks and then split a 50-pound block into two 25-pound blocks. At the end of this chapter there is a diagram of how the card looked and how the block of ice looked (Inclusion #2). With ice tongs, the driver would carry the ice into the house and place it on an icebox that was metal lined.

1918 – 1924: Milk Delivery

We had our own cow so we did not have milk delivered. If you did not have a cow, you could have your milk delivered by horse and buggy. At the end of this chapter is a picture of a horse and buggy that delivered milk in Somerset (Inclusion #3). You would receive the same amount of milk every day unless you left a note telling the milkman or lady to change the amount.

1919: Jennie Vic Barnett Ham's Removal of Her Kidney on the Kitchen Table

As I was growing up, I often wondered what happened to Aunt Ninnie (Jennie Vic) that caused her to use morphine all the time. The following article was written by J. W. Barnett (Wor Wor), Mimi's (Mother) youngest brother, in October 1995, for a Barnett family reunion at Cumberland Falls, Kentucky. Wor Wor had kept up with the family history and wrote interesting articles on all ten children in the N. L. Barnett family. He referred to each of the ten children by number, i.e. the order in which they were born. This is the one that he wrote about Aunt Ninnie.

"#6 – Jennie Vic Barnett Ham (1898 – 1967) was born at 718 East Mount Vernon Street in Somerset, Kentucky. Jennie was named for two of her aunts – Aunt Jennie Brinkley and Aunt Vic Barnett Ellison.

When Jennie was a junior at Somerset High School, she returned home one day after playing a game of basketball. Feeling sick, she went to bed and remained there for three years. Finally, they discovered she had a diseased kidney. There was no hospital in Somerset, nor was there a doctor qualified to perform an operation. Sometime later, a new doctor, Dr. Eugene Beard, a Southern Railroad surgeon, moved to Somerset and took Jennie under his care. When her kidney ruptured, poison was released throughout her body and Dr. Beard said if she didn't have an operation to remove the kidney, she would die.

Not having enough time to take her to Cincinnati, they laid her on our kitchen table. Dr. Beard gave her a shot of morphine to kill the pain and he, with the assistance of Bill Ramsey, removed the kidney. At the time of the operation, it was not known that morphine was habit forming; Jennie remained hooked on it, off and on, for the rest of her life.

Poor Jennie! She was sick and suffered most of her life but did not complain about her misfortune. She married Elmer Ham, who dropped dead while working at the Somerset Vocational School. She lived with #4 (Sis) and #1 (Matt) the last few years of her life and died at the age of 67."

1921: Camping at Age 3

I was three years old in May 1921. My brothers Bill and Jim, six and eight years old, had been taking me to Caney Fork Creek, about one-half mile from where we lived. We had dammed up the creek so that there was a small pool in which to swim. So that they would not have to watch me every minute, they taught me to swim. In those days a person who could swim at three years of age was almost unheard of. Because I could swim, Mimi would let us three boys, and our dog Buck, take a tent and stay at the Creek for three or four days. Dad would check on us two or three times a day.

1921 – 1923: Telephones

I remember my grandparents' old ringer telephone. When you wished to call someone, you had to know how many rings to make. Papa Barnett's ring at work was two rings. Everybody on that line could hear the ring and he or she knew who was being called. If they wanted to listen in on the call, they could, and the caller would never know who was listening. Papa Barnett was the County Judge. I can see Mama going to the phone, giving it two rings to call Papa. He would answer the phone and Mama would say, "Pa, bring home ten cents worth of steak for dinner," or "Pa, we are having company tonight so bring home twenty cents worth of steak."

When we moved to Stanford Pike, we got the modern telephone. It had a mouthpiece on a stand that you either held in your hand or set on the table, and you held the earpiece in the other hand. You could get a private line if one was available, or you might be on a party line. You received your telephone number in the order that the phone was installed. Dad was able to get private lines. His business phone number was 27 at the Gulf Refining Company. It took a while to get a telephone outside the city limits where we lived, so our home phone number was 48. When you picked up the receiver from the phone, the operator would say, "Number, please." You would give her the number and she would plug you into that number and ring the phone. When the operators were really busy, they would sometimes make an error and plug you into another number. You would usually apologize for giving the wrong number or for the operator's mistake.

October 28, 1921: Boston Trip

Dad and Mimi drove to Boston, Massachusetts from Somerset, Kentucky on October 28, 1921, to see the Harvard vs. Centre College football game. The car was called a touring car. The only protection from the weather was to put up the folding top and put on the side curtains. There were no glass windows in car doors in those days. The only glass was the windshield. Side curtains were made with a frame of metal rods covered with leather and, what I remember was called isin-glass, which was the closest thing to plastic in those days. At the end of this chapter (Inclusion #4) is a picture of the car that Dad and Mimi drove to Boston to see Centre College beat Harvard in football.

To travel by car in those days was a real chore. Maps were hard to find and the roads had very few markings. At some intersections you would see a small stone monument that was a road marker. This marker would show you which road to take to the next city and would probably give you the mileage.

October 29, 1921: Harvard vs. Centre College Football

On October 29, 1921, Centre College in Danville, Kentucky, played and beat Harvard in football. Harvard, a powerhouse in football, had won 25 straight games. The Associated Press in 1950 considered this the biggest upset in college football in the half-century.

Centre's Bo McMillin, who later coached at Indiana University and at Philadelphia and Detroit in the NFL, was the hero of the day when he broke loose for a 32-yard touchdown run in the third quarter. Centre also had a formidable football program with a 25-2 record over three seasons leading into this game.

McMillin and James "Red" Roberts, who played without a helmet, were named to Pop Warner's All-American team that season. Bo and Red both played at Somerset High School, Somerset, Kentucky. As I remember the story, Bo's coach from Texas knew Dick Williams in Somerset and sent Bo to Somerset, hoping he could go to Centre College. Dick Williams, Dad, and others got Bo a place to live and sponsored him through high school and Centre College.

The victory by Centre College proved to be a financial windfall for Centre players because a student had been sent to Harvard to place bets. "Bo had more folding money on the night of 29 October 1921, in the lower berth on a Pullman heading back to Kentucky, than could normally be found in a lot of small town banks," sports columnist Earl Ruby reported in The Courier-Journal.

1921 – 1923: First Radio

I can remember the first radio that was in our family. The *World Book Encyclopedia* states: "In 1920 a few hundred amateur-radio fans heard the radio broadcast of the Harding – Cox election returns." The first radio in our family was owned by Dick Ramsey, Dad's half-brother, who was still living at home with his parents, Grandma and Grandpa Ramsey. I remember that Dick's radio had three dials and a very large speaker. On the wall was a large black board where he kept all the information needed to get a radio station. The black board looked something like this:

Station	Dial-1	Dial-2	Dial-3
KDKA	89	91	90

As I recall, KDKA, in Pittsburgh, Pennsylvania, was the first radio station on the air. As new stations appeared, Dick would search his dials and record the station name and dial numbers. It was not very long until a single dial radio was invented, and we soon had a radio.

1924 – 1925: School Teachers

My first grade teacher in 1924 was Mrs. Amelia Saunders, who had also taught my mother and my two older brothers. I understand that Mrs. Saunders taught the first grade in Somerset for about 50 years. She was a local legend, and everyone that she taught had the highest regard for her.

In 1925, I entered the second grade and my teacher was Mrs. Viola Gragg. Mrs. Gragg was a very large woman and very strict. She did not hesitate to spank a student when they did something wrong.

For some reason, I was the teacher's pet. One day I did something wrong, although I do not remember what it was. It was obvious that Mrs. Gragg was upset with me. She told me to come to her desk; instead of spanking me, however, she picked me up and laid me face down on her lap. I could see my fellow students from that embarrassing position. I believe that the same incident caused her to call another student to her desk. She picked him up and laid him on top of me. We stayed in this position for quite some time. I am sure that this taught me a lesson because a spanking was over very quickly, but lying in that position, with someone on top of me, taught me never to do what I had done again.

1926: J. E. Lowhorn

In 1926, J. E. Lowhorn lived next door, and we became very good friends. He would appear at our house looking for me at most anytime. One day, during the week, he came over, knocked on the door, and Mimi answered.

J. E. asked, "Whar's Feller?"

Mimi answered, "He is upstairs taking a bath."

J. E. retorted, "Dis Saturday?"

Another weekday, he came over to play and again he asked Mimi, "Whar's Feller?"

Mimi answered, "He is out on the back porch eating ice cream. Would you like some?"

His response: "Dis Sunday?"

As you can see, J. E. only took baths on Saturdays and only had ice cream on Sundays.

1926: Dad and Frank Barnett Turn a Livery Stable into a Service Station

In 1926, Dad and Uncle Frank Barnett bought a livery stable on the corner of Mt. Vernon Street and Central Avenue in Somerset. Livery stables were places where people stabled their horses, which were fed and cleaned while they were shopping or working. Dad and Uncle Frank were going to turn the livery stable into a service station for care of automobiles. There were not many cars in those days and many people thought that Dad and Uncle Frank were taking a serious risk in trying to sell gasoline and service cars instead of taking care of horses. At the end of this chapter there is a picture of the livery stable and how it looked when converted into a service station (Inclusion #5).

1920s – 1930s: Dad Went to Rotary Club Every Tuesday for Lunch

Dad went to the Rotary Club for lunch every Tuesday. All other days he came home for lunch, and we boys would walk a mile from school to get our lunch. Sometimes Dad would take us back to school, but many times he rested and we would have to walk a mile back to school. On Tuesdays, Mother did not like to cook when Dad was not going to be there. Dad would give each boy 15 cents for lunch. For 15 cents we could buy two hamburgers and a soft drink, such as orange pop, Pepsi Cola, or Coca Cola. I remember when Pepsi Cola came out with its 12-ounce bottle with the jingle:

> *Pepsi Cola hits the spot*
> *Twelve full ounces that's a lot*
> *Twice as much for a nickel too*
> *Pepsi Cola is the drink for you.*

May 21-22, 1927: Lindbergh, the First Man to Fly the Ocean

On May 21-22, 1927, I well remember when Captain Charles A. Lindbergh flew his monoplane from New York to Paris in 33 ½ hours, a distance of 3,800 miles at a speed of 113 miles per hour. As a newspaper said, "The first man in history to go from New York to Paris without changing his seat...his landing tonight made him the greatest of heroes mankind has produced since the air became a means of travel."

1920s – early 1930s: We Had Pigs, Chickens, Cows, Horse or Pony, and a Large Garden

As I was growing up, I had to help take care of the pigs, chickens, cow, horse or pony, and I also had to work in the garden. We had about two acres of land so we had plenty of room for the animals and a garden. Dad raised the pigs, had them slaughtered and cut up, and that was a lot of our meat for the year. We had chickens that laid eggs and young chickens that we would kill to eat. I gathered the eggs almost every day. I learned to milk the cow at a very early age. I remember that we had one cow that would kick over the milk bucket, so Dad bought kicking chains to use on the cow. This solved the problem, but I hated to put on those kicking chains. We had a cat with a curly tail and we called her "Curly." She would always go to the barn with me to milk the cow. Curly would sit up and I would squirt milk, which she loved, into her mouth.

We would cool the milk and drink it. We would churn butter. To make butter, you would save enough cream off the top of the milk and put the cream in a wooden churn. The churn was a wooden cylinder about three feet high and about eight inches in diameter. A removable top was on the cylinder with a hole in the center; a wooden pole came through the hole. On the end of the pole there was a type of paddle. We would sit behind the churn, with our legs around the churn, and raise the pole up and down until the cream got thicker and thicker and finally became butter. This process took quite a bit of time.

As time progressed, we had margarine. You bought it in a block and it looked like a block of lard. It had coloring that came with it. You poured in the color and with your hands you had to mix the margarine and the coloring until it looked like butter. This was very hard and time consuming. Sometimes, after it was supposedly mixed well, you would take a slice of margarine and some of it still looked like lard. Even though the coloring had no taste, most of us would not eat the white margarine that had not been colored.

I hated to work in the garden, but it had to be done. We did not have a very large garden, so it really did not take much of my time, especially when Bill and Jim helped.

We all enjoyed our horse or pony, whichever we had at the time. For years we had one or the other.

About 1928: Trip to Creelsboro, Kentucky

Around 1928, Grandpa Ramsey wanted to go to Creelsboro, Kentucky, about 45 or 50 miles away on the Cumberland River in Russell County, to visit some of his close relatives that he had not seen for some time. He did not have a car so he was going by horse and buggy (just like the one in Inclusion #3 that delivered milk). He asked me to go with him. The time was either late spring or early fall. Grandpa bought me a pack of Juicy Fruit gum to keep me occupied. We left about 3 a.m. and arrived there in the late afternoon.

Some of the roads were washed out and were not wide enough for the buggy to pass. I remember Grandpa Ramsey telling me to lead the horse, keeping it very close to the upper bank, while he put his feet on the hubs of the buggy, on the upper bank side, and held the uprights to the buggy top to balance the buggy, which had two wheels hanging over the washed-out portion of the road. In this way we managed to get through those bad places.

This was a very interesting trip for a young boy - one that I will never forget. I chewed the entire pack of gum on the way down and back.

About 1928: Jim Was in the Eighth Grade and Got a Spanking

I will always remember when Jim was in the eighth grade and his teacher was Aunt Della Ramsey, who was the wife of Ray Ramsey, Dad's half-brother. Aunt Della was a great teacher, but she was tough on her students. One day she thought that Jim had done something wrong so she gave him a spanking. In those days, they always called the mother or father to tell them what had happened.

When Dad came home and found out about the incident, he called Jim into the bedroom and asked him what had happened. Jim told Dad that he had not done anything. This made Dad angry because Dad was sure that Jim had done something wrong and now he was lying. Dad picked up the nearest hairbrush, which had raised places on the back, and gave Jim a very hard spanking. The next day, Jim's rear was black and blue and swollen. After Jim got to school, Aunt Della decided to make further checks on the incident that had happened the day before.

She then found out that Jim was not involved and she apologized for the spanking. She also called home to tell Mimi of her error and that she had apologized to Jim.

Dad was very tough on us, but this was one time that big tears came into his eyes as he tried to make up to Jim for not believing his story.

1924: Somerset Golf Course

In 1924 Dad, Paul Dexheimer, and some other businessmen in Somerset decided to build a golf course. This was before the Depression. They built a nine hole course about one-half mile north of our house. I became a caddy and was paid 25 cents for nine holes, 50 cents for 18 holes. Tipping was never done at that course.

About 1930, I decided that what was needed was a soft drink stand. Dad agreed and bought me an icebox and the first soft drinks and candy to sell. After that I was on my own. Under the porch of the clubhouse, I built a room out of scrap lumber and set up my soft drink stand. On good days, I would make a profit between $1.00 and $2.00, which was more than caddying for 50 cents, and it was not as hard but was longer hours. I did very well until one night someone broke into my stand and stole most of my drinks and candy. Thank goodness I did not keep much stock, but it took me about two weeks to recover my loss.

Late 1920s and Early 1930s: Uncle Olaf Peterson, a Man of Brilliance

I can remember in the late 1920s that my Uncle Olaf Peterson was always coming up with new ideas. In those days, he designed a system to grind up coal and blow it from Rockcastle County, Kentucky, to Cincinnati, Ohio. People thought that he was crazy, but such systems have been studied many times over the years by large companies. Uncle Olaf cooled his house in the summer by using the water from his well. He said that he could heat from the same source, but he never got that far. Such heat pump systems are used today.

1929: Pillow Fight between Jim and Feller

About 1929, Jim and I had a pillow fight in our bedroom. We had beds in the same room. His bed was against the wall and my bed was under the front windows. One night after we were supposed to be going to sleep, we got into a pillow fight. Jim threw a pillow at me but it missed me and hit one of the windows above my bed, breaking it. Of course it made a loud crash.

Mimi came upstairs and asked, "Who broke the window and how?"

We both tried to tell Mimi our story and finally what she heard from me was, "We were having a pillow fight and Jim threw a pillow at me that missed and broke the window above my bed."

From Jim she heard, "I agree that we were having a pillow fight and that I threw the pillow, but it was Feller's fault because he ducked."

Late 1920s: One of Dad's Favorite Stories

In the late 1920s Dad used to tell a story that we used at meals many times. There was a group of people having a meal. The host was an elderly person who was hard of hearing. After the meal was over the elderly host asked one of the guests:

Host: "Have you had enough to eat?"
Guest: "I have had a sufficiency."
Host: "You've been a fishin."
Guest: "I have had plenty."
Host: "You caught twenty."
Guest: "You darned old fool."
Host: "And broke your pole, well that is the luck of a fisher man."

1929: Barnett Family Reunion

In 1929 the Barnett family had a reunion. At the end of this chapter, Inclusion #6, is a picture of those present. The names have been typed on the picture. Wor Wor, the youngest of the ten children, started calling them by number in the order that they were born. That is why the numbers are on the picture.

1929 – About 1932: The Great Depression

The Great Depression started in 1929 and lasted until Roosevelt became President in 1932. Many banks closed and some people lost all of their money. Dad seemed to get along fairly well, but I can remember him cutting out cardboard and putting it in his shoes because the soles were worn out and he could not afford to have new soles. The cardboard would keep his feet from touching the ground where there were holes in his shoe. For two or three years we never had new clothes. I can remember people going hungry and people sharing food with their neighbors. The Depression days are hard to explain unless you went through those rough years.

March 3, 1931: The Star Spangled Banner Became Our National Anthem

As I was growing up, we always sang the Star Spangled Banner as our National Anthem. Francis Scott Key wrote it on September 14, 1814. I well remember March 3, 1931, when Congress passed legislation to make the Star Spangled Banner our official National Anthem.

1920s: Playing the Victrola Was Our Music

Before radios came in, about 1921-1923, and for some time thereafter, the phonograph (victrola) was our main source of music. The victrola was a cabinet about four feet tall and about 18 inches on each side, sitting on four legs. You could raise the top and there was a place to play a record. To play the machine, you had to turn a crank on the right side to wind it up. There was an arm with a round head that had a needle. You would place the needle on the record, push a start switch, and it would play about three records before you had to crank it up again. As I recall, you had to replace the needle after about 10 records were played. If you bought cheap needles, you would have to replace the needles more often. You could tell by the sound of the record when the needle was going bad. Playing a record with a bad needle could ruin a record very quickly. The records and extra needles were stored in the bottom of the cabinet.

About 1930 or 1931: I Had Scarlet Fever

About 1930-1931, I had scarlet fever, which in those days had a high fatality rate. I was a very sick boy and I understood that my chances of survival were very slim. I can well remember how all of my skin peeled off and my bed looked as if it were filled with dandruff. I could take large pieces of skin from my feet. All of my hair came out, but as I lost hair, new hair would come in, so I was never bald. As the new hair came in, it turned curly. The doctors and the Good Lord pulled me through this illness, and I never had any lasting results. My hair stayed curly until the early 1940s when I started wearing an Army helmet. The helmet made my hair straight again.

The Ramsey House on Stanford Pike.
Feller with our dog Buck.

INCL. # 1

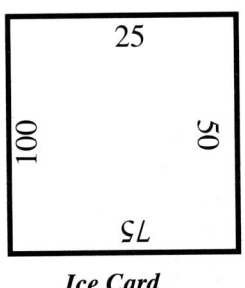

Ice Card

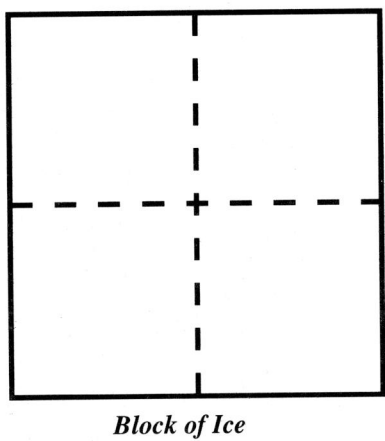

*Block of Ice
Showing
Sawed Grooves*

INCL. # 2

If you did not have a cow so that you could produce your own milk you could have your milk delivered by horse and buggy like the one shown here. You would receive the same amount of milk every day unless you left a note telling the milk man or lady to change the amount.

Minnie Massey delivered milk on the streets of Somerset for 27 years. Sweet milk was 20 cents per gallon and buttermilk was 10 cents per gallon during this time.

INCL. # 3

This is the car that Mimi and Dad drove to Boston, Mass. in 1921, to see Centre beat Harvard in football.

INCL. # 4

The Livery Stable in downtown Somerset. This picture was taken at the "turn of the century". This stable became Frank's Service Station which is pictured below.

Frank Barnett, operator of Frank's Service Station, in 1926. Frank's Service Station was on the corner of East Mount Vernon Street and South Central Avenue, and sold Indian Gas which later became Gulf Gas.

INCL. # 5

INCL. # 6

CHAPTER 2

HIGH SCHOOL, 1932 – 1936

1932 – 1936: Blue Bird Swimming Pool

Blue Bird swimming pool was on old route U.S. 27, about three miles north of Somerset, Kentucky. It was operated by Clyda and Ray Reid and it cost 15 cents to swim. Some of my friends and I would go there when we did not go to the river. Before Dad had the houseboat, I would go there more often. The pool had a low diving board, a 10-foot high platform, and a rope swing with a ramp to climb up to get a swing. My brothers had taught me to swim at age three, so by 1932 I was a very good swimmer and had taught myself how to dive. I learned the following dives: swan, jack knife, forward flip, 1 ½ forward flip, ½ gainer, full gainer, back dive, back flip, and back 1 ½ flip.

I could do some of these things coming off the rope swing. Some of my friends could do some of these dives but not all of them. On Saturdays and Sundays, we noticed that more people were coming to swim, but mostly to observe our diving from the low board, high platform, and the rope swing. They would buy refreshments. One day Ray Reid told me that because my diving was drawing more people to the pool to swim or watch, I could swim for free. None of my friends received that offer.

Strange Use of the Alphabet

Sometime during my high school days I learned about the strange use of the alphabet. You can either say or write the following, and then ask what it says. Very few people could make sense of the letter.

ABCD – Goldfish
LMNO – Goldfish
SMR – Goldfish
CM – Goldfish

Translated:
Abbie, see the gold fish
Hell, them no goldfish

Yes, them are goldfish
See them goldfish.

Another strange use of the alphabet made a Christmas card:
ABCDEFGHIJKMNOPQRSTUVWXYZ.

Most people could not make anything out of these letters. But if you asked them if any letters were left out, they would say yes, there is no L. You are right, that is a Christmas card– NOEL.

Another strange use of the alphabet is called Alfalfa language. It went something like this:

Dil fid yul ulfunder stal fand me'l fe?
(Did you understand me?)

Yel fes I'l file dil fid.
(Yes I did.)

To speak this language you had to do the following: put an L after the first vowel, then put an F in front of the same vowel, such as the first word in the example. Did becomes Dil fid.

After my children were born, Lloyd Ann and Judi picked up this language very early, and I could converse easily with them but no one else would understand us.

1932 – 1936: Dad Built a Houseboat on the Cumberland River

Dad always had some kind of boat on the Cumberland River. The first boat that I remember was named "KAZAN." I believe this boat was built by Ralph Longsworth, who had a lumber yard in Somerset. The boat had an old Chevrolet engine that was left uncovered. You could carry as many as eight or ten people on board.

Dad then decided that he wanted a houseboat. He bought an old wooden barge about 50 feet long and 10 feet wide. We all helped build the houseboat, which had three bedrooms, a kitchen, a dining room, and a large covered deck about 14 x 20 feet square. There was a walkway on each side of the boat that hung over the barge. At the end of one walkway was a toilet that hung over the water (not very sanitary). Two of the three bedrooms had bunk beds. Mimi and Dad's bedroom was large enough for a double bed. Each room had a pitcher and a wash pan so that you could wash your face and hands. The kitchen had a three burner kerosene stove with an oven and a few shelves to store the dishes, glasses, and food. It had an icebox, which would hold about 25 pounds of ice. All of the rooms and the deck were lighted with kerosene lamps. (I have one of those lamps somewhere in storage.) We either had to bring water to the houseboat or get it out of springs along the river.

We tied up most of the time at the Cascades, which was about one-half mile down the river from Burnside, Kentucky. The water coming out of the Cascades was good drinking water. Our other most used location was a place called Slate Branch, about one-half mile down the river from Waitsboro or about three miles from Burnside. The water at Slate Branch was also good to drink. To move the boat we would pull it with the KAZAN. When we were not on the houseboat, we left it at Waitsboro, where the ferry people that Dad hired would take care of it. A picture of the houseboat is at the end of this chapter (Inclusion #1).

There is a small houseboat tied to the back of Dad's houseboat.

In addition to the ferry at Waitsboro, there were two ferries at Burnside. One took cars and wagons across the Cumberland River on U.S. Highway 27. The other took cars and wagons across the South Fork River on Kentucky Highway 90. All ferries were guided across the river by a wire line that went through pulleys on the ferry. These wire lines dropped deep enough so that motor boats could cross over them. The ferries were moved by a small boat attached to the ferry. The boat was powered by a Model T Ford engine and had to be cranked to start. The boat was tied to the ferry at the front end of the boat. After each crossing the boat would be swung around and would push the ferry in the other direction. The Model T Ford engine had a direct drive to the propeller so the motor had to be stopped before the end of each trip and then hand-cranked for the next crossing. I do not remember the cost to cross, but it was either 25 or 50 cents for cars and 50 or 75 cents for trucks. The ferry could haul three cars or two trucks.

After spending some time on the river, I decided that the KAZAN should be remodeled. Dad gave me permission to put on a roof and to enclose the motor. The roof would make the boat more comfortable in the hot sun. Enclosing the motor would make the ride less noisy and would look much better. I had to change the steering wheel from a side wheel to a front wheel drive.

Dad bought a small outboard motor that we could use on the rowboat that he had built. This worked well for moving back and forth, but I wanted more speed. I found a homemade hull that had buckled so badly the owner did not believe it could be fixed, so he gave it to me. I took it to our barn and worked slowly and methodically to cut out some of the buckles. I then used long screws to pull the remaining part of the buckle down and put in caulking (hemp) until it looked as if it were sealed. Water tests proved that it was sealed.

I put Dad's outboard motor on this boat, and it was amazing how fast the boat would travel. I then decided that it was time for an aquaplane. I checked on the cost and it was more than I could afford so I made my own aquaplane. It worked well. The small boat would pull the aquaplane but it needed more power. Starling Gregory and I went together and bought a much larger outboard motor which had enough power to pull the aquaplane with no problem. This was the only aquaplane on the river. People would come from miles around on the weekends to see Starling and me ride it. My dog, Chief, loved to ride on the aquaplane with me. He could ride alone as long as we went straight, but on a turn, you had to lean on the board and Chief could not do that. I could stand on my head on the aquaplane. A picture of me doing just that is at the end of this chapter (Inclusion #2).

1932 – 1936: Dad Got Another Boat

Dad wanted a boat that was larger than the KAZAN. I am not sure whether he had the new one built or whether he bought it from someone. It was larger than the KAZAN and had a top and side curtains. You could spend the night on this boat, as we boys did many times. Dad named the boat JO JO after his first grandchild. The JO JO was much more comfortable than the KAZAN and had more speed, but it was not very fast. A picture of the JO JO is at the end of this chapter (Inclusion #3).

1932 – 1936: Fannie Brown's Restaurant, Burnside, Kentucky

Fannie Brown had a restaurant in Burnside, Kentucky, about five miles south of Somerset. It was near the Cumberland River ferry crossing on U.S. Highway 27. The restaurant was very close to the river. Fannie had one long table that would seat about 16 people, where she would serve the food family style. You could eat all you wanted for 25 cents. The men from around the river, we called them river rats, would come in, and there would be a large crowd for about an hour. Fannie was a heavy-set lady. She ran the cash register and barked out the orders to her husband, who did all the work in the kitchen. Fannie kept the one dollar bills in the cash register and kept the larger bills in her stocking. I am told that she did this for safety. They tell the story that she was held up more than once and had given the robber the money in the cash register. The robbers usually knew the other money was in her stocking and wanted that money also. She told them if they wanted the money, they would have to take it from her. The story goes that no one ever took any money from her stocking and would leave with a few one dollar bills from the cash register.

1932 – 1936: High School Band

I played in the high school band for four years. My main instrument was the E-flat tuba, although I could play other instruments.

In 1933, the state contest for musical instruments was held in Lexington, Kentucky. For some reason, our band director signed me up to try out for a place in the E-flat tuba contest. As far as I was concerned, I was not qualified to play that kind of instrument. When we arrived in Lexington, we discovered that the person responsible for loading the bus had failed to load my tuba. The band leader finally was able to borrow an E-flat tuba in time for me to practice a little. I found the mouthpiece to be very different from the one that I had used. With very little practice and a different mouthpiece, I was sure that I did not have a chance even to place in the contest. Since I felt that I had no chance, I was not worried and played my song as I had never played it before. To my great surprise, when they announced the winning places, I was number one. Can you imagine me, a poor instrument player and playing on a borrowed instrument, winning the Kentucky state contest with the E-flat tuba?

February 1935: Guilty Verdict Regarding Lindbergh's Son

Captain Charles A. Lindbergh, who was the first man to fly the Atlantic on May 21, 1927 (see previous remarks regarding Lindbergh in Chapter 1), learned that his infant son, who had been kidnapped, had been murdered.

On February 13, 1935, a jury in Flemington, New Jersey, found Bruno Richard Hauptmann guilty of first degree murder in the kidnap and death of the infant child. Hauptmann was later executed.

1932 – 1936: My High School Days

Inclusion #4 is taken from the 1936 Homespun "Scrapbook," published and printed by the Somerset High School Press. I was deeply involved in school activities, but some of the dates are not correct. These are the correct dates.

Freshman Chorus – 1933
Football – 1932, 33, 34, 35
Captain Football – 1935
Basketball – 1933, 34, 35, 36
    (played very little in 1936 but will discuss reason later)
Male Chorus – 1934, 35, 36
Jolly Tars – play – lead part – 1933
Chonita – play – lead part – 1934
H.M.S. Pinafore – play – lead part – 1935
President Home Room – 1933, 35
President Junior Class – 1935
President Senior Class – 1936
Track – 1933 (We did not have track after that.)
Male Quartet – 1934, 35, 36
S Club – 1933, 34, 35, 36; President – 1936
Hi-Y – 1933
Science Club – 1934
Latin Club – 1934

Mixed Chorus – 1933, 34, 35, 36
Mikado – play – lead part – 1936
Mixed Quartet – 1935, 36
    Band – 1933, 34, 35, 36
        (was the drum major when needed)
    Won State contest for E-flat bass horn (tuba) – 1933
    Vocal Solo – 1935, 36

May 29, 1934: My 16th Birthday

On May 28, 1934, we went to the houseboat for the first time since the winter. Mimi and Dad were very happy to get down there again and to get the boat cleaned up and ready for summer use. The next day, May 29, was my 16th birthday. I woke up that morning expecting Dad to come in, give me a small spanking, and then roll me under the bunk (bed) as he always did to us three boys. All day went by without a word, so I expected that maybe they were going to surprise me with something. About bedtime, as we were sitting on the deck, I stood up and tearfully said, "Thank you for a very nice 16th birthday." Of course, Mimi and Dad were crushed that they had forgotten my birthday because of the opening of the houseboat for the summer. For the next few days I was treated like a king.

1932 – 1936: Painted Gasoline Pumps and Other Equipment during the Summer

During my high school days, when they could get me off the river, Dad, who owned the local Gulf Refining Company distributorship had us painting gasoline pumps and other equipment. That was very hot work in the sun. We made $1.00 a day. Even so, I did not miss many days either at the river or the swimming pool.

1932 – 1936: Dad Bought into Another Business

Between 1932 and 1936, Dad and two other men set up a new business - The Denny-Murrell-Ramsey Funeral Home. I believe that Dad did fairly well in this business because it was needed in Somerset at that time. They had a town hearse and a country hearse. The country hearse was used when they had to bury someone who lived on the bad country roads.

One day they had to deliver a casket over some bad country roads. Milford Waddle, who worked at the funeral home, asked me to go with him. It was not a day for swimming so I agreed. After we delivered the casket, we had engine trouble with the hearse. We finally pulled into a grocery store with one gasoline pump and asked the owner if he could tell what was wrong. He said he was not sure, but if we tried to drive it any farther the motor would freeze. Milford asked where the nearest phone was. He was told that it was at a house about a mile down the road and that there was no transportation available. Milford said that he would go make a call and that I could wait at the store. I decided to climb into the hearse and take a nap. While I was sleeping, two men walked up and saw me. While looking at me, the owner came out and told them how I was killed. About that time, I woke up and moved. When I got out of the hearse, the owner showed me the two men running down the road. He then told me the story that he had told them.

1935: Drove from Somerset, Kentucky to Orlando, Florida in a Model T Ford

In 1934-1935, I was dating a girl from Longwood, Florida, near Orlando, who had come to Somerset to live with her uncle and to attend high school for a year. During the summer of 1935, she had returned to Longwood. A friend of mine and I decided to drive there for a visit. I owned a Model T Ford, and we decided to drive that to Florida. A Model T Ford would not go more than 35 to 40 miles per hour, and Florida was a long way. We were doing fine until the timing gear stripped a cog. We had no money to get it fixed, but we managed to get to a used car lot. The owner was very nice and helped us get a timing gear off an old car. We looked like we needed help so he sold us the part for $1.00 and then took the time to explain how to replace the gear. We did exactly what he told us to do and it worked.

The Model T Ford did not have a gear shift. It had three pedals to shift from low to high and reverse. The pedals used pads that had to be replaced a number of times during the trip. We knew that the pads would wear out so we kept some in stock. That was some trip. I would never try to travel that far again in a Model T Ford.

1935: Going to Lock 21 on the Jo Jo, We Killed a Six-Foot Shovel Bill Catfish

In the summer of 1935, a group of us decided to boat to Lock 21, about 20 to 25 miles away. We were almost to the locks when the propeller hit something. I was the pilot, and I immediately stopped the propeller to reduce any further damage. I reached over the end of the boat to see if a log had been caught between the propeller and the boat, which happened often. To my surprise, I felt flesh, and I wondered if it was a person. I told the people in the boat what I felt and said that I was going to bring it up. When I got it up, we found out that we had hit and killed a shovel bill catfish. The fish was about 4 ½ feet long, and the shovel bill was about 1 ½ feet long, for a total of six feet. Some of the old fishermen told me that it was not unusual for a shovel bill catfish to strike at a shiny moving propeller. However, most of them were no more than about two feet long. This was the longest one that the old fishermen had seen or heard of.

1935: Football Team, Elected Captain

I was elected captain of the 1935 Somerset High School football team, known as the "Briar Jumpers." We played nine games, won seven, tied one, and lost one, and we won the Central Kentucky Conference (CKC) championship. There is a picture of the football team at the end of this chapter (Inclusion #5). At Inclusion #6 there is a picture and write-up about me and a team article. At Inclusion #7 there is an article on the 1936 "All CKC Team." I received an honorable mention.

I had the reputation of being one of the best blocking backs in the CKC and was developing into a better ball carrier. I did all the kicking (kick-offs, punts) and extra points. During the season, my right leg started to hurt. The doctors could not find anything wrong. Since this was my fourth year of playing football, and being captain of the team, they were sure that I was having trouble, but they could not help me. I played the season in pain and had a good season, but I believe that I could have done better had I been free of pain. In late December 1935, I was practicing basketball, still in pain, getting ready for the season. I went in for a lay-up, and when I came down, my right leg collapsed and I went down. I went to our team doctor and he could see a large indentation in my upper thigh. He sent me to a Lexington doctor who said that I had a ruptured thigh muscle that could be corrected with surgery.

1935: Social Security Act

I remember when President Roosevelt signed the Social Security Act of 1935. Many people thought that it was too expensive while others thought that the system would improve retirement benefits.

I remember when Uncle Hampie, Mimi's older brother, retired from the railroad. They did not have to pay into Social Security; however, after he retired, he was on some board and paid into Social Security. When he drew his first Social Security check, he drew more money in his first check than he had paid into Social Security. That was at age 65, and he drew Social Security until he died in his 80's.

1935: Basketball Winner of the 36th District Tournament

At the end of this chapter (Inclusion #8) is a picture of me and other members of the 1935 Somerset High School basketball winners of the 36th District Tournament. I played first string guard on the team.

January 1936: Good Samaritan Hospital, Lexington, Kentucky

In January 1936, I went to the Good Samaritan Hospital, Lexington, Kentucky, for the operation on my leg. The operation went well. The most interesting thing that happened to me while I was there was the number of visitors, cards, and letters that I received. I will only mention a few. Of course Mimi and Dad were there most of the time. On some days, Dad would drive to Somerset to work and drive back at night. The preacher Lee Davis Fisher from the First Christian Church in Somerset was known as everybody's preacher. He was one of my first visitors and came back every day or so while I was there. Another frequent visitor was Elvis Stahr, President of the Lambda Lambda Chapter, Sigma Chi, at the University of Kentucky. He heard or read about my reputation in high school and started recruiting me for Sigma Chi, which I joined in the fall. Elvis was an outstanding student and a Rhodes Scholar. He later became Dean of the University of Kentucky Law School, President of West Virginia University, Pennsylvania

University, and then the University of Indiana. He also became the Secretary of the Army and later President of the National Audubon Society. He served in the army for a while during World War II. While he was in the army, we renewed our contact, and we kept in touch with each other from then on. As I recall, Elvis received around 50 honorary degrees. In Washington, D.C., about 1998, Elvis was receiving another award and invited me to attend. During his speech to over 300 people, he referred to me as his best and oldest friend and then went on to say some nice things about my military career. Then he asked me to stand up and be recognized. What a thrill from such an outstanding person!

I was thrilled to receive a letter from my English teacher, Mildred Ellis. A copy of her letter is included at the end of this chapter (Inclusion #9).

I also received a letter from Chris Purdom, my high school principal for three years, who had moved to Lancaster, Kentucky as superintendent before my senior year started. He was a very thoughtful man. A copy of his letter is included at the end of this chapter (Inclusion #10).

Three Awards That I Received in High School

A few awards were given by various organizations in Somerset. In four years I received three. They are shown at the end of this chapter (Inclusion #11). The three awards were:

> The Freshman Citizenship Prize - $2.50
> Senior Efficiency Prize - $10.00
> The George Dugan Convese Athletic Prize - $5.00.
> Senior Year – Selected as "Best All-Around"

During my senior year in high school, my classmates were very good to me. In addition to being elected captain of the football team and president of my class, I was selected as the male "Best All-Around" student. To me, this was a great honor. At the end of this chapter is a picture that shows the "Best Students" and "Best All-Around" (Inclusion #12).

Commencement Program

The commencement program for the Somerset High School graduating class of 1936 is at the end of this chapter (Inclusion #13).

1937: Trip to Arizona to Pick Up Mama Barnett and Take Her to Gary, Indiana

In the summer of 1937, Mama Barnett, Mimi's mother, had been visiting in Arizona with her son, N. L. Barnett. She had been there for some time and wanted to be picked up and taken to Gary, Indiana, to visit with her daughter, Delia Barnett Naive. Jim and I said that we would make the trip if we had a car. Demra Taylor, husband of Mimi's youngest sister, offered his car for the trip. Aunt Estelle Peterson from Somerset went with us. We departed Somerset, Kentucky, on June 4, 1937, and returned about the middle of July.

Mama Barnett wanted to see California, so we had a very long trip. In Los Angeles, we stopped at the Rose Bowl. Mama stayed in the car because it was too far for her to walk. When Aunt Estelle, Jim, and I returned, we noticed that Mama appeared to be upset. She then told us what had happened. A man saw our car from Kentucky and he was from Kentucky so he came over to speak to Mama. He introduced himself and Mama said that she was Mrs. N. L. Barnett from Somerset, Kentucky. The man said that he used to work on the railroad with a man by the name of Bob Barnett, and he thought that he was from Somerset and asked Mama if she knew him. Mama said that she repeated the name and said that she did not know a Bob Barnett. After the man left, Mama said that she kept thinking about this Bob Barnett, and it finally dawned on her that it was her son, Robert, who she always referred to as Robert and never Bob. The man had been gone for some time, so it was too late to correct her mistake.

About 1936: First Baptist Church – Dad Was the Choir Leader

Dad was the choir leader of the First Baptist Church, Somerset, for many years. Brother Hunter was the preacher for many of those years. Once or twice a year, Brother Hunter would preach on prohibition, the evils of alcohol, or some subject involving whiskey. In those days, we had no air conditioning. Men always wore a coat and tie and never removed their coats in public, regardless of the heat. In the pews, there were always enough fans for everyone to have one. Many women brought their own fancy fans to use in church.

On one hot Sunday in July, with everyone using their fans, Brother Hunter had been preaching one of his sermons on the evils of alcohol. As we perspired, we could hear the town clock strike 12. Shortly thereafter, he ended his sermon by saying: "If I had all of the barrels and bottles of wine, whiskey, and beer in this world, I would take them down to the banks of the Cumberland River (the Cumberland River was about seven miles away), and I would take a sledge hammer and break the barrels and bottles and let them pour into the river."

He then turned to Dad and said, "Brother Ramsey, what shall we sing?"

Dad replied, "Page 72, 'Shall We Gather at the River'!"

This story has been told on Dad for many years as a true story. You must remember that the song selections were always made before the sermon and printed on the bulletin, so it could have happened.

Old Houseboat from Far away

Top Photo: The houseboat that Dad and all of us built. A smaller houseboat is tied to the rear of Dad's houseboat.
Lower Photo: This shows the large deck that was on the houseboat. The deck was about 14'x20'.

INCL. # 1

*Feller standing on his head
on a homemade Aquaplane.*

INCL. # 2

The JoJo

INCL. # 3

LLOYD RAMSEY
Freshman Chorus '33; Football '33 '34, '35, '36, Captain '36; Basketball '33, '34, '35, '36; Male Chorus '34, '35 '36; Jolly Tars '33; Chonita '34; H. M. S. Pinafore '35; Pres. of Home Room '33, '35; Pres. of Junior Class '35; Pres. of Senior Class '36; Track '33; Quartet '34, '35, '36; S Club '33, '34, '35, '36; Hi-Y '33; Science Club '34; Latin Club '34; Mixed Chorus '33, '34 '35, '36; Mixed Octet '34, '35, '36; Mikado '36; Mixed Quartet '35, '36; Band '33, '34, '35, '36; Won State Contest of E Flat bass Horn (Tuba) '33; Vocal Solo '35, '36

VIRGINIA TAYLOR
Freshman Chorus '33; Painist for Freshman Chorus; Girl Reserves '33, '34, '35; Glee Club '34, '35, '36; Chonita '35; Dramatic Club '35; Social Social Science '36.

CARL RANDALL
Football '33, '34, '35, '36; Reserve Basketball '33, '34; S Club '33, '34, '35; Dramatic Club '34, '35; Male Chorus '36; Track '34; Science Club '33.

REATHA TURNER
Girl Reserves '33, '34, '35, '36; Home Ec Club '35.

RUTH SCHENCK TIBBALS
Freshman Chorus '33; Freshman Quartet '33; Glee Club '34, '35, '36; Annual Staff '36; Dramatic Club '34; Physical Ed '35; Pep Club '36; Soial Science '36; Girl Reservec '33, '34; Pres. of Home Room '33, '34; Mixed Chorus '35, '36.

EDGAR RUSSELL
Football '33, '34, '35; S Club '34; Hi-Y '34; Science Club '35; Male Chorus '35, '36; Social Science Club '36; National Honor Society '36.

EVELYN VAUGHT
Glee Club '33, '36; Latin Club '33, '34; Girl Reseves '33, '34; Physical Ed '34; Art Club '35; Dramatic Club '36; Social Science Club '36; Annual Staff '36; National Honor Society '36; School Rep. in Biology '35; School Rep. in World History '34.

JAMES SMITH
Hi-Y '33; Vice-Pres. Home Room '34; Sec. of Home Room '35; Radio Club '35, 36; Science Club '35, '36; Library Staff '35, '36.

INCL. # 4

C. K. C. Champions, 1935

FOOTBALL LETTERMEN, 1935

Lloyd Ramsey, Captain
Lyle Nice
Albert McClure
Leslie Baker
Fred Greene
Ed Kiser
Charles Ritter
Harold Davis
Jack Hamilton
Cecil Murphy
R. B. Waddle, Coach

Dick Waddle
Bernell Heaton
Abel Benelli
Vole Gardner
Curl Randall
Harvy Thomas
John Chamberlain
Ed Tucker
Willard Trimble
B. I Tucker, Manager
Dick Brown, Asst. Coach

INCL. # 5

GENERALSHIP LEADS JUMPERS TO VICTORY

LLOYD RAMSEY

The generalship of Captain Lloyd Ramsey had much to do with the victory of the Somerset High Briar Jumpers over the Lexington High eleven here last Friday afternoon. He ran the team like a veteran, mixing his plays so as to completely keep his opponents guessing. Ramsey was considered one of the best blocking backs in the CKC last year. This season he has developed into an outstanding ball carrier. He is a senior.

Special to The Courier-Journal.

Somerset, Ky., Nov. 20.—The Somerset High School Briar Jumpers, champions of the Central Kentucky Conference, enjoyed one of the most successful seasons this year it has had for many seasons. The Jumpers this year have played nine games, winning seven, losing one and tying one. In the nine games they have scored 114 points to their opponents' 33.

Conference games were won this year from Paris, Mt. Sterling, Irvine, Lancaster, M. M. I, and Lexington. The Jumpers were held to a 7-7 tie by Stanford in a conference engagement. Somerset's unexpected victory over the Lexington Blue Devils completed a record of two consecutive years without defeat in the conference. A total of eighteen conference games have been won by Somerset since the Jumpers last tasted defeat by a C. K. C. foe in the Lancaster game in 1933.

At the opening of the season this year there were few seasoned players on the squad and the team averaged only 147 pounds in weight, about 20 pounds per man lighter than the elevens that had represented Somerset on the gridiron in recent years. Only two regular players from the 1934 squad were left for service on this year's team and only four of the present squad had played enough to win letters last season.

Under the training of Coaches Bob Bruce Waddle and Dick Bourn, the Jumpers developed this season into a speedy, smart and dangerous eleven. Their rating, under the Dickinson System, is one of the highest in the conference in recent years.

INCL. # 6

EIGHT SCHOOLS PLACE MEN ON ALL-C. K. C. TEAM

Somerset, Carlisle and Lawrenceburg Each Gain Two Berths; Green Leads

Coaches' All-C. K. C. Selections

FIRST TEAM	POS.	SECOND TEAM
Armstrong, Carlisle	End	Fudold, Paris
Sorg, Frankfort	Tackle	Parson, Carlisle
Cunningham, Lexington	Guard	Puckett, Shelbyville
Sanders, Harrodsburg	Center	Watts, Winchester
Lykins, Paris	Guard	Wiseman, Irvine
Heaton, Somerset	Tackle	Racel, Maysville
Trent, Lawrenceburg	End	West, Madison
Mullin, Versailles	Quarter	Gregg, Shelbyville
Green, Carlisle (Capt.)	Half	Johnson, Lexington
Yates, Lawrenceburg	Half	(Capt.) Goodman, Paris
Ritter, Somerset	Full	Denham, Maysville

Third Team: Ends—Thiessen, M. M. I., and Ledford, Lancaster; tackles—Boles, Lexington, and Birkle, Lawrenceburg; guards—Baker, Somerset, and Walker, Nicholasville; center—Proctor, Lexington; quarterback—Carroll, Georgetown; halfbacks—Berry, Stanford, and Kinnaird, M. M. I.; fullback—Wadlington, Shelbyville.

Honorable mention: Ends—Whitaker, Shelbyville; Tucker, Somerset; Clarence Wilder, Versailles; Dozier, Versailles; Porter, Georgetown; tackles—Coombs, Shelbyville; Moore, Irvine; Traylor, Georgetown; guards—Blount, Carlisle; Ewalt, Paris; Lyons, Maysville; Wright, Maysville; Craig, Versailles; center—VanArsdall, Georgetown; backs—Shannon, Shelbyville; Blackburn, Versailles; Mitchell, Frankfort; Carroll Wilder, Versailles; Best, Harrodsburg; Conn, Lancaster; Levy, Lexington; Vinson, Irvine; Greene, Mt. Sterling; Croorcft, Maysville; Cochran, Irvine; Horton, Paris; Ramsey, Somerset; Barnes, Mt. Sterling.

INCL. # 7

Ladies and Gentlemen .... The Winners!

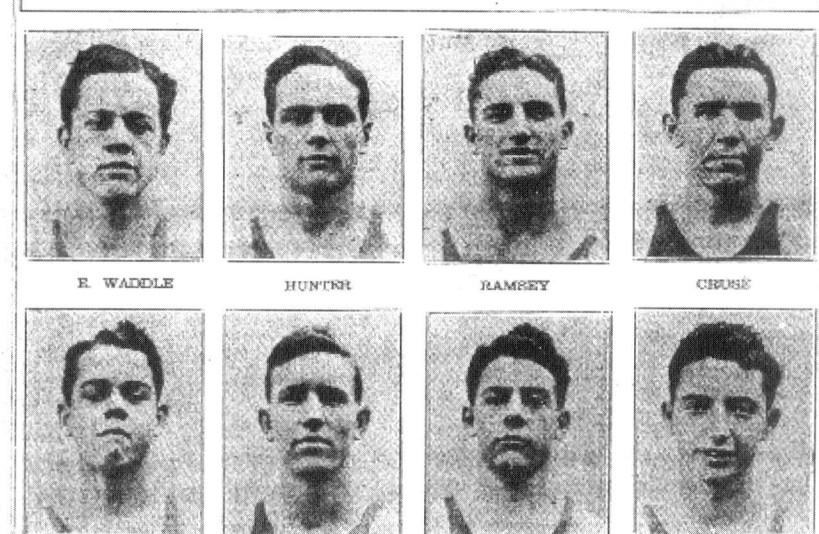

R. WADDLE   HUNTER   RAMSEY   CRUSE

N. WADDLE   MURPHY   NOEL   HICKS

Above are the eight players who represented Somerset High School in the Thirty-sixth District Basketball Tournament here last week and won the championship. They will meet McKinney in the opening game of the Regional Tournament at Stanford Friday afternoon. The Briar Jumpers will probably meet Danville in the finals if they get by the first game.

At school
Thursday afternoon

Dear Lloyd,

Please excuse all errors of any kind, but I knew that you could not read this at all if I wrote it by hand. I am using my vacant period to write this letter, aren't you proud of me?

I really am very lonely without you, because after all it does take sweet smiles to make the world go round, and you are about the most cheerful thing I know of. Joe has been out the last two days because of the death of his grandfather. So you see I am really in need of somebody to sit up near my desk and give me moral and physical support.

We had a letter from Frank this morning saying that he had been over to see you. It came as a great surprise to me, because he will not go near a hospital as a rule. It must be your magnetic personality, there has to be something to get old Ellis to a place he doesn't care for.

After so long a time I find that I have been writin part of this letter single space and part of it double space. That is the way my mind works on a typewriter. I neither look before nor after.

Mr. Allen has just come in here looking like the great stone face I always think he is going to get me for something. I think if it ever came to a showdown I could get the best of him, but I feel I must always listen if he is around just so that I can argue if he starts something.

INCL. # 9

SOMERSET PUBLIC SCHOOLS
F. B. HOPKINS, Superintendent
SOMERSET, KENTUCKY

Mr. Jones will be pleased to death to have me use his paper. (This darned thing has started that double spacing aga

He ,Mr. J., is out of school, has bronchitis. He was out all day yesterday and is not to come back until Monday. So you see that you really should come back and get this place under control. We need some sort of control, I cannot run everything by myself.

We are having a jolly good time in class diagraming. If you do not know anything about it, you had better stay away, 'cause I keep them in if they do not know their lessons. Much to my surprise, I do not think that they enjoy it much.

I did not go to the game the other night. By the time I get through my church work and go to Bank Night, I have done about all that I can.

Nellie needs her typewriter, so I had better let you rest for a little while. I am so glad that you got along so splendidly keep up the good work. Tell Bob Singleton that I hope he feels much better by now. Of course he will not have the faintest idea who I am, you can explain that it is just one of your old maid teachers.

I really miss you, so hurry back to see me. Very best wishes to a sweet child.

Mildred L. Ellis

INCL. # 9-2

LANCASTER PUBLIC SCHOOLS

C. H. PURDOM, SUPERINTENDENT

LANCASTER, KY.

February 6
1936

Dear Lloyd:

I had read that you were going to Lexington to be examined but that you had been operated on I had not the slightest knowledge. I am delighted to hear that the operation has been successful and I am sure that it will not be long until you are your old self again. From the reports in the papers the Basketball teams seems to be missing your services I hope that you will be able to get about by tournament time as I plan on being in Somerset to see the finals of the Tournament.

We had planned on being in Lexington this week end with the Floods but he was called to Knoxville so I guess we shall have to delay our visit. However if I do get there I will be around to see how you are getting along with all of the pretty nurses.

I had thought of getting one of the girls here to write you but maybe that would not be the wise thing as maybe you would have to do a good amount of explaining and I know that can be a hard thing some times.

I sincerely hope that you will soon be out and I know that you will. With best wishes to you and I hope that I may be able to see you soon,

As ever,

Chris H. Purdom

INCL. # 10

THE FRESHMAN CITIZENSHIP PRIZE - $2.50

This prize is awarded by the local chapter of the Daughters of the American Revolution to the Freshman showing throughout the Freshman year, outstanding qualities of citizenship, such as initiative, self-reliance, reliability, self-control, industry, determination, open-mindedness, unselfishness, loyalty, tolerance, cooperation, respect for authority, ideals, and character.

Lloyd Ramsey wins this prize.

Senior Efficiency Prize - $10.00

Given by the Somerset Rotary Club. The Senior Efficiency Prize is awarded to the outstanding senior in character, scholarship and leadership on the basis of four year's record in high school. The winner is Lloyd Ramsey. The winner of this prize is selected by the Faculty of the Somerset High School.

The George Dugan Converse Athletic Prize

Lloyd Ramsey - $5.00

INCL. # 11

53

BEST STUDENTS

Hershell Parmley   Thelma Hayes

BEST ALL AROUND

Betty Phelps   Lloyd Ramsey

INCL. # 12

COMMENCEMENT PROGRAM
May 24-28, 1936

BACCALAUREATE SERVICE
Methodist Episcopal Church, South
Sunday, May 24, 11:00 A. M.

Prelude
Invocation .... Reverend C. H. Talbot
Hymn .... Congregation
Prayer .... Reverend A. R. Perkins
Announcements .... Superintendent P. H. Hopkins
Special Music
Sermon .... Doctor R. V. Bennett
Hymn .... Congregation
Benediction .... Reverend W. E. Hunter
Postlude

CLASS DAY
Methodist Episcopal Church, South
Monday, May 25, 2:30 P. M.

LLOYD RAMSEY, President
NEIL WADDLE, Vice President
FERNE REYNOLDS, Secretary
HAZEL PERKINS, Treasurer

To Greet the Spring, Mendelssohn .... Girls' Sextet
Class History .... Ruth Gover
Clarinet Solo .... Fred Greene
Class Prophecy .... John Prather
Class Poem .... Evelyn Vaught
By the Bend of the River, Edwards .... Mixed Quartet
Class Knocker .... Ruth Tibbals
Presentation of Gift .... Amelia Pumphrey
Violin Solo .... Thelma Kidd
Key of Knowledge .... Lloyd Ramsey
Class Will .... Vola Gardner
Announcements .... Principal W. B. Jones
Till We Meet Again, Whiting .... Senior Class

GRADUATION EXERCISES
Methodist Episcopal Church, South
Tuesday, May 26, 8:00 P. M.

Special Music .... Band Ensemble
Invocation .... Reverend L. D. Fisher
Come to the Fair, Martin .... Girls' Glee Club
Commencement Address .... Doctor W. P. King
Night (Liebestraum), Liszt .... Boys' Glee Club
Awarding of Prizes .... Superintendent P. H. Hopkins
The Nightingale, Tschaikowsky .... Mixed Glee Club
Awarding of Diplomas .... Principal W. B. Jones
Benediction .... Reverend T. C. Duke

INCL. # 13

SENIOR CLASS ROLL

Albertson, Wilbert
Allen, Irvine
Baker, Laslie
Beeler, Eleanor
Biers, James
Boone, Billy M.
Burdine, Rupert
Carr, Mary Katherine
Carter, Martha D.
Catron, Cloda
Coggins, Delmas
Coggins, Neil, Jr.
Collier, Margaret
Colyer, Christine
Colyer, Ray
Crockett, Virginia
Cummins, William
Curtis, Evelyn
Curtis, Jack
Denham, Dorothy
Denny, Charles
Dodson, Marcus
Dolen, Fionnie
Dutton, Gwendolyn
Early, Jack
Entzminger, Luce
Ewers, Louise
Fabel, Jacqueline
Fisher, Hazel
Floyd, Curtis
Gardner, Ola
Gardner, Vola
Garland, Virginia
Girdler, Chrystal
Godby, Marie
Gossett, Kathleen
Gover, Roy
Gover, Ruth
Greene, Fred
Gribbin, Owen Tibbals
Hahn, Edna

Hahn, Velera
Hall, Willard
Hayes, Thelma
Heaton, Bernell
Hines, Mary Ellen
Hines, Robert E.
Holladay, Louise
Hopper, Ruth
Huffman, Kathyrn
Hurt, Robert
Jasper, Pauline
Jones, James Everett
Keeney, Beryl
Keith, Clarence
Kidd, Thelma
Kiser, Edward
Latham, Nina Jean
Leonard, Bud
Lewis, Ben P.
Lewis, Edna Kate
Lewis, Zola
McClure, Albert
McCracken, Mary E.
McDaniel, William
McKenzie, Edsel
McNamer, Frank
Massey, Ruth
Meece, Marcella
Meece, Okra
Merrick, Bonnie
Miller, Berta M.
Morgan, Bill
Mounce, Lillian
Mullenix, Ruby
Neely, Mildred
Neikirk, Glen
Nelson, Virginia
Noel, Lyttleton
Parmley, Ella
Parmley, Hershel
Pennington, Edna

Perkins, Hazel
Phelps, Bettie
Phillpott, Pearl
Ping, Jean
Poynter, Eleanor
Prather, John G.
Pumphrey, Amelia
Ramsey, Lloyd
Randall, Carl
Rayborn, Kathleen
Reynolds, Ferne
Ross, Kate G.
Russell, Edgar
Russell, Nancy
Sheneman, Joe D.
Silvers, Katharyn
Simpson, Clark
Sims, Carley
Sims, Charles
Sims, Clarence
Smith, James
Smith, Naoma
Stevenson, Doris
Sutherland, Hazel
Tanner, Mary Ola
Taylor, Virginia
Tibbals, Ruth
Turner, Reatha
Vaught, Evelyn
Waddle, James
Waddle, Neil B.
Waddle, Louise
Wahle, Joan
Warren, Marie
Watson, Alvin
Weddle, Virginia
Weddle, Mildred
Wild, Noy Lee
Williams, Mary Evelyn
Yates, Harold

INCL. # 13-2

CHAPTER 3

COLLEGE PERIOD, 1936 – 1940

1936: College Freshman Football

I wanted to go to the University of Kentucky and play football. Practice started in August, so I went to the university to see if I could get a football scholarship. I met with Frank Mosely, the freshman coach and varsity backfield coach. In those days, football teams had very little money and most coaches had to perform more than one task. I showed Mosely some of the write-ups of our team winning the CKC championship, with me as captain, and my reputation as a blocking back and running back. This did not seem to impress him. Mosely asked me how much I weighed, and I told him 143 pounds. He said I was too small to play college football. I told him that I recalled he was an All-American quarterback at Alabama and only weighed about 160 pounds. I asked him if he weighed 143 pounds as a freshman. (In those days, freshmen could not play varsity football; the freshmen had their own games.) With those questions, he told me that he would accept me as a "walk on," and if I could make either the first or second freshman team, he would give me a scholarship. When I went out for practice the first day, there were about 15 people trying out for quarterback, only three of whom were on scholarship; the rest were "walk ons."

As time passed, I became the first string quarterback and was elected captain of the freshman team by my teammates. I was then put on a full scholarship, but I had already paid my tuition, room, and books, so all that I received for the first semester was my meals and laundry. By the end of the first semester, there were only two quarterbacks on scholarship, myself and one of the three that started on scholarship. I was the only "walk on" quarterback who made it.

It is interesting to note that in those days the same players played both offense and defense. If you were taken out of the game, you could not return until that quarter ended. Many players would play all 60 minutes of the game. Another interesting thing about football in those days: the quarterback ran the offense completely. Even if you sent in a substitute, he could not enter the huddle because he might give a play from the coach. The quarterback would have to step out of the huddle with the incoming player and give him the play. If a coach was caught giving a signal from the bench, his team would be penalized.

Fall 1936: Rushed by a Number of Fraternities – Pledged Sigma Chi

During the fall of 1936, many fraternities were rushing freshmen and upper classmen who had not joined a fraternity. As I recall, Elvis Stahr was at the university waiting to go to England as a Rhodes Scholar. He was there to help Sigma Chi in rushing, and he had come to see me when I was in the hospital in January. He tried to persuade me to pledge Sigma Chi. My friend Sherman Heinkebein was a sophomore and played center on the varsity football team. Sigma Chi was rushing him also, and we decided to pledge Sigma Chi.

Fall 1936: Joined the University of Kentucky Swimming Team

During football season, Sherman Heinkebein told me that he and another man had organized a swimming team the previous year. He had heard about my swimming from someone, and he asked me to join the team and to help get it operating. His previous helper had passed away. I agreed to join and to help recruit swimmers. The University of Kentucky had no swimming pool so we had to travel about 25 miles each way to the pool at Eastern Kentucky State Teachers College in Richmond (now Eastern Kentucky University) to get some practice. Heinkebein had made arrangements with the college for us to practice there, but we had no transportation to get back and forth. Some students from Lexington could borrow the family car now and then. I told Dad about our problem. Good old Dad, with his interest in athletics, came to Lexington and bought me a new Dodge for the team to travel in. Dad said that since I was on a full football scholarship, he would use the money that he would have spent on my college to pay for the car. Heinkebein made himself coach and captain of the team and made me the assistant coach. I had gotten to know Jim Shropshire on the faculty, so I asked him if he would be our faculty advisor and help us arrange meets. He accepted and was a great help to us.

Early Spring 1937: Initiated into Lambda Lambda Chapter Sigma Chi

In the early spring of 1937, Heinkebein and I had to go through "Hell Week" with the other pledges before we could be initiated into Sigma Chi. Since we were both in spring football practice, we got out of a lot of "Hell Week" that the other pledges had to perform. The last event during "Hell Week" was at night. Each pledge was blindfolded, put in a car, driven around, and told to find his way home. As I recall, pledges were let out at different places in groups of three. You did have some choice about who you were going to be with. Heinkebein and I managed to go together. We had some idea of this event and when it was going to happen. I got a friend of mine to stake out the Sigma Chi house, and, using my car, follow the car that carried Heinkebein and me. The friend followed at a safe distance and picked us up after the other car left. We managed to get back to the Sigma Chi house before the driver who had let us out. Was he surprised to find us sitting in the living room when he returned! Since both of us were football players, and Heinkebein weighed about 200 pounds, they decided that they would not try to drop us off in the country again.

1937: Spring Football Practices – I Suffered a Broken Neck

In the 1937 spring football practice, I did very well as quarterback. The quarterback of the 1936 season was graduating, and it was between the two quarterbacks that came up from the freshman team as to who would be the first string quarterback for the 1937 season. The other quarterback was Joe Shepard from Manual High School in Louisville. I was never told, but based on the line-up and playing time, I believe that I was the starting quarterback. The system that we used made the quarterback position primarily a blocking back. We did carry the ball and throw some passes at times.

One day in practice I was blocking and the runner caught up with me and hit me in the back of the neck with his knee. It hurt but I continued to practice and did not tell the coach. That evening I was a referee at a basketball game at Woodlawn Park, where I worked to earn extra money. My neck was hurting, and the more that I tried to turn, the worse it got. However, I did finish officiating the game. I went back to the dorm and told my roommate Jim, my brother, what had happened and said I thought the best thing for me to do was to get some rest. I slept well that night, but when I woke up the next morning, the pain was so bad that Jim had to help me out of bed. With Jim's help, I was able to get dressed. He then took me to the dispensary where they checked me over and sent me to the Good Samaritan Hospital. Dr. Brown, an orthopedic surgeon, had an X-ray taken and determined that I had broken the third cervical vertebrae in my neck. He told me that I was very fortunate that no further damage was done since I continued to practice and then officiated a basketball game that night. He explained to me what had to be done so that I would recover completely: I would be put in a cast from the top of my head to my waist; I would have to wear the cast for approximately six to eight weeks; and if I healed well, then I would have to wear a brace for another four to six weeks. Would you believe that all of this was done in the morning and that I went to my classes that afternoon without pain? At the end of this chapter is a poor picture of me in the cast (Inclusion #1).

1936: My Major Was Physical Education

When I started to school in the fall of 1936, I had decided that I wanted to be a football coach; therefore, I majored in physical education (PE). With a broken neck in the spring of 1937, I could not do very much PE. When we had to take a test on leading a class in exercises, the professor told me I could wait a few weeks before taking the test. I told him that I could not demonstrate all of the exercises in spite of my cast, but that I was ready to give all the commands for the exercises. Each person did this in front of the class. When I finished my turn, the professor congratulated me on an outstanding performance. He said that he could not find any mistakes and that he had never seen anyone go through so many exercises without making a mistake. Also, he had never given a perfect grade so he was going to give me a 99+. Of course I was thrilled with such a comment and grade.

1937: Removing the Cast, Putting on a Brace

My doctor was very pleased with my progress during the spring of 1937, and, as I recall, he removed the cast in slightly less than six weeks. I was placed in a brace that came over my shoulders, had two braces behind my head, and one brace under my chin. This let me breathe more air than with the cast, which was great, but it was harder to eat and sleep. Even so, it was great to get out of the cast.

I had been in the brace for almost three weeks when one of my classmates fell from a rope swing and landed on his head. They called the medical office immediately and a nurse came over. The nurse determined that the injured person must get to the hospital soon but did not need an ambulance. I had my car available, so I took him and the nurse to the hospital. We saw Dr. Brown, who took X-rays and gave him a thorough examination. He had some very serious neck injuries that would require a brace. They searched the Lexington area, by phone, and could not find a brace. It would be two or three days before a brace would arrive. Dr. Brown turned to me and said that my brace was the only one available. He said that I had been a very good patient, but he needed my brace. Before taking it from me, I had to agree that I would not turn my head for one week; otherwise, the man would have to be put into the hospital and placed in traction. Hospitalization under these conditions would be very expensive. I agreed to it. The injured classmate could not thank me enough for what I had done for him so that he could continue going to class and save him from paying a large hospital bill.

1937: Football Season – I Took Movies of the Games

During the 1937 football season, I could not play because of my broken neck. I was still on a full athletic scholarship. Bernie Shively, the line coach and athletic director, knew that I liked photography, so he asked me if I could take movies of the games. I told him that I thought I could, but the equipment would be expensive. He authorized me to buy a camera and projector, leaving the cost up to me. I purchased a very good camera and projector, and then started making arrangements to buy film at a discount and to send it off after a game on Saturday, to have it returned on Monday. This was the first time that the University of Kentucky had ever taken movies of their games.

On games out of town, Shively would call ahead and make arrangements for me to take movies. I would get to the stadium early so that I could find a good location (usually on top of the press box). This was fine until winter when it was cold and the wind was blowing. Most of the time I was the only person taking movies, and I did a pretty good job of it, which helped the coach and players.

1937: Glenda Moved to the University of Kentucky from Georgetown College, Kentucky

When the school year started in 1937, Glenda came to the University of Kentucky from Georgetown College, Kentucky, where she had been going for the previous two years. She was a hometown girl I knew very well, and we had been to many parties at the same places while we were in high school, but since I was one year behind her in school, we had never dated. She was very nice looking, so I thought that I would be nice and try to help a hometown girl. I showed her around the university and told her that if she were asked for a date and she wanted to know more about the person, she should call me. She did this often because it was not long until she was very popular. At some functions at the university, which she should attend, I would check with her to see if she had a date. If she did not, I would offer to take her to the function.

In 1939, her senior year, she lived with six other girls in a house not very far from the university. The six were all very beautiful girls. When you telephoned for one of them, they would answer, "Dunbarr House of Charm," then give their name. I must agree that those six girls made it a house of charm. Trying to be nice to Glenda and help her get around became a little more than trying to be nice. The more I saw her, the more I enjoyed being with her. (This finally led to our marriage on February 22, 1941.)

1938: Football Season

I was able to play football in 1938. We got a new coach that year – Ab Kirwin. He came from Manual High School in Louisville, Kentucky, and gave special attention to players from Manual. The man that I beat out as a freshman, Joe Shepard, was the quarterback the previous year, 1937 when I was injured, and was from Manual. Because of the expense of injuries, the athletic department having little money, and Joe Shepard being from Manual, I seldom got to scrimmage, even though I became the second string quarterback.

I played very little football. The last game of the season was with the University of Tennessee, and six inches of snow were on the ground. Tennessee was so far ahead at the half that the first team came out in the second half in their civilian clothes. Since it was a miserable day and we had already lost the game, Kirwin put me in the game to play the second half. On defense I was playing safety. A Tennessee runner got loose and I tackled him on the 10-yard line and we slid over the goal line. The ball was brought back to the 10-yard line. As I recall, the score was 46 to 0.

To the best of my knowledge, all the second string players received a letter except me. Many of my teammates were very concerned that I had not received a letter, especially after having played in a number of games and playing the entire second half of the Tennessee game. At the end of this chapter are pictures of the 1938 football team (Inclusion #2).

To take my place in shooting movies, they hired a professional. After the first game, they could not get any pictures to show. They called me to come over to see if I could do anything to help. Some rolls were blank or blurred because they had not been loaded correctly into the camera. The rolls that were good had not been loaded into the projector correctly. I had to teach a pro how to use both the camera and the projector.

1938 – 1939: Swimming Team

I was elected coach of the team for the swimming season of 1938 – 1939. We had an undefeated season for the first and only time in my four years on the team. At the end of this chapter is a picture of the swimming team and a write-up of the 1938-1939 season (Inclusion #3). At Inclusion #4 is a picture: "…Lloyd (Feller) Ramsey of Somerset, winner of the Freeburg plaque for high-point honors last year and student 'coach' of the team this season, who was elected at the banquet as 1940 captain: Herb Hillenmeyer of Lexington, retiring captain of the Wildcat-fish; and Frank B. Roberts of Lexington, who took the high-point laurels this year and was chosen by teammates as 'coach' for next season."

July 1939: ROTC Summer Camp

If you took advanced ROTC, you had to go to summer camp at

Fort Knox, Kentucky, for four to six weeks. They made it tough training, but I learned more about the military and how to fight a war during that short period than I learned during four years of ROTC at the University.

In addition to our tough training, we had time for intramurals. Our company did very well in all the activities. I was on the softball team, and as I remember, we came in second. I was on the swimming team where I won the 100-yard freestyle event and was on the 200-yard relay team that won. I also entered boxing and wrestling and won each match to the finals. On the day of the finals, both events were scheduled for the same day. Unfortunately, I got up that morning with a temperature of 102 degrees. That was on a Saturday, and we did not have to train that day. I went to the doctor and he said all that I needed was some aspirin. I told him that I was scheduled to have a boxing and wrestling match late in the afternoon and evening. He said there was no reason that I could not participate, but I might be very weak, especially having to enter two matches. The wrestling event came first. It took all of my strength to win that match. When it came time to box, I was tired but I did the best that I could. I lost the match on a 2 to 1 vote by the judges. I was proud of my accomplishments under the conditions.

August 1939 – June 1940: My Senior Year

This was a busy, exciting, and rewarding year.

1939: Ab Kirwin, the Coach, Wanted Me to be the Freshman Backfield Coach

Since I did not receive a letter for play during the last season, I was determined to work harder and earn a letter this season. On the first day of practice, Coach Kirwin called me aside and said that he wanted me to coach the freshman backfield, plus do some scouting at high schools for next year. I told the coach that I preferred to play football. He then reminded me that I did not play very much last year because of my neck, even though I was the second string quarterback. He then told me that last year's freshman quarterback would now be the second string quarterback and that I would play third string. I could see from this information that I had very little chance of playing in a game; therefore, I accepted his offer and thanked him for having that much confidence in me. At the end of this chapter is a picture of the 1939 coaching staff (Inclusion #5).

This position kept me very busy. Every Friday, I would go with one of the other coaches to watch a high school game to scout for players for next year. On many Saturdays I would go with another coach to a game being played by a team that we were to play in the future. We would scout their plays, bring the information to our team, and try to be prepared to stop their offense. During football season, I seldom went to a Friday or Saturday class. This made it very difficult to keep my grades up.

1939: Elected Vice President (Pro Consul) of Sigma Chi Fraternity

I was honored by my fraternity brothers who thought enough of me to elect me Vice President (Pro Consul) of the Sigma Chi fraternity. James J. Wine was elected President (Consul). You will note that he and I both earned a few honors during our senior year. At the end of this chapter is a picture of the Sigma Chi fraternity (Inclusion #6).

1939: Appointed Cadet Colonel of the Corps of Cadets, ROTC

Shortly after school started for my senior year in 1939, the PMS & T (Professor of Military Science and Tactics) ROTC, Lieutenant Colonel Howard Donnelly, published the list of officers and noncommissioned for the Corps of Cadets. The top positions usually went to those who had served in the Pershing Rifles drill team. They were considered the elite in the ROTC. Since I was an athlete, I did not have time to participate in the Pershing Rifles. I hoped that I would at least be appointed a captain or maybe a field grade officer. To my great surprise, I was appointed Cadet Colonel of the Corps of Cadets. At the end of this chapter is a picture of the Regimental Staff (Inclusion #7).

1939: Elected Captain, Scabbard and Blade, National Honorary Military Organization

Not long after I was appointed Cadet Colonel, the list came out of those selected for Scabbard and Blade, National Honorary Military Organization. I was honored by my cadet classmates who elected me captain of Scabbard and Blade. Note that James J. Wine was selected for this honor. At the end of this chapter there is a picture of those in Scabbard and Blade (Inclusion #8). At Inclusion #9 is a picture of me and Jane Baynham under arch of sabers. Jane was crowned Military Queen at Scabbard and Blade's annual formal.

1939: Appointed to the Student Union Board

Being appointed to the Student Union Board was considered a highlight in your college career. You will note that James J. Wine was also appointed to the board. At the end of this chapter (Inclusion #10) is a picture of the Student Union Board.

1939: Appointed to the Student Legislature

I do not remember the exact method of getting this appointment, but I believe that each college appointed a certain number to the Student Legislature; the Education College had one appointment, and they appointed me. At the end of this chapter (Inclusion #11) is a picture of the Student Legislature.

1939: Appointed to Lamp and Cross – Senior Honorary for Men

It was a great honor for me to be selected into this group. The purpose of this group states: "To recognize qualities of leadership among outstanding members of the senior class." At the end of this chapter (Inclusion #12) is a picture and list of Lamp and Cross. I am not in this picture, but I am listed as the Vice-President and as a member.

1939: Inducted into Who's Who Among Students in American Universities and Colleges

Being selected for Who's Who in American Universities and Colleges was another great honor for me. I had done the leadership requisites, but I was not sure that my scholastic standing was good enough. At the end of this chapter (Inclusion #13) is a picture and a list of those who made Who's Who from the University of Kentucky. You will note that James J. Wine was on this list. At Inclusion #13-2 is a letter from Who's Who that was sent to my parents and gives details regarding the selection. It states: "This selection was an unprejudiced and unbiased one by a committee from the institution which he attends."

1939: Selected for Omicron Delta Kappa, Men's Leadership Fraternity

In 1939, I was selected to be a member of Omicron Delta Kappa, Men's Leadership Fraternity. To me this was the ultimate honor. First, you must earn enough points by holding positions of leadership. Second, you must attain a certain grade average; as I recall, the grade average had to be a 1.7 on a three-point scale, or almost a B average. I maintained a 1.8 to 1.9 average. Third, you must be selected to membership by the circle. It was interesting to note that two or three professors had finally earned enough points, and, of course, they had the grades to be selected that year to Omicron Delta Kappa. They were extremely pleased to receive this honor. You will note that James J. Wine received this honor. At the end of this chapter (Inclusion #14) is a picture and list of those who made Omicron Delta Kappa. At Inclusion #14-2 is a letter from the Dean of Education telling me: "I was delighted to see you made a member of Omicron Delta Kappa."

1939: Physical Education Club

If you were a physical education major, you were automatically a member of the Physical Education Club. It was a very good club and had a number of activities. I was honored when my classmates elected me club President.

1939 – 1940: Swimming Season

I was elected Captain of the team for the swimming season of 1939–1940. We had a very good season, but not the undefeated season that we had the previous year when I was the coach. At the end of this chapter is a picture of the swimming team and a write-up of the 1939-40 season (Inclusion #15).

1940: "Down in Front" – An Article About Me in the Lexington Paper

Larry Shropshire, of the Lexington, Kentucky, paper, wrote a very nice article about me. The article is at the end of this chapter (Inclusion

#16 and #16-2). He made some nice comments about me, such as: *"Scouting around for information and you quickly find that there is not one but quite a number of reasons for his popularity. Among the chief ones are his genuine friendliness, his fine spirit, and, above all, his complete unselfishness."* He then went on to write about my entering a boxing match in Washington, D.C., after driving 16 hours to get the boxing team to Washington. I was not scheduled to fight, but since the other team had advertised that there would be a light heavyweight fight, they insisted that one of our boxers enter that fight. Coach Frank Mosely knew that I had boxed intramural so he talked me into entering the fight. At Inclusion #16-2, you can see me in an embarrassing position, but at Inclusion #16-3, you can see that I really floored my opponent, Jimmy Brown. After the match, Jimmy came to my locker room to see me. In his very conceited way, he advised me that he had never lost a heavyweight match in the area and that he had worked hard to lose enough weight so that he could fight light heavyweight. He said this was the first time he had been knocked down in his boxing career, and then he congratulated me. That made me feel real good about my fight.

In the second part of the article, "Phooey On a Broken Neck," he wrote about my playing football again after breaking my neck and about my swimming.

In the third part of the article, "When a Fellow Needs a Friend," he wrote about how I helped Bill Boston – who had received a very serious knee injury in football and could hardly walk – and how I helped him get to class with my car.

1940: ROTC Interviews for Regular Army Commission

The Professor of Military Science and Tactics (PMS & T) announced interviews for applicants for the regular army that would be held in February 1940. Since I was a physical education major and wanted to be a football coach, I did not apply for a regular army commission. When PMS&T Lt. Col. Howard Donnelly did not find my application, he called me to his office and said that I had a greater opportunity to get a regular army commission than any other ROTC cadet in the Corps. I told him that I was not interested in a regular army commission because I wanted to be a football coach. He then asked me – as a favor to him since he appointed me Cadet Colonel – to apply, even though I was not making a commitment. I agreed, knowing that I would not be accepted. Colonel Donnelly said that I would need a letter of recommendation from a faculty member so I asked M. E. Potter, Head, Department of Physical Education, for such a letter. He wrote a very complimentary letter, which is Inclusion #17 at the end of this chapter.

I had made no preparations for the interview. One of the first questions was regarding world events. I told them that I knew very little of world events because I had very little time to read newspapers and magazines. They then asked me why I did not have time to read. I named many of the things that I was involved in and that led their questions to events that I knew about. Even though I did well after the first question, I was sure that they would not give me a very good evaluation. To my great surprise, my mother and father received a letter a few days later from Virginia Elliot Williams, the wife of Colonel J. B. Williams, the Commanding Officer, Fort Knox, Kentucky. Colonel Williams and Virginia came from Somerset, my hometown. The handwritten letter follows:

Dear Mary Ella and Bill,

Colonel Vesely, who was on the board of officers interviewing college boys for commission in the Army, told me last night Lloyd was at the top of the list and was sure of a commission.

I only wish you could have heard the nice things he said about your son. I was proud for both of you. They interviewed the cream of the crop and he said Lloyd was the outstanding one of them all.

I do hope the Army will be lucky enough to get him – at the same time it's a grand career for a young boy.

Congratulations to you both, in which Jake joins me.

Sincerely,

Virginia Elliot Williams

The regular Army appointments came from the Fifth Corps Area of six states, which included Kentucky. To my great surprise, I was at the top of the list. My mother and father had never told me about the letter from Mrs. Williams. The PMS&T Lt. Col. Donnelly was very proud that one of his cadets headed the list.

I told Colonel Donnelly that I was honored to be selected for the regular Army, but since I went to school to learn how to be a football coach, I thought it best that I go into that profession and not accept the regular army commission. After much discussion with Colonel Donnelly, Major Irvine Scudder, and Sergeant Perkins, and days of consideration, I finally agreed to try the Army for a year. If I did not like it, I would resign and go into coaching.

1940: College of Education Graduation Picture

At the end of this chapter (Inclusion #18) is my college of education graduation picture. You will note that the list of my activities is larger than the others on that page, and not all of my activities are listed.

May 29, 1940: Military Field Day and ROTC Graduation Exercises

On May 29, 1940, we had our Military Field Day and ROTC graduation exercises on Stoll Field (football field). The program for this event is at the end of this chapter (Inclusion #19). As Cadet Colonel, this was quite a day for me. At this function, I received two awards:

ROTARY CLUB TROPHY – Awarded to the graduating member of the Second Year Advanced Course, Reserve Officers' Training Corps, who is selected by vote of the Advanced Course students as excelling in the requirements of good citizenship.

Awarded to: Cadet Colonel Lloyd Brinkley Ramsey,
Somerset, Kentucky.

AMERICAN LEGION CUP, MAN OF WAR POST – Awarded to the graduating cadet officer selected by a board of Regular Army Officers as outstanding and possessing in marked degree those inherent qualities in the making of an officer and gentleman.

*Awarded to: Cadet Colonel Lloyd Brinkley Ramsey,
Somerset, Kentucky.*

I was listed on the program along with eight other cadets as "HONOR GRADUATES."

Letter to Dr. Frank L. McVey, Retiring President

As the Cadet Colonel of the regiment, I wrote the following letter to President McVey and presented it to him during the Military Field Day.

May 29, 1940

*Dr. Frank L. McVey, President
University of Kentucky*

Dear Doctor McVey:

The R.O.T.C. Regiment parading before you today for the final time as our commander-in-chief salutes you as our leader, our counselor, and our friend.

May the retirement from long years of outstanding public service, which you have so justly earned, be years of happiness, peace, and good health.

We bid you farewell with regret, and trust that you will always be present to receive our "Present Arms" in the future.

Sincerely Yours,

*Lloyd B. Ramsey,
Cadet Colonel, Commanding.*

June 1940: Received the Sigma Chi Fraternity Province Balfour Award

During the second semester of my senior year, the Sigma Chi Fraternity selected me to apply for the Province Balfour Award, the highest honor the fraternity is capable of bestowing upon one of its members. The Province included all Sigma Chi chapters in Kentucky and Tennessee. This would require me to prepare a paper covering the activities in which I had participated in college, especially in a leadership roll. I also would have to give my grades and discuss what I had done to earn a major. I spent hours preparing this paper and had some of my fraternity brothers to review it and make suggested changes. James J. Wine, our President, was of great help to me on this project. After much time and effort, one of the brothers typed the paper for me, and we sent it in.

To my great surprise and amazement, I was selected to receive the Province Balfour Award. At the end of this chapter (Inc.lusion #20) is a letter from the Grand Praetor, Kentucky-Tennessee Province, advising me that I had been selected for the award. The letter reads as follows:

Dear Brother Ramsey:

I am delighted to state that the committee which I asked to judge the papers submitted on representatives of the active chapters in this province unanimously voted in favor of your receiving the Balfour award for the Kentucky-Tennessee province. Permit me to congratulate you, sir, and to wish you every success in your further preparation for service in our great country.

In the bonds of Sigma Chi, I am

Fraternally yours,

Ullin W. Leavell

At Inclusion #20-2 is an article from the Somerset paper about my receiving the Balfour Award.

Glenda and I at a Formal Dance at the University of Kentucky

The picture of Glenda and me at the end of this chapter (Inclusion #21) is at a formal dance at the Student Union Building, University of Kentucky. I am not sure whether the picture was taken at the end of the school year 1939 or 1940. Glenda graduated in 1939 but came back to certain functions to be with me during my senior year.

Burma Shave Signs

For those of you who never saw the Burma Shave signs, here is a quick lesson in our history of the 1930's and 1940's. Before the interstates when everyone drove the old two-lane roads, Burma Shave signs would be posted all over the countryside in farmers' fields. They were small red signs with white letters. Five signs were placed, about 100 feet apart, each containing one line of a four-line couplet and the obligatory fifth line advertising Burma shave, a popular cream. I will quote a few that I have found:

1. *Drove Too Long*
   Driver Snoozing
   What Happened Next
   Is Not Amusing
   Burma Shave

2. *No Matter the Price*
   No Matter How New
   The Best Safety Device
   In the Car Is You
   Burma Shave

3. *Passing School Zone*
   Take It Slow
   Let Our Little
   Shavers Grow
   Burma Shave

4. *A Guy Who Drives*
   A Car Wide Open
   Is Not Thinking
   He's Just Hoping
   Burma Shave

5. *Both Hands on the Wheel*
   Eyes on the Road
   That's the Skillful
   Driver's Code
   Burma Shave

*Not a very good picture,
but this is what I looked
like in my cast.*

Top Picture: 1938 Football Team, University of Kentucky. Lloyd
Ramsey, Number 20.
Middle Picture: some of the individual pictures of players.
Bottom Picture: Shows the type of headgear we used.

INCL. # 2

Seated -- Riddell, Phillips, David, Triplett, Ramsey, Curtis, Stephenson, Sellers.
Standing -- Manager Sumpter Lewis, Hinkebein, Hillenmeyer, Doyle, Roberts, Scott, Adrian Shoopman.

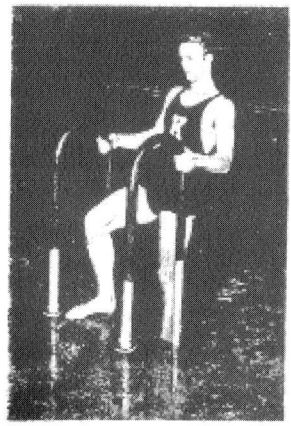

Swimming

Captain Hillenmeyer Emerges

Kentucky's "dry land" swimming team finished an undefeated season in a blaze of glory by leaving Berea College and Eastern Teachers College stranded as they stroked to their fourth consecutive state title at the Richmond pool late in March. This victory was the climax of a season which saw the Wildcats drench nine opponents, score an average of 56 points per meet, while holding their foes to an average of 15 points, and establish five new state records, which brings their total up to 6 of the 8 existing marks.

Lloyd Ramsey, coach and member of the team, called the tanksmen together a little after Thanksgiving and, early in January, the Cats ducked Eastern easily. In February the boys took Maryville, Tennessee, and Georgia Tech.

The remainder of the season saw the Kentucky mermen outswim all competitors including two very strong mid-western teams, Depauw and Butler. In their final scheduled meet of the season and their second with Eastern the Wildcats submerged their foes under the top-heavy score of 60-15.

Frank Roberts heads the list of record holders as he holds the 50-yard mark at :25 and the 100-yard mark at :57. Ikod Scott cut his own state record for the 150-yard backstroke to 1.53.2. Sherman Hinkebein reduced his own record for the 200-yard breaststroke to 2.50. Against Georgia Tech, Kentucky's crack 300-yard medley relay team churned the distance in 3:21.9, a time which bettered the state mark by five seconds and also eclipsed the Southeastern Conference mark. The sprint relay team reduced their mark to 3:54.5 for a new state record.

The prospects for another great team next year are very bright despite the loss of Captain Hillenmeyer and Sherman Hinkebein. Returning for further competition will be such holdovers as Ramsey, Roberts, Triplett, Scott, David, Curtis, Stephenson, Riddell, and Lewis.

INCL. # 3

(Caption Reads:) "SPLASHING STARS--Three leading memebers of the University of Kentucky's undefeated swimming team, which formally closed the 1939 season with a banquet Tuesday night at Harrodsburg, are pictured above. Left to right: Lloyd (Feller) Ramsey of Somerset, winner of the Freeburg plaque for high-point honors last year and student "coach" of the team this season, who was elected at the banquet as 1940 captian; Herb Hillenmeyer of Lexington, retiring captian of the Wildcat-fish; and Frank B. Roberts of Lexington, who took the high-point laurels this year and was chosen by teammates as "coach" for next season.*

INCL. # 4

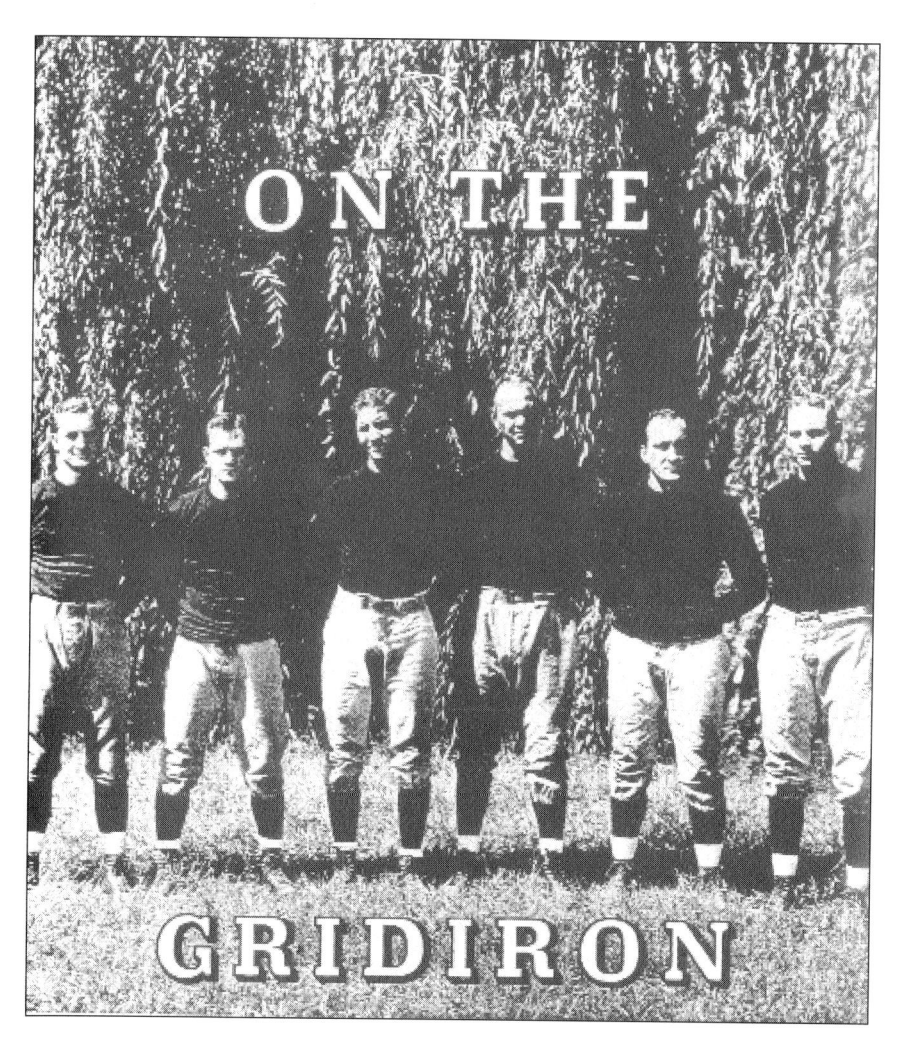

Coaching staff, 1939
Lloyd Ramsey, Frank Moseley, Ab Kirwin, Bernie Shively, Gene Myers, Joe Rupert

INCL. # 5

SIGMA CHI

National Social Fraternity

**LAMBDA
LAMBDA**
Left to right:

Row one
Stephenson
Easton
Wine
Ramsey
Palmer

Row two
Miller
Doerr
Haley
Colbert
Rawlins

Row three
Carl
Combs
Stark
Jones
Curtis

Row four
Liles
C. Trapp, Jr.
J. Routt
Pierson
Dingus

Row five
Caudill
W. Routt
C. Trapp
Funk
Rogers

OFFICERS

James W. Wine	President
Lloyd B. Ramsey	Vice-President
Hilary J. Boone	Secretary
R. Douglas Montondo	Treasurer

INCL. # 6

80

Regimental Staff

Front: Cadet Colonel L. B. Ramsey
Second Row: Cadet Lt. Colonels W. J. Drummy, R. T. Scott, L. T. Rouse, T. W. Spickard.
Third Row: Cap't G. P. Carter, Cadet Majors J. O. Bell, R. T. Sweeny, Cadet Cap't, J. C. Bode.
Fourth Row: Cadet Sgt's., Curtis, Combs, Hickey, Robards
Fifth Row: Cadet Sgt's., Lawrence, Butler, Gaines, Courtney

INCL. # 7

SCABBARD AND BLADE

NATIONAL HONORARY MILITARY ORGANIZATION
D COMPANY, FOURTH REGIMENT

Founded at University of Wisconsin in 1904
Installed on campus in 1925

PURPOSE

"Believing that military service is an obligation of citizenship and that greater opportunities afforded college men for the study of military science place upon them certain responsibilities as citizens, we cadet officers in various colleges and universities conferring baccalaureate degrees do form this Society and adopt this constitution in order to unite in closer relationship the military departments of American universities and colleges; to preserve and develop the essential qualities of good and efficient officers; to prepare ourselves as educated men to take a more active part and to have a greater influence in the military affairs of the communities in which we may reside; and above all to spread intelligent information concerning the military requirements of our country."
— Preamble of the constitution of the National Society of Scabbard and Blade.

FACULTY ADVISER
Lieutenant Colonel Howard Donnelly

MEMBERS IN FACULTY

Major Eugene N. Morrow   Major A. W. S. Sanders   Major W. S. Harrow

OFFICERS

LLOYD B. RAMSEY		Captain
FRANK B. ROBERTS		First Lieutenant
LOGAN CALDWELL		Second Lieutenant
JOHN C. TUTTLE		First Sergeant

MEMBERS

Charles Aitkin	Joe Burnette	William Drumny	Albert Hoskins	Frank Roberts
Harry Alexander	Logan Caldwell	Fred J. Fischer	Roger Lyons	Austin Triplett
Virgil Beasley	W. G. Coblin	Harry Gordon	Robert McGill	William L. Tudor
James O. Bell	Elbert L. Cooper	Joseph Greenwell	John Mylor	John C. Tuttle
John C. Bode	Harry Denham	Marshall Guthrie	P. T. Porterfield	Harris Walker
Thomson Bryant	Robert Dickerson	Robert Hansen	Lloyd B. Ramsey	James Wine

Military Queen Jane Baynham . . .

Courtesy Herald-Leader

. . . emerges with Cadet Colonel Lloyd Ramsey from an arch of ROTC sabers. Miss Baynham, who was crowned at Scabbard and Blade's annual formal Saturday night, is a Lexington sophomore and a member of Kappa Kappa Gamma sorority. Attendants chosen were Peggy Denny, Independent, Lexington; Peg Tallman, Kappa Kappa Gamma, Miami, Fla.; Dorothy Hillenmeyer, Delta Delta Delta, Lexington; and DoAnn Young, Chi Omega, Glencoe, Ill.

INCL. # 9

STUDENT UNION BOARD

PURPOSE

The activities of the Union Building are divided into separate committees. The Board of Directors brings the different chairmen together in order that greater efficiency and unity can be effected in the operation of the Union.

UNION DIRECTOR	ASSISTANT DIRECTOR	STUDENT ASSISTANT
James S. Shropshire	Ronald Sharpe	Vincent Fanelli

MEMBERS IN FACULTY

Sarah Blanding	T. T. Jones	M. E. Potter

OFFICERS

Dorothy Hillenmeyer . . . . President
John H. Clarke . . . . Vice-President
Frances Hannah . . . . Secretary-Treasurer

MEMBERS

John H. Clarke	Frances Hannah	Susan Jackson
John Conrad	Dorothy Hillenmeyer	Lloyd Rumsey
Vincent Fanelli	Murry Holroyd	James Wine

STUDENT LEGISLATURE

Installed on campus in September, 1939

PURPOSE

The purpose of the Student Government Association is to enact and enforce such legislation as is hereinafter set out, with a view to a harmonious coordination of the various organizations on the campus, to effect a centralized student government, better faculty-student cooperation, and to promote the general welfare of the student body.

OFFICERS

WILLIAM DUTY	President
ROBERT NASH	Men's Vice-President
JEANNE BARKER	Women's Vice-President
RUTH CLAY PALMER	Secretary
C. P. JOHNSON	Treasurer

MEMBERS

Agriculture College
Robert Booton
John Clore
Sam Triplett

Arts and Sciences College
Robert Allen
James Caldwell
Mary Duncan
Llewellyn Holmes
John Hunsaker
Ruth Clay Palmer
Sarah Randell
Harry Zimmerman

Law College
Arthur Bryson

Graduate School
Marie Harris
Lillian Gaines Webb

Ex-officio Members
Dorothy Hillenmeyer
Patricia Stein
Crittenden Lowry

Commerce College
Howard Davis
Mary Catlyn Gregory
C. P. Johnson

Education College
Lloyd Ramsey

Engineering College
David Blythe
Carl Staker

Freshmen
Robert Ammons
Dorothy Angle

The New

INCL. # 11

85

LAMP AND CROSS

SENIOR HONORARY FOR MEN

Founded in 1903

PURPOSE

The purpose of this organization is to recognize qualities of leadership among outstanding members of the senior class.

FACULTY ADVISER
T. R. Bryant

MEMBERS IN FACULTY
Kurt Peek   J. Richard Johnson   Ab Kirwan

OFFICERS

CRITTENDEN LOWRY . . . . President
LLOYD B. RAMSEY . . . . Vice-President
GLENN N. STANFORD . . . . Secretary
EDDIE DAVID . . . . Treasurer

MEMBERS

Logan Caldwell, *Phi Delta Theta*
David Knox Blythe, *Triangle*
Eddie David, *Phi Kappa Tau*
Lloyd B. Ramsey, *Sigma Chi*
Richard Vincent Fanelli, *Phi Kappa Tau*
Franklin R. Frazier, *Alpha Gamma Rho*

George W. Kusocheh, *Independent*
Crittenden Lowry, *Sigma Alpha Epsilon*
Phillip K. Phillis, *Alpha Tau Omega*
Glenn N. Stanford, *Delta Tau Delta*
John Bruce Sullivan, *Independent*
Harry Johnson Weeks, *Independent*

Clifton Powell Johnson, *Lambda Chi Alpha*

WHO'S WHO

AMONG STUDENTS IN AMERICAN UNIVERSITIES AND COLLEGES

Founded at the University of Alabama in 1934

PURPOSE

"The idea of creating one national basis of recognition for students, devoid of politics, initiation fees, and dues was conceived by its founders a number of years ago. For four years it has published a book containing the biographies of outstanding students in American Universities and colleges as well as every phase of activity in the college world. It is designed to be a book of value to the college library, to the business and social world, and to the students themselves."—Foreword, 1940 Who's Who.

MEMBERS

COLLEGE OF EDUCATION
Margaret Purdom, Hazard
Lloyd Ramsey, Somerset
Mary Lou McFarland, Lexington

COLLEGE OF LAW
Alan Vogeler, Lexington
James W. Wine, Charleston, W. Va.

COLLEGE OF ENGINEERING
Harry Weaks, Water Valley
George Kurschek, New York City

COLLEGE OF COMMERCE
William L. Tudor, Lexington
Fivelus Hunter, Buffalo, N. Y.

COLLEGE OF AGRICULTURE
Franklin Frazier, Upper Tygart
William Duty, Winchester

COLLEGE OF ARTS AND SCIENCES
L. T. Iglehart, Hopkinsville
Harriet Hendershot, Louisville
John H. Morgan, Madisonville
Jeanne Barker, Louisville
Crist Lowry, Princeton
Barbara MacVey, Canton, N. Y.
David Scott, Kent, Ohio
Dorothy Hillenmeyer, Lexington

Who's Who

AMONG STUDENTS IN AMERICAN UNIVERSITIES AND COLLEGES

H. Pettus Randall
Editor

University, Alabama

Dear Parent:

Your son has been selected as one of the outstanding students in America. This selection was an unprejudiced and unbiased one by a committee from the institution which he attends. The biography is being printed in the college publication of the 1939-40 Who's Who Among Students in American Universities and Colleges, in which nearly every college in the United States is represented.

This means of recognition is the only recognition that a student receives while attending college that is devoid of politics, initiation fees and dues. It is also the only means of recognition which is used so that the student may directly benefit from it. If you will read the enclosed pamphlet, you will note the high requirements that are necessary for one's biography to appear in this publication. This honor is the highest honor that a student can achieve while in college, because only a very small number of seniors and juniors are selected from each institution. We congratulate you on being the parent of such a student.

We are sending the biographies and pictures of these students to their respective home town newspapers in order that they may receive more recognition which they rightly deserve.

Besides the honor that students receive from having their biography appear in the publication they will be placed before the business world and others who annually recruit outstanding students. It is because this is such an honor and because we think that you should be proud of your son that we write you.

Again--Congratulations on being the parent of such a student. We wish him all of the success in the world.

Sincerely yours,

The Editor.

THIS PUBLICATION HAS NO CONNECTION WITH THE UNIVERSITY OF ALABAMA OR ANY OTHER UNIVERSITY, BUT IS PUBLISHED THROUGH THE COOPERATION OF ALL AMERICAN UNIVERSITIES AND COLLEGES.

INCL. # 13-2

J. Johnson   Wine   Tudor   Morgan   Vogeler   C. Johnson
Duty   Iglehart   Holcomb   Ramsey   Lowry   Clure
Clark   Scott   Bryant   Hunter   Blythe   Hunsaker

OMICRON DELTA KAPPA

MEN'S LEADERSHIP FRATERNITY

NU CIRCLE

Founded at Washington and Lee University in 1914
Established on campus in 1925

PURPOSE

A national organization which recognizes outstanding junior and senior men in the various phases of campus life. Men are selected on an earned point system and elected to membership by the circle.

The circle recognizes men who have attained a high standard of efficiency in collegiate activities and inspires others to strive for conspicuous attainment along similar lines.

FACULTY ADVISER
R. D. McIntyre

MEMBERS IN FACULTY

Albert Kirwan   George Muransky   Roy Moreland   James May   Thomas P. Cooper
Adolph Rupp   J. Huntley Dupre   R. D. McIntyre   Bernie Shively   William S. Taylor
R. W. Spicer   Henry Beaumont   M. E. Potter   Frank L. McVey   Edward Wiest
James Shropshire   C. N. Melcher   H. H. Downing   W. D. Funkhouser   W. E. Freeman
Gene Myers   L. C. Robinson   G. Davis Buckner   Paul P. Boyd   L. J. Horlacher

OFFICERS

JOHN MORGAN . . . . President
WILLIAM DUTY . . . . Vice-President
JOE R. JOHNSON, JR. . . . . Secretary
M. E. POTTER . . . . Treasurer

MEMBERS

David Blythe   William Duty   L. T. Iglehart   Crittenden Lowry   David Scott
T. R. Bryant, Jr.   Merry Holcomb   Joe R. Johnson, Jr.   John H. Morgan   William Tudor
John Clarke   John Hunsaker   C. P. Johnson   David Pettus   Alan R. Vogeler
John G. Clure   Freelon Hunter   Lloyd Ramsey   James Wine

INCL. # 14

UNIVERSITY OF KENTUCKY
LEXINGTON

COLLEGE OF EDUCATION
OFFICE OF THE DEAN

December 4, 1939

Dear Mr. Rumsey:

I was delighted to see you made a member of Omicron Delta Kappa. You have made an excellent record at the University of Kentucky both scholastically and in your extra-curricular activities. You have been a good leader and I want to tell you that we very genuinely appreciate it.

Very sincerely yours,

William S. Taylor

Mr. Lloyd B. Ramsey
343 Harrison Avenue
Lexington, Kentucky

INCL. # 14-2

SWIMMING

Under the leadership of Captain Lloyd Ramsey, the University of Kentucky "pool-less wonders" splashed through a fairly successful season.

A repetition of last year's undefeated season just "wasn't in the books" for the Mermen this year. Finishing ahead of six opponents, behind four, and tieing one in seven dual meets and two triangle meets was the fate of the swimmers. The orphans won from Eastern, Georgia Tech, and Armour Tech in dual meets. They lost to Florida and Georgia, the first and third ranking teams in the Southeast, respectively, and to DeMurray and Tusculum and split with Tennessee.

The local Y. W. C. A. pool replaced Eastern's tank as training quarters this year. The pool being under the regulation length and width and lacking proper diving facilities proved somewhat of a drawback. Its proximity to the college enabled the men to work out more frequently. By diligent practice the club managed to average 42.5 points per meet as compared with their opponents averaging 35.5.

Comprising this year's team were: Sprints and sprint relays - Frank Roberts, Lloyd Ramsey, Walter Reid, Henry Hillenmeyer and Gilberrt Wymond; breast stroke - Edwin David and Gene Riddell; back stroke - James Scott and Carl Colby; distance - Gilbert Wymond, Jack Lewis and Jim Doyle; divers - Letelle Stephenson and Houston Curtis.

First place winners during the season were: Roberts and Scott, six; Stephenson, five; David and Ramsey, four; Wymond, two; Curtis and Hillenmeyer, one. Together with the relay teams, these point winners furnished the nucleus of the scoring. The medley relay team of Scott, David, and Ramsey, and the dash relay team of Wymond, Hillenmeyer, Roberts, and Ramsey were each victorious seven times and defeated twice during the season. Georgia and Florida had the distinction of being the only two teams in five years of competition to defeat the medley relay team.

Reid, Hillenmeyer, Wymond, Scott, Curtis, and Stephenson are the only veterans who will answer roll call next year. Though the loss of Roberts, Ramsey, David, Riddell, and Colby will weaken the squad severely, some promising freshmen are expected to fill their vacancies.

Individual champions on the team include: Roberts, fifty and hundred yard free style; Scott, 150 yard back stroke; and Curtis, one meter diving. The above titles are Kentucky Intercollegiate championships, which were established last year in the state meet. Scott also hold the Kentucky A. A. U. hundred yard back stroke championship. Ed David, Kentucky's most versatile swimmer holds the Kentucky A. A. U. fifty yard free style championship, although he has swum distance and breast stroke solely in collegiate competition. Letelle Stephenson holds the Kentucky A. A. U. open and the A. A. U. mid-states open championship from the three meter springboard.

Seated: Stephenson, Riddell, Ramsey, James S. Shropshire, Advisor; Hillenmeyer, David, Curtis.
Standing: Roberts, Wymond, Reid, Colby, Scott.

INCL. # 15

DOWN in FRONT

BY LARRY SHROPSHIRE

TODAY'S FLOURISHING big bow goes to a very personable young collegian, Lloyd Ramsey, who hails from down in the briar-jumping country, specifically Somerset. There must be a reason why "Feller," as he is commonly known, is easily one of the most popular students at the University of Kentucky.

Start scouting around for information and you quickly find that there is not one but quite a number of reasons for his popularity.

Among the chief ones are his genuine friendliness, his fine spirit and, above all, his complete unselfishness.

A typical Ramsey performance popped up just a few days ago. The U. K. boxing team was going to Washington for a match and a couple of cars were needed for the trip. Coach Frank Moseley furnishes one. "Feller" volunteered to take the rest of the Wildcat boxers in his.

The trip to Washington took 16 hours, a journey hard enough to leave the fighters in anything but top condition for their scraps. They reached their destination at 2 o'clock in the morning, Ramsey having been at the wheel of his car all the way.

That night, still stiff and tired from the long ride, the Wildcats took their turns in the ring. No one had been taken along to fight in the light-heavyweight class, so "Feller," although he had fought only a few times in intramural bouts and was not in training for boxing, volunteered to represent Kentucky in that division.

Not only that, but he made a great showing and gave plenty of trouble to his opponent, a trained-down former 186-pound heavyweight who outweighed the Somerset boy eight pounds when they entered the ring.

In the first round Ramsey was caught off balance and knocked off his feet. That, he admitted later, kinda got his dander up, so shortly he hung a solid smack on his foe that sent the latter to the canvas, a shocking blow that made the Washington boy glad to stay down for a count of nine before he got back to his feet to outpoint the less-experienced U. K. battler during the rest of the bout.

"Feller" had no business in the ring, but he went into the bout anyway, trying his best to win a point for Kentucky.

---o---

Phooey On A Broken Neck

Young Ramsey, hitting the scales then at only 168 pounds, played in several football games with the Wildcats last fall, and you never could have told from the way he played that a couple of years ago, as a freshman, he received a broken neck in spring grid practice. The injury made him wear a cast for four weeks, then a brace on his neck for five more.

He laid out of football the next season, but last fall came out for the squad again, having more enthusiasm and energy than ever.

You'd hardly expect Ramsey to be any different from what he is as his dad, Bill Ramsey, is one of the most loyal supporters the University has. Although not a U. K. alumnus, he has probably traveled more to watch Kentucky play the last few seasons than any other fan.

The elder Ramsey, too, commodore of the Somerset Boat Club, is looked upon as the "father" of the U. K. swimming team. He attends most of the tank meets, he's helped the team in a material way more than once, and furnishes the car that his son uses regularly to take part of the team to Richmond to practice in the Eastern pool and to make the trips for their various meets.

The son, star dash man of the team for two years, is serving this season also as coach of the swimmers.

The Kentucky team has no pool and no hired coach, and when outside work this year prevented Sherman Finkelson, breaststroke, ex-from handling the coaching duties, young Ramsey was nominated for the job. He took it—not because he thought he was particularly qualified to serve as coach, but because someone has to carry the responsibility of organizing the team and directing it in competition.

LLOYD RAMSEY

When A Fellow Needs A Friend

Another insight into the fine character of "Feller" was revealed in a conversation the other day with Bill Boston. One of his legs having been badly injured in spring football practice a year ago, Bill was in the hospital several months and also was compelled to miss school the first semester.

Now back in school for the second semester, he was asked how his leg was coming along. As uncomplaining as ever, he replied:

"It's doing all right, except that my foot won't heal up. I limp pretty badly in this leg, but I don't have to use crutches anymore, and that's the main thing. And I don't have any trouble going to school. 'Feller' Ramsey takes me from one building to another for every one of my classes and all the walking I have to do is just up and down stairs."

Ramsey doesn't help Bill to get around because he was assigned to do it. It just seems to be his nature to help a friend whenever he can.

Yes, it's a lucky day when there comes along a fellow like "Feller."

Caption Reads:

When A Feller Needs A Friend
  Another insight into the fine character of "Feller" Was revealed in a conversation the other day with Bill Boston. One of his legs having been badly injured in spring football practice a year ago, Bill was in the hospital several months and also was compelled to miss school the first semester.
  Now back in school for the second semester, he was asked how his leg was coming along. As uncomplaining as ever, he replied:
  It's doing all right, except that my foot won't heal up. I limp pretty badly in this leg, but I don't have to use crutches anymore, and that's the main thing. And I don't have any trouble going to school. 'Feller' Ramsey takes me from one building to another for every one of my classes and all the walking I have to do is just up and down stairs."
  Ramsey doesn't help Bill to get around because he was assigned to do it. It just seems to be his nature to help a friend whenever he can.
  Yes, it's a lucky day when there comes along a fellow like "Feller."

Looking for That Decision He Dropped to Columbus U.

The Posts photographer snapped the Kentucky's light-heavyweight, Lloyd Ramsey, in an embarrasing pose last night at Turner's Arena. At first glance it appears that Ramsey might be looking for something, while opponent Jim Brown hovers over him, and Referee Charley Reynolds brings up the rear. this was Ramsey's second time on the canvas in the first round. Between trips he put Brown down once for a nine-count with a brisling right hook to the jaw. Brown eventually won a decision.
Post staff photo.

INCL. # 16-2

He Ain't Resting on Purpose

Jimmy Brown, Columbus University's slugging light heavyweight, is about to come in violent contact with the deck, onto which he was unceremoniously dumped last night when his jawbone collided with Loyd Ramsey's right fist. Brown, who had just floored Ramsey, got up and did it again, however, thereby rating an "a" on effort. Jimmy also won the decision.

Caption reads:

Jimmy Brown, Columbus University's slugging light heavy weight, is about to come in violent contact with the deck, onto which he was unceremoniously dumped last night when his jawbone collided with Loyd Ramsey's right fist. Brown, who had just floored Ramsey, got up and did it again, however, thereby rating an "a" for effort. Jimmy also won the decision.

INCL. # 16-3

UNIVERSITY OF KENTUCKY
LEXINGTON

COLLEGE OF ARTS AND SCIENCES
DEPARTMENT OF PHYSICAL EDUCATION

COPY

December 5
1 9 3 9

Colonel Howard Donnelly
Military Department
University of Kentucky

Dear Colonel Donnelly:

I am writing you at the request of Mr. Lloyd Ramsey, who informs me that he is an applicant for a commission in the United States Army.

Mr. Ramsey has majored in the Department of Physical Education during his undergraduate work at the University of Kentucky. As a student in this department, Mr. Ramsey's scholastic work has been well above average. In addition to his scholastic work, this young man has been a most active participant in many of the extracurricular affairs of this department and the University. It is significant to note in this connection that in practically all of his extracurricular activities, he has been elected or appointed to positions of leadership.

Attention is called to the fact that among many other honors at the University, Mr. Ramsey has received the following: membership in Omicron Delta Kappa, men's honorary leadership society; president of the Physical Education Club; captain of the University swimming team; and assistant football coach of the freshman varsity football team.

Beyond reason of doubt, Mr. Ramsey possesses many qualities of leadership that should serve him well as a commissioned officer in the United States Army. He is a young man of fine personal appearance. His character and moral conduct are of the very best. It is a pleasure indeed to recommend this young man to the position for which he is applying.

Cordially yours,

M. E. Potter, Head
Department of Physical Education
MEP O'C

INCL. # 17

E D U C A T I O N

MARY ELIZABETH MOORE
Etowah, Tennessee
Glee Club; Y. W. C. A.; Phi Beta;
Future Teachers of America

REX OSTEEN
Sigma Alpha Epsilon
Hopkinsville
Blue and White Orchestra; Radio Ensemble

JEAN ANN OVERSTREET
Kappa Delta
Lexington
Women's Glee Club; Y. W. C. A.

RENA PEDEN
Lexington
Physical Education Club; Spanish Club; W. A. A. Council; Future Teachers of America

FRANKLIN REED PERKINS
Lexington

BETTIE GIBSON PHELPS
Kappa Delta
Somerset
Y. W. C. A.; Glee Club; Choristers; Madrigal Singers; Phi Beta

MARGARET PRUITT
Owensboro
Future Teachers of America; W. A. A.; Physical Education Club; Y. W. C. A.; Modern Dance Club

MARGARET PURDOM
Kappa Kappa Gamma
Hazard
President Mortar Board; Phi Beta; Y. W. C. A.; Junior Round Table; Glee Club; Student Union Committee

LLOYD B. RAMSEY
Sigma Chi
Somerset
Cadet Colonel R. O. T. C.; Captain Scabbard and Blade; President Physical Education Club; Captain Swimming Team; Football, Track; Board of Directors Student Union; Vice-President Lamp and Cross; Vice President Sigma Chi; Y. M. C. A.; Omicron Delta Kappa

ELIZABETH RAND
Kappa Delta
Foley, Florida
Physical Education Club; W. A. A.; Modern Dance Club; Y. W. C. A.

INCL. # 18

Twenty-first Annual

Military Field Day and R.O.T.C. Graduation Exercises

Wednesday, May 29, 1940
Stoll Field

University of Kentucky

Lexington

INCL. # 19

Program

I. ASSEMBLY of the Reserve Officers' Training Corps Regiment, 6:30 p. m.

II. PASS IN REVIEW BY THE REGIMENT In Honor of the President, University of Kentucky.

III. COMPETITIVE COMPANY DRILL for the Colonel Freeman Trophy.
 Company E, Cadet Captain Frank Bryant Roberts, Lexington, Kentucky, Commanding.
 Company K, Cadet Captain Roger Lee Lyons, Cave City, Kentucky, Commanding.

IV. DEMONSTRATION—Sponsors Training Company.
 Captain Mary G. Hayworth, Lynch, Kentucky, Commanding.

V. INDIVIDUAL COMPETITIVE DRILL for Scabbard and Blade Trophy.
 Company A: Cadet Corporal Leslie Van Hoy, Henderson, Kentucky.
 Company B: Cadet Corporal Howard Moffett, Jr., Lexington, Kentucky.
 Company C: Cadet Corporal John Wesley Hinkle, Lexington, Kentucky.
 Company E: Cadet Corporal William Dixon Maxedon, Lexington, Kentucky.
 Company F: Cadet Winfield Webb Ward, Lexington, Kentucky.
 Company G: Cadet Corporal Albert Joseph Spare, Covington, Kentucky.
 Company I: Cadet Corporal Joseph Bolnuk, Northampton, Massachusetts.
 Company K: Cadet Corporal Addison Wolcott Lee, III, Louisville, Kentucky.
 Company L: Cadet James Ivan Potts, Shelbyville, Tennessee.

VI. EXHIBITION DRILL—First Platoon, Company C, First Regiment, Pershing Rifles.

VII. AWARD OF TROPHIES.

VIII. ADMINISTRATION OF OATH OF OFFICE as Second Lieutenants, Officers' Reserve Corps.

IX. GRADUATION PARADE. In honor of Reserve Officers' Association of the Kentucky Military Area.

List of Awards

UNIVERSITY CUP — Awarded to the Company attaining the highest scholastic average in Military Science during the academic year 1939-1940.
 Awarded to: Company C, Cadet Captain Joseph William Bailey, Lexington, Kentucky, Commanding.

COLONEL FREEMAN CUP — Awarded to the Company winning the drill competition this evening.

ROTARY CLUB TROPHY — Awarded to the graduating member of the Second Year Advanced Course, Reserve Officers' Training Corps, who is selected by secret vote of the Advanced Course students as excelling in the requirements of good citizenship.
 Awarded to: Cadet Colonel Lloyd Brinkley Ramsey, Somerset, Kentucky.

AMERICAN LEGION CUP, MAN O' WAR POST — Awarded to the graduating cadet officer selected by a board of Regular Army officers as outstanding and possessing in marked degree those inherent qualities necessary in the making of an officer and gentleman.

Awarded to: Cadet Colonel Lloyd Brinkley Ramsey, Somerset, Kentucky

RESERVE OFFICERS' ASSOCIATION TROPHY — Awarded to the graduating member of the Second Year Advanced Course, Reserve Officers' Training Corps, having the highest standing in all his university work.

Awarded to: Cadet Major Thomson Ripley Bryant, Jr., Lexington, Kentucky.

PHOENIX HOTEL TROPHY — Awarded to the member of the Second Year Advanced Course, Reserve Officers' Training Corps, having the highest average in Military Science for academic year 1939-1940.

Awarded to: Cadet Major James Olin Bell, Hopkinsville, Kentucky.

LAFAYETTE HOTEL TROPHY — Awarded to the member of the First Year Advanced Course, Reserve Officers' Training Corps, having the highest average in Military Science for the academic year 1939-1940.

Awarded to: Cadet Sergeant Roy Winston Mullis, Lexington, Kentucky.

KIWANIS CLUB TROPHY — Awarded to the member of the Second Year Basic Course, Reserve Officers' Training Corps, having the highest average in Military Science for the academic year 1939-1940.

Awarded to: Cadet Corporal Albert Joseph Spare, Covington, Kentucky.

PERSHING RIFLES TROPHY — Awarded to the member of the First Year Basic Course, Reserve Officers' Training Corps, having the highest average in Military Science for the academic year 1939-1940.

Awarded to: Cadet Corporal Richard Keating Young, Winchester, Kentucky.

LIONS CLUB TROPHY — Awarded to the member of the Reserve Officers' Training Corps Rifle Team having the highest record in team competition.

Awarded to: Cadet Corporal Maurice Edward Mitchell, Campbellsville, Kentucky.

SCABBARD AND BLADE CUP — Awarded to the winner of the basic individual drill competition this evening.

Awarded to: Cadet ....

Honor Graduates

Cadet Major James Olin Bell, Hopkinsville, Kentucky.
Cadet Major Thomson Ripley Bryant, Jr., Lexington, Kentucky.
Cadet Captain George Philip Carter, Louisa, Kentucky.
Cadet Captain Robert Louis Dickerson, Lexington, Kentucky.
Cadet Lieutenant Colonel William Joseph Drummy, Lexington, Kentucky.
Cadet Lieutenant Marshall Beck Guthrie, Lexington, Kentucky.
Cadet Captain Roger Lee Lyons, Cave City, Kentucky.
Cadet Colonel Lloyd Brinkley Ramsey, Somerset, Kentucky.
Cadet Lieutenant Colonel Robert Tackett Scott, Lexington, Kentucky.

Sigma Chi Fraternity

Founded at Miami University, Oxford, Ohio, June 28, 1855

GRAND PRAETOR
Kentucky-Tennessee Province
DR. ULLIN W. LEAVELL
George Peabody College for Teachers
Nashville, Tennessee

June 5, 1940

Mr. Lloyd B. Ramsey
Sigma Chi Fraternity
Rose & Kalmia Streets
Lexington, Kentucky

Dear Brother Ramsey:

I am delighted to state that the committee which I asked to judge the papers submitted on representatives of the active chapters in this province unanimously voted in favor of your receiving the*award for the Kentucky-Tennessee province. Permit me to congratulate you, sir, and to wish you every success in your further preparation for service in our great country.

In the bonds of Sigma Chi, I am

Fraternally yours,

Ullin W. Leavell

UWL:MA

*Baltur

INCL. # 20

LLOYD RAMSEY GETS FRATERNITY AWARD

It was learned here this week that Lieut. Lloyd B. Ramsey, son of Mr. and Mrs. W. H. Ramsey, has been awarded the Balfour Province Award of the Sigma Chi fraternity for the year 1939-40.

The award, in the form of a gold key bearing the insignia of the fraternity, was accompanied by a leather bound, engraved certificate stating that he has been selected as the most representative undergraduate of the Kentucky-Tennessee province of Sigma Chi on the basis of scholarship, personality, fraternity service and student activity.

Lieutenant Ramsey graduated from the University of Kentucky in June where he was a member of Lambda Lambda chapter of Sigma Chi. He won the Pershing Medal for being the outstanding R.O.T.C. cadet in the Fifth Corps Area, U. S. Army, and on the basis of this achievement was given the rank of lieutenant in the regular army. Lieutenant Ramsey is now stationed at Fort Bragg, N. C.

The Balfour Province Award is the highest honor the fraternity is capable of bestowing upon one of its members.

This Award concerns the Balfour award.
The article was in the Somerset, Ky. paper in early Aug. 1940.
I am extremely proud of what the last paragraph states:
"The Balfour Province Award is the highest honor the fraternity is capable of bestowing upon one of its members."

INCL. # 20-2

INCL. # 21

CHAPTER 4

JULY 1, 1940 ENTERED ARMY – WORLD WAR II
DECEMBER 7, 1941 – NOVEMBER 14, 1943

July 1, 1940: Appointed Second Lieutenant Regular Army

When I graduated from the University of Kentucky in May 1940, I received an appointment as a Second Lieutenant, Reserve Corps. I had been notified that I would receive an appointment as a Regular Army Second Lieutenant on July 1, 1940 and that I would report to the 10th Infantry, Fort Thomas, Kentucky, on July 15, 1940 for my first assignment. Copy of my official orders are at Inclusion #1 at the end of this chapter.

I reported to Fort Thomas on July 15, 1940 as ordered. I was given a nice set of bachelor quarters, but I was told that I would not have time to fix up my quarters because I was being sent to Fort Knox, Kentucky to join some demonstration troops there that were from Fort Thomas. I left the next day for Fort Knox and was there for a few days and then returned to Fort Thomas. I started to fix up my quarters when I received orders on July 27 transferring me to the Ninth Infantry Division, Fort Bragg, North Carolina. My orders gave me two days to get there. When I arrived, I found out that the Ninth Infantry Division was just being organized. As I recall, within the first week we had about eleven second lieutenants and two lieutenant colonels, plus a number of non-commissioned officers that would make up the cadre. The two lieutenant colonels would be the Division G-3 and Division G-4. We were assigned to regiments that did not exist except on paper.

Three of us were assigned to the 39th Infantry. We were all given additional duties to get the division organized. We were going to live in a tent camp. I was assigned the duty of division construction quartermaster with the mission of building the tent camp for the division. I was assigned a number of very fine non-commissioned officers, many with some construction experience. Our job was to build frames and floors for a four-wall tent. Each tent would house four enlisted men or two officers. For the division that meant that we would have to build about 3,000 frames and floors. A survey crew kept in front of us so we knew exactly where to build the frames. After one week, I was relieved by a Quartermaster Lieutenant Colonel with a much larger crew to complete the work. Very soon there was a contract made to build wooden barracks and offices for the Division. We started moving into them in January, 1941.

In the fall, I was selected to attend an Infantry Officers Communications Course at Fort Benning, Georgia. I returned in time to live in those cold tents even though we had coal stoves in the tents.

February 1941: Received Leave to Get Married

Glenda and I had been planning to marry, and we finally set a date of February 22, 1941, George Washington's birthday. I was given two weeks leave to get home, get married, and have our honeymoon. We wanted a very small wedding so we were married in the parsonage of the First Baptist Church, Somerset. The pastor of the church, D. L. Hill, conducted the services. Glenda's sister, Edna Mason Burton, was the bridesmaid, and Starling S. Gregory, one of my closest friends and a neighbor, was the best man. Pictures are at the end of this chapter (Inclusions #2 and #3). The Somerset newspaper had a nice article about our wedding. A copy of the article is at the end of this chapter (Inclusion #4).

Our Honeymoon – Not So Good

We immediately took off on our honeymoon. The first night we stayed in Chattanooga, Tennessee. Glenda was not feeling very well so we did not do much celebrating. The next morning she felt better so we headed for Florida. As the day passed, Glenda started to feel worse. By the time we had reached Lake City, Florida, she was feeling pretty bad. We stopped and asked for a room at a hotel and the clerk, in a rather strange tone, said, "Let me check." She came back and said that they had one room left that we could have. (The clerk told me later that they had already turned people away, but that Glenda looked so sick she went to the manager and requested that we give her their last room and he agreed.)

By the time we got to the room, Glenda was feeling very bad. I called the front desk and asked what was the best way for her to see a doctor. They said that they had a doctor that would come by and see her within an hour. The doctor was there within 30 minutes. He said that Glenda had a bad case of pneumonia and should go to the hospital for at least one day. He let her out the next afternoon but said that she could not travel for at least two days and that he would check her then. I called my regiment, explained my problem, and told them that I might be a day or so late returning from leave. They were kind enough to give me an open-end leave to cover whatever time I needed. In two days the doctor released Glenda. The bills came to $100.00, but since Dad had given me $100.00 for our honeymoon, I had enough money to pay them. I then wondered how much the hotel would charge me. Once again, to my surprise, the lady at the desk said because of our problem they were giving us a special rate of $5.00 per day, and since Glenda was not in the room one night, they would only charge me half price or $2.50 for that night. Total cost, $12.50. Then to top things off, they lent me three pillows and two blankets so that Glenda could get comfortable in the back seat while we were traveling back to Fort Bragg. They did ask that we send the pillows and blankets back to them, but they would not let me sign a receipt that I had them. We were treated like royalty by the doctor, the hospital, and the hotel.

Training Was Very Rigorous for the Next Few Months

Trying to get a division organized and training the men for combat was a difficult job for all. Our training days were usually very long and very hard. I was probably in the best condition that I had ever been – even when I was playing football – because we had long hikes and took other exercises with the troops on a daily basis. Conditioning was a very important part of training.

Promotions to 1st Lieutenant

With the Army growing rapidly, promotions were coming more frequently. On October 10, 1941, to my surprise, I was promoted to the rank of 1st Lieutenant. Many of the Reserve Corps second lieutenants that I was serving with were envious of my having a Regular Army Commission. When these promotions came through, they were now sorry for me instead of being envious. The reason: a Regular Army Officer could only receive the pay of his Regular Rank except in time of war. That meant that I would as a 1st Lieutenant be drawing a 2nd

Lieutenant's pay, which was about $25.00 a month less. On December 7, 1941, Pearl Harbor Day, my pay was automatically increased because war had been declared.

December 7, 1941: Pearl Harbor Day, Fort Bragg, North Carolina

On December 7, 1941, Glenda and I were babysitting for my company commander and his wife, Captain and Mrs. O. Z. Tyler. They had out-of-town guests and all wanted to play golf but could not find a babysitter. The Tylers had been very nice to Glenda and me so when I learned of their problem I called Glenda and we volunteered to sit with their two children, a boy and a girl, so that they could play golf. We brought the children to our small apartment for the day.

When we first heard the news on the radio that Pearl Harbor, Hawaii, had been bombed by the Japanese (there was no TV in those days), we thought it was one of those programs that try to scare people. It was not long until we learned that it was the real thing. The Tylers received the word on the golf course and came to pick up the children very soon. It was not long until we were called to our units to prepare for deployment. Although I had been in O. Z.'s company for some time, I was now commanding the anti-tank company as a 1st Lieutenant.

As time passed, we learned that the Japanese bombed Pearl Harbor with complete surprise with fighter planes from an aircraft carrier. Most of our aircraft were destroyed while still on the ground. Nineteen of our warships were destroyed or damaged in Pearl Harbor. There were 2,300 people killed. Many of the casualties were on the USS Arizona, a battleship that was sunk with all of its crew on board. The United States declared war on Japan on December 8, 1941 and also on Germany, who had been at war since 1939. Germany declared war on the United States on December 11, 1941.

Early the next day, my company was deployed to Salisbury, North Carolina. Salisbury had large railroad shops and many bridges that terrorists could destroy or damage. My company was given the mission of guarding the railroad shops and certain bridges. My uncle Robert Barnett lived in Salisbury and worked at the shops. He invited me to sleep at his house, then called Glenda, and she came up and stayed there also. I spent most of my time inspecting troops at these various guard locations, both day and night, but did have enough time to enjoy a meal with Glenda and my Uncle Bob and Aunt Mary Stella. We stayed there about one week and then moved back to Fort Bragg.

April 1, 1942: Allotment

On April 1, 1942, I made an allotment to the Citizens National Bank, Somerset, Kentucky, to our joint checking account for $170.00 per month. This allotment for Glenda's living expenses was in case I was ordered overseas or someplace else in the United States where she could not go. I would not write checks on this account. I believe that I had $20.00 left on payday to buy the essentials that I needed to live on.

May 21, 1942: Promotion to Captain

I was promoted to Captain on May 21, 1942, with a date of rank of February 1, 1942, by War Department order dated May 21, 1942, S.O. #133. I did not receive any additional pay for the period February 1 to May 21, 1942.

August 1942: Fayetteville, North Carolina

Glenda and I lived in a part of someone's home. It was dark and gloomy with little space. We found an apartment below a friend of ours. The place was originally a two-car garage with an apartment above. To make the apartment large enough, they had built two small rooms behind the two-car garage. They had now taken one garage and the two rooms behind the garages and made a second apartment. The garage became the living room, the kitchen was immediately behind the garage, and the other room became the bedroom. At the end of this chapter (Inclusion #5), there are three pictures: (1) Glenda and me; (2) Mimi, Glenda, and me; (3) Dad and me. They came down to visit us in August 1942. The picture of Glenda and me (#1) shows our apartment in the background. We had the downstairs.

September 1, 1942: Promotion to Major

In order to be eligible for promotion to Major, you had to be in grade for six months. Since my promotion to Captain on May 21,

1942 had a date of rank of February 1, 1942, I was eligible for promotion. I was the S-3 of the regiment, which was a Major's position, so I received my promotion to Major on September 1, 1942. I was very lucky. Many of my friends were promoted in May with me but did not receive an early date of rank; therefore, they had to wait until they were in grade for six months to be promoted.

September 1942: Secret Orders

Glenda's mother, father, and brother Sonny, 11 years old, had been down to see us. I believe it was August 1942. By then we were wearing uniforms all the time and were expected to go overseas anytime. Therefore, I sent all my civilian clothes home with them.

Just before my promotion the regimental commander called me in one day and told me that we had secret orders to leave on September 17, 1942, for Washington, D.C. and then to London, England. The orders included the regimental commander, myself (the S-3), and the S-1. Our flight to London would be on a civilian airline that would land in Ireland, where we could not wear uniforms because it was a free state and they could intern us for the duration of the war. I could tell Glenda when I was leaving but not where I was going. I did tell her that I had to have civilian clothes but could not tell her why and that we would have to buy some because I did not have enough time to get them from home.

We arranged with the Army for a moving van to move our belongings to Somerset. Glenda had to drive herself to Somerset and do everything that I would normally do or at least assist her in doing. We had no idea when we would see each other again, if ever. This was a very sad departure. Glenda moved in with her mother and father for the duration of the war.

In Washington, D.C. we were told that we were going to London to make plans for a landing in North Africa in November, 1942. We were also told that our regiment, the 39th Infantry, 9th Infantry Division, would be moved to England in late September or early October in time to practice for the landing in North Africa.

We flew to London, were given a place to live and work, and

started making our plans to land in Algiers, North Africa, on November 8, 1942. The 39th Infantry would be under the Headquarters of the 34th Infantry Division, with one regiment of the 34th Division and a Brigade of British. We worked long hours studying maps and getting intelligence information about the area where we were to land. At this time, London was being bombed by the Germans and at night everything was blacked out. It was most difficult to move around after dark. The only time that we were out after dark was to get to our living area, which was very close.

Our regiment arrived in England in early October and immediately started practice landings. We were not permitted to tell anyone in the regiment where we were going to land until we embarked and were on the high seas. Our plans had to include detailed briefings of our landing sites and the projected enemy situation.

October 17, 1942: Loaded Ships in England to Leave for North Africa

On October 17, 1942, we loaded our ships and moved from England to the Mediterranean with no problem. Shortly after we arrived in the Mediterranean, the USS Stone, which had a battalion of the 39th Infantry aboard, was hit by a torpedo from a German submarine. Before the ship sank, they were able to unload the landing craft with everyone aboard. This worked fine for a while but the seas started to get rough. One by one the landing craft would receive a large wave and would start to sink. A destroyer, which was escorting the landing craft, would pick up those on the landing craft. Finally, all the landing craft were sunk and an entire infantry battalion plus the crew of the Stone were aboard the destroyer.

The 3rd Battalion, 39th Infantry was on the USS Leadstown and the headquarters for the 39th Infantry were also on this ship. The day before we were to land in Algiers, the commanding officer called me in and stated that he was assigning me as the Executive Officer of the 3rd Battalion because he did not trust the present battalion commander. He felt that I could influence his moves and help keep the battalion moving so that it could reach the Miason Blanc airport and secure it. Our fighter planes were leaving from Gibraltar to give us needed support and they had to land in that area because they did not have enough fuel to return to Gibraltar. I had been the S-3 since August and had seen the poor leadership given by the battalion commander. I told the commander that he was putting me in a bad situation and could cause me to receive bad reports. He said that he realized that but that he had faith in me and felt that this move was necessary. I suggested that he relieve the battalion commander and assign me as the commander. He said he would like to do that but he needed more facts to relieve him.

November 8, 1942: Landed in North Africa

The battalion came ashore on November 8, 1942, without any enemy resistance and was well-organized to secure the airport. Before we moved toward the airport, the USS Leadstown was hit by a German torpedo and sank in shallow water. Most everyone was off the ship, and since the water was shallow, we were able to get most of the equipment off the ship. There were no casualties.

The battalion secured the airport, without any resistance, but it took some urging on my part to keep the battalion moving.

December 1942: Souk Ahras, Algeria

In early December, the 3rd Battalion, 39th Infantry, was moved to Souk Ahras, Algeria, to protect our line of supply to our front line troops. This was a difficult task because we had very little to do. I tried to get the battalion commander to conduct more training but had little success.

February 19, 1943: Move into Battle in Kasserine

The famous battle of Kasserine Pass was a very serious situation. During the night of February 18/19, the 3rd Battalion, 39th Infantry, received orders to move to Kasserine as soon as they could. With great effort, we got the battalion ready to move by mid-morning. The battalion commander was the only one to receive the message to move, and most of what he received he kept to himself. I tried to get information from him, but all that he would tell me was that it was my duty to bring up the rear to insure that we lost no trucks or equipment.

When it started to get dark, the column stopped and a messenger in a Jeep came looking for me. The message was for me to report to the battalion commander immediately. When I did, he was in a great hurry, saying that he had just received orders to report to Corps Headquarters immediately. He ordered me to take the battalion into Kasserine and said that "someone" would meet the battalion there. I asked him about the enemy situation, but he knew nothing. I asked who would meet us and where but could get nothing from him. He departed, so he said, for Corps Headquarters.

I checked to see what security we had out and found that we did not have any security anywhere. I immediately put out a point guard with a radio and put radio patrols to the right and left of the front of the column of vehicles. It was not long after we moved out, and it was getting dark, that the patrol was stopped by a waiting patrol from the 1st Infantry Division. We were still quite a few miles from Kasserine. Since we had radio contact, I went forward and talked to the officer in charge. He took me to the regiment to which our battalion would be attached. His first question was where was the battalion commander? When I told him what had happened, he was shocked. It was a very dark night, so it was difficult to move. The regimental commander brought me up-to-date on the enemy situation and showed me on the map where he wanted me to deploy the battalion, but stated that I should not try to deploy until daybreak. Meanwhile, I should bed down the troops for the night with plenty of security.

During the night, I studied the map of the area with my staff, and we made plans to deploy the troops. I had the company commanders in before daylight, and we went over the plans. At daylight, the battalion commander had not shown up so I gave the order to move the troops into the defensive positions. After we were in position, the battalion commander showed up. He did not like the way that I had deployed the battalion but he did nothing to change the deployment.

February 1943: Selected to be the American Aide-de-Camp to the British General H. R. L. G. Alexander

In the prime of the battle, I received orders from the regimental commander to report to the G-1 at Corps Headquarters. I immediately complied and was told that I had been selected to be the American Aide-de-Camp to the British General H. R. L. G. Alexander. He had come to North Africa from the Middle East to be General Eisenhower's Deputy and the Commander in the field. I was to report to Allied Forces Headquarters in Algiers as soon as I could get there. I told the G-1 that I was highly honored for being selected for such a position and that it was a great opportunity for me; however, if I left the battalion with the present battalion commander in command, the whole battalion would be lost. After hearing my stories about the battalion commander, he agreed. I suggested that they assign a new battalion commander and then I could be on my way. The G-1 departed, after some time, came back and said that they did not have a battalion commander available.

He asked me if Allied Forces Headquarters would let me report a few days late would I be willing to stay with the battalion? Once again, as I had done earlier with my commander while at sea, I asked that I be made the battalion commander. The answer was that I must leave within a few days and if I was the commander it would be more difficult to get away. For the good of a battalion of soldiers, I had no choice but to stay.

Shortly after I returned to the battalion, the Germans started an attack. The company commanders had asked permission to withdraw but no one could find the battalion commander. I checked with regiment and they gave me permission to withdraw. With the enemy on the attack, we had to use artillery to a great extent to protect our troop withdrawal. We managed to reach a fairly good defensive position without very many casualties and dug in for the next attack. By this time, the battalion commander showed up and stated that he had been captured by the enemy while visiting one of the companies. If he had been visiting a company, he did not tell any member of the staff where he was going, which a commander must always do. He then stated that he had just now been able to escape from the enemy. Isn't it amazing how the battalion commander managed to be away every time that we reached a critical situation?

February 20, 21, and 22 were tough days of fighting at Kasserine. I did not average over an hour or two of sleep each night. On February 23, things calmed down and the enemy withdrew a short distance. With the enemy situation changed, the Corps G-1 called me and gave verbal orders to report to Allied Forces Headquarters as soon as I could get there.

I reported to Allied Forces Headquarters immediately. When I arrived, I was told that they had assigned Lieutenant Colonel Theodore J. Conway as temporary Aide-de-Camp to General Alexander and that General Alexander wanted me to get well-organized with the headquarters so that I would know my way around when we visited there. In order to meet the senior staff, I worked out of the protocol office and met all of the senior officers. I was invited to lunch with General Eisenhower and other senior officers on many occasions and knew them well when I visited the headquarters with General Alexander. I could not have asked for any better preparation for the assignment.

April 13, 1943: Reported to General Alexander as His American Aide-de-Camp

I reported to General Alexander's headquarters on April 13, 1943. This was the 18th Army Group consisting of the First and Eighth British Armies, under the command of Lieutenant General Kenneth Anderson and General Sir Bernard Montgomery, and the U.S. II Corps under Lieutenant General George S. Patton. I was immediately introduced to General Alexander, who greeted me warmly. During our conversation, he informed me that he had a military assistant, a major, a personal assistant, a captain, and that I was the Aide-de-Camp. He said that I would accompany him on most of his visits to the field or other headquarters. My duties would be to assist him as needed, which he said was not very specific, but he thought that I would learn fast.

He then introduced me to his Chief of Staff, a British Major General Richardson, and his Deputy Chief of Staff, an American Brigadier General, U.S. Army Air Corps. The Air Corps General was soon replaced by Army Brigadier General Lyman L. Lemnitzer. I soon learned that General Alexander had a very high regard for General Lemnitzer. As I saw it, the two of them worked out the war plans and then had the staff to do the detail work. I well remember when the two of them holed up in General Alexander's trailer and worked on the plans to conclude the Tunisian campaign. After the staff filled out the details, General Alexander sent a copy to General Eisenhower and a copy to Prime Minister Churchill. By this time, I had learned that Churchill thought very highly of General Alexander.

I well remember General Alexander's personal copy of his map.

On this map, he put dates along phase lines that he used as his objective to finish the Tunisian campaign. With his military assistant, we had a chance to check this map very often. As I recall, General Alexander never missed a phase line by more than one or two days and finished the campaign on May 13, 1943, within days of his prediction. From my position of seeing him prepare plans and visiting with him in the field, I would say that General Alexander was one of the greatest strategic and tactical planners of World War II.

We left Tunisia on May 14, 1943 to set up a new headquarters in Algiers to plan for the invasion of Sicily. We were called 141 Force Headquarters during the planning but became the 15th Army Group Headquarters for the invasion.

May/June 1943: Visit of Prime Minister Churchill to See the Troops

Prime Minister Churchill came to North Africa in late May or early June to visit the troops after the Tunisian campaign. General Alexander was his host and was responsible for the entire tour. The party consisted of about 16 people, and I was the only American in the party. Since we were going to visit U.S. troops, General Alexander wanted me to be along. We visited U.S., French, and British troops. One of our last visits was to the British Eighth Army headquarters, commanded by General Sir Bernard Montgomery. General Montgomery stayed very close to the Prime Minister as we moved around. When it came time to review the troops by vehicle, General Alexander was well in the background. The Prime Minister stepped up on the running board and called out to General Alexander, saying, "Alex, would you please join me for this review." This meant that General Montgomery would sit in the front seat and General Alexander would sit next to the Prime Minister. I observed that that really did hurt General Montgomery's feelings.

Our last stop on this visit was designed to give the Prime Minister some rest and relaxation. We went to a village called Hammamett, in Tunisia, where Air Marshall Coningham had acquired a villa. The Air Marshall commanded the Northwest African Tactical Air Force. The Air Marshall explained to the Prime Minister that the place was completely secure and that there were no women in the area. We were standing near a swimming pool and the Air Marshall explained to the Prime Minister that he could swim in the pool or in the Mediterranean Sea, which you could see from the pool, either in the nude or that there were bathing suits in the upstairs bedroom. The Prime Minister headed for the bedroom while we all waited. He soon came down dressed as follows: his hat, his cigar, his shirt, and his shoes. He headed for the sea. We all followed, and we undressed on the beach. As a good Aide, I watched everyone as if I was a lifeguard. I noticed that Anthony Eden, the Foreign Minister, had swum out quite far. I swam out to him. Pretty soon, all were on the shore, dressing and heading for the house. I suggested to Mr. Eden that we go in. When we arrived on shore, I had left my clothes too close to the incoming tide, and they were all wet. Mr. Eden said, "I say Major, let's wring the clothes out, hang them on a meskit bush to dry, and take another dip." Can you imagine me, a Major in the U.S. Army, wringing out my clothes with the British Foreign Minister? This we did, and my clothes were dry within minutes.

June 1943: Visit of King George VI of England

King George VI of England came to visit the troops in North Africa shortly after Prime Minister Churchill was there. Once again, I was the only American in the party. The King's visit was very short, and he only visited British troops. At Inclusion #6 is a picture that shows General Alexander, British Major General Clark, and myself, and states: "rode in the car immediately behind the one in which the King rode."

June – July 10, 1943: Making Plans for Sicily Invasion

141 Force Headquarters was located on a hill just outside of Algiers. General Alexander kept very busy making plans for the invasion of Sicily. One of my biggest problems was trying to keep up with him when he had some spare time. He enjoyed taking a swim in the sea. He might tell his military assistant that he was going for a swim, but neither the MA nor the General told me, and I would find out that the General had left, driving his own Jeep and swimming alone. I had to go looking for him and he was difficult to find. I tried to convince him that he should not be alone in this type of situation, but I never succeeded.

As the time came closer to the invasion date, which was secret at the time, General Alexander invited General Montgomery, the British Eighth Army Commander, to his headquarters to receive a complete briefing of the plan. This went well, and General Montgomery left the same day. He then invited the U.S. Seventh Army Commander, Lieutenant General George S. Patton, to come for a briefing. Since General Patton's headquarters were much farther away, he asked General Patton to spend the night. Again, the briefing went well. After a late dinner, which was normal for the British, we all sat around talking until finally everyone started to leave for the evening. I suggested to General Patton that I would show him to his van where he would sleep. This was then about 10:00 p.m. General Patton said, "Major, I would like to chat with you for a few minutes." For the next two hours, General Patton poured the questions to me about how the British operated and how the U.S. could work with them; he tried to find out everything that I knew about the British. He never said anything about the British, but it became obvious to me, by his questions, that he did not think very much of General Montgomery. On the other hand, he showed great respect for General Alexander and his plans. I was honored that General Patton would try to learn something from me.

June 1943:   Visit of Prime Minister Churchill

About this same time, Prime Minister Churchill sent a message that he would like to spend a few days with General Alexander prior to the invasion of Sicily. The Prime Minister arrived late one afternoon. That evening 14 or so dined with General Alexander, and I was the only American because the U.S. Deputy C/S was on a mission. General Alexander said, "Major, since you are the only American present, would you please sit next to the Prime Minister." That was a great honor for me.

The next day, Commander Butcher, General Eisenhower's Aide, called me and said that General Eisenhower would like to invite the Prime Minister, General Alexander, and an Aide for each to dinner. The dinner party consisted of the following: General Eisenhower, the host, Prime Minister Churchill, General Alexander, General Patton, General Bradley, and five aides, of which I was one. Prime Minister Churchill was usually the person to carry the conversation; however, on this occasion, General Eisenhower carried the conversation as much as the Prime Minister. This was an evening that a young Major – me – would never forget.

During the dinner, someone suggested that we sign a short snorter bill for each of us. (A short snorter bill was a regular or script bill that was used in the theater. You were authorized to sign this after you passed the international date line.) A copy of the short snorter bills used that night is at the end of this chapter (Inclusion #7).

June 9, 1943: Lloyd Ann Was Born

Sometime in mid-July, I received a letter from Glenda telling me that we had a daughter born on June 9, 1943. Since I was overseas, she decided to name the girl after me. So she named her Lloyd Ann. In those days, it would take a few weeks to receive mail from home. She had previously written to me that she was pregnant. She also explained that due to limited medical facilities in Somerset, Kentucky, she would have to go to Lexington, Kentucky, to have the baby. Later I learned that she stayed in a private home for about two weeks, waiting for labor pains, so that she could call a cab to take her to the hospital. While waiting, she had to walk two or three blocks to the Kentucky Hotel to get her meals.

Glenda was a true soldier at this time, having to go through all this alone. I was so thrilled with the news that I reported it to General Alexander. He asked me if I had wired my wife a message? I told him that there were no such facilities available and that a letter would take four to six weeks to reach her. He called in his secretary and dictated a message to Field Marshall Sir John Dill, Combined Joint Chiefs of Staff, Washington, D.C. The message was somewhat as follows: "Dear Sir John Dill, My American Aide's wife has just delivered a baby. Would you please send a message to Glenda B. Ramsey, 205 Vine Street, Somerset, Kentucky as follows:" The General then turned to me and told me to fill out the rest of the message, but keep it short. In a day or so, Glenda had a message from me that was sent to her by Field Marshall Sir John Dill's office, in Washington, D.C., thanks to General Alexander.

Prior to going to Sicily, General Eisenhower called a meeting of his Major Commanders at his headquarters in Algiers. His staff made out an agenda which General Eisenhower would follow. Prime Minister Churchill had urged General Alexander to try to get the Allies to invade, what he called, the soft underbelly of Europe (i.e. a landing in Albania). This item was on the agenda. When the item came up, an American General made a motion to table this item. General Eisenhower asked if all agreed, and they did, including General Alexander. They then went to the next item on the agenda. General Alexander then turned to me – I was sitting directly behind him – and said: "Major, what is going on? I thought they were going to table that item." I told General Alexander that in our language when you table a motion you put it on a table over in the corner and forget about it. He told me later that he thought when you tabled a motion you put it on the table and took action on that motion immediately. General Alexander never brought up this subject again.

July 10 – August 8, 1943: Sicily

The troops landed in Sicily on July 10, 1943. After we moved our headquarters to Sicily, I got the impression that General Alexander did not have much confidence in the U.S. troops' ability to win battles in the early days of the campaign. After some time, however, he seemed to change his feelings. As an example, General Alexander visited General Montgomery's headquarters in Augusta, on the East coast. During the briefing, it became clear that General Montgomery's troops were not moving. We then went to Palermo on the north coast to visit General Patton, where we received an outstanding briefing. It showed how much the U.S. troops had moved and were still moving. During the evening meal, General Alexander would sometimes talk about his visits to the field. On this particular evening, after visiting the two headquarters, General Alexander talked about his visits and then made a statement somewhat as follows: "Sometimes I wish that Monty was not so conservative and would move out rapidly like Georgi." To me, this was a great compliment to the Americans. From that day on, General Alexander showed great respect for the U.S. forces because they had shown their ability to produce.

General Alexander did a lot of traveling to visit the troops in the field. He asked me if I thought that I could get him a couple of small U.S. fixed wing aircraft that would save him time in driving so far. I got in touch with Brigadier General Hobart Gay, General Patton's C/S, and explained to him what General Alexander wanted. General Gay said that he would look into the problem and would get back to me.

General Gay called me back in a few days and said that the Seventh Army could loan two liaison aircraft to the 15th Army Group Headquarters, but that they could only furnish one pilot, a sergeant. He suggested that one of the pilots, of the C-47 that the U.S. had furnished General Alexander, could fly the other plane. I told him that I would talk to the C-47 pilots and get back to him. I talked to the pilots and both said that with some refresher training from the sergeant, they could fly the liaison aircraft. I called General Gay and made arrangements for the aircraft to be flown to our headquarters. General Alexander was very pleased with the arrangements that I had made. The two pilots received the refresher training in the next few days and the aircraft was used often.

On the days that the aircraft was not being used, the sergeant suggested that he teach me to fly. I discussed this with General Alexander, and he approved. After a few hours of instruction, I made my solo flight. Some days, when the General was busy doing paper work, I would continue to get more hours of flying time. According to the sergeant, I was doing extremely well in flying the aircraft.

General Eisenhower's Commanders Meeting at General Alexander's Headquarters

General Eisenhower called a meeting of his Major Commanders at General Alexander's headquarters in Sicily. The meeting was to be held at 10:00 a.m. General Alexander told me to prepare lunch for the entire group. The meeting went well, ending about 12:00 noon. As the meeting ended, General Eisenhower headed to his car to take him to his aircraft. General Alexander was right behind him and I was following. When we reached the car, General Alexander told General Eisenhower that all the commanders were staying for lunch, and they hoped that General Eisenhower would join them for some conversation and relaxation. General Eisenhower continued to get into his car and said to General Alexander, "Alex, I have to get back to Algiers for a meeting. Please give me a rain check." As the car pulled away, General Alexander turned to me and asked the meaning of "a rain check." I explained to him that when a baseball game was called off because of rain, you received a rain check to see the game when it was replayed.

August 18, 1943: Messina, Sicily

Messina, Sicily was supposed to be taken by the British Eighth Army. With General Patton's U.S. Seventh Army moving so rapidly, General Alexander gave him the authority to take Messina. This did not set too well with General Montgomery but made General Patton very happy. The campaign in Sicily ended on August 18, 1943.

September 3, 1943: Italy Surrenders

After many negotiations, Italy signed the surrender documents on September 3, 1943. On that day, the British Eighth Army moved troops to Calabia, Italy. The U.S. Army landed at Salerno on September 18, 1943.

Move to Bari, Italy

I do not remember the date that we moved our headquarters to Bari, Italy. However, I do remember one part of the move that put me on the spot. General Alexander needed his C-47 and one of the small aircraft soon after arriving in Bari. That left one small aircraft to be flown to Bari, which was on the east coast of Italy. The sergeant said that he had faith in my ability to fly the small aircraft from Sicily to Bari, about a 250-mile flight. The sergeant made out my flight plan, including places to land to get gasoline. I made the trip as planned with one exception – the airfields where I was to get refueled had been closed. I had to land along a highway and get gasoline from jeeps and trucks passing by. I had to do this two or three times to have enough gasoline to get me to Bari. I was very proud of what I had accomplished.

In Bari, the small aircraft were used often. One day a British Major General and his aide were visiting our headquarters and wanted to get to the front and back but had very little time. The sergeant and one of the C-47 pilots were ill, so that left only one pilot to fly the General and his aide to the front. The British C/S called me in and asked me to fly the aide. I told the C/S that I was not a certified pilot and should not take passengers on my aircraft. I tried my best to get out of this flight, but he insisted that I fly the aide and then accompany the General on his visit. While we were away, the pilot was told to move the aircraft. He moved one aircraft with no problem, but when he started to move the second aircraft, he climbed into the front seat when he should have been in the rear seat for balance. When he started to taxi, he hit a small bump and the aircraft nosed over breaking the propeller. When we arrived back, the British Major General refused to fly with the pilot who had caused the accident. He insisted that I fly him back, saying the aide could get someone to drive him back. I protested but finally gave in. It was getting late and we ran into a very strong headwind. By the time we reached the airfield it was almost dark. Luckily, I made a smooth landing and the General was very pleased. The next day, the British C/S called me in and thanked me for what I had done; then he told me that I was not to take senior officers as passengers in my aircraft anymore, which I was pleased to hear.

General Alexander was always very nice to me and I learned a lot from such an outstanding soldier. He mixed pleasure with business. I will never forget that he taught me the true definition of golf:

Golf is an ineffectual effort
To place an insignificant pellet
Into an obscure hole
By using completely inadequate weapons.

At the end of this chapter (Inclusion #8) is a picture of General Alexander reviewing troops of the 3rd Infantry Division. Date of picture is unknown.

By November 1943, after having been with General Alexander for about seven months, I felt that I should get back to troop duty again. I discussed this with General Alexander, and he agreed to release me after we got a suitable replacement. I then went to General Lemnitzer, who said that he could get a suitable replacement. He then told me to pick the division that I wished to be assigned to and he would get me to that division. I had been watching what each division was accomplishing and there was no doubt that the 3rd Infantry was by far the best. I thought it would be better to go with the best division and do an outstanding job there. If I went with a division less than the best, I could do an outstanding job there, but I would prefer to do it with the best division.

General Lemnitzer arranged for my replacement and got me assigned to the 3rd Infantry Division. I left General Alexander on November 14, 1943. Prior to my departure, he presented me with a decoration, "M. B. E. – Member of the British Empire," and said some wonderful words about my service with him. It was difficult to respond to such a nice departure.

Major Ramsey's Citation of the "MBE"

Major Ramsey joined my personal staff as A.D.C. in March 1943 and continued as such till November. During the whole of that period he thought only of how he could be of the greatest assistance to my staff and me. He was always cheerful and tireless even after the most exhausting journeys and I was able to place complete reliance in him on all matters of a confidential nature.

(sgd) H. R. Alexander General
General Officer Commander-in-Chief, 15 Army Group

WAR DEPARTMENT
THE ADJUTANT GENERAL'S OFFICE
WASHINGTON

IN REPLY AG 201- Ramsey, Lloyd Brinkley
REFER TO (6-15-40)O WGP PEC 1603   July 1, 1940.
Subject: Appointment in the Regular Army.

Thru: Commanding General,
            Fifth Corps Area.

To: Second Lieutenant Lloyd Brinkley Ramsey, Inf-Res.

    1. The President has appointed you this date, second lieutenant of Infantry, Regular Army, with rank from July 1, 1940. It is desired that you execute the oath of office on the form inclosed for that purpose. Your serial number will be O-23553.

    2. Under the provisions of the Act of July 25, 1939, (Public No. 202, 76th Congress), the Secretary of War, under such regulations as he may prescribe, may revoke the commission of any officer appointed since the enactment of that Act, who has less than three years continuous commissioned service prior to the date of such revocation.

    3. You are assigned to the 10th Infantry with station at Fort Thomas, Kentucky, and will report to the commanding officer for duty on or before July 15, 1940. In this connection you should communicate by letter at once with that officer relative to such assignment. The delay herein authorized is in the interest of the public service. You will be required to defray your travel expenses to first station.

    4. It is directed that you forward to this office at an early date a photograph of yourself, taken in uniform as an officer of the United States Army. The photograph should be unmounted, not smaller than 5 inches in width and 7 inches in height, and not exceeding 8 inches in width and 10 inches in height, and should show upon the back thereof your name, rank and organization plainly written or printed, and as nearly as possible the date when taken. Finger-print record as required by AR 345-120, May 1, 1939, is also desired.

    5. The attached forms, Designation of Beneficiary and Historical Record should be accomplished and returned to this office at once.

    6. Attention is invited to paragraph 3 (1) (i), AR 600-100, W.D., 1929, as amended by Changes No. 2, September 1, 1933, relative to the provisions governing United States Government Life Insurance.

                                      By order of the Secretary of War:

3 Incls.

AGO Form 0337
AGO Form 0337-A
AGO Form 41.   Adjutant General.

INCL. # 1

For some reason we did not take pictures of our wedding. This is the only picture of Glenda and me.
Leaving the Parsonage of the First Baptist Church Somerset, Kentucky 22 February 1941

INCL. # 2

A few at the wedding
Morris W. (Sonny) Burton, Glenda's Brother
Mason E. Burton, Glenda's Father
Minnie May Burton, Glenda's Mother
Starling S. Gregory, Feller's friend and best man
Edna Mason Burton, Glenda's Sister and the only attendant
W.H. Ramsey, Feller's Dad
Mary Ella (Mimi) Ramsey, Feller's Mother

INCL. # 3

BURTON—RAMSEY

The marriage of Miss Glenda Burton, daughter of Mr. and Mrs. M. E. Burton, to Lieut. Lloyd B. Ramsey, son of Mr. and Mrs. W. H. Ramsey, was solemnized Saturday afternoon at the Baptist parsonage in Somerset, with the Rev. D. L. Hill officiating.

The bride, given in marriage by her father, wore a powder blue suit trimmed in mink, brown accessories, and a shoulder bouquet of sweetheart roses.

Miss Edna Mason Burton, sister of the bride, was her only attendant. She was attired in a blue ensemble and wore a shoulder bouquet of red roses. Mr. Starling Gregory served as Lieutenant Ramsey's best man.

Mrs. Burton chose for her daughter's wedding an aqua crepe dress with black accessories, and a shoulder bouquet of gardenias. Mrs. Ramsey was attired in an ensemble of gold and brown with a shoulder bouquet of talisman roses.

Immediately following the ceremony Lieut. and Mrs. Ramsey left on a trip to Silver Springs, Fla., and after Feb. 28 will be at home at Fort Bragg, N. C.

The attractive bride is a graduate of the Somerset High School and the University of Kentucky, where she was a member of the Chi Omega sorority. She is a popular member of the younger set.

The groom also graduated from the Somerset High School and received his A. B. degree from the University of Kentucky where he was a member of the Sigma Chi fraternity, Cadet Colonel of the R. O. T. C. regiment, member of Omicron Delta Kappa, captain of Scabbard and Blade, honorary military fraternity, and received a permanent appointment as second lieutenant with the regular army. He was also captain and coach of the swimming team, and freshman football coach.

He captained the Somerset High School football team that won the C.K.C. championship in 1936.

Out of town guests for the wedding were Mr. and Mrs. Brinkley Barnett, Miss Roberta Wilson, Lexington; Mr. and Mrs. Elmer Haan of Monticello; and Miss Ernestine Hieatt of Louisville.

This article is from the Somerset, Ky. newspaper.
It covers the wedding of Glenda and me.
22 February, 1941

INCL. # 4

Glenda and Feller. Our house in Fayetteville N.C. We had the down stairs apartment. August 1942

Mimi, Feller and Glenda

Feller and Dad

INCL. # 5

(Caption reads:) **WITH THE ALLIED GENERALS** is Major Lloyd Ramsey, son of Mr. and Mrs. W. H. Ramsey of Somerset. Major Ramsey, at right, is seen with General Sir Harold Alexander of the British Army, left, who has served as commander-in-chief of the Allied forces in Sicily; and General Clark, of the British Army. The picture was made in Tunis in June when King George VI of England visited Africa. Major Ramsey, who is aide to General Alexander, and the two generals rode in the car immediately behind the one in which the King rode.

INCL. # 6

Top Right
G. Patton Jr.
Lt. Gen. later
General

H.R. Alexander
General – British
Later Field Marshall
O.N. Bradley
Lt. General later
General of the Army
Dwight D.Eisenhower
General laterGeneral
Of the Army later
President of the
United States

L.L. Lemnitzer
Brig. General
later General
Chairman JCS

Left bill under
STATES OF
W.C. Churchill
Prime Minister
Great Britian

INCL. # 7

INCL. # 8

CHAPTER 5

WORLD WAR II – NOVEMBER 14, 1943 – MAY 7, 1945

Explanation of war

As I get into the war-time situation (i.e. my fighting the battles of war), I would like to quote from an article regarding war by General Frederich J. Kroesen, U.S. Army, retired, in Volume XI, No. 2, *The Cottonbaler*, Spring 2001. Fritz commanded the 196th Brigade of the American Division just before I assumed command of the division in June 1969. Fritz later commanded the division.

"...war is the most inhumane of all human endeavors, the most tragic, the most wasteful, the most destructive, the most terrifying. Wars provide the culminating points for the evil that men do. When William Tecumseh Sherman said 'war is hell,' he was not exaggerating, and so any decision to go to war must be made with the understanding that participants are to be committed to a holocaust in the making. I also learned that there are worse things than war. When personal freedom is denied, when fear is a constant, when lives and livelihoods are spent under threat, and when trust and confidence in fellow men, even among families, are undermined by the subjugation of a populace to an absolute regime, the human spirit suffers degradation and destruction. People are reduced almost to an animal-like existence...I learned that war is the most complex and complicated human endeavor. No other activity demands a greater mental and physical commitment over an indefinite time span than that required to man, equip and train forces needed for combat, then to employ them for as long as it takes to reach a decision."

This, in a few words, explains the problems of a commander in war.

November 14, 1943 – January 30, 1944: G-3 Section 3rd Infantry Division

When I reported to the 3rd Infantry Division on November 14, 1943, I was assigned to G-3, doing staff duty. I remained there until after we made the landing at Anzio on January 22, 1944. The 3rd Infantry Division route of advance during World War II is at the end of this chapter (Inclusion #1).

January 30, 1944 – May 7, 1945: Some of My Combat Situations During This Time

In this chapter, I will discuss a limited number of combat situations that I was involved in that were very dangerous for me or my command. These events should give the reader some idea of what combat is all about. The reader should understand, however, that these events only lasted a few minutes or a few hours at the most, whereas the battle would continue for days or even weeks, and we would continue to be fighting with the enemy. The reader should also understand that there were many other combat situations during this period.

As a battalion commander, I commanded three rifle companies, a heavy weapons company, and a headquarters company, for a total of about 900 men when at full strength. Sometimes a tank company would be attached to me, which was most helpful. I always had a forward observer artillery officer with me, which would give me at least the fire support of one artillery battalion. I could usually get air support by calling Regiment who would call Division to arrange support.

As the battalion commander, I was responsible for all combat actions in my area of operations. I was also responsible for getting food, ammunition, and clothing to my troops. In combat, troops had to live on "C Rations" much of the time. This came in a can, and you usually ate it out of the can cold. The troops always carried a "D Ration," which was a chocolate bar that was very bitter, but it had the proper food elements to keep you going until you could get some better food. I would always try to get hot food to my troops whenever possible.

Living conditions: The troops had to live with what they could carry on their back. The "Colmar Pocket" was one of the worst. It got down to about 5 degrees at night with as much as 10 to 12 inches of snow on the ground. You fought, you rested, you ate, you shaved under these conditions. (Most good troops kept shaven in combat when they could find time.) Every now and then you could get some troops into a house or barn for some cover, but they always had to have security well out from the house or the barn. The battalion command post could get into a house more often so that we could lay out the maps and better control the combat situation.

As for the American soldier, no words can ever explain how great he was. He was concerned for his fellow man, for his country, and for his own life. In combat it did not take long for a commander to learn if you took care of your troops, your troops would take care of you.

One of the most heartbreaking events for me was to see a soldier being carried away on a stretcher. When I stopped and talked to them, many of the better soldiers would apologize to me for getting wounded and then add, "But sir, I will come back to my company."

January 30 – March 13, 1944: 1st Battalion, 7th Infantry – Anzio

On January 30, 1944, Lieutenant Colonel Frank M. Izenour, C.O. 1st Battalion, 7th Infantry, and his Executive Officer were wounded and evacuated. Colonel Sherman, the regimental commander, called the division commander, Major General Truscott, and told him what had happened. General Truscott told Colonel Sherman that he was assigning me to the 7th Infantry, and he thought that I would be a good commander. By the time I arrived at the 7th Infantry, Colonel Sherman had decided to assign his S-4 as the battalion commander and I would be his Executive Officer. The S-4, a major, was senior to me so I had no choice. It became apparent very quickly that S-4 knew nothing about tactics or commanding troops. For all practical purposes, I took command of the battalion.

January 31, 1944 was a tough day. *The Seventh Infantry History, From Fedala to Berchtesgaden*, pages 81-82, explains these battles very well:

"At 0045, 31 Jan. the Red Battalion (First Battalion) was the target for still another counter-attack coming from the north and northeast. The attack was heavier than the preceding one. The enemy used mortar and small arms fire and tried to infiltrate through the 'Cotton Baler' positions. The fight was continuous throughout the night with heavy losses sustained by both sides. With no thought of surrender or relaxation against the enemy, the Red Battalion (First Battalion)

troops lived up to the finest traditions of the 'Cotton Baler' Regiment. It was kill or be killed and the feats of heroism performed at the risk of life above and beyond the call of duty will always be remembered and revered..."

"In spite of all it had been through, the Red Battalion (First Battalion) continued the offensive and attacked at 1400 on the 31st. With determination to achieve the objective, the troops advanced in the face of withering fire laid down by the enemy. It is impossible to understand how anything that moved could survive through that fire. Firing their weapons while running in a half crouched manner, at times creeping and crawling in the slimy ooze that made them blend indistinguishably with the surrounding terrain, the advance elements overran two enemy 105s in the orchard that was to become famous. A group of men under the command of Captain William Athas of Company "D" turned the weapon around and used it to good effect on the enemy. (I brought Captain Athas to these guns to see if he knew how to fire them. Captain Athas was the heavy weapons commander and probably knew more about these type of guns than any other person in the battalion.) Shortly thereafter the First Battalion assault troops crossed the railroad tracks northwest of Cisterna di Littoria, an outstanding accomplishment that day that was not to be repeated until four months had passed. This was the farthest advance made by any unit on the beachhead during the attacks of 30-31 January 1944 and testifies to the superb fighting ability of the 'Cotton Baler' troops. After reaching that exposed position, the battalion stuck out like a sore thumb and was counterattacked from the rear. As the First Battalion troops fought fiercely to beat off the enemy, the Second Battalion moved up behind the First and established contact near midnight with First Battalion Headquarters Company."

"The Red Battalion (First Battalion) troops fought with grim determination against the enemy on all sides."

This was a real baptism of fire – my first combat since Kasserine in February 1943. Once again, as the assigned Ex. Off. of a battalion, I had to actually command the battalion. In order to make things look normal, most of my orders were given through the battalion commander. (On March 13, 1944, a change in command will show the true commander.)

February 1944: Company CP in Tunnel on Anzio

There was one company in the battalion that we could visit in the daytime without getting shot at. The Company Command Post was in a tunnel that had been built by the Germans. The opening was through a small hole that went straight down by ladder. The tunnel was deep enough to give good protection from artillery, and it also had been vented so that you received fresh air. The tunnel led to the far side of the hill, where there was an opening that gave a good view of the front lines.

One rainy day after visiting the company, I had climbed the ladder to return to the battalion command post. As I was exiting the hole, I heard an 88mm German shell coming in. They had a sound that was terrifying and gave you one or two seconds to hit the ground. I immediately tried to get back into the hole, but my canteen and pistol caught on the rim of the hole and prevented me from getting into cover. The shell landed within 15 feet of the hole; I was splattered with mud and knew that I was dead. But, if I were dead, why did I know that I had been splattered with mud? It took me a few seconds to figure out that the 88mm shell that landed so close to me was a dud (i.e. it did not explode). Luck and the Lord were with me once again.

March 3, 1944: Company A, Captain Athas and Company B, Major Ramsey

On March 3, 1944, the enemy made an attack on the 3rd Battalion that caused me to make a crucial decision. I will quote from the book, *Anzio Beachhead* (22 January – 25 May 1944), by The Batter Press, Nashville, page 102:

> *"At dawn on 3 March the enemy renewed his attack on the 3d Battalion, 7th Infantry, southwest of Ponte Rotto. Tanks and armored infantry of the 25th Panzer Division broke through Company L's position astride the road, forcing a slight withdrawal. Colonel Sherman sent Company A, under Captain Athas, and Company B, under Maj. Lloyd B. Ramsey, up the road toward Ponte Rotto to recapture the contested bridge and restore the 7th Infantry's former positions."*

(Comment: Colonel Sherman asked the 1st Battalion for a recommendation. Our company commanders were completely worn out. I talked to Captain Athas, the heavy weapons company commander, and suggested that he and I command A and B companies on this attack. He agreed and Colonel Sherman approved the recommendation.)

"The division artillery poured smoke shells into the area ahead of the troops before the attack was launched at 1330. Some of the smoke drifted over beyond Ponto Rotto, giving the 15th Infantry the impression that it was the enemy who was preparing to attack. The 15th Infantry expended a lot of ammunition laying down defensive fires across its front until a call to 7th Infantry headquarters clarified the situation. The smoke was thin at first, then it improved, and the two companies moved forward. Company B, attacking on the north side of the road, reached its objective northwest of the bridge without difficulty; two platoons of Company A, attacking along and to the south of the road, reached the crater where the engineers had created a road block. There they were met by tank fire and a terrific concentration of artillery. Captain Athas was killed, and when the two platoons withdrew to reorganize, only thirty men were left. Although the enemy still held the contested bridge, the counterattack served its purpose of stopping the enemy attack."

March 13, 1944: I Take Command of the 3rd Battalion, 7th Infantry

On March 13, Frank Izenour had recovered from his wounds and returned to command the 1st Battalion. The new regimental commander, Colonel O'Mohundro, assigned me to command the 3rd Battalion, 7th Infantry and left the major that was commanding as the Executive Officer of the 1st Battalion. This was a great compliment to my ability and showed what Regiment thought of my actions as the Executive Officer of the 1st Battalion. On March 26, 1944, a Lieutenant Colonel was assigned as the Battalion Commander, and I became the Executive Officer. The Battalion Commander was about 45 years of age and could not stay awake at night when most of the action took place. Once again, I had to command the Battalion.

April 5-12, 1944: Vacation in Sorrento

On April 5, 1944, I was given a vacation to go to the resort area of Sorrento, an island just off the coast of Naples, Italy. Lieutenant Colonel John J. Toffey, Jr., the Regimental Executive Officer, and I went together. We stayed at Hotel San Vittoria. John did not drink much and was not interested in women, so the two of us had a week of rest and relaxation, which was needed and enjoyed.

April 18-19, 1944: Walked Into a Minefield

On April 18, 1944, Colonel O'Mohundro started an operation which would cause the 3rd Battalion to move Company K to a forward position on April 19. This would be a much better defensive position. Since we could not move around in the daytime because the enemy could see our every move and would bring some type of fire on us, I went to Company K on the night of April 18 so that the Company Commander, Captain Frank Petruzel, and I could observe the front in the daylight and finalize our plans for the move on the night of April 19, 1944.

At daylight we were on the front line with our soldiers. There was a barbed wire fence along the front. We were at the point where the troops would move through that night. We had studied our maps, checked for mine fields that had been charted, and were now making a last reconnaissance. We asked the soldiers on the front if they had ever seen anyone laying land mines in the area. They had not. We could not see much from where we were. There was a small hill a short distance in front of us, so I suggested to Captain Petruzel that we move there for better observation. We would have to cut the barbed wire, and the front line troops would be our cover in case of enemy fire.

We had cut the wire and walked a short distance when a land mine went off; either Petruzel or I had hit a trip wire and set off the mine. I received only minor wounds, but Petruzel was badly wounded. One wound was in the upper right leg, which was bleeding badly. I had to tear some of his clothes and make a tourniquet to put on his leg to keep him from bleeding to death. The front line troops started to come and help us, but I ordered them to stay at their positions because there might have been more land mines in the area. I picked Frank Petruzel up and put him on my shoulder. Our foot marks were barely visible so I tried to step in the same place in order to not set off another landmine.

Reaching our lines safely, I immediately called for the medics. Since we had started our venture so early, it was still hazy enough that we were able to evacuate Frank without any problem.

I went back to headquarters and immediately arranged for engineers to clear that minefield before the troops moved out at 2100 hours. The engineers were able to clear the minefield and our move was made without a single casualty, except for Frank and myself. However, if we had not hit that mine, it is possible that there would have been many casualties. When troops are moving, especially at night, and someone hits a land mine, they will many times panic and run to get out of the area, causing more soldiers to be wounded.

After the operation was complete, the Regimental Commander called me and gave me hell for walking into a minefield. He told me that he was going to have his S-2 make an investigation to find out why a Major would not know where the minefields were located before he ventured into one. After a few weeks, the Regimental Commander told me that S-2 had determined that between the U.S. and German forces there were more than 10,000 mines in a 1,000 yard square that were not charted. He apologized for his harsh words to me and then congratulated me for what I accomplished by making that reconnaissance and for saving Frank.

Harvey R. Keeler, Corporal, and William Rodriguez, T/5

As Executive Officer of a Battalion, I was authorized an orderly and a driver for my jeep. As my orderly, I was assigned Harvey R. Keeler, Corporal, who had worked for Colonel Izenour. Keeler was of small stature, not more than five feet seven inches tall. He could, however, carry more than men much larger than he. Wherever we went, Keeler always seemed to be carrying what I needed. Keeler became more than my orderly; he was my right hand, my assistant, my bodyguard, my guide, my helper in every way. He kept up with the situation and knew where the troops were located and the location of the enemy (i.e. as well as we knew it). Keeler would never walk beside me because he felt if one of us got hit by artillery, maybe the other one would not be wounded. When we got close to the front lines, Keeler would move in front of me and say, "Sir, follow me." He knew where we were going and wished to protect me. I can't say enough about this fine soldier and how well he took care of me throughout the war. He was wounded once and evacuated, but returned to take care of me.

My driver was William Rodriguez. On Anzio I could not use a jeep. Every night Rodriguez would bring the mail and any other things that we needed. In southern France and Germany, Rodriguez was another right hand, like Keeler. I had complete confidence in him and knew that he would always be at the right place at the right time and do what was needed to be done.

April 21-22: Change of Battalion Commanders

On April 21, 1944, the present Battalion Commander was relieved, and the new Lieutenant Colonel was placed in command on April 22. The new Lieutenant Colonel was a West Point graduate and gave me the impression that he would be a very fine commander. I judged wrong.

May 1, 1944: Letter to Dad

On May 1, 1944, while sitting in the battalion headquarters bunker on Anzio Beachhead, where we could not move much in daylight without bringing enemy artillery fire on us, I decided to use the battalion headquarters' typewriter to write a letter to Dad (my father). The bunker was completely enclosed and our only light was by kerosene lanterns. Not being a typist, I did the best that I could. I wanted to tell Dad about my experiences in the last few months so that he could tell Glenda, my wife, and Mimi, my mother, what he thought they should know. The letter covered my walking into a minefield with the company commander, covered previously in this chapter, and the wound that I received while being taken to the 1st Battalion, 7th Infantry by a Lieutenant when we were shelled and he was killed. A copy of the letter is at the end of this chapter (Inclusion #2). The letter also praised the "dogface soldier."

May 23, 1944: Breakout of Anzio

On May 23, 1944, at 0630, we made our attack to breakout of Anzio. At first, enemy resistance was light. By 0815, however, we ran into heavy machine gun, mortar, and artillery fire. When the artillery fire came in on us, the Battalion Commander told me to tell the companies to take cover and to halt the attack. I told the Battalion Commander that the enemy had us located and that they would continue to pour the artillery on us if we did not move. I told him that we must move forward and get as close to the enemy as we could before the artillery would stop. The Battalion Commander would not move. I told him that I was moving the battalion forward and that he could catch up with us. The Battalion Commander finally caught up with us, and I thought he would take over and give out the proper orders. Once again, I assumed command of the battalion. I did not know that anyone knew this except my staff until I read: *U.S. Army in World War II, Mediterranean Theater of Operations, Cassino to the Alps*, pages 134-137:

"The 3d Battalion in the meantime remained throughout the afternoon on the Colle Monaco. At last convinced that the commander was no longer able to control either himself or his unit, the executive officer, Maj. Lloyd B. Ramsey, assumed command and made plans for a two-company attack to start shortly after nightfall at 2100. When the armored support Ramsey requested failed to appear, he postponed the attack to 2130, but before that hour arrived, enemy tanks made a second appearance. Leading a small infantry force, several German tanks approached to within 250 yards of Ramsey's right front. Although the tanks failed to attack, their presence was enough to prompt Ramsey to cancel his plans and go on the defensive for the night, while awaiting reinforcement by the regiment's reserve battalion. By the end of the first day, only the 2d Battalion of O'Mohundro's 7th Infantry had made any significant penetration of the enemy's defense, that to within 600 yards of Cisterna. Antitank minefields had severely limited the close-in fire support so desperately needed by the infantry in the first hours if the momentum of the attack was to be maintained. Moreover, the day's gains had been as costly as they were disappointing. Of the regiment's more than 200 casualties, 54 men had been killed...Some indication of the effectiveness of the enemy's defensive fires could be seen in the high losses incurred by the division on the first day. Of a total of 1,626 casualties, 107 were killed in action, 642 wounded, 812 missing, and 65 captured."

On May 24, 1944, the 3d Battalion was passed through by the 1st Battalion, giving them support by fire. The Battalion Command Post was in a German trench about five feet deep, which we thought was a very safe place. A German artillery shell burst directly above our position in the trench. The artillery liaison officer was lying in the trench with his head near mine. Fragments hit him in the back with severe wounds. Our Battalion surgeon was also in the ditch with us. He took one look at the artillery officer and said that we must close the chest wound immediately, but he doubted that he could save his life. After closing the gaping wound in his back, we turned him over and saw that one of his legs did not turn below the knee. The doctor amputated the leg and closed that wound. I was sure he would die before he could be evacuated, but I was later overjoyed to find out that he lived.

After getting the artillery officer taken care of, I told the doctor that I had been hit in the leg. I did not realize how large the wound was. The fragment went through my leg, and you could feel it under the skin on the inside of my leg. The doctor said that I must go to the hospital. With the battalion commander problems, I tried to get the doctor to take care of my leg, but he said he could not do that in the field and that I must go to the hospital. That night at the hospital a nurse came to tell me that my Battalion Commander from the 7th Infantry had just been brought in with a serious wound in the knee. His wound was so bad that he never returned to combat.

June 6, 1944: D-Day in Northern France

I remember well June 6, 1944, which was known as D-Day. I was in the hospital in the Naples area, recovering from my wounds on Anzio, when I read that thousands of soldiers, sailors, airmen, and marines of the Allied Expeditionary Force had landed in the Cherbourg-Harve area and that the casualties were very high. At the end of this chapter (Inclusion #3) is a copy of the message that General Eisenhower sent to all the troops. At Inclusion #3-2 and #3-3 are messages that he wrote in case of failure.

June 22, 1944: Command of the 3d Battalion, 7th Infantry and Promotion to Lieutenant Colonel

I was in the hospital from May 24 until June 21, 1944. I guess this proved that the battalion surgeon was correct when he said that I should go to the hospital. I returned to the 7th Infantry on June 21, 1944. The 7th Infantry, at this time, was training in the Bagnoli-

Pozzuoli area. On June 22, 1944, I was again given command of the 3d Battalion. In about one week, when we were in the field training, a messenger came and told me that the Regimental Commander wanted to see me right away. I reported to him as soon as I could get there, wondering if once again he was going to tell me that a Lieutenant Colonel would be taking command. When I reported, he took one look at me and made a statement to the effect that he would not allow officers in his regiment to be out of uniform. Hearing such a statement, I looked down to see if I was out of uniform. The Colonel then reminded me that I was at attention and should stay that way until he ordered otherwise. This type of talk went on for a few minutes, and I was quite concerned about my dress. The Colonel then turned to the adjutant and asked him for help to get me into proper uniform. The adjutant pulled out some silver leaves, which meant that I was being promoted to Lieutenant Colonel. The Colonel then told me that I had been out of uniform since June 19, 1944, the day that my promotion was effective. I was very surprised because I did not know that I had been recommended for promotion.

Since I had been wounded and did not get into Rome, the Regimental Commander suggested that I take a few days off and visit there. Rodriguez drove me to Rome on July 21, and we returned on July 23. We had a very interesting visit in Rome.

June 22 – August 11, 1944: Training for Invasion of Southern France

From June 22 until August 11, 1944, we trained for a landing in southern France. This was the first time since joining the division that we had a fairly long training period. When General Lucian K. Truscott was the Commanding General, he started a program in training that became known as the "Truscott Trot." In this program, each battalion had to march five miles in one hour at the start of each training day. Then once a week, each battalion would have to march 25 miles in eight hours. Since we were marching five miles in one hour, most battalions would march the 25 miles in six to seven hours. This was a very good program to get the troops in condition, and it sure made a difference in southern France when we had to make some forced marches.

On August 12 we sailed out of Naples for the landing in

southern France on August 15, 1944. Winston Churchill passed through the line of craft in a launch, displaying his famous "V" for victory sign. The soldiers really did enjoy seeing the Prime Minister and appreciated his efforts to wish them success.

August 13 or 14, 1944: Aboard Ship to Southern France

While we were en route to our landing, August 13 or 14, 1944, I was relaxing in the Ward Room when an officer ran in very excited. In a nervous voice, he explained that there was a soldier on the deck who had pulled the pin of a hand grenade, thrown the pin aside and was now holding the live grenade in his hand. I immediately went to the deck. I tried to be calm, walking normally, even though I was scared, in order to show that soldier and others that there was no problem. I ordered the deck cleared. I then began to talk to the soldier, trying to convince him that he did not want to harm himself or any of his fellow soldiers. As I got closer to him, I could see that he was concerned and he said that he did not want to hurt anyone. When I was close enough to him to receive the grenade from him, he started to cry and said that he was sorry. I kept pleading with him not to release the spoon on the grenade as it would explode in about five seconds, possibly killing us. As I reached for the grenade, he released the spoon and handed me a live grenade. I knew that I had about five seconds to get rid of the grenade. I was too far from the side of the ship to throw it overboard, so I ran toward the side of the ship counting 1000/1, 1000/2, 1000/3, and threw the grenade as far as I could. It exploded in the air, below deck level, and no one was hurt. The Battalion Surgeon said the soldier had a mental problem and had to be put in the aid station under guard. The Navy would take care of him after we landed.

After the episode was over, I talked to the officer who told me about the man with the grenade. He said that there were very few people who realized that the man had a grenade. I told him to get those people together and tell them not to discuss the incident with anyone because it might give other soldiers an idea of how to get out of combat.

August 15, 1944: Landing in Southern France

The 3rd Battalion, 7th Infantry landed on Red Beach at 0800, August 15, 1944. The 7th Infantry Battle Patrol was attached to the

3rd Battalion. We had very little resistance except for the Battle Patrol, whose objective was to clear Cavalaire-sur-Mer and the cape. A Sergeant James P. Connor earned a Medal of Honor for his outstanding bravery in helping to take the objective.

August 16, 1944: My Award of the Silver Star

The next day, August 16, 1944, the enemy became stubborn in their resistance. The citation for my award of the Silver Star for that day pretty well outlines the problems we were facing.

GENERAL ORDERS)
HEADQUARTERS   THIRD   INFANTRY   DIVISION
NUMBER 299)   :   APO #3   27 December 1944

Award of the Silver Star

    1. – <u>Award of Silver Star.</u> Under the provisions of Army Regulations as amended, a Silver Star is awarded each of the following named individuals:

    LLOYD B. RAMSEY, 023553, Lieutenant Colonel, Infantry, Headquarters Third Battalion, 7th Infantry Regiment. For gallantry in action. On 16 August 1944, Lieutenant Colonel RAMSEY EXPOSED HIMSELF to artillery and point-blank small arms fire, in order to direct a successful attack by his battalion near ***, France. When his assault company was held up by about 150 Germans re-enforced with approximately 10 machine guns and with bazookas, Lieutenant Colonel RAMSEY directed a flanking maneuver up a mined hillside. Moving 500 yards through artillery fire that had disorganized one of his units, he reorganized two leading platoons and started them moving forward. Later, when this unit reached the top of the hill and came under artillery and intense small arms fire at 100 to 200 yards range, Lieutenant Colonel RAMSEY helped the company commander place his men in position. He then led a platoon of another company up the hill under the enemy fire. As a result of his courageous leadership, the battalion wiped out the enemy stronghold, killing 21 and capturing 75. Residence; Somerset, Kentucky.

August 29, 1944: The Slaughter North of Montelimar, France

On August 29, 1944 there was a slaughter of Germans and destruction of equipment north of Montelimar. The *Seventh Infantry History, From Fedala to Berchtesgaden,* page 142 explains:

"The enemy was trapped with Seventh Infantry troops to the right and rear of them and the Rhone River on the left. Heavy concentrations (artillery) were placed at the head of the column. There was no way out. Artillery of the 36th Division finally joined in the shoot and eventually friendly fighter bombers of the air support got in on the work of destruction. It was veritable hell for the trapped enemy as bullets and shells dropped on them, smashing the vehicles and trains, killing the horses, men and women, there were a few present, and setting fire to the vehicles...the ambush of the enemy in the Montelimar pocket by the speedy and aggressive Seventh Infantry and other units brought 2000 live enemy into the prisoner of war cages. Hundreds were killed, 1000 horses were killed and nearly 2000 vehicles were destroyed or captured. In the booty was included the big railway guns, 300 trailers, 12 dreaded 88mm guns, 24 guns of lesser caliber, 30 tanks and an unestimated amount of lesser material."

The 3d Battalion, 7th Infantry, which I was commanding, was in the middle of this entire operation. I was directing artillery fire, my own mortar fire, and had my troops deployed so that they could shoot into the trapped area. I believe that this was the worst death and destruction that I saw at one time during the entire war. It was a horrible sight to see. Pictures of destruction are at the end of this chapter (Inclusions #4 and #4-2).

September 6-7, 1944: Besancon, France

The night of September 6-7, 1944 was a very rough night. Again, I quote from the *Seventh Infantry History*, page 148:

"During the night of 6-7 September 1944, near Besancon, the forward observation and command post of the Third Battalion came under attack by a platoon of German Infantrymen. The enemy had infiltrated through the battalion's forward companies and attacked the command post with machine guns, machine pistols and grenade fire at ranges as

close as ten yards. Lieutenant Colonel Lloyd B. Ramsey, the battalion commander and members of his staff who were present were in great danger of being captured or killed. In telling of the happenings that night, Lieutenant Colonel Ramsey said...'A rupture of communications with the assault companies, which were then meeting strong resistance, might easily have been disastrous.' Technician Fifth Grade Robert D. Maxwell, a wire corporal, radio operator Private James P. Soblensky, wire chief Technician Fourth Grade Cyril F. McCall, and wireman Private First Class James P. Joyce were in the post with the battalion commander."

(Comment: I always had communication men with me; without communications you can fight a battle, but you have very limited control and you cannot get assistance if needed – as we needed it in this situation.)

"The enemy Platoon, supported by 20mm flakwagon, and machine gun fire virtually surrounded the post and came within ten to fifteen yards of the building. They raked the doors and windows with a hail of bullets. 'Through all this fire,' said radio operator Soblensky, 'there was one man who just sat there calmly observing out into the darkness, taking pot shots at every Kraut he saw. It was Technician Fifth Grade Robert D. Maxwell, one of the wire corporals. He was the coolest customer I've ever seen. Tracer bullets were just barely clearing his head, yet he didn't seem to notice it.'"

"Despite the hail of fire from the enemy's automatic weapons and grenade launchers Technician Fifth Grade Maxwell aggressively fought off advancing enemy elements and by his calmness, tenacity and fortitude, inspired fellow soldiers to continue the unequal struggle. Lieutenant Colonel Ramsey realized that his small force could not hold the post against the enemy superior in numbers, so he ordered a withdrawal to another location. When suddenly an enemy grenade came over the wall and landed in the midst of the group, Technician Fifth Grade Maxwell unhesitatingly hurled himself on it, using his blanket and his unprotected body to absorb the full force of the explosion. Private First Class James P. Joyce said: 'I lay still for a few seconds partially stunned by the concussion, then I realized that I wasn't hurt. Technician Fifth Grade Maxwell had deliberately drawn the full force of the explosion on himself in order to protect us and make it possible for us to continue

at our posts and fight.' Technician Fifth Grade Maxwell was severely wounded and maimed, but his act of instantaneous heroism saved the lives of his comrades and facilitated the maintenance of vital military communications during the temporary withdrawal of the battalion's forward headquarters. For his action of that night Technician Fifth Grade Maxwell was awarded the Congressional Medal of Honor."

My comment: Maxwell's heroism no doubt saved me and others from injury or death. Now it was my duty to get the injured Maxwell and the other men to safety. The following actions were directed by me and the company commanders. Having communications with my company commanders was a lifesaver. It was not very long until we got Maxwell to our battalion surgeon.

"Private First Class Wilbur D. Springer, machine gunner of Company "M" and his assistant Private First Class Paul D. Clever, Jr., knocked out an enemy machine gun and killed several supporting riflemen after a duel at one hundred fifty yards range. When a second machine gun and about 25 riflemen thirty-five yards away suddenly opened fire on them, the two men held their ground and returned fire. Despite bullets that kicked dirt over them and hand grenades that exploded ten yards away, the two soldiers killed the remaining riflemen in the first group and forced the second enemy group to take cover in buildings. The tracer bullets they then directed at the buildings guided the fire of a friendly tank, and enabled Blue Battalion (3d Battalion) riflemen to seize them.

"The lead elements of the Blue Battalion (3d Battalion) pressed their advance. At 2145 Company "K" knocked out a 20mm flakwagon and an ammunition truck with bazooka fire. Seven enemy were killed and the battalion continued to advance. At 0110, 7 September, Company "K" ran into an enemy convoy in the process of forming by a road junction on the northwestern outskirts of the city. Again a bazooka round knocked out a truck, setting it afire. Enemy activity became intense and "King" and "Love" Companies went into defensive positions. The fire fight continued until about 0400 hours. The enemy used two self-propelled guns and a flakwagon as well as small arms, grenades and machine guns. At 0400 hours 7 September, Lieutenant Colonel Ramsey ordered a withdrawal of the companies to more advantageous positions and directed a heavy shelling on the vacated positions. At 0700 the Blue

troops (3d battalion) jumped off in the attack again and skirted the city. At 1130 hours the battalion motor pool personnel engaged in a fire fight that lasted for an hour and resulted in the capture of eighteen prisoners. By 1530 the Blue troops (3d battalion) were at A la Baraque and road junction northeast of Besancon, having skirted around the city. An hour and a half later the battalion less Company "K" progressed to the hill northeast of the city between the railroad and highway and made ready for another assault. The battalion then pressed forward against small arms and mortar fire and entered Besancon at 2015, 7 September. Fifteen minutes later the battalion was assembled near the railroad station in the city just northeast of the loop."

My comment: The battalion had been fighting for over 36 hours without rest and with very little food. The troops were able to rest from about 2030, 7 September to about 0930, 8 September. I received very little rest because I was making plans for our next move.

September 15-16, 1944: Vy-Les-Lures, France

This was a terrible battle with many casualties. Captain Ralph J. Yates, L Company Commander, performed in an outstanding manner against a determined enemy. The 3d Battalion launched an attack on Vy-Les-Lures, France at 1330 hours, September 15, 1944. The enemy was determined to overrun our forces, but time and time again our troops held their positions. In the early evening of September 15, the enemy made a last, desperate attack on Company L. I was confronted with a very tough decision. It appeared that the enemy would overrun Company "L". They were so close that if I used artillery I might kill some of our own troops. If I did not use artillery, I might lose many more troops. I made the decision to use artillery. I informed Company "L" Commander to take cover as well as they could and that the artillery would start firing soon. We would fire one round to get the range and Company L could adjust the range. We would then fire for effect and continue to fire unless Captain Yates asked us to adjust our range or cease fire. I quote from the *Seventh Infantry History*, page 157:

"...the enemy gathered his forces for a last desperate attack and surged forward to overrun and destroy the remnants of Company "L". As the fanatical German force advanced, round after round of friendly artillery fire pounded the area. Shells burst within ten feet of

the Command Post, their concussion shaking the earth. The German assault force almost reached its goal only to be cut to pieces by this withering concentration of fire. Thirteen Germans, all of them clutching hand grenades, lay dead when the massed artillery fire ceased. Some of these Germans were within twenty feet of the Command Post.

"Approximately four hours later, at 0150 hours, a patrol from Company "K" and the Battle Patrol, Seventh Infantry, broke through the enemy cordon and reached the Command Post of the surrounded company. Although many of the men were completely out of ammunition and the rest averaged a rifle clip each, Company "L" had held on grimly to the toe-hold of Vy-les-Lure, which had been won at such a heavy cost in blood. The weary, gallant men of the company remained on the alert all night, their bayonets fixed, waiting for another counterattack which the defeated enemy was too weak to deliver."

My comment: Although we had many casualties, as far as we could determine, none came from our artillery. My tough decision proved to be the right one.

September 1944: My Remarks to the Commanding General, General O'Daniel

Sometime in September 1944 – the exact date unknown because the 7th Infantry history does not cover this action – two battalions of the 7th Infantry were moving forward, but my 3d battalion had met heavy enemy resistance and was held up. Major General "Iron Mike" O'Daniel came to my battalion command post to see why I was not moving. It was not unusual for the C. G. to make such visits. When he arrived, I was at the top of a hill where I could see the entire front. Upon his arrival, he started raising hell with me for not moving forward. This was one time that I, as a battalion commander, was using almost every weapon available to me. I had laid down smoke across the front so that my troops could move without being seen. I had at least two battalions of artillery firing into the German positions. To my left, you could see a company of tanks making a flanking movement on the enemy. You could see my mortars shooting over our head. I had requested fighter bomber support and you could hear them coming. I pointed all of this out to him and he still raised hell with me. I got so exasperated with his comments that without really thinking, I turned to him and said, "General, if you can run this battalion better than I can, why don't you take over and I will go home." After this comment, the General turned and walked away, heading for his Jeep. I then realized what I had said. My first thought was how soon will it be before I am relieved of command?

It was not long until I was notified that the 30th Infantry Regiment would relieve the 3d Battalion. When the 30th Infantry took over, it did not take them long to discover that the enemy force consisted of a German Regiment. It took the 30th Infantry almost three days before they could move forward. My Regimental Commander, Colonel Ben Harrell, who supported my actions, reminded the Commanding General that it took a regiment almost three days to perform what I could not do in one day.

I should never have made the comment to the commanding general that I did, but it was probably the best thing I ever did. From then on it appeared that I could do no wrong. (Comment: In later years, at Fort Benning, Georgia, when I was the Aide-de-Camp to General O'Daniel, he seemed to enjoy telling Glenda how I had told him off in combat.)

October 14 – December 19, 1944: Rest and Relaxation to the United States After 25 Months Overseas

I received orders dated October 9, 1944 for 30 days rest and relaxation in the United States after being overseas for 25 months. We were in the vicinity of Vagney, France. Colonel Ben Harrell, the Regimental Commander, called me in and told me that I had been overseas longer than anyone else in the regiment and that he was giving me a 30 day rest and relaxation to visit my family in the United States. I departed the 7th Infantry on October 14, 1944, and returned to the regiment on December 19, 1944.

It was great to get home. Lloyd Ann had been born June 20, 1943, and this was the first time that I had seen my daughter. However, just having left combat, never having anything to do with a child before, and not having seen my wife for over two years made this a very difficult period for me; I am sure that it was for Glenda also. But Glenda was still a true soldier and made me feel at home and loved very much.

I made many speeches while I was home and was treated like a war hero, which I was not. A man in uniform in those days was given first class treatment by everyone. One day, in Somerset, Kentucky, we were walking down the sidewalk and passed a jewelry store. Glenda stopped and said that she would like to look in the window. She saw a man's diamond ring and said, "Isn't that a beautiful ring?" I said that it was beautiful, but only sissy men wore diamonds. That evening I was presented with that beautiful ring and was my face red because she reminded me of what I had said about men wearing diamonds. The ring had a diamond in the middle with six diamonds outside. A beautiful ring from a beautiful, lovely, sweet and adorable wife. Sometimes in combat, I wondered if I should be wearing the ring. If I were captured, that would be the first thing they would take from me.

I saw a lot of Mimi and Dad and, as Lloyd Ann called Mr. and Mrs. Burton, Mamma and Pappap, who treated me like a son. I saw all of my relatives in that area. My brother Bill never had to go into the Army. Jim went into the Army rather late and spent his entire service in the United States.

When it was time for me to return overseas, I asked Glenda to go to New York with me because I was told that when I arrived in New York I would be there at least three days after reporting for return overseas. We drove our 1939 Pontiac to New York. This was taking a chance because gasoline was rationed, and if you needed a tire, it was very hard to acquire. We checked into the New Yorker Hotel, and our room was magnificent. It was a large corner room that was divided into a living room and a sleeping area. I took one look at the room and knew that I could not afford such luxury, but I thought that I might never see Glenda again, so someway I would pay for the room. To check in for return overseas all that I had to do was make a phone call. I was told to stay in my room every day until 1100 hours. If I had not received a phone call by then, I was free to do anything until the next morning.

With this information we made our plans to go to a night club every night. At 1100 hours I would call a night club and make a reservation for that evening. Although we called late for a reservation, my being in the military always got us a ringside table, where we had a good view of the floor show. Many nights someone would pick up my bill and leave a message with the waiter to "tell the officer thanks for his combat service." One night a man came to our table and wished to see my diamond ring. He was wearing a very large diamond, and he said that mine sparkled more than his and he had to see why. He was amazed that my ring with small diamonds sparkled so much. He only took a very few minutes of our time, and again I did not receive a check.

A Doctor Gilmore from Somerset lived in New York. He found out that we were there and invited us, along with two ladies from Somerset who were working in New York during the war, to dinner. We met at his apartment, where he showed us pictures of many of the Siegfeld Follies dancers whom he had dated over the years. The doctor was hard of hearing, but even so, he showed us a wonderful evening on the town.

After three days in the hotel, I thought that I had better pay my bill in case I was called to return overseas the next day. I dreaded to see the cost. What a pleasant surprise I received: the hotel room was $5.00 a day, and, as I recall, there was no tax in those days. (Five dollars was the going rate for a small room in a standard hotel in those days. Being in the military was the reason that we got a larger room for that price.) Glenda and I stayed there for seven days before I was called for overseas movement. Poor Glenda had to drive all the way back to Somerset by herself. I think, however, that the drive was worth the wonderful week that we had together in New York.

December 19-20, 1944: Return to 7th Infantry – Strasbourg, France

I once again took command of the 3d Battalion, 7th Infantry on December 20, 1944. We were relieved of our defensive positions along the Rhine River on that date. On December 21, 1944, we moved to the fringe of the Colmar Pocket.

December 21, 1944 –February 15, 1945: Colmar Pocket, France

The *Seventh Infantry History*, page 201, states: "During the 'Colmar Pocket' Campaign the Seventh Infantry fought the bitter cold and deep snow of the Vosges Mountains as well as the enemy." As I recall, the snow got to 12 inches deep and the temperature got down to five degrees. Seldom did the troops have a chance to get into a building for some warmth. I remember trying to get some rest in the snow on a bitter cold night with nothing more than you could carry on your back. The good Lord gave you the strength to live under those conditions.

January 23-23, 1945: Crossing the Fecht River

I quote from *History of the Third Division in World War II*, page 304: "*The 7th and 30th Infantry Regiments, commanded by Lt. Col. John A. Heintges and Col. Lionel C. McGarr, respectively, began their crossing of the Fecht River by stealth at Guemar at 2100, on a front measuring less than 1000 yards in width. It was a repetition of the Meurthe stunt, and it worked. In the 7th zone, two platoons crossed just prior to H-Hour and seized bridgeheads. Artillery fell on both bridges of the 7th, and enemy heavy mortar fire fell on 1st Battalion, 30th Infantry, but enemy infantry resistance was negligible.*

The 3d Battalion, 7th Infantry, commanded by Lt. Col. Lloyd B. Ramsey, after crossing the river swung southeast and encountered enemy small-arms and machine-gun fire in the Bois Communale de Guemar. After overcoming this resistance the battalion, with Company I on the right and Company L on the left, moved swiftly across the east-west road which runs along the northern edge of the Foret Communale de Colmar.

Clearing the woods as they advanced, Colonel Ramsey's men continued past Ostheim and to a small wooded area, Brunnwald, where they beat off an enemy counterattack consisting of tanks and infantry which came from the east. Our artillery and mortar fire played an important part in stopping the German counter-thrust while elements of Lt. Col. Glenn F. Rogers' 756th Tank Battalion supported the battalion all along the route of advance..."

January 24, 1945: Lt. Garlin M. Conner, My S-2; an Act of Heroism

I quote from *Combat Medic* by Isadore Valenti, pages 154-155.

"*Ex-private, but now Lieut. Garlin M. Connor, formerly of Company K, now with the 3d Battalion Headquarters was scheduled to go home, i.e. to the U.S.A. Lt. Col. Lloyd B. Ramsey, 3rd Battalion C.O., said, 'For his safety, I decided to bring Lieut. Connor to the 3rd Bn. Hqs.*

where he might be a little safer. I made him my S-2.' And added, 'He has more silver stars and purple hearts than anyone I know.'"

"The 3rd Battalion was slowed down by a fierce enemy counterattack. Enemy formations were converging on the battalion's position and were in danger of being overrun by a powerful enemy force of more than 500 German fanatics.

"At this point, Col. Ramsey was discussing the seriousness of the 3rd Battalion's situation, with his staff when Lieut. Connor approached him. Connor said he would take a patrol out, and see if he could direct artillery strikes on the advancing enemy. Taking a radio and a wire line with field phone, in case of radio problems, Lieut. Connor moved out with his patrol.

"Connor and his men soon found themselves at a point with nothing in front of them but Germans, and under intense automatic weapons fire. Connor called for artillery fire support which he directed on the Germans as their advance rolled forward. Col. Ramsey said, 'I personally stayed in radio, or telephone contact with Garlin Connor.' He added, 'Fortunately, they both worked all the time.'

"For more than two hours Connor remained there as artillery observer directing one artillery strike after another on the advancing Germans as they surged forward. At times, Connor remained there as enemy soldiers began edging around his position, wounding his assistant. Each time the German fanatics were stopped just short of his position.

"At one time, Lieut. Connor had to leave his position. He radioed Col. Ramsey that he would be out of action for a few minutes. When he returned he told Col. Ramsey he had spotted two German tanks, and had gone over to a tank destroyer (TD) to point them out. The German tanks were knocked out by the TD.

"At another time, Col. Ramsey, concerned with Connor and his patrols safety, asked if he were bringing the artillery fire too close to his position. Connor's answer was that the artillery fire had already been on his position; that the artillery fire was now behind him, i.e. between his position and that of the battalion's command post. He continued to direct the accurate shell fire of the 10th Field Artillery until the German attack was shattered and broken.

"For this action, Lieut. Connor received the Distinguished Service Cross. He was responsible for killing and wounding over 150 enemy soldiers."

My comment: This award should have been a Medal of Honor. I quote from a letter that I sent to my father in February 1945.

"I just sent one of my officers home, he was my S-2 (Intelligence Officer), Lt. Garlin M. Conner, who is from Aaron, Kentucky. I'm really proud of Lt. Conner, he probably will call you and, if he does, he may not sound like a soldier, will sound like any good old country boy, but, to my way of seeing, he's one of the outstanding soldiers of this war, if not the outstanding. He was a Sergeant until July and now is a First Lieutenant. He has the D.S.C. which should have been, I believe, a Congressional Medal of Honor, but, he was heading home and we wanted to get him the highest award possible before he left. He has a Silver Star with 4 clusters, a Bronze Star, Purple Heart with 6 clusters and is in for a French medal. On this last push, within two weeks he earned the D.S.C., a cluster to his Silver Star and Bronze Star. I've never seen a man with as much courage and ability as he has. I usually don't brag much on my officers but, this is one officer nobody could brag enough about and do him justice; he's a real soldier."

January 25, 1945: My Wounds in the Colmar Pocket

I quote from *Combat Medic* by Isadore Valenti, pages 157-158.

"LIEUT. COLONEL LLOYD B. RAMSEY – 3RD BATTALION COMMANDER – AN EXTRAORDINARY MAN.

"During the late afternoon of 25 January, Company K was ordered to set up a roadblock northeast of Houssen. During this momentarily fixed position, I worked my way back to the battalion aid station, situated in the cellar of an old French railroad station within ear shot of small arms fire.

"The Germans had been shelling our positions all afternoon. I had run low on critical medical supplies. The ground was covered with fresh snow; the wind had a frosty edge. Darkness was fast approaching.

"My medical kits now filled with fresh supplies, I was about to crawl out of the cellar and head back to Company K, when I noticed – in the distance – a figure of a man trudging toward the aid station.

"As he approached the entrance I pulled aside the blanket to let him in. It was then I recognized him. It was Lieutenant Colonel Lloyd B. Ramsey, our 3rd battalion commander, who had just recently returned

from an R and R leave from the States.

"Earlier in the day, Col. Ramsey had set up a forward observation post, from where he directed his overall, battle plan objective. Col. Ramsey's post came under a heavy, German mortar barrage during one of several German counterattacks. Col. Ramsey, along with several others, was caught in the barrage. Col. Ramsey received multiple wounds in the back from slivers of razor-edged shrapnel."

My comment: Some of these wounds were from mortar fire, but the razor sharp ones came from German Potato Mashers. A Potato Masher is a percussive grenade that is normally used in fox holes or tunnels. It primarily puts out a percussion, to bounce off walls, but it does produce some slivers of tin that are very sharp. We had run into a German patrol only a few feet away, and I must assume that Potato Mashers were the only ammo that they had left. When the first German grenade was thrown at us, I picked it up and threw it back at the enemy. Another one came in about the same time and I did not get it back to the enemy in time; as it exploded in the air, I hit the ground. We then killed the three-man German patrol.

The Combat Medic quote continued:

"Captain Frank J. Syladek, our genial, six-foot tall battalion surgeon, asked me to lend a hand. I helped Col. Ramsey remove his shredded combat jacket, and prepared a stretcher for him to lie on. While I held a gasoline lantern over the Colonel, Captain Syladek dug out over a dozen pieces of ragged-edged shrapnel, some deeply embedded, from Col. Ramsey's back. The shrapnel was removed without anesthesia.

"Lieut. Col. Lloyd B. Ramsey was as extraordinary man. He came through the surgery remarkably well, other than a couple of grunts. The 26 year old Lieut. Col. came in on his own power and he left on his own power, returning to his observation post.

"Company K, still short a medic, was dug in about 150 yards up ahead. Before I left the aid station, Captain Syladek had me prepare a Purple Heart report on Col. Ramsey, his fifth Purple Heart."

My comment: As I recall, Keeler was with me when we killed the enemy patrol, and he helped me find the aid station. Keeler was not wounded in this action.

February 2-4, 1945: K and L Company Battle

I quote from *Combat Medic* by Isadore Valenti, pages 162-164:

"In spite of our depleted strength, the 7th Infantry Regiment, following an artillery saturation of positions, jumped off into a new attack at dawn, 2 February 1945. The objective – crossing of the Rhone Canal.

The third Battalion took up the right flank in the attacking wave. Company K, under the able command of Captain Kret, met and fought off fanatical enemy resistance.

Company K was cut in two, and forced to take cover in trenches. Several attempts by the 7th Infantry Battle Patrol to rescue the trapped men of Company K failed. Bitter fighting raged on between Germans and the trapped American troops.

Troops of the 1st and 3rd Battalions tried to move in near the vicinity of the trapped K Company soldiers, only to find themselves locked in battle with the Germans inside the nearby graveyard. Troops from all three battalions were committed in the rescue attempt of Company K, but failed because of devastating enemy fire over the flat terrain.

The commander of L Company was killed during one of the rescue attempts. The enemy now concentrated 80MM mortar, artillery and flakwagen fire on the town of Biesheim, which was now partly occupied by Company L, and on the road leading to the trapped Company K.

Lieut. Connor was still with 3rd Battalion Headquarters when Company L's CO was killed. Lieut. Col. Lloyd B. Ramsey called a staff meeting to select his replacement. Again Lieut. Connor came forward and volunteered to act as Company L's CO. 'No words can express the outstanding leadership qualities that Lieut. Garlin Connor had, always willing to do more than his part' said Col. Ramsey, 3rd Battalion CO.

Company L, now under command of First Lt. Garlin M. Connor, though badly shaken, continued the rescue assault. After engaging the Germans in hand-to-hand combat, in which more than 12 enemy soldiers were killed, other elements of the 3rd Battalion, during the night, made contact with the trapped Company K.

By 4 February, the bitter fighting in Biesheim was over. A great many Germans were killed and were captured. Company K lost over ten men KIA, and as many wounded, including Capt. Kret., Company K's C.O. who was hit by a chunk of shrapnel from an exploding 81MM cannon shell.

When I got to Captain Kret he was already going into shock. His breathing was rapid and he had lost much blood.

His shattered arm barely hung on by several strands of muscular tissue had to come off. Captain Kret appeared to be sinking deeper into shock. I had to act quickly.

I immediately lifted two woolen blankets from the back packs of two nearby dead G.I.'s. I wrapped the blankets around Captain Krets body to help keep him warmer.

I gave Captain Kret a shot of morphine, and pinned the empty capsule to his shirt as evidence of a morphine injection.

I had Company K's C.P. contact the battalion aid station for litter bearers and more blankets. 'And hurry!'

I saturated the gaping shoulder wound with a heavy coating of sulfa powder to prevent serious infection and covered the ghastly wound with heavy dressings to staunch further loss of blood and keep the wound clean."

My comment: Valenti, who wrote Combat Medic, was Company K's medic, and he was doing his best to save the life of his company commander. Valenti asked me to write a comment about his book, Combat Medic, which I did, and he placed it in the back of his book.

What One of My Company Commanders Thought of Me

I quote from Autobahn to Berchtesgaden by Lieutenant Colonel Sherman W. Pratt, page 565: "...I arrived at the battalion command Post. The company commanders had been summoned there for briefings by the battalion commander, Lt. Col. Lloyd Ramsey. Ramsey had been the battalion commander earlier during the winter but had been away on a special assignment and had just returned to take over from Major Flynn. Ramsey was a most likeable individual.

Col. Ramsey was friendly, military in his bearing and pleasant in his approach to everyone with whom he came into contact. No matter what their rank or job, he both commanded, and earned, the respect of subordinates and seniors alike. He was in every sense the type of military person that literally exuded confidence and respect. I doubt there was any member of his command who was not especially proud and eager to serve under him in whatever capacity."

My comment: Pratt was one of the finest soldiers, NCO and Officer, that I had the honor to command. I helped him to get his battlefield commission. When he wrote his book, *Autobahn to Berchtesgaden*, he asked me to write the Foreward, which I did, and he published it in his book.

Pratt sent me an autographed copy and printed the following: WITH BEST WISHES TO LLOYD RAMSEY – A GREAT AMERICAN AND A PROVEN HERO MANY TIMES OVER AND WITHOUT WHOSE LEADERSHIP AND INSPRIRATION I WOULD NOT LIKELY HAVE SURVIVED TO WRITE THIS NARRATIVE!
Sherman Pratt
Arlington, VA
Dec. 92

February 26, 1945: I Become the Executive Officer of the 7th Infantry Regiment

On February 25 I became the Executive Officer of the 7th Infantry Regiment. In this position, I was not in daily contact with the enemy as I had been before. However, I had to be prepared to assume command of a battalion at any time, day or night, in case one of the battalion commanders was wounded.

My duties were to assist the Regimental Commander in any way that he wanted. I would visit at least one or two battalions every day or night and try to help them as needed. I could give advice, from my experience as a battalion commander, or I could help get the needed support, i.e. tanks, artillery, or even fighter bomber support. I could also assist in getting ammo, rations, or clothing to the battalion and/or companies as needed.

May 4, 1945: Finding a Bridge Across the Saalach River

On May 4, 1945, the Second Battalion, 7th Infantry, entered Salzburg, Austria, by crossing the Saalach River in boats and was the first Allied troops into Salzburg. Berchtesgaden was not far away, but we needed a vehicle bridge to get our trucks and tanks across. Colonel Duncan, C.O., 2nd Battalion, had sent a patrol out during the night to see if there was a bridge still standing. The patrol came back, not being able to find a bridge, and the information was reported to Regiment. Colonel Heintges and I had been studying the maps, which showed that there was a railroad crossing the river. He sent me to see Col. Duncan and find the bridge to see if it was still standing. I told Colonel Duncan that night patrols sometimes think that they have been a long way but have actually covered a very short distance. I suggested that he and I take a patrol to see if we could find the bridge. Colonel Duncan was reluctant for two lieutenant colonels to be on a night patrol. He had a very good point, but I felt that the enemy was weak and was surrendering very fast; therefore, he agreed that we take the patrol.

It was not long until we found the railroad bridge. The enemy had spread the tracks in the middle of the bridge and run an engine out on the bridge until it fell to the cross ties. I immediately called Colonel Heintges, who got the engineers to remove the engine.

I quote from the *Seventh Infantry History,* pages 278:

"Early in the morning of 4 May 1945 reconnaissance discovered that a railroad bridge over the Saalach near Piding had a locomotive engine on it. A small wooden bridge was also discovered nearby which was undamaged and strong enough to permit passage of foot troops and jeeps.

With its Second Battalion already across the river into Austria and in possession of much of Salzburg and by a stroke of luck in possession of two bridges, the Seventh Infantry was in a most favorable position to swoop down on Berchtesgaden and capture Hitler's hideaway, Der Berghof Obersalzberg. No one realized this any sooner than the Third Division Commander. On the right the 101st Airborne Infantry Division and the Second French Armored Division, which divisions had direct orders to seize Berchtesgaden, had not yet reached the Saalach.

Early 4 May Major General O'Daniel took matters into his own hands and decided to send the Seventh United States Infantry out of the Third Division zone of action to steal Berchtesgaden and Hitler's hideaway, Der Berhof Obersalzberg, from the American paratroopers and French armored forces, who technically were supposed to capture those places. Only Salzburg, Austria, had been definitely assigned to the Third Infantry Division but that place was already in hand. It had been expected that Salzburg would be a last enemy stronghold before Berchtesgaden and would be a hard nut to crack, like Nurnberg had been, but as stated, hardly a shot had been fired in that city and it capitulated early.

Major General John W. 'Iron Mike' O'Daniel, Commanding

General of the Third Infantry Division, had tried unsuccessfully to get Berchtesgaden as an objective for his division. However, he decided not to let slip from his fingers the golden opportunity of adding the Bavarian mountain town, made famous by Hitler's hideaway, to the long list of towns and cities captured by the 'Rock of the Marne' Division. He then ordered Colonel John A. Heintges to drive the 'Cotton Baler' Regiment with all possible speed and to capture Berchestgaden, the prize and pearl of all military objectives at that time.

Colonel Heintges, who the night before had dreamed and hoped for that very opportunity and had conceived his 'Orange Plan' to put into execution should the chance occur, quickly issued his orders to push the First and Third Battalions over the bridges. The Commanding General, to assure himself of success, had ordered Colonel Heintges to place heavy guard on the two bridges and to permit no one, or any vehicle to pass over them except Seventh Infantry personnel and vehicles."

My comment: the *Seventh Infantry History* says that First Lieutenant Nathan W. White and Lieutenant Robert Miller were put in command of the bridge. Lt. White wrote the *Seventh Infantry History* but he did not care for me because, as the Executive Officer of the Regiment, I had kept after him to keep the history up-to-date. General O'Daniel told Colonel Heintges to put me in charge of the bridge and to allow no one, except the Seventh Infantry, to cross that bridge without his approval directly to me. White and Miller were assigned to me. I assume that White's dislike for me is why Colonel Duncan and I are not mentioned in the Seventh Infantry History as leading the patrol that found the bridges. The history says on page 278: *"Early in the morning of 4 May 1945 reconnaissance discovered that a railroad bridge over the Saalach near Piding had a locomotive engine on it."*

Everything went fine until the Second French Armored Division arrived. When I saw them coming, I put 2 ½ ton trucks across the road in front of the bridge so that they could not cross. It was not long until Major General LeClerc, the Division Commander, arrived. When I reported to him, he informed me that he had seen General O'Daniel and that the General had authorized him to cross the bridge . I told him that General O'Daniel's instructions to me were that such approval must come directly from him to me. After much discussion, General LeClerc went off to find General O'Daniel.

It was not long until General O'Daniel arrived at the bridge. I asked him if he had authorized General LeClerc to cross the bridge. His answer: "Yes, I did. Did you let him across?"

I said, "No, sir. My orders were that any crossing, other than Seventh Infantry, must come from you directly to me."

His reply, "It is a good thing that you followed my orders."

General O'Daniel left and said that he would be back to talk to General LeClerc when he returned to the bridge. The two generals returned about the same time. By this time, General O'Daniel learned that the Seventh Infantry was in Berchtesgaden, about four hours after they had crossed the bridge. He then allowed the Second French Armored Division to cross the bridge.

I quote from the *Seventh Infantry History*, pages 820-281:

"In Berchtesgaden, at Hermann Goering's Staff Headquarters, General Der Fleiger (Lieutenant General) Gustav Kastner-Kirkdorf was found dead in his bedroom adjoining his office. According to a female employee at the headquarters, who was questioned, he was a member of Adolf Hitler's Staff and had arrived at Goering's Headquarters in Berchtesgaden on 2 May. He committed suicide shortly after Seventh Infantrymen entered the town, as did one other German general.

"Included in the bag of prisoners caught in Berchtesgaden was Colonel Fritz Goering of the Luftwaffe, a nephew of the number two Nazi, Hermann Goering. He personally surrendered to Colonel Heintges and handed his pistols to the Commanding Officer, who personally questioned him on the whereabouts of Adolf Hitler, Hermann Goering, and other Nazi officials, as it was hoped that some of them could be captured. The German Colonel stated he did not know of his uncle's whereabouts because Hitler had had Hermann Goering arrested a few days before because he had wanted to quit the war. Neither did he know anything of Hitler's whereabouts. He told Colonel Heintges that he would like to turn over to the Seventh Infantry Commander the property of Hermann and Frau Goering which was quite considerable. That which interested the 'Cotton Baler' Colonel most was some 18,000 bottles of the finest liquers and two automobiles: the Field Marshal's two seated roadster and a fourteen passenger, bullet-proof sedan.

"According to the headquarters commander of Field Marshal Albert Kesselring's General Staff, who was also taken prisoner in Berchtesgaden that day, the 'Cotton Balers' had missed the commander in chief of all German forces on the Western Front by just several hours. The Field Marshal had been in Berchtesgaden and had left the town the previous night with hundreds of his troops. However at 2000B on 4 May an armistice delegation from Field Marshal Kesselring entered the Second Battalion lines in Salzburg, Austria. The delegation consisted of General of Infantry Foertsch, Commanding General of the First German Army, at the head, and Colonel Zolling, Major Hay, Major Forker, and Major Von Orloff of the German General Staff Corps as well as a Major Koelle, Captain Behrendt, Captain Castillieri, First Lieutenant Von Weber, Sonderfuehrer Schoeningh and Colonel Collosius of the Luftwaffe..."

The capture of Berchtesgaden on May 4, 1945 for all practical purposes ended the war in Europe for the 3rd Infantry Division. On May 9, 1945, all fighting in Europe ceased.

May 5, 1945: Ceremony Celebrating the Capture of Berchtesgaden

A proud Colonel John A. Heintges, Commanding Officer 7th Infantry Regiment, on May 5 wanted to have a ceremony celebrating the capture of Berchtesgaden on May 4 and to raise the American flag over Hitler's hideaway. The French strongly objected since they were supposed to have taken Berchtesgaden. Colonel Heintges spoke both German and French. He told the French that we would have a very short ceremony, raise the American flag, and then immediately lower the flag. After a long discussion, he got the French to agree, except they would not let us raise the flag to the top of the pole. Colonel Heintges did not like this arrangement, but he thought that it was better than no ceremony at all.

A picture at the end of the chapter (Inclusion #5) shows some of the destruction at Obersalzburg, near Berchtesgaden, the ceremony, and how high the flag was flown. Colonel Heintges is in the front, and I am to his immediate right rear. At Inclusion #5-2, there is an enlarged picture of the ceremony.

May 6, 1945: Move to Salzburg, Austria

Since the 101st Airborne Division and the French were supposed to have taken Berchtesgaden, the 7th Infantry on May 6 turned the whole place over to the 506th Parachute Regiment, 101st Airborne Division, and to the French. The entire 7th Infantry moved to Salzburg, Austria, on May 6, 1945.

May 7, 1945: The End of the War in Europe

From the *History of the Third Infantry Division*, page 372: "At 2:41 A.M., Monday, May 7 at Reims, France, General of the Army Dwight D. Eisenhower turned to his deputy commander, British Air Marshal Tedder and said, 'Thank you very much, Arthur.' Then he held up two pens with which surrender had been signed and made a 'V' for victory. Peace had officially come to Europe."

Wounded Five Times

I had been wounded five times since joining the 3rd Infantry Division on November 14, 1943. It was a relief to know that I would not hear another shot fired in anger in World War II.

A "Quote" That I Lived By in World War II

"Accept a man for what he is, not for what you want him to be."

I do not remember the source of this quote, but I learned it very early in World War II. I lived by what the quote says, and I was able to use the officers and NCO's under me in such a way that it helped them and it helped me to accomplish our objectives. The quote is at the end of my biography in Marquis' Who's Who in America.

7th Infantry Regiment

At the end of this chapter (Inclusion #6) there is a short write-up of the 7th Infantry Regiment. At Inclusion #7 is a list of Regimental Commanders, Regimental Executive Officers, and Battalion Commanders.

September 2, 1945: World War II Ends

I remember well the date of September 2, 1945. On that date World War II ended. Although the war in Germany had ended on May 7, 1945, with unconditional surrender by the Germans, the war in the Pacific continued.

The Japanese started the war in the Pacific by their attack on Pearl Harbor, Hawaii, on December 7, 1941, and they were dedicated to protect their homeland from invasion at almost any cost. President Truman made the decision to drop the atomic bomb on Hiroshima on August 6, 1945 and on Nagasaki on August 9, 1945. The number of casualties at Hiroshima and Nagasaki was estimated to be between 80,000 and 100,000 civilians. Many others died later from radiation. These figures, in civilian casualties, were much lower than the estimated American lives that would have been lost had we been forced to invade Japan. I have seen estimates that as many as 500,000 U.S. servicemen may have been killed or wounded if we had taken this action.

President Truman announced the surrender of Japan on August 14, 1945. The actual signing of the surrender papers was aboard the USS Missouri in Tokyo Bay on September 2, 1945. General Douglas MacArthur signed the surrender agreement for the United States of America.

I have seen estimates that during World War II there may have been as many as 75 million deaths around the world. Sixteen million Americans served in the Armed Forces during World War II. There were 53 nations involved in World War II, according to the *Encyclopedia Britannica*. Military losses by some of the largest nations are as follows:

United States	292,100	1 of every 450 population
Great Britain	544,559	1 of every 150 population
USSR	7,500,000	1 of every 22 population
France	210,671	1 of every 200 population
Germany	2,850,000	1 of every 25 population
Italy	300,000	1 of every 150 population
China	2,200,000	1 of every 200 population
Japan	1,506,000	1 of every 46 population

All figures in this paragraph are subject to question. Other encyclopedias and computer printouts show different figures, some of which vary considerably. As an example, I show 16,000,000 Americans served in the Armed Forces, whereas *Encyclopedia Britannica* shows 12,000,000.

An Interesting Poem

The following poem was supposedly found in a guard hut on the British fortress at Gibraltar:

> *God and Soldier we adore*
> *In time of danger, not before*
> *The danger passed, and all things righted*
> *God is forgotten, and the soldier slighted.*

December 1985: Christmas Card from a Soldier Who Served Me in September – October 1944

In Chapter 5, I mentioned that Corporal Harvey Keeler was my right-hand man. Keeler received a minor wound in September 1944 and had to be evacuated, but he insisted that he would return. I needed a man like Keeler so I got Louis Sumien from L Company to replace Keeler until he returned. Evidently, Sumien had seen my name and address in the 3rd Infantry Division newsletter, as Chairman of the 3rd Infantry Division Memorial Committee, and decided to drop me a line. This excerpt is from his card:

Dear General,
Over 40 years ago, it had been my pleasure to serve my Lt. Col., as a "Part Time" Dogrobber, near Remirmont, France and I tried, and I think…succeeded in making you the finest-looking officer – because you were…and are still, 'The Best There Is.' Do you remember?

> *Louis Sumien*
> *L Co., 3d Bn*
> *7th Inf.*

Now, our goal is our monument.

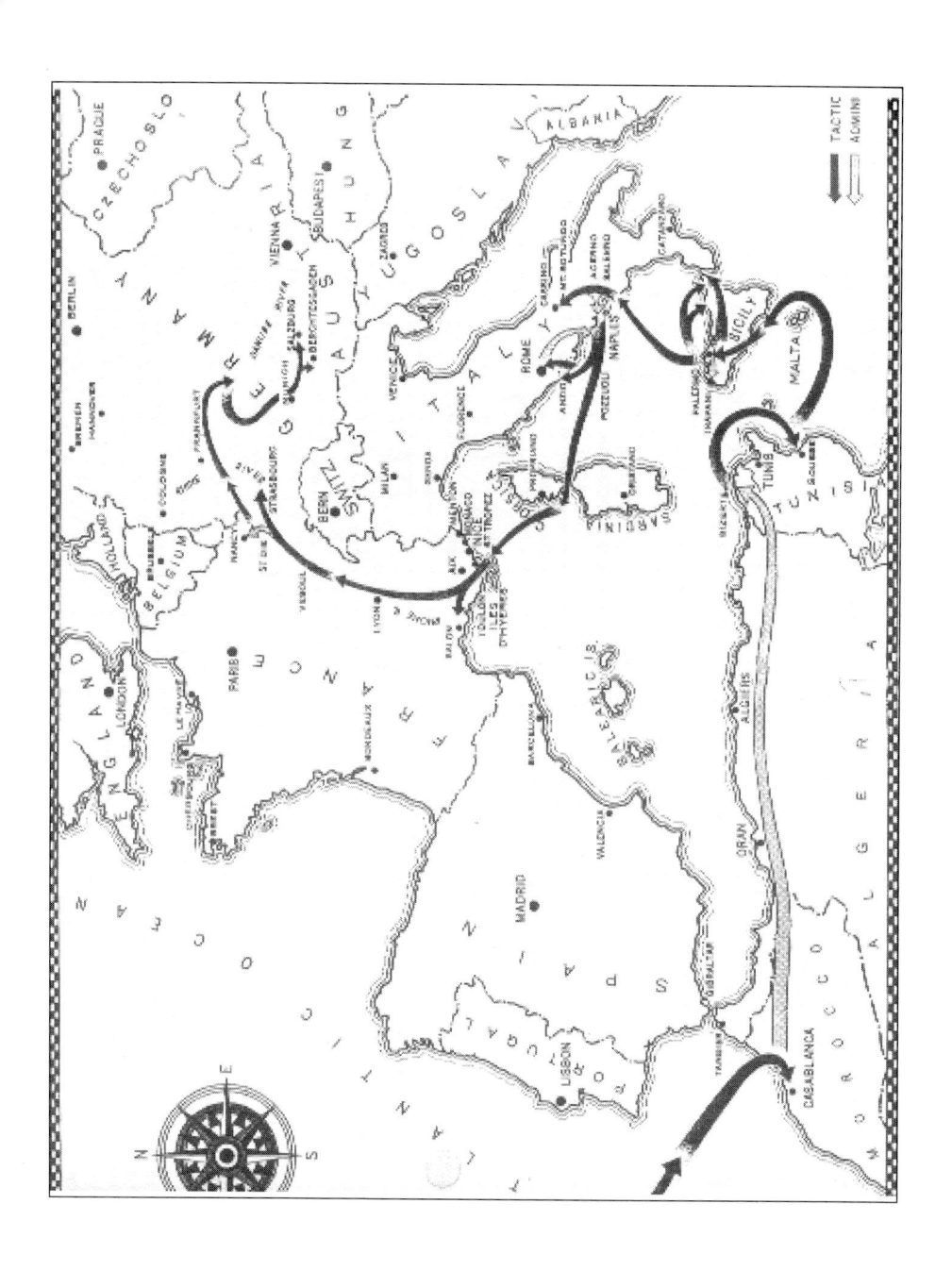

INCL. # 1

May I, 1944
Anzio Beachhead

Dear Dad,
    Thought I would try to give you a few of my experiences in the last few months and let you tell Mimi and Glenda about them if you think it would be alright.
    First of all I have been wounded a second time but up to now I never said anything about it because the last time that I had a little wound it seemed to me that you all believed that I was wounded pretty bad and I actually wasn't so I have been holding this one off so I could explain the whole thing, and again it was omly a scratch, thank God. One day a captain and myself were out on a recon. in front of our lines, places we probably shouldn't have been but I still say that I can go anywhere that I have to send my men. We were looking for routes and also how the ground would suit us for a little fight, well all of a sudden there was an explosion and we both were knocked to the ground. After looking around to see what it was I got up but the captain didn't, he was wounded seriously in the legs. I then found out that we were in the middle of a German mine field and we had hit a trip wire that set off the mine. The mine that went off was only about three feet from us and we were lucky that even got out of it alive. The only trouble with me was that I was shook up a little from the explosion and had a very small piece of fragment that went in the back of my thigh. I had to carry Pretruzel, the captain, out of the mine field and God only knows how I kept from hitting another mine. Got him back to the aid station pretty quick and he was rushed to the hospital. They thought for a while that he would lose his leg but now he is getting along fine and no chance to lose his leg. As for me, my small wound has healed completely, and I never did even quit duty it was so small. I certainly did give thanks to the Lord for watching over me and taking care of both of us during that time. There is only one consolation about Pretrauel being wounded and that is that we had planned to use that route for our troops and after this incident we changed our route and not one man was wounded during the move whereas if we had gone out there we would probably have had quite a few men killed and wounded.
    I never told you how I got my other wound but that time too only God knows how I came out alive. It was my first day in my present regiment, I was on my way pp to join my battalion and was being led by a Lt. who was going back up after a trip to regiment H.Q. On the way up we started receiving some very heavy shelling and of course we were hitting the ground but had to keep moving as fast as we could because we were needed very much. Once we heard a shell coming in and we hit the ground about ten yards apart and bang, the shell landed between us. I raised up and hollerd at Buzzby but received no answer. I had trouble in trying to get up because the concussion had stunned me. I finally got and felt a little blood running down my throat, but when I felt it I could tell it was only a scratch. I went to Buzzby, turned him over and noticed that he had been hit in the throat, there was very little chance for him. I cut his pack off and put a bandage on him. He then tried to talk to me and the only words that I heard

INCL. # 2

was " Tell H_____ that I love her". I didn't even get her name but knew that it was his wife. I got a soldier to stay with him and told him that I would go for the Medics, but when the Medics returned it was too late. Only God could have taken care of me in such dangerous situations and I have given prayers of thanks many times since then.

Another close call that I had was one day I was out inspecting on the front lines and some artillery started falling. I got in a fox hole and stayed there until I thought the shelling was over. The hole that I was in had a very small entrance so I started worming my way out. I got about half way out and got my pistol and canteen stuck so I couldn't move and about that time I heard another shell coming in. I tried to get back in but couldn't budge, and then a deep thud went off right next to me and mud splattered all over me. I wiped the mud out of my eyes and about ten feet from me was a big hole in the ground and in the bottom was an unexploded shell. I guess a cat with only nine lives could be so lucky sometimes.

Some people around here try to tell me that I have more guts than brains but its not guts at all because I'm as scared as anybody else is and probably a little more, but when I see these Dogfaces up there in a fight and see what they go through and how they fight it is only a small thing that I can do in going around and trying to help them and give them an inspiration because they think its something when they see some guy wearing a leaf on his collar and coming up on the front lines just to sit down and talk to some of them and dodge a few bullets with them. I've learned to love these GI's and as long as an officer will lead them and take care of them they will fight for you till the finish and never say a word. If they are wounded they will lay there for hours/and/never/say/a/word/ after hour without moaning about some one not picking them up. You can say what you want to about the glamour boys of the air corps who do a good job and are decorated from head to foot and you can talk about the armoured corps who can tell about what they can do with their iron monsters, but no matter what you say or what you hear the dogface soldiers are the heroes of this and all other wars, he's the queen of the battle, the guy that lives in the mud without eating or sleeping, fights on his guts when completely fatigued and then comes out with a smile.

I could rave for hours about the infantry soldier who to me will always be known as a dogface soldier. there was a song written by some one in the division which to me is a wonderful song.

> I wouldn't give a bean
> To be a fancy pants Marine
> I'd rather be a dogface like I am
> I wouldn't trade my old OD's
> For all the Navy's dungerees
> For I'm the walking pride of Uncle Sam
> All the posters that I read
> Say the army builds men/~~They~~/
> They're tearing me down
> To build me over again
> I'm just a dogface soldier
> With a rifle on my shoulder
> And I eat a Kraut for breakfast every day
> So feed me amunition
> Keep me in the Third Division
> Your Dogface soldier boy's O K.

These are just a few of the things that happen here Dad but I'm afraid to write Glenda because I'm almost inhuman at times from the things that I see that never bother me, and I wouldn't want to worry her for anything in the world. I'll leave it up to you to tell these things to Mimi and G;enda if you think it alright. Please don't be putting anything ~~like/that~~ in the paper about me being wounded or anything like that save the papers for the dogfaces, you can't write enough or say enough about him.

                                        Love,

                                            "Feller"

INCL. # 2-3

SUPREME HEADQUARTERS
ALLIED EXPEDITIONARY FORCE

Soldiers, Sailors and Airmen of the Allied Expeditionary Force!

You are about to embark upon the Great Crusade, toward which we have striven these many months. The eyes of the world are upon you. The hopes and prayers of liberty-loving people everywhere march with you. In company with our brave Allies and brothers-in-arms on other Fronts, you will bring about the destruction of the German war machine, the elimination of Nazi tyranny over the oppressed peoples of Europe, and security for ourselves in a free world.

Your task will not be an easy one. Your enemy is well trained, well equipped and battle-hardened. He will fight savagely.

But this is the year 1944 ! Much has happened since the Nazi triumphs of 1940-41. The United Nations have inflicted upon the Germans great defeats, in open battle, man-to-man. Our air offensive has seriously reduced their strength in the air and their capacity to wage war on the ground. Our Home Fronts have given us an overwhelming superiority in weapons and munitions of war, and placed at our disposal great reserves of trained fighting men. The tide has turned ! The free men of the world are marching together to Victory !

I have full confidence in your courage, devotion to duty and skill in battle. We will accept nothing less than full Victory !

Good Luck ! And let us all beseech the blessing of Almighty God upon this great and noble undertaking.

Dwight Eisenhower

INCL. # 3

On the eve of D-Day June 6, 1944: The night before the invasion of France, the Allied Supreme Commander, General Dwight D. Eisenhower, wrote a short note and tucked it into his pocket. It was only to be released to the press in the event the invasion was a failure. In the rush of the moment, he wrote July on the bottom, rather than June. In one of history's fascinating "what ifs," the text of the note is reproduced below. This handwritten document is now on display at The National D-Day Museum in New Orleans.

"Our landings in the Cherbourg-Havre area have failed to gain a satisfactory foothold and I have withdrawn the troops. My decision to attack at this time and place was based upon the best information available. The troops, the air and the Navy did all that Bravery and devotion to duty could do. If any blame or fault attaches to the attempt it is mine alone. — July 5"

INCL. # 3-2

Our landings in the Cherbourg – Havre area have failed to gain a satisfactory foothold and ~~I have withdrawn the troops.~~ ~~this particular~~ ~~Juncture~~ My decision to attack at this time and place was based upon the best information available. The troops, the air and the Navy did all that ~~~~ Bravery and devotion to duty could do. If any blame or fault attaches to the attempt it is mine alone.

July 5

INCL. # 3-3

Part of an enemy truck convoy which was partly destroyed south of Montelimar. The chief scene of destruction was north of the town.

One of the 380mm German railway guns abandoned by the enemy in the battle of Montelimar. There were also four 280mm guns abandoned.

INCL. # 4

Top photos show how some of the bodies of dead Germans appeared after destruction of the enemy convoys north of Montelimar. Center photos show the highway after bulldozers plowed a path through the wreckage. Two of the large enemy railway guns are shown in the lower photos.

INCL. # 4-2

At Obersalzburg, the Nazis' retreat near Berchtesgaden, the RAF bombs had caused considerable destruction as evidenced by this photo.

The United States flag is raised at Obersalzburg, above Berchtesgaden, by Pvt. Bennet A. Walter and Pfc. Nick Urich of the 3rd Division's 7th Infantry, after capture of the Village.

INCL. # 5

The United States flag is raised at Obersalzburg, above Berchtesgaden, by Pvt. Bennet A. Walter and Pfc. Nick Urich of the 3rd Division's 7th Infantry, after capture of the Village.

INCL. # 5-2

7TH INFANTRY REGIMENT

The "Cotton Balers," who gained that nickname for the use they made of cotton bales in the battle for New Orleans during the war with Britain 1812-1814, were first organized in 1798, mustered out in 1800, and re-organized in 1808, with continuous service dating from that time. As such they are the second oldest regiment in the United States Army.

The 7th received its baptism of fire against the British at Villiere's Plantation, Louisiana, in December, 1814. Two weeks later it won undying fame in the Battle of New Orleans. From 1815 to 1846 the regiment was stationed at Fort Gibson, now the site of Muskogee, Okla., and participated in numerous operations against the Indians.

Between 1839 and 1842 it took part in the Florida War against the Seminoles and their chief Osceola.

In 1846, when difficulties with Mexico became serious, the 7th Infantry was concentrated at Corpus Christi, Texas, then moved to the Rio Grande. The regiment next went to Monterrey. It joined in the siege of Vera Cruz, which ended in the Mexican capitulation in March, 1847. The 7th marched into the interior, winning recognition for capturing the heights of Cerro Gordo, carrying the entrenchments of Contreras and Churubusco, and finally the works of Chapultepec, it entered Mexico City on Sept. 14, 1847.

The 7th Infantry served throughout the Civil War, and participated in the following engagements: Mesilla, 1861; Valverde, Corinth, Fredericksburg and Murfreesboro, 1862; Chancellorsville, Hoover's Gap, Gettysburg, Chickamauga, Siege of Chattanooga and Missionary Ridge, 1863; Resaca, New Hope Church, Neal Dale Station and Siege of Atlanta, 1864.

It also participated in many Indian campaigns and is remembered as the regiment which was sent to relieve Custer. The 7th Infantry's last operation against the Indians was in 1891.

During the war with Spain the 7th fought in Cuba, at El Caney and San Juan Heights, and followed that with service in the Philippines and Alaska.

On Nov. 23, 1917, the 7th Infantry became part of the 3d Division and has been a member of the Division ever since. In World War I it fought with distinction in the Aisne Defensive, Champagne-Marne Defensive, Aisne-Marne Offensive and the Meuse-Argonne Offensive. For its great fighting on French soil the regiment was awarded the Croix de Guerre with Star by a grateful French government.

After serving in the Army of Occupation in Germany the regiment returned to the United States in August, 1919. Following brief stays at a number of posts the 7th moved to Vancouver Barracks and was stationed at Fort Lewis, Wash., when war was declared Dec. 8, 1941.

446

INCL. # 6

178

7TH INFANTRY*

Regimental Commander

(Highest rank held)	Held pos. from	To	(Highest rank held)	from	To
Col. Robert C. Macon		18 Feb 1943	Col. Wiley H. O'Mohundro	11 Mar 1944	21 Aug 1944
Col. Harry B. Sherman	19 Feb 1943	16 Feb 1944	Col. Ben Harrell	22 Aug 1944	1 Dec 1944
Col. William O. Darby	17 Feb 1944	18 Feb 1944	Lt. Col. Frank M. Izenour	2 Dec 1944	3 Dec 1944
Col. Wiley H. O'Mohundro	19 Feb 1944	26 Feb 1944	Lt. Col. Clayton C. Thobro	4 Dec 1944	4 Dec 1944
Col. Harry B. Sherman	27 Feb 1944	10 Mar 1944	Col. John A. Heintges	5 Dec 1944	

Regimental Executive Officer

(Highest rank held)	from	to	(Highest rank held)	from	to
Lt. Col. John O. Williams		11 Feb 1943	Lt. Col. Wiley H. O'Mohundro	27 Feb 1944	10 Mar 1944
Lt. Col. Rafael L. Salzmann	12 Feb 1943	28 Feb 1943	Lt. Col. John J. Toffey, Jr.	13 Mar 1944	2 June 1944
Lt. Col. John O. Williams	1 Mar 1943	15 July 1943	Lt. Col. Victor E. Sinclair	17 June 1944	1 Sept 1944
Maj. William B. Rosson	16 July 1943	24 July 1943	Lt. Col. Jesse F. Thomas	2 Sept 1944	14 Sept 1944
Lt. Col. Roy E. Moore	25 July 1943	6 Jan 1944	Lt. Col. Frank M. Izenour	15 Sept 1944	4 Dec 1944
Lt. Col. James E. Breth	7 Jan 1944	10 Jan 1944	Lt. Col. Clayton C. Thobro	5 Dec 1944	25 Feb 1945
Lt. Col. Roy E. Moore	11 Jan 1944	4 Feb 1944	Lt. Col. Lloyd B. Ramsey	26 Feb 1945	
Lt. Col. Ashton H. Manhart	5 Feb 1944	13 Feb 1944			

1st Battalion Commander

(Highest rank held)	from	to	(Highest rank held)	from	to
Lt. Col. Roy E. Moore		11 Feb 1943	Lt. Col. Frank M. Izenour	13 Mar 1944	14 Sept 1944
Maj. Everett W. Duvall	12 Feb 1943	28 Feb 1943	Lt. Col. Jesse F. Thomas	15 Sept 1944	14 Oct 1944
Lt. Col. Roy E. Moore	1 Mar 1943	24 July 1943	Maj. Benjamin C. Boyd	15 Oct 1944	30 Oct 1944
Lt. Col. Frank M. Izenour	25 July 1943	29 Jan 1944	Lt. Col. Kenneth Wallace	31 Oct 1944	
Maj. Frank C. Sinsel	30 Jan 1944	12 Mar 1944			

2d Battalion Commander

(Highest rank held)	from	to	(Highest rank held)	from	to
Lt. Col. Rafael L. Salzmann		3 Mar 1943	Lt. Col. Everett W. Duvall	23 Oct 1943	10 Nov 1943
*Maj. Everett W. Duvall	13 April 1943	28 June 1943	Maj. John A. Elterich	11 Nov 1943	9 Jan 1944
Maj. John A. Elterich	29 June 1943	3 July 1943	Lt. Col. Everett W. Duvall	10 Jan 1944	15 July 1944
Maj. Everett W. Duvall	4 July 1943	23 Sept 1943	Lt. Col. Clayton C. Thobro	16 July 1944	3 Dec 1944
*Lt. Col. Everett W. Duvall	5 Oct 1943	17 Oct 1943	Maj. Robert D. Marsh	4 Dec 1944	5 Dec 1944
*Maj. John A. Elterich	18 Oct 1943	22 Oct 1943	Lt. Col. Jack M. Duncan	6 Dec 1944	

3d Battalion Commander

(Highest rank held)	from	to	(Highest rank held)	from	to
Maj. Eugene H. Cloud		11 Nov 1942	Maj. Lloyd B. Ramsey	13 Mar 1944	25 Mar 1944
Lt. Col. Robert C. Williams, Jr.	12 Nov 1942	11 Feb 1943	Lt. Col. William A. Weitzel	26 Mar 1944	21 April 1944
Maj. Carroll A. Plaquet	12 Feb 1943	28 Feb 1943	Lt. Col. Arthur J. Smith, Jr.	22 April 1944	24 May 1944
Maj. Carroll A. Plaquet	4 Mar 1943	24 April 1943	Maj. Glenn E. Rathbun	25 May 1944	21 June 1944
Maj. Mark E. Cory, Jr.	25 April 1943	27 April 1943	Maj. Lloyd B. Ramsey Lt. Col.	22 June 1944	14 Oct 1944
Maj. Carroll A. Plaquer	28 April 1943	31 May 1943	Maj. Ralph M. Flynn	4 Dec 1944	15 Dec 1944
Lt. Col. Frank M. Izenour	1 June 1943	3 July 1943	Capt. Robert V. Horton	16 Dec 1944	17 Dec 1944
Lt. Col. John A. Heintges	4 July 1943	17 Nov 1943	Maj. Ralph M. Flynn	18 Dec 1944	19 Dec 1944
Lt. Col. William B. Rosson	18 Nov 1943	23 Feb 1944	Lt. Col. Lloyd B. Ramsey	20 Dec 1944	25 Feb 1945
Lt. Col. John A. Heintges	24 Feb 1944	3 Mar 1944	Maj. Ralph M. Flynn	26 Feb 1945	4 May 1945
Maj. Clayton C. Thobro	4 Mar 1944	12 Mar 1944	Capt. Robert V. Horton	5 May 1945	

INCL. # 7

CHAPTER 6

GERMANY, JUNE 1945 – FORT BENNING, GEORGIA, APRIL 1946

June 1945: Move to Bad Hershfeld, Germany

We stayed in Salzburg, Austria until about the middle of June. We then moved to Hershfeld, Germany to continue "The Occupation of Germany." About this time, General O'Daniel left the division and Brigadier General W. T. Sexton took command.

July 25, 1945: New Assignment

About the middle of July, Colonel Heintges called me in to his office to tell me that I was going to receive a new assignment. He had been told by Colonel Johnson, the division Chief of Staff, that Colonel Lionel C. McGarr, Commanding Officer, 30th Infantry, would become the Assistant Division Commander. He was also told that the division G-3, Lieutenant Colonel William B. Rosson, and I were being considered for command of the 30th Infantry. If Colonel Rosson took the position, I would become the G-3. Colonel Johnson emphasized that a new regulation had just come out, making the division G-3 a Colonel; therefore, we both would be in a position where we could be promoted, if promotions became available. (It was not long until this regulation was withdrawn and the G-3 reverted to Lieutenant Colonel.) Colonel Rosson took the 30th Infantry, and I became the G-3 on July 25, 1945. The 3rd Infantry Division headquarters was located at Bad Wildungen, Germany. The Corps headquarters decided that that was a very fine location for a headquarters so they moved us out, and we moved to Rhinhardshousen, Germany, just a few miles away.

August–September 1945: Logistical Problems with the Russians

After the war in Europe ended on May 7, 1945, the Army began to have logistical problems with our supply line. These problems were caused by the Russians. The ships from the United States would deliver supplies to the port of Bremmerhaven, which was in the British area of occupation. From there they were loaded onto trains, which went through the British zone into the American area of occupation. Before the trains would reach a main railroad station in the American zone, they had to go a short distance, about 3,000 meters, through the Russian area of occupation, which was adjacent to the 3rd Infantry Division's area of occupation. The Russians would stop the trains and hold them up for hours, allegedly to check the trains. At the end of this chapter (Inclusion #1), Map 1 shows the boundary between East and West Germany and the area of agreement. Inclusion #1-2, Map 2, shows the area of agreement and the railroad, which was originally in the Russian zone, but now shows it in the American zone. They never took anything, but the delay was causing many logistical problems. In August 1945, the Army gave the 3rd Infantry Division the task of trading land with the Russians in order that the railroad would be completely in the American zone. As the G-3 operations officer, I would be the principal staff officer responsible for making the plans to transfer the land.

(I am not sure how we received this order. I discussed this with the U.S. Army Center for Military History, starting in August 2000. As of May 2002, the Military History could find no record of such an order, but they did find the agreement. Since the Military History could find no order, I must assume that we received the order verbally.)

When we received the order from the Army, the Chief of Staff, Colonel Charles E. Johnson, called a meeting of the staff so that we could discuss the problem and it could give me some guidance for planning. The first thing that we needed was a Russian-speaking liaison officer, with necessary staff, to live in the area near the Russian zone, where he could be in immediate contact with the Russians. Colonel Johnson said that the Army had provided us with a very fine Russian-speaking officer, Captain Michael Burda. I believe that Captain Burda had already moved into the "Kalhof," the home of Mr. and Mrs. W. von Scharfenberg, in Wanfried, on another intelligence mission, and we could use that as a place for our meetings with the Russians.

According to a German newspaper, September 18, 1985, *"von Scharfenberg and his wife were not allowed to enter their home. His mother and the janitor, Wilhelm Franke and his wife, Anna, the cook, were permitted to work for the Americans. But, according to the now 70-year old President of the Chamber of Agriculture and Forestry, who is still addressed as 'Herr President,' the relationship became more relaxed, and more of a friendship developed between himself, his family and the Americans."* The 3rd Infantry Division was very fortunate to have Captain Michael Burda as our liaison. He was friendly with the Germans and got along extremely well with the Russians. His friendship with the von Scharfenbergs is still very close. According to a German newspaper, July 1, 1945, *"Between the family and Michael Burda a close friendship developed. In 1946 the American even stood godfather to daughter Veleska."*

After we got the liaison set up, we had Captain Burda contact the Russians to advise them that he would be the contact for the 3rd Infantry Division to negotiate with them to trade some land so that the railroad would be in the American zone. The railroad covered a distance of about 3,000 meters in the Russian zone. I thought that we should offer much more land to the Russians than we wished to take in order to get the railroad in the American zone. For the first meeting, I drew new boundaries on a map so that we would have something to discuss. General Sexton, the CG, and Colonel Johnson, the C/S, agreed with my recommendation and also agreed that we could afford to give up more land if necessary. In the area that we wished to occupy were the villages of Werleshausen and Neuseesen. In the zone that we wished to trade with the Russians were the villages of Weidenbach and Vatterode. I left out the villages of Sickenberg and Asbach so that we would have room to negotiate. I later learned through a source, which seemed to be reliable, that the Russians were interested in getting some cities, especially Vatterode, in their zone because these cities had some electrical equipment that they depended on for electricity in the Russian zone. These cities are on the three pages of maps at the end of this chapter (Inclusions #2 through #2-3).

When I gave this information to Colonel Johnson, C/S, he was most interested and hoped that the source was reliable because the Russians would then want something like we did. Colonel Johnson told me that he did not want anyone to know this except the two of us because he did not want the word to get back to the Russians. He told me that he was primarily concerned with our G-2. He was a very fine G-2; however, he was inclined to drink too much at social functions, and after each meeting with the Russians, one side or the other would host a cocktail party. The G-2 was inclined to talk too much after a few drinks. He kept saying that the Russians wanted the high ground. A study of the map showed that the high ground the Russians would gain was very little. Colonel Johnson said if the Russians thought that we were giving them the high ground, we should continue our negotiation with that in mind. After each meeting, we seemed to be getting closer to agreement, and, by this time, we had offered the villages of Sickenberg and Asbach to be in the Russian zone. I told Mike Burda that he should try to get a Russian typewriter just in case we needed to type out an agreement. Mike informed me that he already had one. Colonel Johnson told Captain Burda that he thought we were getting close to an agreement and that we should draw up an agreement so that Captain Burda could type it in Russian. Between Colonel Johnson, Captain Burda, our Judge Advocate General, and myself, we drew up an agreement and had Captain Burda type it in Russian. Captain Burda took it to the Russians for consideration at out next meeting.

September 17, 1945: Wanfried, Saxony, Germany – Agreement Between United States and the Union of Soviet Socialist Republic

We met with the Russians on September 17, 1945, and they were ready to sign the agreement that we had prepared. I had everything with me that I needed for the signing, except for a draftsman; therefore, I had to do all of the drafting. All the printing and lines on the map were done by me. Colonel Johnson had brought the 30th Infantry Commander, Lieutenant Colonel Rosson, and told him to be prepared to move troops to the new boundary in the Russian zone just in case we reached an agreement. He should also be prepared to withdraw his troops to the new boundary in the American zone.

The agreement, at the end of this chapter (Inclusion #3 through #3-5), was signed by:

COMMANDING GENERAL THIRD INFANTRY DIVISION
BRIGADIER GENERAL W. T. SEXTON

COMMANDING GENERAL 77TH GUARD INFANTRY DIVISION
HERO OF THE SOVIET UNION GUARD MAJOR GENERAL
V. S. ASKALIPOV

The agreement witnesses:
>American:
>>Charles E. Johnson, Col. GSC
>>Lloyd B. Ramsey, Lt. Col. GSC
>
>Soviet:
>>Guard Colonel Tarasov
>>Guard Lt. Col. Paschenko

During our celebration of the event, Colonel Johnson got Brigadier General W. T. Sexton, Commanding General, 3rd Infantry Division, to talk to Major General Vasil S. Askalipov, Commanding General, 77th Guard Infantry Division, about our troops moving to their new areas. General Sexton suggested that we start as soon as each side was ready and further stated that we were ready. General Askalipov agreed that we should get the move completed as soon as feasible and said that he would talk to his commanders and staff that were present and have them to meet with the American commander and staff to get the move started. From this conversation, the staff and commanders present got together and made plans for places and times to meet and start the move. According to the agreement, the move had to be completed by 1800 hours, 19 September 1945. Movements were started on the 17th and were completed on the 18th. Our mission from the Army was accomplished.

A copy of the treaty, covering five pages, is at the end of this chapter (Inclusion #3 through #3-4). You will note that Lieutenant Colonel Lloyd B. Ramsey was a witness to the treaty. As of this writing, April 2003, I am the only American still living that signed the treaty. Lieutenant Colonel (now General) William B. Rosson signed the map.

The three pages (Inclusions #2 through #2-3) are taken from the map that became a part of the treaty. The original map showed the old boundary in blue and the new boundary in red. The copy of the map shows the old boundary wide and the new boundary narrow.

September 1976: 31st Anniversary Luncheon of Boundary Changes

Michael Burda was very proud of what we had accomplished with the Russians (i.e. getting a boundary change so that the railroad would be in the United States Zone of Occupation). Mike had kept the Russian typewriter that he had used to type the agreement in Russian. In September 1976, Mike had a "31st Anniversary Luncheon" to celebrate the signing of the treaty with the Russians on September 17, 1945. Mike had kept in touch with the von Scharfenbergs through the years and arranged with them for their son to be present at the luncheon. I believe the son was about 6 years of age when the treaty was signed.

Mike had many high-ranking government officials attend the luncheon, which was an outstanding affair. He also had the Russian typewriter present and prepared a handout for the guests. A copy of the handout is at Inclusion #4 through #4-6 at the end of this chapter. The last page of the handout (Inclusion #4-6) has a picture of General Askalipov and Captain Burda and states: "Captain Burda was in charge of negotiating this agreement for the United States." This is not correct. The Commanding General, 3rd Infantry Division, was in charge of negotiating this agreement for the United States. Colonel Johnson, Chief of Staff, was the Commanding General's principal advisor, and I, as the G-3 operations officer, was the action officer. Captain Burda assisted greatly in the negotiations and his ability to get along with the Germans and Russians was invaluable.

Trips – Before and After the Russian Negotiation

On May 29, 1945, I flew to Rome with the Commanding General to participate in a Memorial Day Ceremony at Anzio, Italy. This is where the 3rd Infantry Division fought from January 30, 1944 until the breakout of Anzio on May 23, 1944. I received a wound on May 24, 1945 and had to be evacuated to the hospital. I represented the 7th Infantry in a ceremony that was attended by the Commanding General, 3rd Infantry Division, and six other officers representing other units of the division.

On August 12, 1945, I flew to Nice-Cannes, France, with the Commanding General, three other officers, and two enlisted men to participate in a ceremony at St. Tropez on August 15, 1945 in commemoration of the Allied Landings and the liberation of that city on August 15, 1944. After the ceremony, the weather between there and our station in Germany turned bad, and we had to spend a couple of days at the U.S. Riviera Recreation Area. This turned out to be a very nice, unplanned vacation.

On November 10, 1945, I accompanied the Commanding General and his aide by car to Berlin to attend a football game between the 3rd Infantry Division and the 82nd Airborne Division on November 11, 1945. In a second car, the General had invited two enlisted men and two Red Cross girls, who had served the division so faithfully. I am happy to report that the 3rd Infantry Division won the football game.

On November 14, 1945, I was given seven days leave to go to Switzerland as a part of the Seventh Army quota. Major Dan Wickersham, the G-1, and I traveled together, and we had a very enjoyable vacation.

Planning My Return to the United States on R & R

By January 1946 I had been overseas since September 1942, with home leave in October 1944 for 30 days, called R & R. Our war-time Commanding General, Major General "Iron Mike" O'Daniel and his Chief of Staff, Colonel Charles E. Johnson, were now stationed at Fort Benning, Georgia and had asked for my assignment there. They had made official requests to Headquarters, Army Ground Forces, for my assignment without success. Our Adjutant General had made many attempts to get me transferred to the United States since I had been overseas so long, also without success.

The Adjutant General, Major Jack Dwan, was a very good friend of mine. He suggested that he could send me home on a 45-day R & R and hoped that Fort Benning could get me assigned there while I was visiting in the United States. I discussed the matter with the Chief of Staff, Colonel G. E. Bruner, and then the Commanding General, Major General William R. Schmidt. (It is interesting to note General Schmidt was my commanding officer for a while when I was in the 39th Infantry, 9th Infantry Division, Fort Bragg, North Carolina.) They agreed that it was time for me to go home. Orders were published on February 25, 1946 for my return to the United States on 45 days R & R and then return to my overseas assignment. Copies were sent to Colonel Johnson at Fort Benning, Georgia.

Lieutenant Colonel Dick A. King, the G-4 of the division, had also been requested to be assigned to Fort Benning and had received his orders. We were able to travel together on this trip. Our orders were to report to Camp Herbert Tareyton, Le Havre, France. (All of the camps that were processing troops home were named after cigarettes.)

Early March 1946: Arrival at Camp Herbert Tareyton, Le Havre, France

When we arrived at Camp Herbert Tareyton by automobile, an MP told us where to report. We reported to that location and a Sergeant was sitting at a desk. He looked up, ordered us to give him a copy of our orders, go across the street to pick up our bedding, go to tent number, etc. I don't know who started on the Sergeant first – me or Dick – for treating two Lieutenant Colonels, who had been in combat for almost three years, as if we were privates. After some very harsh words from us, he apologized and offered to help us get our bedding and show us to our tent. After getting the bedding, we walked a long way down a muddy street to our tent. The tent was full of holes, had one small light, a wood stove, and two cots with mattresses that should have been in the dump. He then showed us where to go to get wood to build a fire.

By this time both Dick and I had had enough of Camp Herbert Tareyton, so we demanded to see his commanding officer. The Sergeant took us to a Captain who was very nice and respectful. He looked at our records and made the statement that he had never seen two officers with so many points going through this processing center. (Points were given for the months you were overseas, decorations, combat vs. administration, and other areas. The points determined how soon you would get on a ship home.) The Captain arranged for us to stay in a hotel, in separate rooms, and also gave our driver a room so that we would have transportation to the ship rather than having to ride a bus. He told us that we would be leaving in not more than three days.

The hotel was very nice, and the food was fair. The next day a Sergeant came to my room and asked me to sign a certificate that I did not have any firearms in my baggage. Since I did not have any firearms, I signed the certificate. He then asked me to open my baggage to look for weapons. I told the Sergeant that he had my certificate that I had no firearms and that he would have to return my certificate if he wished to inspect my baggage. The Sergeant said that he was required to do both. I told the Sergeant to talk to his commanding officer. Very soon a Captain appeared and pleaded with me to allow them to do both. I told the Captain that this was a very serious problem with me and that I would do either but not both.

The Captain left, came back shortly, and said the Colonel would like to see me. When I reported to the Colonel, he immediately started raising hell with me for not abiding by their rules. He ordered me to go back to my room and allow the Sergeant to inspect my baggage and keep the certificate. I reminded the Colonel that we were alone and that he would have to put his order in writing or call in an unbiased witness to hear the order before I would obey it. The Colonel made a statement to the effect that I might be there longer than expected. I then told the Colonel that I had been overseas for almost 3 ½ years and a few more days would not make much difference for me to stand on a principle. I also told him that I had been Aide-de-Camp to General Alexander, British, for seven months, had gotten to know General Eisenhower very well, and still knew many Generals on the staff in Allied Forces Headquarters. I told him that I was not making a threat, only stating a fact. If I were delayed one day, I would immediately call Allied Forces Headquarters and ask for an immediate investigation by the Inspector General. By this time the Colonel had completely changed his views about my position. He stated that my baggage would not be inspected and that I would be on a ship home not later than the next day. He went on to say that he admired my attitude and could see why I had been a successful commander in combat. He wished me success in my future assignments. The next day (I do not have dates for this area) Dick and I were moved to Camp Home Run APO 895. We then boarded the vessel Chapel Hill Victory and sailed from Le Havre, France for the United States.

March 12, 1946: Arrived New York Port of Embarkation

We arrived at the New York Port of Embarkation on March 12, 1946. On March 13 I received orders as follows:

AFS, NYPE, CAMP KILMER, NEW BRUNSWICK, NEW JERSEY, 13 March 1946
2. Above named officer WP by rail fr this Sta to Reception Sta no.

6, Cp. Atterbury, Ind., during the period of 13 to 14 March 1946, for TDY thereat in connection with recuppration. (Sic)

March 17, 1946: Home Again

On March 17, 1946 I received orders from Camp Atterbury, Indiana for 45 days R & R in Somerset, Kentucky. I arrived home that day to see my family once again. What a wonderful reunion we had! Lloyd Ann was almost three years old and I had only seen her for about 30 days in October/November 1944 when I was home on a 30-day R & R. Although I was very busy enjoying Glenda and Lloyd Ann, I had to do some work to try to ensure that I would stay in the United States. On March 18, 1946, I called Colonel Johnson at the Infantry School, Fort Benning, Georgia. He told me that the Infantry School had renewed its request for my assignment there. He also suggested that I write a letter to Army Ground Forces regarding the Infantry School's request and indicate my desire for this assignment.

April 16, 1946: Received Orders to Yale University, on TDY, for an Orientation Course

On April 16, 1946, I received orders placing my TDY, from Infantry School, to Yale University, New Haven, Connecticut, on April 29, 1946 for the purpose of attending an orientation course in psychology. I had received a call from Colonel Johnson advising me that I was being assigned to the Infantry School, but I had not received any orders. He also told me that the War Department wished to send six combat arms officers (two infantry, two cavalry, and two artillery) to Yale with the mission of designing a way to teach leadership at their respective schools. He also advised me that I had been selected as one of the two officers from the Infantry School because I was going to teach leadership at the Infantry School upon my arrival there. The course would be about three weeks in length.

The course at Yale was quite interesting. Yale had three psychology professors who had studied the theory of leadership and had used rats in many of their experiments. The professors conducted an orientation of their theory and then tried to see if it fit in with leadership in actual combat experience. The professors soon realized that there was very little comparison between their theory and actual combat. We then attempted to come up with a definition of leadership. This subject caused a great amount of discussion by all concerned. We never agreed on a definition of leadership, but the professors seemed to like one that one professor, another officer, and I had suggested: "Leadership is the ability to influence others to achieve a common goal." We tried to emphasize that this could be done by actions or by words.

This definition was not accepted by the other officers. We then attempted to come up with a way to teach leadership. This caused more discussion than the definition of leadership. Once again we failed to reach agreement. During the three weeks that we were there we had some very interesting discussions. I believe that we all learned more about leadership, but we were not able to come up with a method to teach it in the military schools. I am sure that the psychology professors learned more about leadership than the six officers present.

April 22, 1946: Received Orders Assigning Me to the Infantry School, Fort Benning, Georgia

I finally received orders assigning me to the Infantry School, Fort Benning, Georgia. The orders were dated April 22, 1946. Glenda, Lloyd Ann, and I arrived at Fort Benning on May 27, 1946 and were assigned quarters on post, 217 Miller Loop. My new Commanding Officer, Colonel William Blandford, had called me in Somerset, Kentucky and told me that he would arrange to get quarters for my family. He told me, when we arrived, to come to his quarters. He would have the keys and show us our quarters. We met him and his wife, and both were very nice to welcome us to Fort Benning.

They offered us a cool drink and a snack. They then took us to our quarters on Miller Loop. At the quarters, they had arranged to get three cots with sheets, blankets, and pillows so that we would have a place to sleep until our furniture arrived. They had also brought in some groceries, napkins, paper cups, and plastic utensils so that we could eat. A table and some chairs were in the kitchen. Colonel Blandford told us that this was always done before the war. We paid them for the groceries and other things that they bought and thanked them over and over again for all the things they had done for us. Our furniture arrived the next day, May 28, 1946. I had been in touch with Fort Knox, Kentucky, and they had arranged to pick up our furniture at Glenda's parents' home. That was done before we left Somerset, and the driver said he would deliver our furniture on May 28, 1946, which he did.

April 22, 1946: Orders to Fort Benning, Georgia Ended My Overseas Assignment

The receipt of my orders of April 22, 1946 ended my overseas assignment, which had commenced September 15, 1942. That meant that I spent three years and seven months overseas during and after World War II. It also meant that I had spent four Christmases away from Glenda (1942, 1943, 1944, 1945). Until that time, we had only the Christmas of 1941 together. Being with my family once again was wonderful.

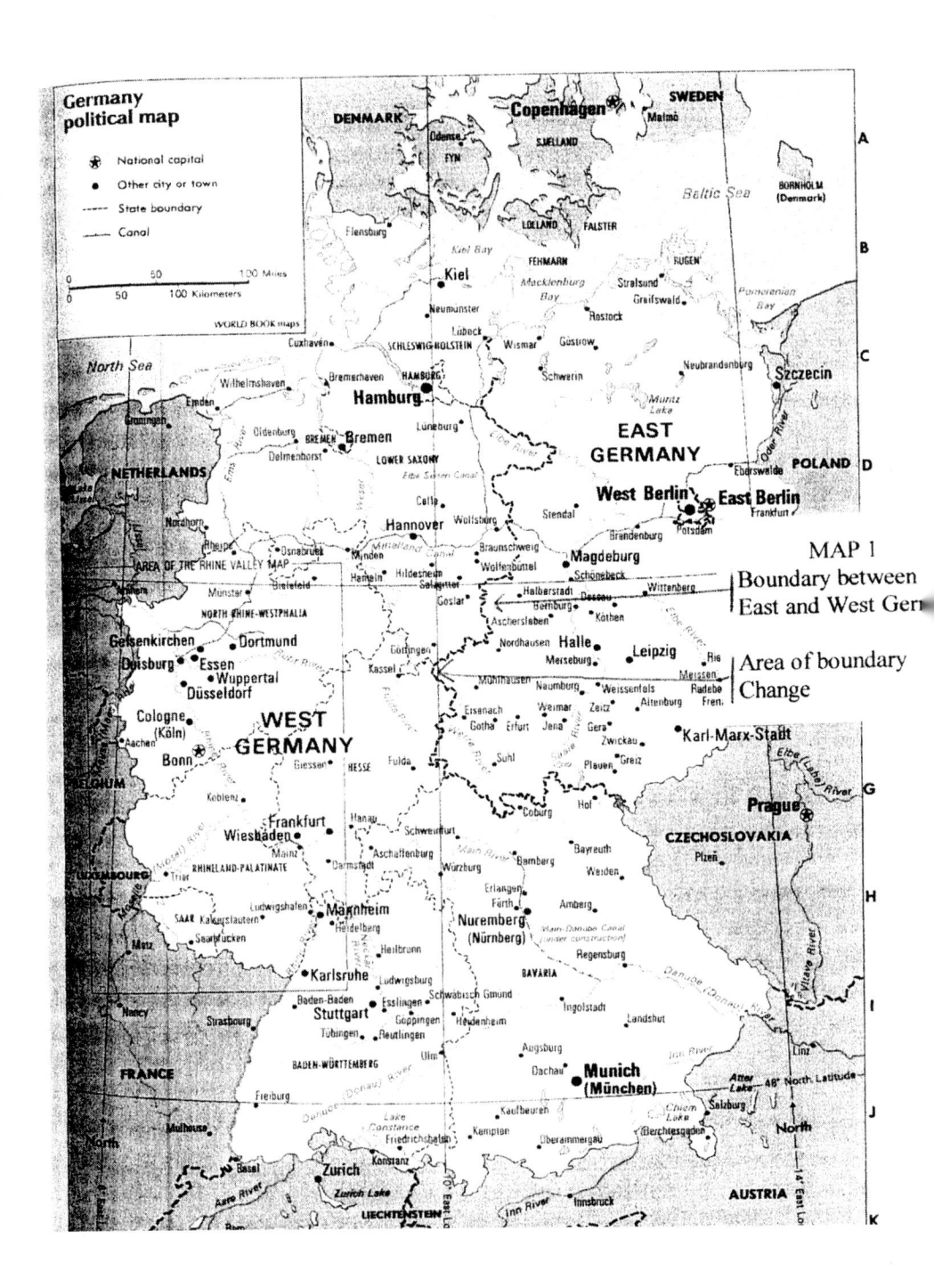

INCL. # 1

MAP 2

Boundary between East and West Germany

Major Rail Line

Area of Boundary change

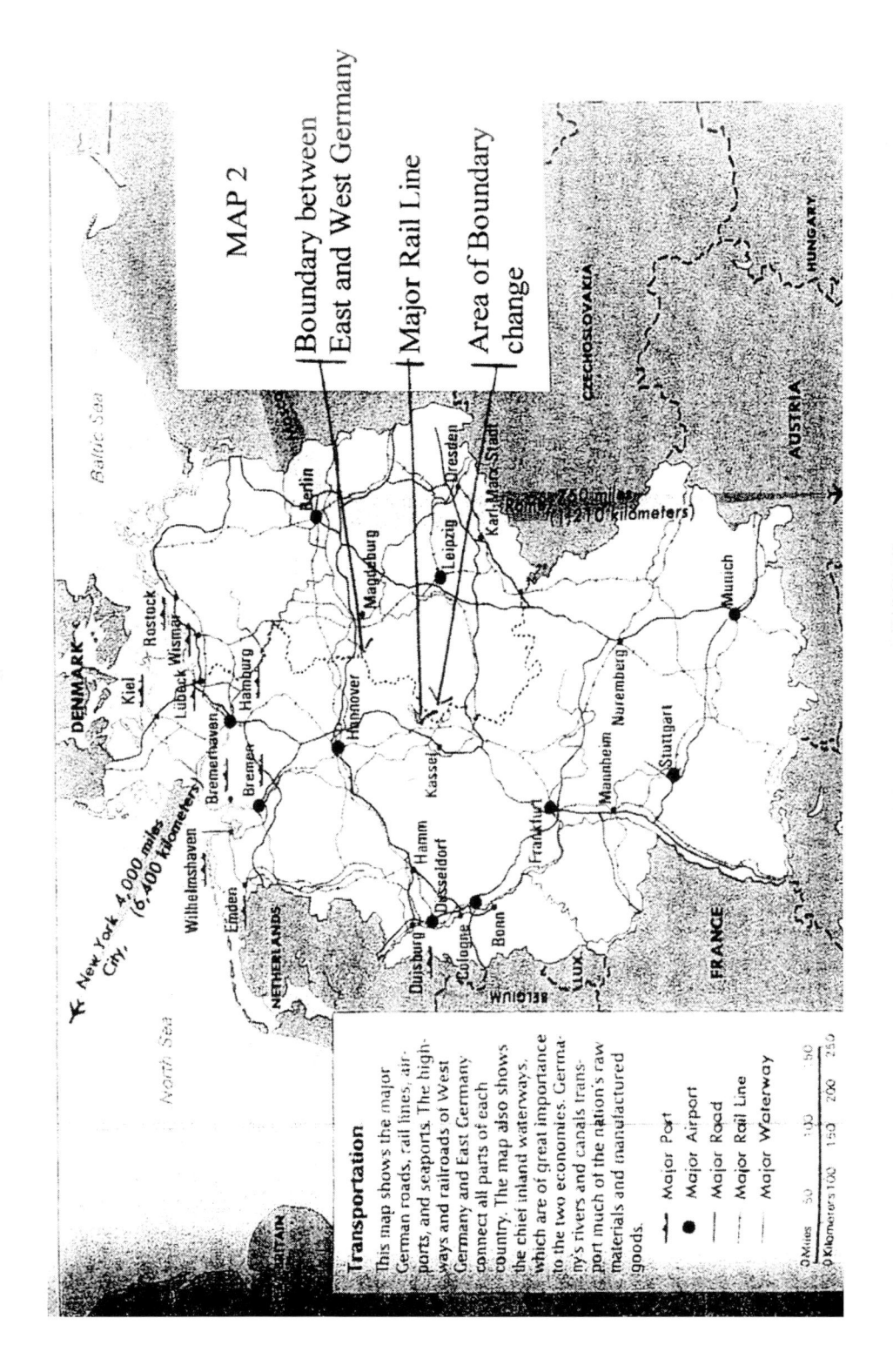

Transportation

This map shows the major German roads, rail lines, airports, and seaports. The highways and railroads of West Germany and East Germany connect all parts of each country. The map also shows the chief inland waterways, which are of great importance to the two economies. Germany's rivers and canals transport much of the nation's raw materials and manufactured goods.

- Major Port
- ● Major Airport
- Major Road
- Major Rail Line
- Major Waterway

INCL. # 1-2

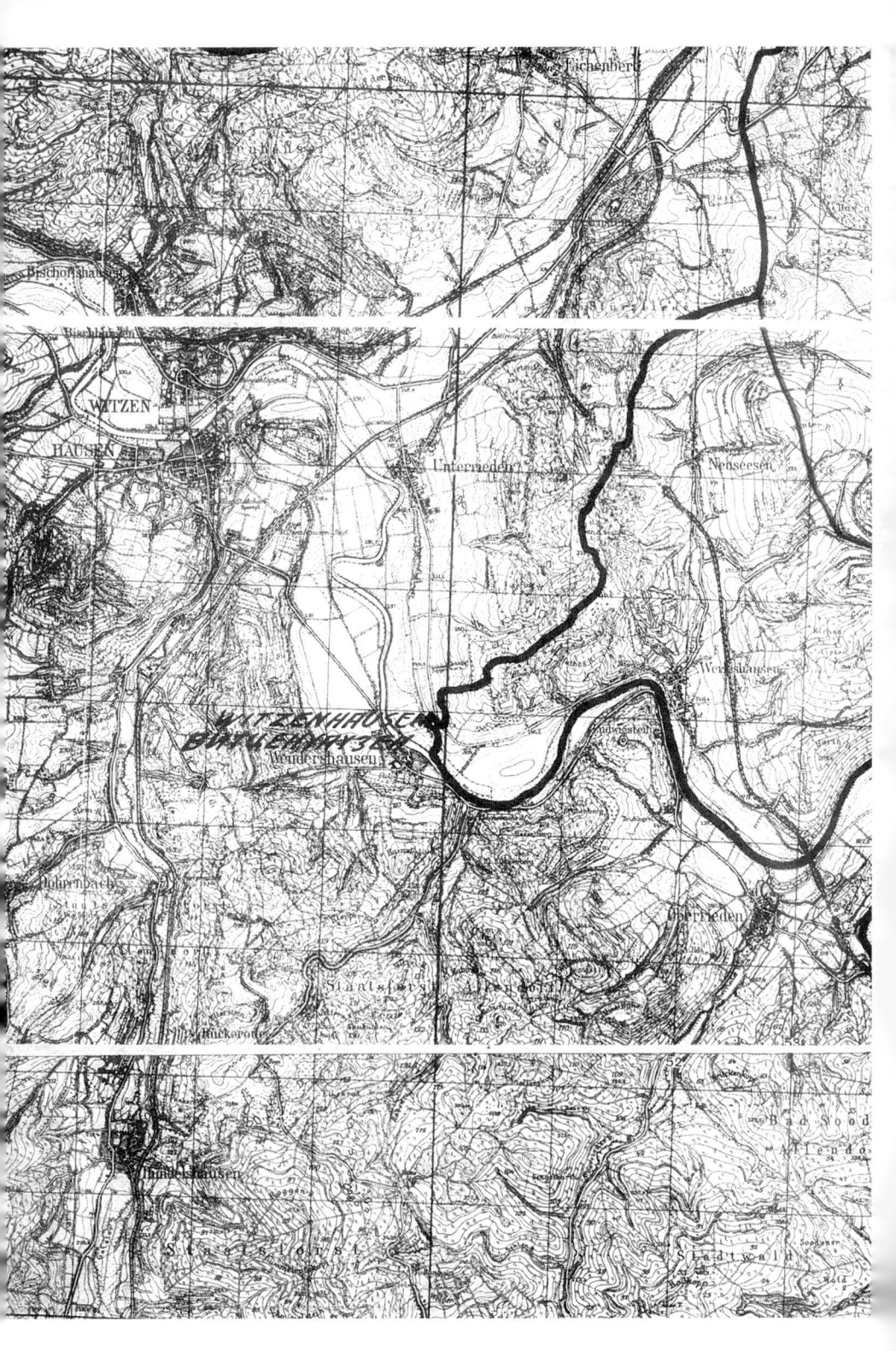

INCL. # 2 A

INCL. # 2 B

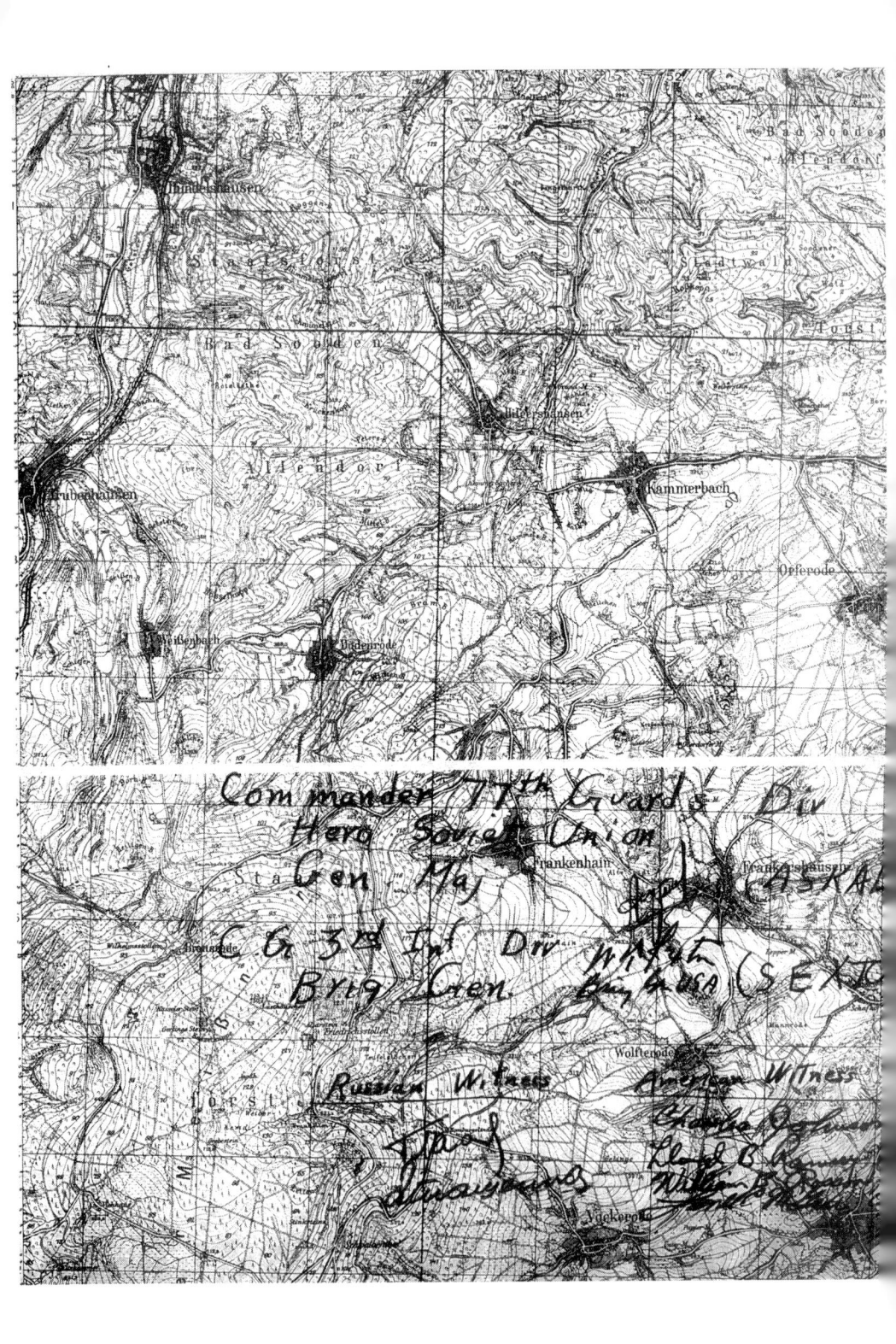

INCL. # 2-2 A

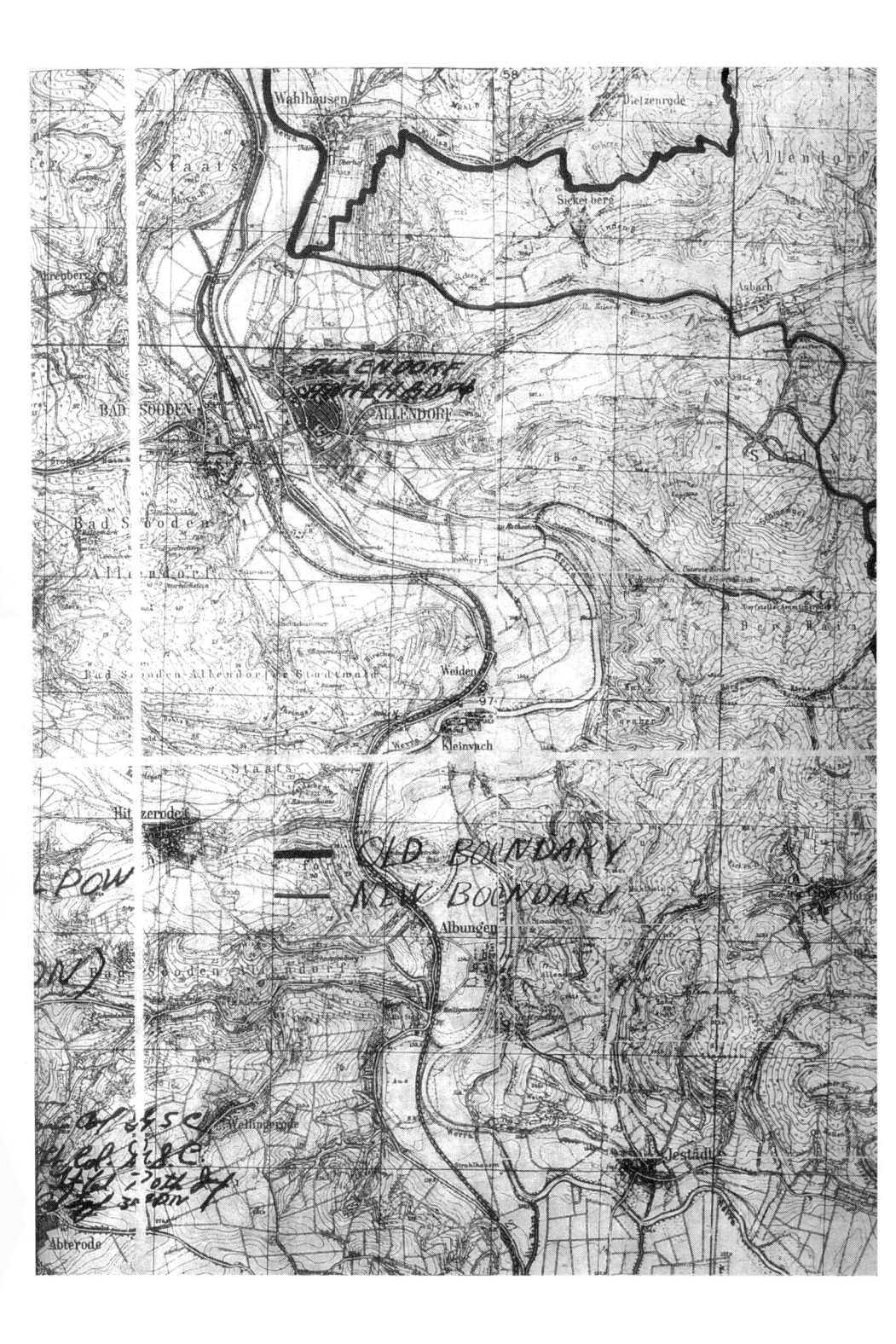

INCL. # 2-2 B

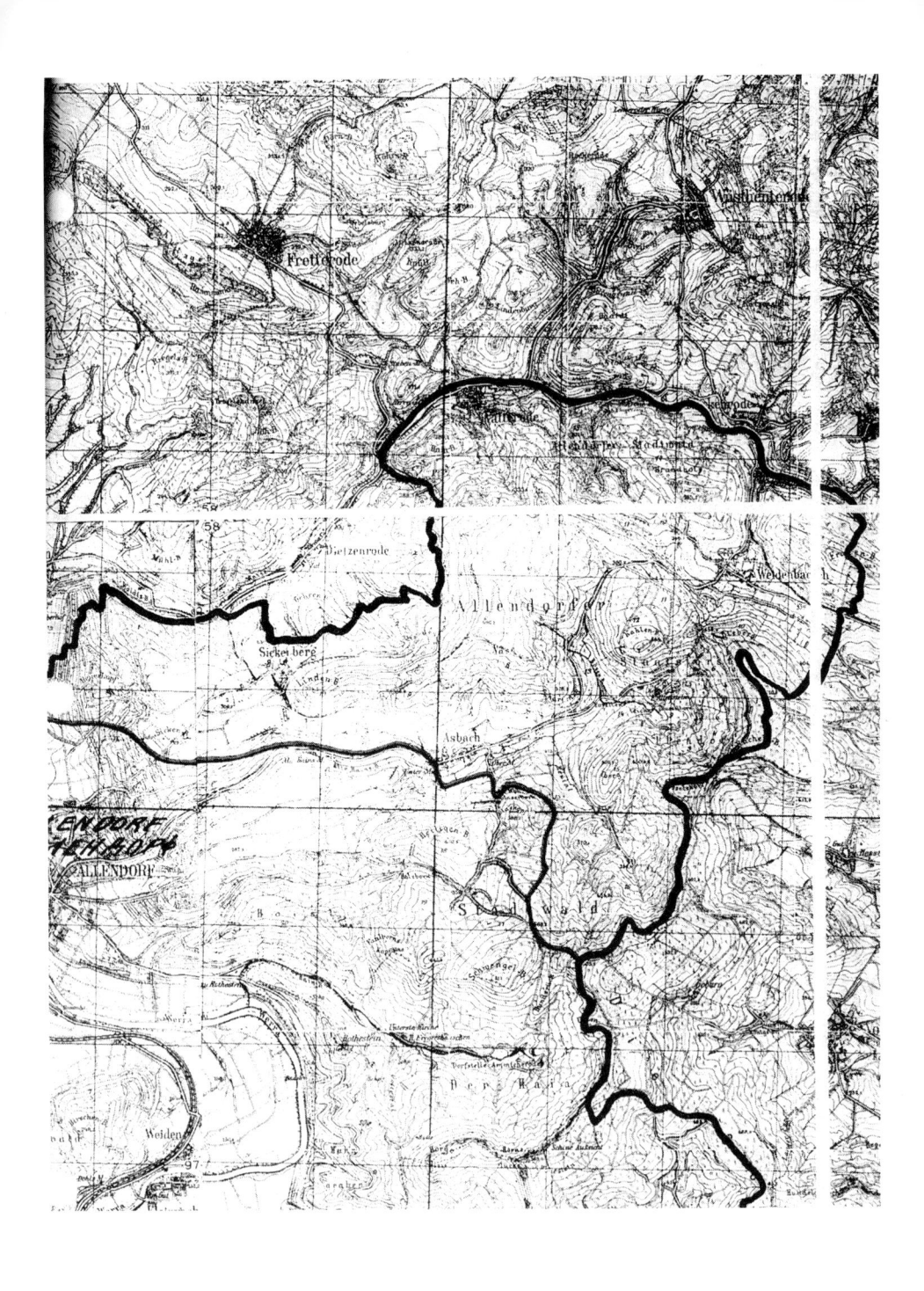

INCL. # 2-3

TREATIES AND OTHER INTERNATIONAL ACTS SERIES 3081

GERMANY

Boundary Changes Between
United States and Soviet
Zones of Occupation

Agreement between the
UNITED STATES OF AMERICA
and the UNION OF SOVIET
SOCIALIST REPUBLICS

- Signed at Wanfried, Saxony, Germany, September 17, 1945
- Entered into force September 17, 1945

INCL. # 3

AGREEMENT

HEADQUARTERS THIRD DIVISION V 3 ARMY

17 September 1945

Brigadier General Sexton, representative of the American High Command, Commanding General of the Third Infantry Division and the representative of the Soviet High Command, Major General Askalepov, Commanding General of the 77th Guard Infantry Division are authorized by their respective governments to alter the existing line of demarcation between the kreises of WITZENHAUSEN, HEILIGENSTADT, and having met in the town of Wanfried, Saxony, Germany on September 17, 1945 have signed the following agreement:

AGREEMENT

1. It is mutually agreed and stipulated between the undersigned, authorized representatives of their respective governments that effective 17 September 1945 the boundary between the United States Occupational Zone in Germany be changed as indicated on the attached map (Annex No 1) — Germany: 1:25000, 3 heets 4525, 4626.

2. The withdrawal of troops to the newly established line of demarcation will be completed by 19 September 1945 1800 hours American time.

3. That the people residing in the areas indicated will remain in place with their property.

S I G N E D :

1. COMMANDING GENERAL THIRD INFANTRY DIVISION

    BRIGADIER GENERAL W. T. SEXTON

2. COMMANDING GENERAL 77th GUARD INFANTRY DIVISION

    HERO OF THE SOVIET UNION GUARD MAJOR GENERAL

    V.S. ASKALEPOV

INCL. # 3-2

1. It is mutually agreed and stipulated between the undersigned, authorized representatives of their respective governments that effective 19 September 1945 the boundary between the United States Occupational Zone in Germany be changed as indicated on the attached map (Annex No 1) — Germany: 1:25000, 3 heets 4525, 4626.

2. The withdrawal of troops to the newly established line of demarcation will be completed by 19 September 1945 1800 hours American time.

3. That the people residing in the areas indicated will remain in place with their property.

SIGNED:

1. COMMANDING GENERAL THIRD INFANTRY DIVISION

    BRIGADIER GENERAL W. T. SEXTON

2. COMMANDING GENERAL 77th GUARD INFANTRY DIVISION

    HERO OF THE SOVIET UNION GUARD MAJOR GENERAL

    V.S. ASKALIPOV

WITNESSES:

AMERICAN:

1. Charles B. Johnson, Col. GSC
2. Lloyd B. Ramsey, Lt. Col. GSC

SOVIET

1. GUARD COLONEL TARASOV
2. GUARD LT. COL. PASCHENKO

INCL. # 3-3

ПРОТОКОЛ
ОТДЕЛЬНОЙ ВОЕННОЙ КОМИССИИ

17 сентября 1945 года.

Представитель Высшего Советского командования командир 77 ГвСД гвардии генерал-майор АСКАЛЕПОВ и представитель Высшего командования Американской армии командующий генерал 3 пехотной дивизии бригадный генерал ДЖОНСТОН уполномочены их соответствующими Высшими командованиями по вопросу об изменении ныне существующей демаркационной линии между округами ВИТЦЕН АУЗЕН, АЛЛЕНГЕЛЬШТАДТ, встретились в г. ВАНФРИД /ГЕРМАНИЯ, провинция САКСОНИЯ/ в сентябре 1945 года и подписали следующее соглашение:

СОГЛАШЕНИЕ

Обоюдно согласно и договорено между ниже подписавшимися уполномоченными представителями соответствующих Правительств, что 17 сентября 1945 года граница демаркационной линии между оккупационными зонами США и СССР будет изменена, как указано на прилагаемой карте /ГЕРМАНИЯ, 1 : 25000. Лист 4625 – 4626/ красной линией.

1. Отвод частей обеих сторон на вновь установленную демаркационную линию произвести 19 сентября 1945 года к 20.00 по московскому времени.

2. Проживающее население в указанных районах с движимым и недвижимым имуществом остается на местах.

ПОДПИСАЛИ:

1. КОМАНДИР 77 ГВАРДЕЙСКОЙ СТРЕЛКОВОЙ ДИВИЗИИ
   ГЕРОЙ СОВЕТСКОГО СОЮЗА
   ГВАРДИЯ ГЕНЕРАЛ-МАЙОР
   /АСКАЛЕПОВ/

2. КОМАНДУЮЩИЙ ГЕНЕРАЛ 3 ПЕХ. АМЕРИКАНСКОЙ ДИВИЗИИ
   БРИГАДНЫЙ ГЕНЕРАЛ
   /ДЖОНСТОН/

ПРИСУТСТВОВАЛИ:

С советской стороны

1. ГВАРДИИ ПОЛКОВНИК ТАРАСОВ
2. ГВАРДИИ ПОДПОЛКОВНИК ПАЩЕНКО

С американской стороны

1. ЧАРЛЬЗ Е. ДЖОНСОН, ПОЛКОВНИК Г.С.
2. ЛЛОЙД В. РАКЗЕЛ, ПОДПОЛКОВНИК Г.С.

Экземпляры составлены на русском и английском языках и являются идентичными.

INCL. # 3-4

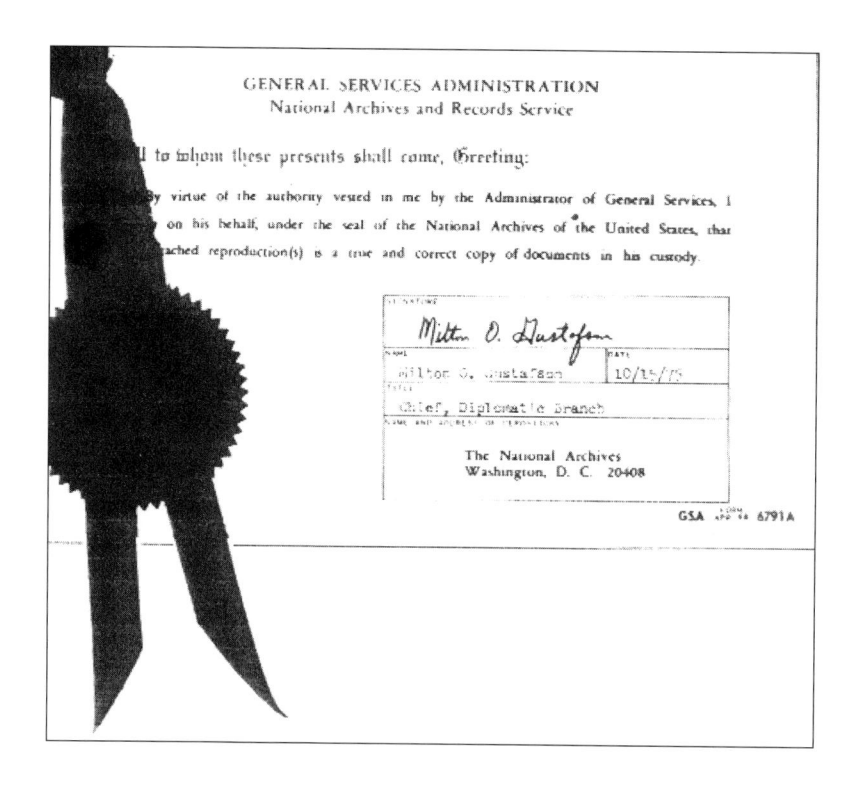

GENERAL SERVICES ADMINISTRATION
National Archives and Records Service

I to whom these presents shall come, Greeting:

By virtue of the authority vested in me by the Administrator of General Services, I on his behalf, under the seal of the National Archives of the United States, that ached reproduction(s) is a true and correct copy of documents in his custody.

Milton O. Gustafson

Milton O. Gustafson   10/15/75

Chief, Diplomatic Branch

The National Archives
Washington, D. C. 20408

GSA 6791A

"Kalkhof"
Home of Mr. and Mrs. D. Von Scharfenberg. Headquarters for the United States Army Russian Liaison Team-- Site of negotiation of this agreement between the United States of America and the Union of Soviet Socialist Republics.

INCL. # 3-5

31st ANNIVERSARY LUNCHEON

GERMANY

Boundary Changes Between United States and Soviet Zones of Occupation

Agreement between the UNITED STATES OF AMERICA and the UNION OF SOVIET SOCIALIST REPUBLICS

- Signed at Wanfried, Saxony, Germany, September 17, 1945
- Entered into force September 17, 1945

THIRD INFANTRY DIVISION

INCL. # 4

MAJOR GENERAL
WILLIAM THADDEUS SEXTON

William Thaddeus Sexton was born in Leavenworth, Kansas, Sept. 3, 1901. He was graduated from the United States Military Academy and commissioned a second lieutenant of Field Artillery June 12, 1924. His first assignment was with the Fourth Field Artillery Battalion at Fort McIntosh, Texas.

In February 1928 General Sexton became assistant and post adjutant at Fort Robinson, Nebraska. He entered the Field Artillery School at Fort Sill, Oklahoma, in August 1929 and completed the battery officer's course. The following June he was assigned to the 24th Field Artillery (Philippine Scouts) at Fort Stotsenburg, Philippine Islands. Three years later he entered the Signal School at Fort Monmouth, New Jersey, and he completed the communication officers' course in June 1934. He then was assigned to the First Field Artillery Brigade at Fort Hoyle, Maryland.

In July 1936 General Sexton became an instructor in the Department of Economics, Government and History at the United States Military Academy. Three years later he entered the Command and General Staff School at Fort Leavenworth, Kansas, and upon graduation in February 1940 was assigned to the 83rd Field Artillery at Fort Bragg, North Carolina.

General Sexton was assigned, in September 1940, to temporary duty in the Intelligence Division of the War Department General Staff. He became Assistant Secretary of the General Staff in February 1941 and was appointed Secretary of the General Staff in March 1943. He entered the Field Artillery School at Fort Sill, Oklahoma, in January 1944 to take a special one month course.

General Sexton went overseas in March 1944 to command the Third Infantry Division Artillery, with which he served in Italy, France and Germany. In May 1946 he was appointed military attache at Teheran, Iran.

He returned to the United States in November 1948, and two months later became Director of the Extension Course Department at the Command and General Staff College, Fort Leavenworth, Kansas. In June 1950 he was appointed Chief of Staff and Deputy Post Commander of the Command and General Staff College.

General Sexton was named Artillery Commander of the 82nd Airborne Division at Fort Bragg, North Carolina, in March 1951. The following August he became Chief of Staff of the Sixth Army with headquarters at the Presidio of San Francisco, California.

General Sexton was appointed Chief of the Military Assistance Advisory Group of Pakistan in July 1954.

In July 1955 General Sexton was named Commanding General, 5th Infantry Division, stationed in Germany, and remained in command of that Division until March 1956.

He was designated Deputy The Inspector General, Department of the Army, on April 16, 1956.

General Sexton has been awarded the Legion of Merit and the Bronze Star Medal with three Oak Leaf Clusters.

MAJOR GENERAL
CHARLES E. JOHNSON, USA RET.

Charles E. Johnson was born in Edgefield, South Carolina, on the 20th November 1911. He was raised in Columbia, South Carolina, which he considers his home. After a year of study at the University of South Carolina, he entered the United States Military Academy, from which he graduated in 1934 and was commissioned in the Infantry.

In 1938 he was assigned to the 3d Infantry Division at Fort Lewis, Washington, in which he was destined to serve for seven and one-half years. He was an infantry battalion commander when the division was deployed to the North African/European Theater in World War II.

General Johnson saw combat with this division in ten campaigns, from the amphibious landings at Casablanca in 1942 through the final advance across Central Europe in 1945. He was promoted to Colonel and Chief of Staff of the Division during the Anzio Beachhead Campaign.

Upon graduation from the Army War College at Carlisle Barracks, Pennsylvania, he was assigned briefly to the Office of the Chief of Information at the Department of Army.

From the Pentagon, he went to Korea, where he commanded the 7th Infantry Regiment, 3d Infantry Division. He was later assigned as Assistant Chief of Staff for Intelligence at Headquarters, Eighth U.S. Army and United Nations Command.

In 1957, after an initial intelligence assignment at Headquarters, USAREUR, General Johnson was named Chief of Staff to the U.S. Commander in Berlin, where he was promoted to brigadier general in August 1959. He was Commanding General of Berlin Command from January 1960 until July 1961, when he was assigned as Director of Foreign Intelligence at the Department of the Army.

After a year in this position, General Johnson was transferred to the Office of the Joint Chiefs of Staff where he first was Deputy to the Special Assistant for Counterinsurgency Operations and then Regional Chief for Europe, Africa, and the Middle East in the Policy and Plans (J-5) Division.

He was promoted to major general in October 1963 with rank retroactive to 4 June 1959.

In May 1964, he was assigned to Headquarters, U.S. Army, Europe, as Deputy Chief of Staff, Intelligence. From this assignment, he went to India as Chief of the Joint U.S. Military Supply Mission.

On 1 October 1966, General Johnson assumed duties as Chief of Staff, First U.S. Army, at Fort George G. Meade, Maryland. In August 1967 General Johnson was named the First Army's Deputy Commanding General.

General Johnson had more than 33 years of active service, during which he earned an impressive list of military decorations. Among them were the Legion of Merit with Oak Leaf Cluster, the Bronze Star with Oak Leaf Cluster, and the Croix de Guerre with Palm.

General Johnson is married to the former Betty Betz from Tacoma, Washington. They have two children—Mrs. Patricia Rice and Charles E. Johnson IV. The Johnsons now reside in Carmel, California.

INCL. # 4-3

MAJOR GENERAL
LLOYD BRINKLEY RAMSEY

Lloyd B. Ramsey was born in Somerset, Kentucky, May 29, 1918. He graduated from the University of Kentucky with a Bachelor of Arts degree in 1940. His military career began July 1, 1940 when he was commissioned a second lieutenant of infantry in the Regular Army. His first assignment was at Fort Thomas, Kentucky with the 10th Infantry. In August 1940 he was transferred to the 39th Infantry, 9th Infantry Division, Fort Bragg, North Carolina, where the division was being organized. He remained with the 39th Infantry until February 1943 when the regiment was in North Africa.

In February 1943 he was selected to be aide-de-camp to General (later Field Marshall) H. R. L. G. Alexander, British, the Ground Commander under General Eisenhower in the North African Campaign.

In November 1943 he was assigned to the 3d Infantry Division and served as a battalion executive officer, battalion commander, and regimental executive officer in the 7th Infantry and later as G-3 of the Division.

In March 1946 he was assigned to the Infantry School, Fort Benning, Georgia to instruct in leadership. He attended a short course in psychology of leadership at Yale University in preparation for this instruction.

He attended the Command and General Staff College, Fort Leavenworth, Kansas in 1949-1950 and upon graduation was assigned to the War Department General Staff in the Office of the Assistant Chief of Staff, G-2.

In August 1953 he was selected for attendance at the Army War College, Carlisle Barracks, Pa. Following graduation in June 1954, he was assigned to the Far East and served as Deputy and later Secretary of the Joint Staff of the United Nations Command and Far East Command.

In July 1957 he was transferred to Fort Benning, Georgia where he commanded the 14th Infantry and later the 1st Infantry Brigade. In September 1958 he became the G-1 of the United States Army Infantry Center.

He returned to the Far East in July 1959 and served as the United States Army Advisor to the Korean National Defense College until August 1960.

In September 1960 he returned to the Department of the Army General Staff serving in the office of The Chief of Legislative Liaison and in April 1963 he became Executive Officer of the newly established Office, Assistant Chief of Staff for Force Development.

General Ramsey became the Deputy Commanding General, US Army Training Center at Fort Leonard Wood, Missouri in October 1964. He was appointed as Deputy Chief of Information, Department of the Army, Washington, D. C. in March of 1966.

In October 1967 he was transferred to Fort McPherson, Georgia where he became Chief of Staff, Third US Army.

General Ramsey departed from the United States and arrived in Vietnam as Deputy Commanding General, Headquarters, 1st Logistical Command in December 1968. He remained in this position until June 1969 when he became the Commanding General of the 23d Infantry Division (Americal).

General Ramsey returned to the United States in March 1970 and was appointed as the Provost Marshal General, US Army in July 1970.

INCL. # 4-4

GUARD MAJOR GENERAL V. S. ASKALEPOV
COMMANDING GENERAL
77TH GUARD INFANTRY DIVISION
HERO OF THE SOVIET UNION

From the very beginning of the battles for Stalingrad and until the final defeat of Marshal Paulus' Army, General Askalepov commanded a Guards Division.

During the great battle of the Kurskoi Bend, General Askalepov commanded the same Guards Division.

For exceptional service during the battles on the Dnepr, General Askalepov was awarded the distinction of HERO OF THE SOVIET UNION.

During the spring and summer 1944, the Guards Division under the command of Guards Major-General Askalepov liberated White Russia and West Ukraina.

General Askalepov was a participant of the heroic battles on Visla for the liberation of Warsaw and for the capture of Berlin.

General Askalepov was awarded the following distinctions and medals by the Government of the Soviet Union:

    Gold Star of the Hero of the Soviet Union
    Three orders of LENIN
    Order of Suvorov 2nd class
    Order of Kutuzov 2nd class
    Medal "20 years of RKKA"
    Medal "For defense of Moscow"
    Medal "For defense of Stalingrad"
    Medal "For victory over Germany"
    Medal "For liberation of Warsaw"
    Medal "For capture of Berlin"

INCL. # 4-5

"Hero of the Soviet Union"
Guard Major General Vasili S. Askalepov with his aide and chauffeur and Captian Michael Burda, United States Army. Captain Burda was in charge of negotiating this agreement for the United States Army.

"Kalkhof"
Home of Mr. and Mrs. D. Von Scharfenberg. Headquarters for the United States Army Russian Liaison Team-- Site of negotiation of this agreement between the United States of America and the Union of Soviet Socialist Republics.

INCL. # 4-6

CHAPTER 7

1946 – 1957 FORT BENNING – FORT LEAVENWORTH – PENTAGON –ARMY WAR COLLEGE – JAPAN

Summer and Fall, 1946: Fort Benning, Georgia

On June 1, 1946, I was assigned to the General Subjects Section, Leadership Committee, under Colonel William Blandford. We had to come up with our own method of teaching leadership. This was a difficult task as I mentioned in my comments about our orientation at Yale. I think that we did come up with some very interesting subjects. Once we started teaching these subjects, the students seemed to learn a lot about leadership. I taught for three years, and I received many compliments for my instructions.

Fall 1946: Infantry Conference, Fort Benning, Georgia

I was just getting myself prepared to teach leadership and had taught a few classes when Major General "Iron Mike" O'Daniel, the Commanding General, called me to his office and advised me that I was going to be his Aide-de-Camp during the upcoming Infantry Conference. He said that he expected Generals Eisenhower and Bradley (five stars) plus a number of four-star generals and a number of other generals to attend the conference. He said that he needed someone who knew how to work with that caliber of the military and that I had the experience since I had been the Aide to General Alexander, British. I asked him if I could teach leadership while being his aide, and he said that I could as long as I did my work for him. Trying to prepare for the Infantry Conference, writing many letters for the General, and performing many other duties, I found that I could not do both. I had already written my presentations so it was not too difficult for one of the officers in the leadership committee to teach my subjects temporarily.

The Infantry Conference went well and General O'Daniel seemed to be pleased with my work. Colonel Ben Harrell, my former Regimental Commander in southern France when I commanded an Infantry Battalion, was General O'Daniel's primary planner for the

Infantry Conference, and he was very pleased with my work. As he told me, if I had not been the Aide he would have had to do much of the work that I did, especially writing letters and helping to take care of senior officers.

After the Infantry Conference was over, I asked General O'Daniel if I could return to teaching leadership. In his rough manner, he informed me that he would let me go when I found an Aide that was acceptable to him. (Although I was a Lieutenant Colonel, he was authorized a Captain as an Aide. However, he told me that due to the visitors that he would be receiving, he wanted at least a Major as his Aide.) I looked around and found Major George Beatty, a handsome officer with a very lovely wife. When I introduced him to General O'Daniel, the General said something to the effect, "You work for a week with Lloyd and then I will let you know if you can be my Aide."

An Inspection by the Commanding General

Before Major Beatty came on board, I was with General O'Daniel one day when he was inspecting different areas on the post. We went to the "Disposal Dump" where excess equipment was being sold. The Captain in charge was showing us around. We came to a location where a man was using a sledgehammer to crush "new" metal footlockers. Before the Captain could explain to the General what he was doing, the General started raising hell about destroying new metal footlockers that had never been used. General O'Daniel was so mad the officer could not say a word. Finally, I was able to ask the General to let me look into the situation and come back to him with a complete and detailed report. He agreed and we went back to the office.

I immediately went back to see the Captain, and a very interesting story came out of this meeting. He had thousands of new metal footlockers. Higher headquarters had ordered him to dispose of all of them at the best price that he could get. He put them out for bid, but the highest bid he received was 10 cents per footlocker. (I am not sure of my figures but they will give you the gist of the story.) He felt that the bidders had gotten together and rigged the bids. He then went to places that bought scrap metal. He asked for bids there and found out that all bidders required that the footlockers be smashed to a width of not more than six inches. (This was so that they could get them into their furnaces.) The highest bidder offered five cents a pound for smashed up metal lockers. The Captain figured out that paying someone to smash the lockers would only amount to pennies per pound. The footlockers weighed 10 to 12 pounds each. In other words, he could sell each footlocker for 50 to 60 cents each, less the labor cost to smash them, and would earn much more money for the Army rather than sell them at 10 cents each for a new locker. When I explained this to the General, I had already written a nice letter to the Captain for the General's signature, congratulating him on his management to get the best price. The General was interested in the explanation and signed the letter, which I delivered to the Captain immediately, and, of course, he was thrilled.

About October 1946: Lloyd Ann Got Dirty in the Sand

Since Lloyd Ann was born while I was overseas, she had lived for three years with her mother, grandmother, and granddaddy. She called the grandparents Mam Maw and Pappap. There were no small children around for her to play with, so for three years she was a young lady. Sonny, Glenda's brother, was still home, but he was 10 years older than Lloyd Ann, so they did not play much together.

After Lloyd Ann entered kindergarten, the teacher became concerned about her because she would not get into the sand pile or do anything outside that might get her soiled or dirty. The teacher discussed this with Glenda, and Glenda explained the problem. One day Glenda received a call from the teacher, who was thrilled because Lloyd Ann had gotten into the sand pile and gotten dirty. This was a big change for Lloyd Ann and from then on she acted like a normal child.

Visits by VIP's and Social Events at Fort Benning

Since I had served under General O'Daniel in combat, and for a short while as his Aide at Fort Benning, plus having been the G-3 under Colonel Johnson in the 3d Infantry Division, and now he was the Chief of Staff at Fort Benning, Glenda and I were invited to most official and social events on the post. Other senior officers and their wives were rotated through these events. Since Glenda and I went to most of them, we were able to meet officers and their wives much sooner.

The three-year period at Fort Benning was one of the finest assignments that Glenda and I had during my career. To make things even better, we were able to get a maid that lived with us for three years. Ann Taylor loved Lloyd Ann, and we had a built-in babysitter so that it was no problem for us to go to social events at night. I paid Ann $12.00 a week. She was off one day a week, but she never took off on a day that we needed her.

May 7, 1947: Larry Was Born

On May 7, 1947, Larry Burton Ramsey was born. It was nice that we now had a girl and a boy. Having Ann there all of the time made it easy for us to continue going to official and social events.

By the time Larry had learned to walk, he wanted to play outside all of the time. He was not like Lloyd Ann; he was dirty all of the time. One thing that he could not stand was a wet diaper. When his diaper became wet, he would come running to the nearest person to change it. One day when I was home, he came to me with a wet diaper. I had him to lie on the rug at the foot of the steps, and I went to the kitchen to get a clean diaper. There were no clean diapers there so I had to go upstairs to get one. I told Larry in a very firm voice to "stay there." When I came back, he had minded well and was still lying there. From then on, when Larry had a wet diaper, he would run to whoever was present and would then go lie down on the rug at the foot of the steps to get his diaper changed.

When we went to the swimming pool, we would set Larry on the side of the pool with his feet in the water, tell him to "stay there," and he would never move. Lloyd Ann loved the pool, but we had to watch her closely. I was trying to teach her to swim. She had reached the stage that she was not afraid of the water and did not mind getting her head under the water.

June 5, 1947: The Marshall Plan

I well remember on June 5, 1947 when General George C. Marshall, the Chief of Staff of the Army during World War II and now the Secretary of State, proposed the European Recovery program, known as "The Marshall Plan." This turned out to be one of the greatest programs in history, restoring European nations after the horrible destruction of World War II.

November 9, 1948: Judy Was Born (As She Was Growing Up She Changed to Judi)

On November 9, 1948, Judy Carol Ramsey was born. It was nice to have three children. And once again it was nice to have Ann there to help raise three small children. As you can see, Glenda was a very busy mother, in addition to being an outstanding wife. It was obvious that Judi was going to be different from the other two. She would get into everything, so you had to watch her every minute. I will explain more of Judi when we get to Fort Leavenworth, Kansas.

July – August 1949: Transferred to Fort Leavenworth, Kansas

I received orders early in the spring of 1949 transferring me to the Command and General Staff College at Fort Leavenworth, Kansas for the school year 1949-50, starting in August 1949. We took a short leave home to Somerset. We had been home once or twice a year while we were at Benning so our family had seen our children.

When we arrived at Fort Leavenworth, we were assigned quarters. Quarters were assigned according to the size of your family and your date of rank. I was fortunate to be assigned to what was called the Bee Hive, 450 Kearney, Apt. No. 6, second floor. It was an old four-story barracks building that had been converted into four apartments on each floor. The apartments were large and had three or four bedrooms per apartment. To rate those quarters, you had to have three or more children and the rank of a Lieutenant Colonel. That came to at least twelve children on each floor; times four floors was 48 plus children in the complex. There were two doors on the first floor into the complex, one in the front and one in the back. The back door was seldom used, so the front door was a very busy place.

If you did not live in the Bee Hive, you had to live in some old World War II converted wood barracks or some other building that I will explain. The barracks were small and gave very little privacy. I will always remember the story of two couples living next to each other, both husbands named Bob. One night after one wife went to bed she called out, "Bob, when are you coming to bed?"

Bob in the next apartment answered, "I am in bed."

There was another story that a husband went to the bathroom and found that there was no toilet paper. He called out, "Honey, bring me some toilet paper." Pretty soon the wife in the other apartment went to her bathroom with some toilet paper, but her husband was not there. He was in the living room reading.

The Army had just built some new houses for students, but due to the size of the class, these three- and four-bedroom houses were converted into two units, making them very small apartments. I remember being in one and the dividing wall came down in the middle of the fireplace.

Our Year at Fort Leavenworth, Kansas

Once again, we were very fortunate and found a babysitter that was available most any time that Glenda needed her. When she came, she would push Judi in the stroller for a long way and Larry loved to walk with them. She had a way with both of them, and they loved when she came. When Judi started walking, she was like Larry, getting all dirty and wanting to be outside. There was one difference however; Larry could not stand a wet diaper, but a wet diaper did not bother Judi. I have seen her come into the house with urine sloshing out of her shoes; she did not want to waste her time by changing her diaper. With all of the children living in our complex, more than 48, when it came 7:00 p.m. you could hear a pin drop because all of the men had to study at least three or four hours per night. It was a good year, but it was a very hard year of studying.

Command and General Staff College Course

Our class was very large. For most of the year, we all attended the same classes. The last month or six weeks we were divided into four sections: G-1 Personnel, G-2 Intelligence, G-3 Operations, and G-4 Logistics. I was assigned to G-2 Intelligence. My entire group was not pleased with the teaching of this section. In fact, the entire G-2 class fell in their class standing from where we stood at the end of the general sessions. I had been in the first quarter of the class for the entire year. After finishing the Intelligence course, I ended up in the second quarter of the class. This should have told the college something because we were not all stupid.

June 1950: Graduation

We graduated on June 30, 1950. War had broken out in Korea on June 25, 1950. Written and verbal orders started coming in immediately, changing assignments to being ordered to Korea or to a unit that was going to Korea. Fortunately, my orders assigning me to the Pentagon, to the office of Assistant Chief of Staff, G-2 Department of the Army, Washington, D.C., stayed in effect. This was probably because I had been overseas for over 3 ½ years during World War II.

After a short vacation in Somerset, we headed for the Washington, D.C. area to look for a place to live while I was stationed at the Pentagon. Some of our friends suggested the area of Falls Church, Virginia. We looked in that area and found a small two story home, three bedrooms, one and one-half baths, kitchen, a small dining room, living room with a fireplace, and a utility room. It cost $15,000. This was as much as we could afford with three growing children. It was located at 709 Woodlawn Avenue, Falls Church, Virginia. Although our address was Falls Church, we actually lived in Fairfax County.

Assignment to A.C. of S., G-2

I reported to the Pentagon on July 19, 1950. My assignment to A.C. of S., G-2 was in the executive office, called Planning and Coordination. My boss was Colonel Hamilton H. Howze, who rose to the rank of four-star General. Colonel Howze was a very fine officer to work for. He was an armored officer and he knew both command and staff. In our office we were involved in everything in addition to being responsible for certain intelligence activities. My primary responsibility was to oversee counterintelligence activities and, as an alternate, to coordinate Army Security Agency (ASA) activities.

I had hardly gotten oriented when Colonel Howze assigned me to work on the Program Advisory Committee (a Department of the Army committee) on the preparation of the Army Program Directive. With guidance from Colonel Howze, I was able to contribute much to the committee. Major General Bolling, the A.C. of G-2, wrote me a nice letter for my work on that committee. A copy of the letter is at the end of this chapter (Inclusion #1).

Silver Platter Story

My desk was in front of Colonel Howze's desk with my back to him. One morning he came in a little later than usual. He had hardly sat down when he said, "Lloyd, turn around. I have something that I want to tell you." His story was that the previous night he and his wife Mary were going through some invitations and found a wedding invitation that they had received some time ago that required a present. They both had a full schedule for the next day and did not have time to shop for a present. He suggested that they send one of the many silver platters that they had received and never used over these many years. He said that he understood many other people did that. They went to the basement to open boxes to find a suitable platter. Every one that they looked at had been engraved. Colonel Howze told Mary that he understood that a jeweler could fill in and engrave the platter again. He said that he had time to take it to the jeweler at the Pentagon, get him to engrave it, and then mail it. Colonel Howze said that he went to the jeweler and asked him if that could be done. After a short inspection of the platter, the jeweler told Colonel Howze that his platter had been engraved so many times that he could not do it again.

The First Computer in the Army

I had been there about one year when we were notified that the Army had installed a computer and was going to demonstrate how it could be used. I was given the mission of attending the demonstration and coming up with a recommendation as to how we could use the computer for intelligence. The computer cost $480,000, could do 100,000 additions in a second, weighed about 30 tons, and filled a 30 by 50 foot room. It had no monitor. Technicians watched 3,000 blinking lights to keep track of an operation. It had no memory. It used 174 kilowatts of electricity a second, enough to power a modern home for more than a week. It required additional air conditioning to keep the area cool. Since it had no memory, I recommended that we had no use for it in Intelligence. This computer came into being in 1946. A picture of the computer, as shown in the *USA Today* of February 14, 1996, also gives some detail about the computer and is at the end of this chapter

(Inclusion #2).

Counterintelligence Files

The headquarters for the Counter Intelligence Corps was located at Fort Holibird, Maryland. I would go there once or twice a month to keep up-to-date in that field. I soon learned that one of our problems was getting an individual's security clearance (i.e. secret, top secret, etc.) because all the courterintelligence files were kept by the Armies and Major Commands. When you needed a security clearance for anyone in the Army, you had to first determine where they had been stationed, and then write to each location to see if was were anything in their file that would keep them from getting a clearance. This was very slow and not always accurate. The Corps had attempted to get the files at one location but was never successful. I discussed this with General Bolling, the G-2. He said that his office had tried to get the files consolidated but failed. I then asked him if I could work out a plan to consolidate the files. He gave me permission to try but gave me very little encouragement.

I kept working with CIC Headquarters but was not getting any good ideas. One day I met a major at Fort Holibird and told him what I was trying to do. He informed me that he had been working on that problem in his spare time for many months, but he could not get anyone to listen to him. I told him that I would listen and that I had the authority to act. He had plans as to how to consolidate the files, where to store them, and how to set up a filing system so that the proper information could be retrieved on one person almost immediately. I told the Major that we needed to brief the CIC Headquarters. The Major was deeply concerned about doing this because he could not get his boss interested in his plan, and now it would appear that he was going over his boss's head. I took the plan, studied it, and then made a presentation to the CIC Headquarters. They thought it was a very good plan and recommended that I get approval of G-2 to put it into effect. I told them that I would need an action officer from Fort Holibird to coordinate all the actions. I then suggested that the Major who had made the plan (without telling them that he made the plans) be the action officer. All agreed, including his boss, who said that he was a fine officer and would do a very good job.

I presented the plan to General Bolling, but he was not very enthusiastic. After much discussion, he finally agreed that I could try to implement the plan. Within six months we had all of the files from headquarters worldwide consolidated at Fort Holibird, and they were filed so that almost immediately you could check a person's background to see if he had anything against him that would prevent him from receiving a security clearance. This file was only one step in securing a security clearance. General Bolling left before this project was completed. I am sure that he would have been very proud of our accomplishment.

June 1, 1952: Soviets Install "Iron Curtain Wall" to Isolate East Berlin, Germany

I well remember June 1, 1952 when the Soviet Union started erecting a wall between East and West Berlin, Germany. I believe their main purpose was to deny East Germans access to West Berlin, where they could go for freedom.

July 1952: Move to Assistant Executive Officer, A.C. of S. G-2

In late spring 1952 the present G-2, Major General R. C. Partridge, brought in as his executive officer Colonel Frederick D. Sharp, an old hand in intelligence. He knew his job very well; however, it soon became obvious that Colonel Sharp was looking toward retirement. It was not long before Colonel Sharp asked me to become his assistant. He told me in no uncertain terms that I would be doing most of the work but must keep him briefed on everything that I did. Colonel Sharp had to sign many documents and originate others. I had to write the documents for him to sign and then brief him. I also briefed him on all the other documents that he signed. Colonel Sharp was very wise. If the briefing did not sound right, he would then read the document. He had an easygoing way but was no pushover. In fact, I would rate him very high as a G-2 executive. I enjoyed working for Colonel Sharp and learned much about intelligence from him. I finished my tour in G-2 in July 1953. I had received my orders to attend the Army War College.

July 27, 1953: Armistice Agreement between North and South Korea

On July 27, 1953, an armistice agreement was signed and the fighting ended in Korea. A buffer zone, called the Demilitarized Zone, divided the two sides. The Demilitarized Zone was 2 ½ miles wide. It was along the final battle lines. A Military Armistice Commission, with representation from both sides, was set up to enforce the armistice terms.

A Very Fine Poem Written after the Korean War

I AM THE INFANTRY

I AM THE INFANTRY – I meet the enemy face to face...will to will. For two centuries, I have been the bulwark of our Nation's defense...I am the Infantry! Follow me!

Both hardship...and glory, I have known. My bleeding feet stained the snow at Valley Forge. I pulled an oar to cross the icy Delaware... tasted victory at Yorktown...and saw our Nation born.

At New Orleans, I fought beyond the hostile hour...discovered the fury of my long rifle...and came of age. I am the Infantry!

I pushed westward with the Conestoga...and marched with the pioneer across the plains...to build outposts for freedom on the wild frontier. Follow me!

With Scott I went to Vera Cruz...battled Santa Ana in the mountain passes...and climbed the high plateau. I planted our flag in the Plaza of Mexico City.

From Bull Run to Appomattox my blood ran red. I fought for both the Blue and the Grey...divided in conflict, I united in peace...

I am the Infantry.

I left these shores with the sinking of the Maine...led the charge up San Juan Hill...and fought the Moro – and disease – in the Philippines.

Across the Rio Grande, I chased the bandit, Villa. Follow me!

At Chateau-Thierry, I went over the top. I stood like a rock on the Marne...cracked the Hindenburg line...and broke the back of the Hun in the Argonne. I didn't come back until it was "over", "over there".

At Battaan and Corregidor, I bowed briefly, licked my wounds and vowed to return. I invaded Tunisia on the African shore...dug my nails into the sand at Anzio...and bounced into Rome with a flower in my helmet.

The Channel and the hedgerow could not hold me. I pushed back the "Bulge"...vaulted the Rhine...and seized the Heartland. The "Thousand-Year" Reich was dead.

From island to island, I hopped the Pacific...hit the beaches...and chopped my way through swamp and jungle. I kept my vow...I did return...I set the Rising Sun.

In Pusan perimeter I gathered my strength...crossed the frozen Han...marched to the Yalu. Along the 38th Parallel...and around the world, I made my stand.

Wherever brave men fight...and die, for freedom, you will find me, I am the bulwark of our Nation's defense. I am always ready...now and forever. I am the Infantry – Queen of Battle! FOLLOW ME!

August 10, 1953: Moved to the Army War College, Carlisle Barracks, Pennsylvania

We sold our house in Falls Church, Virginia for exactly what we paid for it - $15,000. After a short vacation to visit our parents in Somerset, we reported to Carlisle Barracks, Pennsylvania, on August 10, 1953. We had been told that we would get quarters at Carlisle Barracks but that our furniture would go into storage and would be moved in after we arrived. We were only a few hours drive from Carlisle, and I wanted to move our furniture from Falls Church directly to our house at Carlisle. I made a number of phone calls to try to accomplish this, but they said it could not be done.

Amazingly, when we arrived at Carlisle, our furniture had been moved into our house. Of course, much of it was not on the right floor or in the correct room. Glenda and I could move most of the furniture, but we had to hire someone to move the larger pieces. The house had four levels – one half story to each level. The first level was a half basement, where the freezer should have been, but it was put on the second level in the dining area where there was no room for it. The third and fourth levels were bedrooms, and, of course, the beds and other furniture were in the wrong rooms. These were new houses that had never been lived in before. As you would expect, there were many faults in the houses that had to be corrected, and it took time to get things done.

Christmas 1953: Carlisle Barracks, Pennsylvania

Carlisle Barracks was an area which got very cold in the winter and usually received lots of snow. Glenda and I had bought a sled for the children for Christmas. About two or three days before Christmas we received our first few inches snow, which was late for that area. Glenda and I decided to let the children use the sled early and enjoy it. They had a ball with it! The snow was gone by Christmas. All of our friends who had sleds for their children said that we should have waited until Christmas to give them the sled. Would you believe that was the only snow that we received for the entire winter? Glenda and I were so happy that we gave the sled to the children early so that they got to enjoy it. Those same friends who told us that we made a mistake, later told us that they wished they had done what we did.

Army War College School Year

Our class had a wide range of ages. The oldest were West Point graduates from the class of 1933. The youngest were three of us from year group 1940, all ROTC graduates. The other two were a month or so younger than I. Two of us became General Officers, the other General Officer was General William B. Rosson (four stars). He and I served together in the 3d Infantry Division during World War II.

The school year was a great period in my career. We had some outstanding speakers and the faculty was outstanding in every respect. If you did not learn a lot, it was your own fault. We had no exams, but we did have to read a lot, and we had to prepare some papers. Although we were kept very busy, we still had time to spend with our families. One of the most important benefits that I received from going to the War College was the friends that I made during that year. Having such friends and seeing them rise in rank was great, but having them as contacts for the rest of my career was a very valuable asset.

Orders to Korea (My Orders Were Changed in Japan When I Arrived There To Be Assigned to the United Nations Command/Far East Command (UNC/FEC)

Before graduation, in June 1954, I received my orders to Korea, which meant that I could not take my family with me. The house next door to Glenda's mother and father in Somerset was for rent, so we rented it for Glenda and the children to live there for a year while I was in Korea. That would be 207 Vine Street. We got the house set up before I left for Korea.

I left for Korea in late July and had to go through Japan. When I arrived in Japan, I was notified that my orders had been changed and that I was to be assigned to the United Nations Command/Far East Command Headquarters (UNC/FEC Hqs.) which was located at Pershing Heights, Tokyo, Japan. This was a very pleasant surprise because it meant that I could take my family to Japan.

I called Glenda as soon as I could get to a phone for long distance calls. She was thrilled with the news, even though there would be many problems for her: get out of a one-year lease on our house; arrange for our car, a Ford station wagon, to be shipped from Somerset, Kentucky to Tokyo; make arrangements for most of our household goods to be stored, plus decide what should be taken to Japan and arrange for that shipment; make train reservations from Somerset to Seattle, Washington for her and three children. She did all of this like a real Army trooper.

In the meantime, I moved into the Di Ichi Hotel where I lived until my family arrived in December 1954. I applied for government quarters and was told that I would have to go on a waiting list, which would be at least six months and could be as long as a year.

I was assigned to the J-1 section of the headquarters, probably the worst assignment that I had in the Army. I worked for an Air Force Colonel who knew nothing about personnel. When we had a problem, I seemed to be the only person in the section who knew what to do. I received no help from my boss, and I had to plead with the secretary to type my paper. She claimed that she was too busy to do my typing.

I kept looking for a place to put my family when they arrived. The Air Force Colonel that I worked for said that he should get quarters on post in December. If he did, I could rent the place where he and his family were living. It was not too long until he found out that he would get government quarters in December. I arranged with the landlord to take over the rent. The apartment was at 6 Roku Bancho, Chiotu Ku, Tokyo, Japan. It rented for $140 per month. It was 750 square feet, had two bedrooms, one bath, a small living room–including eating area, a tiny kitchen, and a very small maid's room. About mid-December, I moved into the apartment and got some government furniture for the house. I also found a maid, Miki.

Glenda, Lloyd Ann, Larry and Judi Arrived a Few Days Before Christmas 1954

I received word that my family would arrive at the port of debarkation a few days before Christmas 1954. I was there to meet them with open arms. I had arranged for government transportation to take us and our baggage to our new living quarters. On our first night in Japan, I decided that we should go to a very nice Japanese hotel which had both Japanese and American food. We had not been there very long when things suddenly began to shake and the hanging lights began to swing. We were having an earthquake, which was common in Japan. It scared all of us very badly, but at least I had felt an earthquake before.

Getting a Telephone Was a Very Difficult Task

To get a telephone in Japan was a difficult and expensive task. For some people, the waiting period was one year. Certain exceptions were made for the military. In our case, a military family had lived in our apartment so we were permitted to take over their telephone. To do this, the Air Force Colonel and I had to go to the phone company with an interpreter to make the transfer. It could not be done by phone.

After seeing many people, we were told to come back in one week and the paper work would be ready. I was told that the down payment would be $80 in Yen, and it must be paid in cash. One week later, the three of us went back to the phone company. Through the interpreter, I suggested that I pay the releasing officer $80, and his down payment would then become my down payment. They said that such a transfer of funds could not be done. I then gave the clerk $80 in Yen. The clerk put the Yen in the cash drawer and then picked up a stack of Yen and counted out $80 in Yen to the releasing officer. The releasing officer then handed me the $80 in Yen, and I handed him $80 in American Script. I guess this transaction made everything legal. Since the Air Force Colonel had moved on post, he would be using American Script most of the time and I would be using Yen quite often.

January 31, 1955: I Was Promoted to Colonel; Shortly Thereafter, I Was Selected to be the Deputy Secretary of the Joint Staff

I was promoted to Colonel on January 31, 1955 and promoted myself out of a job in J-1. It was not very long until I was selected to be the Deputy Secretary of the Joint Staff. This position was probably one of the best that a new Colonel could have on the UNC/FEC staff. In J-1, I was in the office about eight hours a day, five days a week. In my new job, I would be in the office about ten hours a day and on Saturdays and sometimes on Sundays.

July 1, 1955: We Moved to Government Quarters at Washington Heights

In late May 1955, I received word that government quarters would be available to my family at Washington Heights on July 1, 1955. This gave us time to get out of our rent because we had a clause in the contract that said we could move out, without penalty, with 30 days notice if we received movement orders or government quarters.

The Army had trained a number of Japanese to be maids for American families. Most of these well trained maids worked for Generals or senior Colonels. There was one available that they said I could have. Her name was Sueko. She spoke very good English, knew how to mix and serve drinks, how to cook American food, and how to serve it. She could do all of this for up to ten people and never seemed to be rushed. She loved the children and enjoyed playing with them. She was with us for over a year; then she got married and went to live with her husband. We also had a house boy that came once or twice a week to do the yard work and anything heavy around the house that was too much for Sueko.

After we lost Sueko, we got Toshiko. She was not as well trained as Sueko, but she worked hard to please us. In her spare time, she would study English and then write papers in English and ask me to correct them for her. She really did love the children and would play with them or take them places in Tokyo. She and Mike, the house boy, seemed to get along well. She stayed with us until we left Japan. We gave her our new address and soon after we got home we received a letter from her that said, "I marry up with Mike."

My Duties as Deputy Secretary of the Joint Staff

As the Deputy Secretary, I was responsible for assigning incoming papers to different staff sections with deadlines for completion and then following up to ensure that the staffs met the deadline. As staff papers would arrive for the Commander in Chief's or the Chief of Staff's approval, I would assign the paper to an assistant secretary of the joint staff to prepare a briefing for the Chief of Staff.

Our Commander in Chief (CINC) was General John E. Hull. The Chief of Staff (CS) was Lieutenant General Carter B. Magruder. My boss, Secretary of the Joint Staff (SJS), was Colonel Hank Benson. I did not have much contact with the CINC but met with the CS at least once or twice a day to brief him on activities going on in the staff.

On April 1, 1955, General Hull left to retire and General Maxwell D. Taylor moved up from Command of the Army Forces Far East (AFFE) to be the new CINC. He was not there very long before he was selected to be the Chief of Staff of the Army. General Lymn L. Lemnitzer had taken over command of AFFE, and he moved up to be the CINC, UNC/FEC on June 5, 1955. Colonel Benson left in the fall of 1955, and I moved up to be the Secretary of the Joint Staff.

My Duties as Secretary of the Joint Staff (SJS)

In my new position as Secretary of the Joint Staff, which I took over in the fall of 1955, I had to be at the office by 7:00 a.m. each morning, six days a week, so that I could read all incoming cables, about 250 to 300, and select the important ones for the CINC to read. He would arrive at the office about 8:30 a.m., or sometimes as late as 9:00 a.m. He held a morning staff conference at 9:30 a.m. The cable traffic was always discussed and sometimes I was criticized by the CINC for my selection of cables. Some staff officer would bring up a cable and the CINC would comment that I did not provide him with that cable. I would comment that the cable was in his reading file; he would then comment that I gave him too many cables to read. A few weeks later, the same thing would happen, but this time I had not put that cable in his reading file. He asked why I had left it out, and I told him that I did not think it was that important. He would then comment that I should give him the cables and he would decide what was important. You can see that I was wrong either way; however, this did not happen more than once a month so I did pretty well.

Worked Very Closely with the Chief of Staff

I worked very closely with the Chief of Staff. I sat in on many of the briefings by my officers to the Chief of Staff, consulted with him on actions going on in the staff, and did many other things. One day, late in the afternoon, General Magruder sent a memo to G-3, reversing a decision that he had made on a paper earlier that day. All such memos came through me so that I could keep up with what the Chief of Staff was doing. When I read the memo, he made all types of excuses for reversing his decision. To me this looked bad for young officers and secretaries to see. I dictated a proposed new memo for the CS's consideration. I tried to get in to see him, but he did not wish to be disturbed because he had too much paper work to do. His secretary and aide both pleaded with me to let the memo go as was, or I might be in serious trouble for holding up his paper work. I said that I would not release the memo until I had talked to him, and I asked the secretary to please give him a note that I must see him before he left. I would say that this was about 5:00 p.m. but I did not get to see him until 7:00 p.m. I explained to the CS why I held up his memo and further said that I had taken the liberty of writing a new memo for his consideration. He then said, "Let me see what I said." He read his memo, laid it aside, and then said, "Let me see what you have to say." He picked up his pen and signed the memo that I had written; he then tore up the memo he had written. I thought that he might compliment me for my work. Instead, he said, "That's what you get paid for."

In my new position, I was on all the official guest lists at the headquarters, embassies, and other activities. There were always many social functions going on and General Lemnitzer would try to make as many of those functions as he could. If the party were from 6:00 to 8:00 p.m., General Lemnitzer would change uniforms at the office and leave about 6:45 to 7:00 p.m. I would change uniforms also and would have my driver to pick up Glenda and then pick me up so that we could go together. By the time we got home, the maid had put the children to bed. Because of so many functions, and my long hours at work, I would sometimes go all week without seeing my children. Sunday was an easy day; I would get to the office about 8:00 a.m. and would be able to leave about 2:00 or 3:00 p.m. Many days the General would play golf on Sundays, and I would get away by 12:00 noon, giving me a whole afternoon with my family.

I stayed in this position until July 1, 1957 when the headquarters in Tokyo were closed and a new UNC Headquarters opened in Korea. By this time, I had received orders to command the 29th Infantry at Fort Benning, Georgia, which was the demonstration troops for the Infantry School. My picture as Secretary of the Joint Staff is at the end of this chapter (Inclusion #3).

DEPARTMENT OF THE ARMY
GENERAL STAFF, UNITED STATES ARMY
WASHINGTON 25, D. C.

G2-AP 201 RAMSEY, Lloyd B (O)   6 OCT 1950

SUBJECT: Letter of Commendation

TO: Lieutenant Colonel Lloyd B. Ramsey
        Office of the Assistant Chief of Staff, G-2, Intelligence
        Washington 25, D. C.

    1. At the 39th meeting of the Army Policy Council on 27 September, the Secretary of the Army congratulated the Army General Staff on the excellent work done in preparing the 1951 Army Program Directive. The minutes of that meeting contain the following entry:

> "Mr. Bendetsen invited the attention of the Council to the publication of the Army Program Directive prepared under the direction of the Deputy Chief of Staff for Plans, and said that this is the first time that we have had the basic policy guidance on all Army programs in one document; an important step forward. Mr. Pace said that he had examined the Program Directive himself and considered it a most unusual and valuable effort toward Army leadership in the field of coordinated programming. He said that when the programs have been fully developed, this will constitute a real milestone for the Army. He congratulated the Staff for this very excellent document."

    2. I wish to commend you for the splendid work which you have done as a working member of the Program Advisory Committee on the preparation of the Army Program Directive. Your work as my representative at the important working level has been a source of great satisfaction for me.

    3. A copy of this correspondence will be placed in your official Department of the Army file.

                                                  A. R. BOLLING
                                                  Major General, GSC
                                                  A. C. of S., G-2

TO: Lt. Colonel Lloyd B. Ramsey

      Forwarded with pleasure.

                                                 HAMILTON H. HOWZE
                                                Colonel, GSC
                                                Assistant Executive for
                                                Planning and Coordination

INCL. # 1

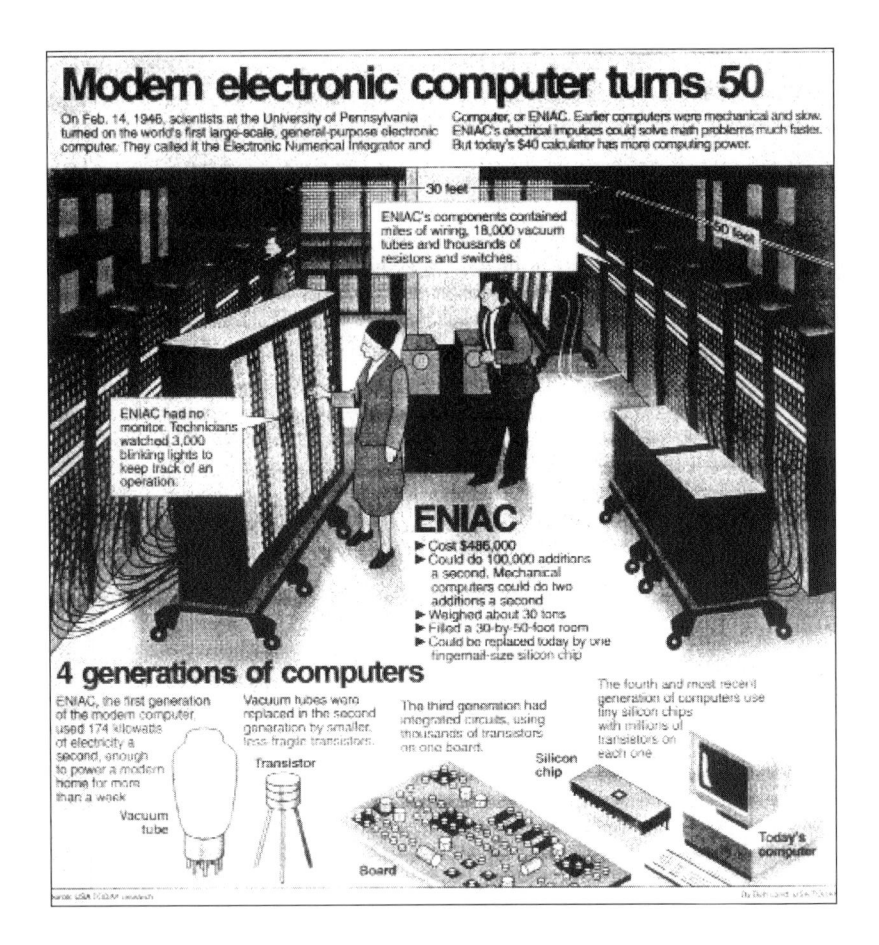

INCL. # 2

INCL. # 3

CHAPTER 8

1957 – 1968   FORT BENNING, GEORGIA – KOREA – PENTAGON – FORT LEONARD WOOD, MISSOURI – PENTAGON –FORT MCPHERSON, GEORGIA

August 1957: Command, Fort Benning, Georgia

By the time that I arrived at Fort Benning, Georgia, about the middle of August, the Army had done away with the Regiments and had organized Battle Groups. The 29th Infantry was split into two groups – the 14th Infantry Battle Group and the 29th Infantry Battle Group, both of which were commanded by the Infantry School Troop Command. The Commanding General selected one of his favorite staff officers to command the Infantry School Troop Command. I was given command of the 14th Infantry Battle Group. It was only a matter of six weeks that the Commanding General learned that the officer he had selected as Commander of the Infantry School Troop Command, who had been an outstanding staff officer, was not a commander. He moved him into a staff position and moved me up to command the Infantry School Troop Command. I was just beginning to get troop requirements, training, and other administrative problems under control in the 14th Infantry.

The Infantry School Troop Command consisted of two Infantry Battle Groups, an Artillery Battalion, a Tank Battalion, an Engineer Company, a Dog Platoon, and some other units. On my first day in command, the S-3 came to me and said that the Infantry School had requested more troops than we could furnish. I then asked him how many troops the Infantry School asked for. He told me they wanted 600 men. Our strength was about 5,000. I said that I could not believe that we could not furnish 600 soldiers to the school from a total of 5,000 soldiers in command. I told him to inform the Battle Group S-3's that they would furnish the required number of soldiers and that every man in this command was available except the 1st Sergeant, the Supply Sergeant, and the Mess Sergeant. In addition, he was to tell the Battle Group S-3's that I wanted an accounting of every soldier that day, by company, on my desk by 10 a.m. the next morning. If there were any questions, Battle Group Commanders were to call me.

When I received the report the next morning, I was shocked. What was happening was that the 1st Sergeants were either furnishing details to activities all over the post so that they could get things they needed for the company or the company was in training and would not change their training program to meet school requirements, which was our primary mission. They were able to convince their company commanders that these details were required by higher headquarters. I put out an order that all requests for details must come through my headquarters.

Because of this horrible situation, I found out that we were doing very little training. We immediately started a training program that kept one battalion in training at all times. The other battalions would furnish the troops to the school and also get in more training than they had been able to do before. Shortly after this happened, I watched a problem that the school was putting on for a class. Seeing many of my men sitting around doing nothing, I went to the head instructor and asked him why these troops were not being used. He replied: "Sir, I always ask for twice the number of men that I need and hope that I get half of them because that is the number I need." He also stated that he had been conducting this problem for over a year, and this was the first time that he had received the number of troops he had asked for. I told him from now on he was to ask for what he needed and that was exactly what he would get. I gave the same information to the operations people, and our requirements were reduced so that we could get more units into training.

After getting many of the troop requirements, training, and requirements for details straightened out, I set as my next goal to change the headquarters from a TD (temporary duty) headquarters to a TO&E (tactical operations and equipment) headquarters. It did not seem proper for a TD Headquarters to command tactical units. I wrote a memo to the Infantry School asking that necessary action be taken through channels to assign a Tactical Brigade number to the Infantry School Troop Command. I received a call from the Infantry School saying that they had already tried but were turned down and that they would not try again at that time.

Since I had been on the Army Staff from 1950 to 1953, I still had many friends there. I called one of them and he agreed that the Headquarters should be a Brigade. He said that he would work with

CONARC (Continental Army Command) and ask them to work with the Third Army Headquarters, Fort Benning's next higher headquarters. It was not long until Third Army was suggesting to Fort Benning that they thought the Infantry School Troop Command should be changed to a Brigade. The Infantry School was very happy that someone above had changed his mind and was going to give the Infantry School a Brigade Headquarters. I never told the Infantry School what I had done. It was not long until a friend from CONARC called me and wanted to know what Brigade headquarters I would like. I told him that I would like "First Brigade" if such number were available. It was, and it did not take long until we became the First Infantry Brigade.

Once I got the Brigade organized for school troop support and set up a training program, the unit became a showpiece for the post. We planted trees, flowers, improved the lawns, and made the parade field a real showplace. This was a great command assignment, but other people on the post would sometimes try to take over some of the troops in my command. They soon learned that they could not do that while I was in command. After one year, around August 1958, the Commanding General decided that I had had enough command time and moved me to be the G-1 (Personnel Officer) of the Headquarters, Fort Benning. In this position, I was involved in many activities on the post.

Retirement of Chief of Chaplains, U.S. Army

The Chief of Chaplains, a Catholic Major General, came to Fort Benning shortly before he retired. He had been the Chief of Chaplains at Fort Benning a few years before. The Commanding General had a luncheon for him at the officer's club. When we arrived, we were greeted by Sergeant Fields. Sergeant Fields had spent most of his Army career at Fort Benning, and most of that time was at the officer's club. He remembered every senior officer who had ever been at Benning and always greeted them like an old friend, hoping to get a good tip. After he and the Catholic chaplain had a nice conversation, Sergeant Fields said, "Chaplain, be sure and give the wife and children my best regards."

January 31, 1958: United States Launched Its First Satellite

I well remember when the Soviets launched Sputnik I, the first satellite into space, on October 4, 1957. On November 3, 1957, they launched a second satellite, Sputnik II. It carried a dog named Laika, the first animal to soar into space. The United States was working very hard to get a satellite into space. On January 31, 1958, the United States launched its first satellite, Explorer I. Then on March 17, 1958, the United States launched its second satellite, Vanguard I.

July 1959: Assigned to PROVMAAGK (Provisional Military Assistance Advisory Group Korea)

I received orders to PROVMAAGK, Korea, to be there by August 1, 1959. We went to Somerset, Kentucky to find a place for the family to stay while I was in Korea. We found a very nice home on College Street, and I had enough time to get the house set up before I had to leave for Korea. I left Somerset in July 1959. My orders assigned me to the PROVMAAGK (Provisional Military Assistance Advisory Group Korea). When I arrived there, I was given a nice set of quarters with two other colonels. We each had our own bedroom and bath. We had a small kitchen and a fairly large living room. The three of us got along well. The only problem was that due to my rank and the position I held, I was a member of the Commander in Chief's mess, and they had to eat at another mess. This was inconvenient for them because they had a good walk to get to their mess. One of the good things about my mess was that I could buy food so that we could cook many of our meals on an open fire at our quarters, which we did often.

I was assigned as the Army Advisor to the National Defense College. It was a long drive every day to get to the college; however, I was furnished a car and driver and that made it easy to get to work. The commander of the College was a Korean, Major General Choi Kwang Nok. He and I got along very well from the first day that I was there. My being a golfer was a great help because he loved golf. He had only been playing for two years and said that he was only a beginner; however, his handicap was ten, which was two strokes better than mine and I had been playing for many years. We played golf quite often, mostly on the weekends.

Having graduated from the Army War College in 1954, I was able to help the college considerably in their academic year. One of my biggest problems was to get their library straightened out. Many of the students could read and write English very well but could not find the book that they wanted. As an example, Choi Kwang Nok used Choi as his last name. If I had written a book and someone wished to find it, they would look under Ramsey, but it would not be there. The Korean would file it under Lloyd. There were lots of small problems like this that I soon straightened out.

I also arranged for high-ranking officers and civilians visiting in Korea to come to the college and make presentations. All of these presentations had to be translated into Korean. The College had some very fine linguists. One day I had asked a civilian from Research and Development, Department of the Army, to make a presentation. When I talked to these people, I would tell them that they should not speak for more than 20 minutes to allow time for translation. I would also tell them to use very simple language to ensure that the linguist could translate. This speaker paid no attention to my suggestion to use simple language. In fact, I could not understand much of what he said. Although I could not understand Korean, I always listened on earphones to be sure that the conference was being translated. On this day, the earphones went dead. When I pointed to my Korean secretary to get them working, he indicated that something was wrong with my earphones. After everything settled down, I went to General Choi and asked him what had happened. He did not want to tell me the truth, but he did. He said that the speaker talked in such technical language and so fast that the linguist could not translate. The linguist told the students that he could not translate but that he could understand enough to tell them when to clap.

December 7, 1959: My Father Passed Away

About December 8-9, 1959 (difference in time), I received a call from home that Dad had passed away. I believe that it was my brother Bill who called. He said that Mimi wanted to hold the funeral until I could get home – that is, if I could be released to get home. I told Bill that I was sure that I could make it home but to give me a little time, and I would call him back. It did not take me very long to get leave and make flight arrangements. Most of my flights would be by military air, so I told Bill to add another day to the schedule I gave him just in case I had travel problems. I got home in two days. When we were in Japan from 1954 to 1957, Dad started to lose his memory; today, we would call it Alzheimer's disease. In those days, they did not know about Alzheimer's. Dad seldom would recognize me after we returned from Japan. When I left home in July 1959 for Korea, Dad did not know that I was his son. That was a very sad day because Dad had always been so proud of me and all the accomplishments that I had achieved in high school, college, and in the Army. I was very grateful to Mimi that she held up the funeral until I could get home. Dad was born June 11, 1890 and died December 7, 1959 at age 69.

I took two weeks of leave so that I could enjoy my family for a short while. I remember that we had an early Christmas, and the children put on a show. Larry was the emcee and Lloyd Ann and Judi put on skits. They all did a wonderful job, and both Glenda and I were very proud of them. It was sad to tell them goodbye once again, but we all had a wonderful time while I was home. I left the day before Christmas to return to Korea and spent Christmas Day in the air. It did not take long until I was back in my normal routine.

In my position, I had contact with many high-ranking Korean military officials and was able to acquire what I thought was some very good intelligence. I reported to the G-2, United Nations Command, but he felt that my sources were not reliable. Some of the things that I did report to him did happen, so my sources were very good.

About March 1960, General Magruder, the CINC, who had been the Chief of Staff of UNC/FEC in Japan when I was the Secretary of the Joint Staff, called me up from PROVMAAGK to assist his people in writing a speech that he was going to give to a number of members of Congress that were going to visit the command. He had made a few notes that he wanted to put in the speech. One note said something to the effect that Korea was the showplace for democracy. I took this out of the speech because, based on my intelligence, this was not true. A few days later we met with General Magruder, and he wanted to know why that statement was not in his speech. I tried to explain why I had taken it out but got nowhere. At his discretion, we put it back into the speech, and within a few days the students led widespread demonstrations against the government. In April, President Rhee resigned. When the Congressmen arrived soon thereafter, I listened to the speech. It did not include anything about Korea being a showplace for democracy.

August 1960: Returned to the United States

While in PROVMAAGK, I received orders assigning me to Legislative Liaison, Department of the Army, the Pentagon, Washington, D.C. I arrived home in August 1960, and we got our things together so that we could move to the Washington area. We found a split foyer in McLean, Virginia that had five bedrooms, three baths, and a large recreation room downstairs. This place was at 6451 Dryden Drive, McLean, Virginia. With this size house, everyone had his or her own bedroom, and Lloyd Ann and Judi shared a bath. Even though this was a new house, it did not have air conditioning. We added air conditioning in the summer of 1961, and it was a real treat.

September 1960: Assigned as the Senior Army Liaison Officer to the United States Senate

When I reported to the Pentagon, I was told that I would be the Senior Army Liaison Officer to the United States Senate. I would have an office in the Pentagon and one in the Senate Office Building, now known as the Russell Building. I would spend most of my time in the Senate. I had two officers and two secretaries working for me.

As the Senior Army Officer, I worked with most of the leadership in the Senate. I would go to Senator Jack Kennedy's office, at his request, to assist him with some Army problems which concerned him. He was running for President, so I did not see him very often. I visited Senator L. B. Johnson, the Majority Leader, quite often, even though he was running for Vice President. After Senator Johnson became Vice President, I made one trip with him and other Senators to a meeting in Paris, France. I got to know Richard Nixon well. After he was Vice President under Eisenhower, he went to California to practice law. He came back to Washington often, and I would see him at various functions. On one occasion when the Senate was having a prayer breakfast, Glenda and I were invited to sit at the table with former Senator and Vice President Nixon and his wife, Pat. On another occasion, after Nixon had moved to New York City in 1963 to practice law, some senators had a meeting in New York City. There were three people that were asked to make comments: General Hershey, head of the draft board; Richard Nixon, and myself. I have a picture that I cannot find of Nixon, General Hershey, and myself. I remember General Hershey making a statement somewhat as follows: "I am the ham between two slices of good bread."

I worked very closely with Senator Richard Russell, Chairman of the Senate Armed Services Committee. I escorted him on a number of trips. I also worked closely with Senator Everett M. Dirksen, the Minority Leader. When I received a call from Senator Dirksen's office and they said that the Senator would like to see me, I always knew that I would see the Senator. Many times I would get calls from other offices that the Senator would like to see me, but when I arrived some staff member would meet me and say the Senator was busy and the staff member would tell me what the Senator wanted.

I will always remember one of the times that I was called to Senator Dirksen's office. As usual, he was waiting for me and greeted me cordially. He said that he had a letter from a very influential constituent who had a son who was a reserve lieutenant on duty in the active Army. The son was being sent to Korea, but he could not get college courses there that he needed, but could get them in Okinawa. The father wanted the Senator to get the son's orders changed from Korea to Okinawa. The Senator was very direct with me and said that he really needed to help this man and anything that I could do would be greatly appreciated.

I immediately got in touch with the people in personnel that would handle such a case. I found out that the son had already talked to these people and they were ready to help him. They assured me that the Lieutenant would go to Okinawa. I went back to the Senator's office to tell him the good news, but he was on the floor of the Senate. His secretary told me that he was taking a beating on the Senate floor and that he needed some good news. She said that I should go to the Senate Chamber and get a Senate page to take him a message that I had some good news and was waiting to see him. I did that and it was not long until the Senator came out to see me. I told him the news, and he was delighted. I also told him that even though the son had done most of the work, he could take credit for the change in orders, which I knew he would do anyway. The Senator then asked me if he had given me a copy of the letter, which was three pages long. I told him that he had, and he said that he could not understand why people wrote such long letters for such a small request. He added: "I will always remember the letter that I received from a Sergeant in Fort Hood, Texas. It read somewhat as follows: 'Dear Senator, I am stationed in Fort Hood, Texas, and I want to be stationed in Fort Sheridan, Illinois. I control 16 votes. Thank you sir.' With that type of information, I went to work to get the Sergeant moved to Fort Sheridan, Illinois."

During my third year in Legislative Liaison, I kept the senior position with the Senate but was also responsible for the liaison people in the House. I did not have to spend much time there, but I did spend enough time to get to know Gerry Ford fairly well. Having worked with General Eisenhower while I was Aide-de-Camp to General Alexander, then working very closely with Senators Jack Kennedy and L. B. Johnson and former Senator and Vice President Richard Nixon as the senior liaison officer with the Senate, and then getting to know Congressman Gerry Ford in the House, I got to know and work with five people that became President of the United States. I consider myself very fortunate to have had this privilege.

January 20, 1961: Invitation to the Inauguration of John F. Kennedy

Glenda and I were honored to receive an honorary invitation to the inaugural ceremonies of President John F. Kennedy on January 20, 1961. A copy of the invitation is at the end of this chapter (Inclusion #1 and #1-2).

September 1961: Selected to Attend "Advanced Management Program" Harvard

During the summer of 1961, I was selected to attend the "Advanced Management Program" at Harvard from September to December. Only two army officers were selected to attend each class of two classes a year. This was a great honor for me. However, I would be absent from my duties on the Hill for three months. I talked to several Senators about my selection and they encouraged me to attend the course, even though it meant a long absence.

When we arrived at Harvard, we were assigned to our rooms and introduced to our classmates. There were four units around a common plumbing facility; two people were assigned to each unit, which had two bedrooms with a study room in between. Since all four units would use the same plumbing facility, we were called "Can Groups." We were "Can Group 12." Our group consisted of the following seven people:

> Robert C. Fields – who became one of the top people in R. R. Donnelly publishing company
> Lou R. Hague – who had his own consulting firm
> John B. Jackson – who became one of the top men in IBM
> Norman J. Kautz – who became President of Bay State Milling Company
> Paul Morel, French – who became President of Aluminum Company of France
> Lloyd B. Ramsey – who became a Major General in the U.S. Army
> Oliver M. Sherman, Jr. – who became one of the top people in Goodyear

This was a very interesting course with emphasis on finance in running a business. Our instructors were outstanding. We never took exams, but we had to study about three hours a night. The instructors would always get participation from the class, and if someone had not studied, it became obvious when he was called on.

We had some free time on weekends, and "Can Group 12" would always go somewhere together. We got along very well. During the last few days of our classes, the wives were invited to come up, and they attended some classes and our graduation. Our "Can Group" with our wives had a great time together. At the end of this chapter is a picture of "Can Group 12" and their wives (Inclusion #2).

February 20, 1962: John Glenn Completes the First U.S. Orbit of the Earth

The Russians were ahead of the U.S. in space, and we were trying very hard to catch up with them. I remember well when John Glenn was sent into space on February 29, 1962 to orbit the earth for the first time for the U.S. I saw as much on TV as could be seen, and it was a thrill.

October 22, 1962: Russia Moved Nuclear Missiles into Cuba

On October 22, 1962, I well remember when President Kennedy appeared on television and stated that Russia had moved nuclear missiles into Cuba, which was a great threat to the United States. He directed Russia and Cuba to remove those missiles immediately. His demeanor made an impression on Russia and it was not long until the missiles were removed. I was Senior Liaison Officer to the United States Senate, Department of the Army, the Pentagon, at this time, and I must say the Army and many senators were deeply concerned. We worked some very long hours on this problem.

April 1963: Assigned to ACSFOR

The Department of the Army was going through a recognition and ACSFOR (Assistant Chief of Staff for Force Development) was organized. The Chief was Lieutenant General Ben Harrell, who had been my regimental commander for a while in World War II and with whom I worked closely during my assignment to Fort Benning, Georgia (1946-1949). He asked DA to assign me to ACSFOR so that I could be his Executive Officer. Having served almost three years in Legislative Liaison, I was transferred to ACSFOR in April 1963, where I became the Executive Officer for Ben Harrell. I was honored that he thought enough of me to fill such an important position.

August 28, 1963: Martin Luther King, Jr. – "I Have a Dream" Speech

On August 28, 1963, I remember well when Martin Luther King, Jr. made his famous speech from the Lincoln Memorial, Washington, D.C., which included "I Have a Dream." This was quite an emotional event for the entire nation. At the end of this chapter are parts of the speech (Inclusion #3).

November 22, 1963: Assassination of President John F. Kennedy

On November 22, 1963, I was working in my office in ACSFOR, under Lieutenant General Ben Harrell, when the news started circulating that President John F. Kennedy had been shot in Dallas, Texas. The President was in an open car coming from the airport. When I went in to tell General Harrell the news, we turned on the television, and we sat there, with others that he invited in, until the President was taken to the hospital and pronounced dead. This was a tragic moment for the nation. It was not long until the alleged assassin, Lee Harvey Oswald, was arrested for the crime.

June 1964: I Was Nominated for Promotion to Brigadier General

In June 1964, I was nominated for promotion to Brigadier General. About that time, the Army wished to increase its enlistments so they came up with a program to study called STEP (Special Training and Enlistment Program). Since I was on the promotion list, I became available to head the study. It was designed to accept soldiers who did not have a high school education but who had a reasonable IQ and could be educated within six to twelve weeks to meet the Army standards of a high school education. It was also designed for men who had minor health problems that could be corrected within six to twelve weeks to meet the Army standards.

I formed a committee to study the program, and we came up with a proposal very soon. When we presented it to the Secretary of the Army, he was pleased. Our next step was to receive Congressional approval. I was to make the presentation to the Senate and House Armed Services Committees, and I would be accompanied by the Vice Chief of Staff, General Creighton Abrams. When we made our first presentation to the Senate Committee, Senator Richard Russell, Chairman of the Senate Armed Services Committee, was present; he and the others listened very carefully and said that they would consider the proposal.

Our next presentation was to the House Armed Services Committee. Chairman Carl Vinson was present, and he immediately took exception to the proposal. He felt that the Army might lower its standards to get more enlistments, even though he said this program was designed to keep our standards up. I had met Chairman Vinson a number of times, and he, being a very fine politician, made a statement somewhat as follows: "If Lloyd Ramsey was going to run this program forever I would probably agree with it, but new people may lower the standards;

therefore, this committee cannot accept your proposal." I was pleased with Chairman Vinson's statement about me, but this was a politician's way of saying, in a nice way, that he disapproved of my proposal. This ended the STEP program.

August 1, 1964: I Was Promoted to Brigadier General

On August 1, 1964, during the study of the STEP program, I was promoted to Brigadier General. If the program had been approved by Congress, the training would have been at Fort Leonard Wood, Missouri; therefore, I was on orders to Fort Leonard Wood.

October 1964: Move to Fort Leonard Wood, Missouri

Since I was on orders to Fort Leonard Wood, Missouri, the Army decided to send me there, and I became the Deputy Commanding General. This was a very interesting assignment, specifically for training soldiers. It kept me in the field most of the time. We conducted basic training and advanced individual training (AIT). Most of the AIT was in engineering subjects, so I had a lot to learn in those areas to give proper supervision to the classes. My commander was Major General Lyle E. Seeman, an engineer. General Seeman was a fine officer to work for. After getting to know me, he put the training responsibility in my hands completely. When we had functions on the post or elsewhere with civilians and someone had to speak, General Seeman would many times call on me to make the remarks because he did not like to make speeches, and he soon learned that I did fairly well. Mrs. Seeman was not very well, so she leaned heavily on Glenda to do many things that the Commanding General's wife would normally do. Glenda did those things well and with ease.

October 1964: SFC Douglas Parks Became My Driver

When I arrived at Fort Leonard Wood, Missouri, I was assigned a driver by the name of SFC Douglas Parks. Parks was an outstanding driver for me, and he was well liked by the entire family. He would do anything for any member of the family. Judi reached the point that if something went wrong with one of her toys, she would ask Parks to fix it for her because Daddy was too busy. Parks stayed with me until I left Fort Leonard Wood in February 1966.

When I moved to Third Army Headquarters, Fort McPherson, Georgia, in late October 1967, I got Parks assigned to me once again. When I left Fort McPherson for Vietnam, Parks asked to go with me, which we arranged. It was great to have him around because he knew exactly what to do for me. After my accident in Vietnam and while I was on sick leave, I was on orders to Fort Polk, Louisiana, and once again I arranged for Parks to go there, but my orders were changed and I became the Provost Marshal General of the Army, stationed in Washington, D.C.

June 1965: Inducted into the "Hall of Distinguished Alumni," University of Kentucky

In the spring, I received notice from the University of Kentucky that I would receive an honor in June 1965, along with some other graduates. I did not have to be present to receive the honor, but they encouraged me to be there. When we arrived at the Student Union Building, there was a very large crowd present. The President of the University announced that they had established a "Hall of Distinguished Alumni" and that 85 graduates, out of many thousands of graduates, would be the first group inducted into the "Hall of Distinguished Alumni." He went on to explain that future selections would be made every five years and that the number selected each time would be very few. I could not believe that I had been selected for this honor. Thrilled and proud when my name was called, I went up in my blue uniform to receive the honor.

November 1965: Received Centennial "K" Medallion

On November 19, 1965, I received the University of Kentucky Achievement Award, the Centennial "K" Medallion, at a ceremony held at the University, however I was unable to attend the ceremony. The University sent information to the Fort Leonard Wood paper, which I quote: "Of the thousands of men who have earned a letter in sports during the past century at the University of Kentucky, only 39 were named distinguished recipients of the Centennial 'K' Medallion." I was highly honored to receive this award. The Fort Leonard Wood article is at the end of this chapter (Inclusion #4).

Fall 1965: New Commanding General, Fort Leonard Wood, Missouri

In the fall of 1965, General Seeman retired and was replaced by another engineer, Major General Thomas H. Lipscomb. General Lipscomb was difficult to work for. There was only one way to do things, and that was his way. He seldom listened to his staff. As soon as I brought up a subject, he would give me a decision. I soon learned never to brief him for a decision. I told him what I was going to do and then justified why it should be done. Using this method, he would listen.

He made many decisions without asking questions. On one snowy day, I went to the field very early. The snow was four to six inches deep. When I went to the office, the Commanding General was not there. I gave orders to cancel training for the day but found out that some troops were already moving. I started out in my jeep to see if I could find those troops. I found them going to the range, and they had already walked more than a mile in the snow. There was a warming tent about one quarter mile away. I told the company commander to get them to the warming tent and that I would get trucks to pick them up. Then, I drove to the warming tent to ensure that the stoves were burning.

When I got back to the troops, they were heading back to the barracks. When I asked the company commander why, he said that General Lipscomb had been there, had given him hell for getting his troops out in the snow, and had told him to get back to the barracks as soon as he could. He said that he tried to tell him about the warming tent, but he would not listen. I told him to follow my orders and that I would tell General Lipscomb what I had done. Once again, he turned around and headed for the warming tent. When I caught up with General Lipscomb and told him what I had done, his comment was that the officer should have told him there was a warming tent close by. I said nothing more.

Glenda and I received many nice compliments from officers and wives about our tour at Fort Leonard Wood, Missouri. Some wrote letters after we left. Glenda saved this one as the best.

December 20, 1965

Dear Mrs. Ramsey!

My husband, Dave Grant, and I, and of course Kenny, our son, wish you, General Ramsey and your family a very Merry Christmas and a successful New Year.

Now that this year is rapidly coming to an end, and we have left Leonard Wood long ago, I feel I can tell you things I couldn't have said at anytime before. My husband and I admire you and General Ramsey very much. Many times at night in those typical husband and wife conversations, we mentioned you and your family, and what a fine example you are. You may laugh now, or think I have lost my senses, but all this comes from the heart and that this is the truth.

As a young couple and as young people who have decided to make the Army their life, we observe, criticize and try to learn. We try not to make the same mistakes, but sometimes with no avail. To me you have been a great help and inspiration. You display a gentleness and kindness which comes from the heart. You have warmth and a lot of femininity, an asset often lacking in older women I met. All these are the obvious things. I am sure you are many more, but to me Mrs. Ramsey, you are a thoroughly admirable lady. I just wanted to say all this. Because so often we feel all those good things but are either too afraid to say them or too embarrassed to speak up. I hope you will forgive my impulsiveness, this comes with youth and I am sure that time or people will take care of that. But, if there should ever be a day, when you would like to remember, please do so, remember that we believe in you and what General Ramsey stand for. The young generations need examples like you.

My husband and I spent 2 of our most happy years in Fort Wood and will never forget this. If my writing is not perfect, please overlook it, English is a lovely language and I am trying my best to master it completely. I hope also that this will find you in good health. We wish you health and happiness in the future years and the realization of your dreams.

Yours Truly, Heidi Grant

Early 1966: I Received My Orders to be the Deputy Chief of Information, Department of the Army, Washington, D.C.

In early 1966 I received my orders to the Pentagon to be the Deputy Chief of Information, Department of the Army, Washington, D.C. I reported to DA in February 1966. Since Judi was a senior in high school, the C.G. said that Glenda could stay on post until Judi graduated. He also allowed Glenda to keep our cook so that he could help her around the house. I lived in a nice set of bachelor quarters at Fort Myer, Virginia while Glenda and Judi stayed at Fort Leonard Wood. I made arrangements for us to be able to move back into our home on Dryden Drive by the time Judi graduated.

In my new assignment, I dealt with correspondents, editors, broadcasters, photographers – all aspects of the media. We made news releases, wrote stories about the Army, and did everything else that you would do in public information. I found this to be a very exciting assignment. When in town, I would spend many hours in the office, usually arriving at 7:00 a.m. and leaving about 7:00 to 8:00 p.m. Saturday was a short day. I would get there at 8:00 a.m. and would usually get away by 2:00 p.m. I did a lot of traveling – many times to make speeches.

My boss was a Brigadier General, on the promotion list, with whom I had served in World War II: Brigadier General Keith Ware, a Medal of Honor recipient from the 3d Infantry Division. Keith was an outstanding officer, and he gave me many responsibilities in this field. We got along extremely well. Keith received his promotion to Major General, but before he was promoted, I was selected for promotion to Major General, which promoted me out of a job. It was not very long until I received my orders to Third Army, Fort McPherson, Georgia. This would be three moves within three years.

1967: Questions and Answers about UK

In 1967 the University of Kentucky published a handout titled "Questions and Answers about UK." In the center of the handout were the pictures of nine of the original 85 "Hall of Distinguished Alumni," selected in 1965. My picture was one of the nine. I quote from the handout: "The University's contribution to the nation's progress is reflected in the many successes of its alumni. Pictured here are but a few of these Kentucky graduates who have brought credit to their alma mater." I was honored that the University would include me among such a distinguished group that ranged from 1886 to 1940, my year of graduation. Part of the handout is at the end of this chapter (Inclusion #5 and #5-2).

October 1967: I Was Assigned to Third Army, Fort McPherson, Georgia, as the Chief of Staff

In October 1967, I was assigned to Headquarters Third Army, Fort McPherson, Georgia, as the Chief of Staff of Third Army. Third Army was responsible for most of the Army installations in the southeast. This included, but was not limited to, such facilities as Fort Benning, Georgia; Fort Rucker, Alabama; Fort Jackson, South Carolina; and Fort Bragg, North Carolina. This was a very large task. My Commanding General was Lieutenant General John L. Throckmorton. He was an outstanding officer to work for, and he and his wife were a delightful couple to be with. As his Chief of Staff, I had complete control over staff and, in most cases, I made the presentations to him for decision. This left him the time he needed to visit the installations to see firsthand what was going on.

April 4, 1968: Reverend Martin Luther King, Jr. Was Shot and Killed

I will always remember when Reverend Martin Luther King, Jr. was killed by a sniper on April 4, 1968 on the balcony of the Lorraine Motel in Memphis, Tennessee. This was in the Third Army's area of responsibility; therefore, we had to prepare for most anything, which we did. The assassination touched off race riots in more than 100 cities and set off one of the largest U.S. manhunts for the alleged killer, James Earl Ray. Ray was convicted and sentenced to 99 years in prison. There has long been speculation that James Earl Ray did not act alone.

July 1, 1968: Promoted to Major General

On July 1, 1968, I was promoted to Major General. General Throckmorton, the Commanding General, and Glenda pinned the stars on my shoulders. A picture of the ceremony is at the end of this chapter

(Inclusion #6).

November 1968: Received Orders to Vietnam

Glenda and I were enjoying a nice vacation on a beach in Florida in November 1968 when I was paged to come to the telephone. When I did, it was General Throckmorton. He told me that he had just received verbal orders that I was being sent to Vietnam and was to arrive there not later than December 28, 1968. This gave me about six weeks to move, find a place to live in Somerset, Kentucky, and get Glenda and the family settled before I had to leave. We were very fortunate to find a house on College Street, and I was able to get the family fairly settled before I had to leave for Vietnam. At the end of this chapter (Inclusion #7) is a picture of Lieutenant General and Mrs. Throckmorton with Glenda and me at a party they gave us after a farewell review. I had received the Legion of Merit at the review, which I am wearing. At Inclusion #8 is a picture of Glenda, Judi and me.

The Inaugural Committee

requests the honor of your presence

to attend and participate in the Inauguration of

John Fitzgerald Kennedy

as President of the United States of America

and

Lyndon Baines Johnson

as Vice President of the United States of America

on Friday the twentieth of January

one thousand nine hundred and sixty one

in the City of Washington

Edward H. Foley
Chairman

INCL. # 1

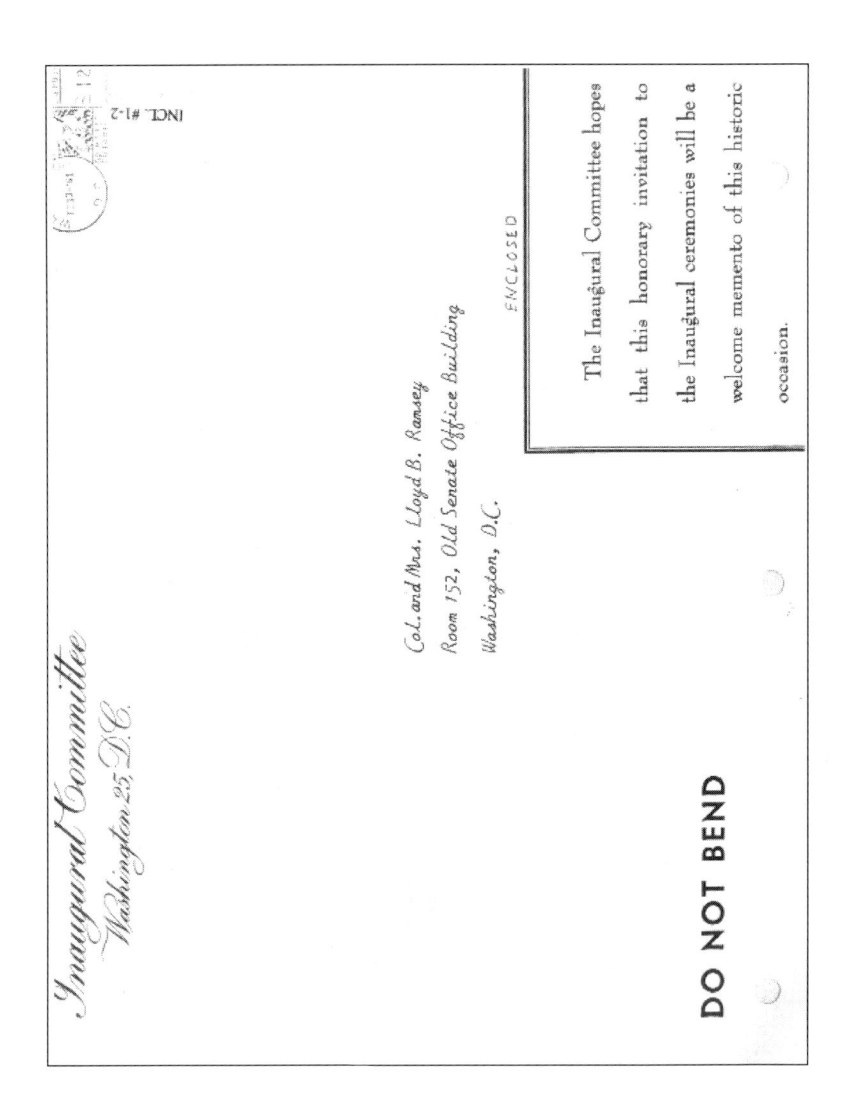

Inaugural Committee
Washington 25, D.C.

Col. and Mrs. Lloyd B. Ramsey
Room 152, Old Senate Office Building
Washington, D.C.

INCL. #1-2

ENCLOSED

The Inaugural Committee hopes that this honorary invitation to the Inaugural ceremonies will be a welcome memento of this historic occasion.

DO NOT BEND

INCL. # 1-2

From left to right: Emily & Jerry Sherman, Re & Lou Hague, Velma & Bob Fields, Mrs. and Paul Morel, Faun & Norm Kautz, Glenda and Feller Ramsey, Putsie and John Jackson.

INCL. # 2

The "I Have a Dream" Speech

Below are parts of the speech Dr. Martin Luther King Jr. gave on Aug. 28, 1963, at the Lincoln Memorial in Washington, D.C.

"I say to you today, my friends, so even though we face the difficulties of today and tomorrow, I still have a dream. It is a dream deeply rooted in the American dream.

"I have a dream that one day this nation will rise up and live out the true meaning of its creed: 'We hold these truths to be self-evident, that all men are created equal.'

"I have a dream that one day on the red hills of Georgia, sons of former slaves and sons of former slave owners will be able to sit down together at the table of brotherhood ...

"I have a dream that my four little children will one day live in a nation where they will not be judged by the color of their skins, but by the content of their character.

"I have a dream today!

"I have a dream that one day down in Alabama ... little black boys and little black girls will be able to join hands with little white boys and white girls as sisters and brothers ...

"This is our hope. This is our faith that I go back to the South with ... With this faith we will be able to work together, to pray together, to struggle together ... knowing that we will be free one day ...

"This will be the day when all of God's children will be able to sing with new meaning, 'My country 'tis of thee, sweet land of liberty, of thee I sing. Land where my fathers died, land of the pilgrims' pride, from every mountainside, let freedom ring.' And if America is to be a great nation, this must become true.

"So let freedom ring from the prodigious hilltops of New Hampshire; let freedom ring from the mighty mountains of New York; let freedom ring from the heightening Alleghenies of Pennsylvania; let freedom ring from the snowcapped Rockies of Colorado ...

"Let freedom ring from every hill and mole hill of Mississippi. 'From every mountainside, let freedom ring.'

"And when this happens, and when we allow freedom to ring, when we let it ring from every village and every hamlet, from every state and every city, we will be able to speed up that day when all of God's children, black men and white men, Jews and Gentiles, Protestants and Catholics, will be able to join hands and sing in the words of that old Negro spiritual,

" 'Free at last! Free at last!
" 'Thank God Almighty, we are free at last.'"

Dr. King waves to crowd of thousands from the steps of the Lincoln Memorial.

INCL. # 3

254

HEADQUARTERS SPECIAL TROOPS, U.S. ARMY TRAINING CENTER, FT. LEONARD WOOD, MISSOURI

DECEMBER 1965

Gen Ramsey Honored By Alma Mater

Brigadier General Lloyd B. Ramsey, deputy commanding general of Fort Wood, received the University of Kentucky Achievement Award, the Centennial "K" Medallion, in ceremonies held there on Nov. 19.

Brigadier General Lloyd B. Ramsey

The Award was presented to former University of Kentucky lettermen who have distinguished themselves in their chosen profession following graduation. The award was sponsored by the University of Kentucky Athletic Association and was announced at their centennial banquet last month.

General Ramsey, who was graduated in 1940, was on the football and swimming teams. He was freshman backfield coach of football his senior year, coach of the swimming team during his junior year and captain of the swimming team his senior year.

Of the thousands of men who have earned a letter in sports during the past century at the University of Kentucky, only 39 were named distinguished recipients of the Centinnial "K" Medallion. Among the recipients were such people as Richard C. Stoll, Sr., football star of the 1890's for whom the University of Kentucky football field is named; Elvis J. Starr, Jr., Secretary of the Army during the Kennedy Administration, who

(Continued on Page 4)

BRIG GEN RAMSEY
(Continued From Page 1)

lettered in tennis during the '30s and Frank V. Ramsey, Jr., a letterman in basketball and baseball who later played professional basketball with the Boston Celtics.

Dr. John W. Oswald, President of the University of Kentucky, said in a letter to the former athletes that "Success in any field of endeavor does not come easily, it has to be won with dedication and hard work, and the athlete learns well how to pursue this goal."

General Ramsey was also chosen as an initial member of the newly created Hall of Distinguished Alumni of the University of Kentucky during the centennial year. He was among 85 alumni nominated to the Hall for distinguishing themselves in their devotion to the University.

The general was graduated with a Bachelor of Arts degree. He earned his commission as a second lieutenant through the Reserve Officer's Training Corps at the University.

INCL. # 4

255

INCL. # 5

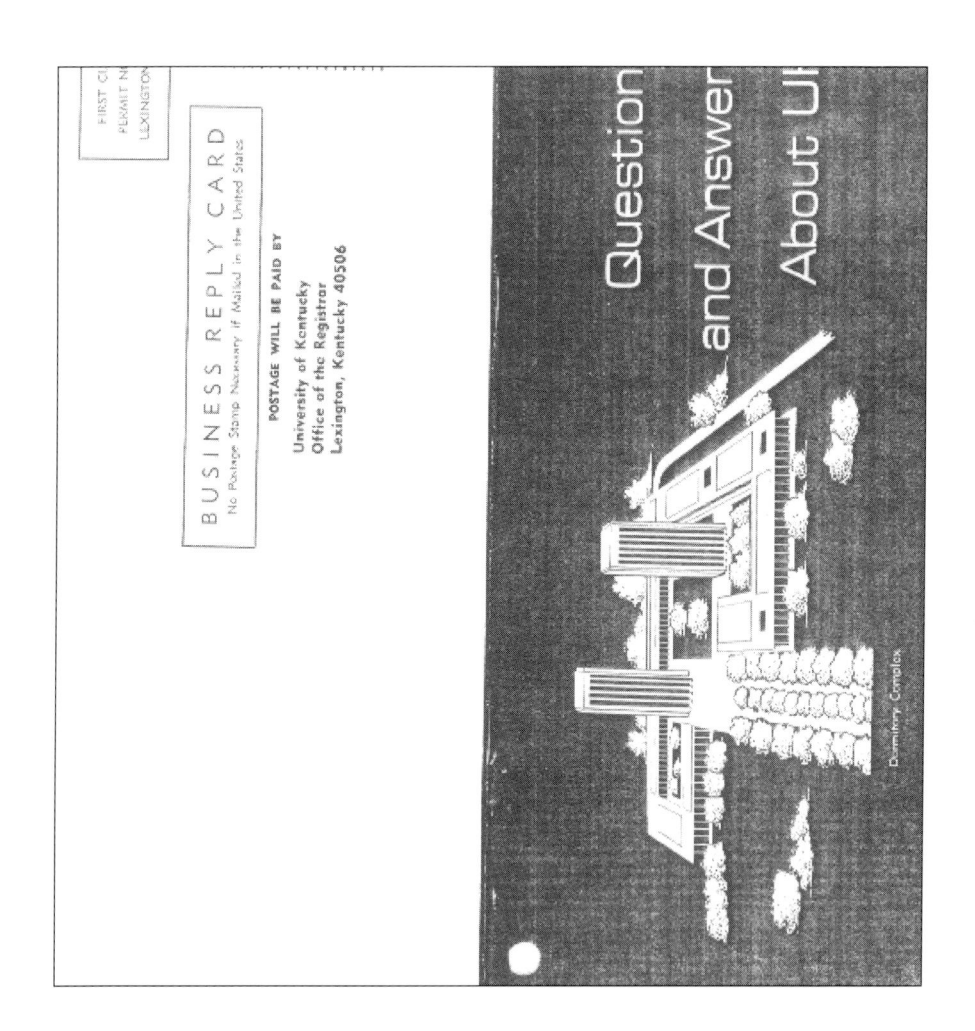

DISTINGUISHED ALUMNI

The University's contribution to the nation's progress is reflected in the many successes of its alumni. Pictured here are but a few of those Kentucky graduates who have brought credit to their alma mater.

INCL. # 5-2

(Caption Reads:) **THIRD ARMY PROMOTION--Third U.S. Army CofS, MGen Lloyd B. Ramsey, receives insignia of his new rank, with LGen J. L. Throckmorton, Third Army C.G. and Mrs. Ramsey doing the honors. Before his present assignment, General Ramsey was Deputy Chief of Army Information.**

ARMED FORCES JOURNAL, 20 July 1968

INCL. # 6

INCL. # 7

INCL. # 8

CHAPTER 9

VIETNAM, 1968 – 1970

December 1968: Arrived in Vietnam – Assigned as Deputy Commanding General, 1st Logistical Command

I arrived in Saigon, Vietnam, on December 28, 1968 and reported to Headquarters, U.S. Army, Vietnam (USARV). I was immediately taken to the Army Commander Lieutenant General Frank Mildren, whom I knew very well because we had served together in the office of the Assistant Chief of Staff Force Development (ACSFOR), Department of the Army, the Pentagon, in 1963-1964. He told me I was being assigned as the Deputy Commander, 1st Logistical Command. He said that he knew that I was not a logistician, but the command needed help, especially in command and security. While I was there, he called in his housing people, and I was assigned a set of quarters. He then escorted me to my new set of quarters, with my baggage, and then took me to meet my new boss, the Commander, 1st Logistical Command, Major General Joseph Heiser.

General Heiser was an expert in logistics, but it became obvious that he did not know much about command or security. His commanders kept asking for MP's or Infantry troops to secure their logistical installations, and he was giving them support for their requests. I soon learned that most of the logistical troops were working eight to ten hours a day with at least one or two days off a week. With proper scheduling, and an increase in work hours, they could furnish their own security of the logistical installations. I convinced General Heiser that this could be done, and he agreed. We put out an order to accomplish this; however, by the time that I left five months later, very little had been done, and I could not get General Heiser to enforce his order. Even though he would not force his commanders to use their troops for security, I was able to improve security in other ways during my five months in the Logistical Command.

April 10-17, 1969: Met Glenda in Hawaii

A General officer was supposed to serve in Vietnam for 18 months.

During that time we were allowed one week in Hawaii, or some other place, and two weeks, plus travel, to go home. Glenda and I planned to meet in Hawaii from April 10 to 17, 1969 before I took command of the Americal Division on June 1, 1969. The Army housed us in a villa at Fort DeRussy, just off Waikiki Beach. A good friend of mine from the 3d Infantry Division days of World War II, Colonel Winston Whall, was on the staff in Hawaii and lent me his second car. Between having a very nice place to stay and having a car, Glenda and I had a lovely week in Hawaii. We ate at many nice places, toured the island, and spent many hours lounging on the beach. Sadly, the week passed fast and once again we went our separate ways, not knowing when and if we would see each other again. It was an emotional departure for both of us.

June 1, 1969: Became the Commanding General, Americal Division

In May 1969, I received orders to take over the Americal Division (23d Infantry Division) with headquarters at Chu Lai on June 1, 1969. The Commander was Major General Charles Gettys. The division was by far the largest division in Vietnam with a strength of about 24,000 men. This included many units attached but was not an integral part of the Division. When I assumed command, a Brigade of the 101st Airborne Division, another 5,000 men, was attached to the Americal Division, making the total strength of the division close to 30,000 men. The Americal Division was under the command of the III MAF (III Marine Amphibious Force) commanded by Lieutenant General Herman Nickerson, U.S. Marine Corps.

At the ceremony for me to take command of the Americal Division, General Nickerson and his Marine Division Commander were present. During the reception after the ceremony, the Marine Division Commander told me how hard it would be to work for General Nickerson. I did not find this to be true. I worked closely with General Nickerson, and we got along very well. I received outstanding support from him and could always depend on him in supporting most operations that I proposed. My picture as the Division Commander is at the end of this chapter (Inclusion #1).

Major Colin Powell Was My G-1

It is interesting to note that when I took command of the Americal Division, my G-1 (Personnel Officer) was Major Colin Powell, who became the Chairman of the Joint Chiefs of Staff and then later became the Secretary of State. It was obvious that Major Powell was an outstanding officer. At the end of this chapter is a copy of a letter that I received from General Powell (Inclusion #2). This letter is in response to my letter of congratulations to him when he was nominated for Secretary of State, and I also informed him of Glenda's death.

Americal Division Area of Operation

The Americal Division's area of operation, in the northern part of South Vietnam, was about 125 miles long. The area included the Provinces of Quang Ngai, Quang Tin, and part of Quang Nam. We could not travel very far by road because we never knew where the enemy was located. The brigades had fire bases throughout the area, usually on top of a hill where we had control of the ground around us. I would visit as many fire bases as I could each day, especially where the action was taking place. I would leave my headquarters between 7:00 and 8:00 a.m. each day, including Sundays, depending on the length of the morning briefing regarding what went on the night before, and would return by 5:00 to 7:00 p.m. each day, depending on the daylight hours. I preferred not to fly after dark unless it was necessary. A map of the northern part of South Vietnam is at the end of this chapter (Inclusion #3).

My orders from General Nickerson were very general. I was to keep the areas that I controlled secure, and to expand the areas when it appeared feasible for the benefit of the civilian population so that they would have more land to cultivate. The latter part of my mission – to expand the areas – was more difficult. In some areas, we were able to clear trees and growth so that the enemy would not have a place to hide. This helped the farmers and they liked what we had done. I was also given the order to support my counterpart – the 2d ARVN Division – to the best of my ability. I quickly learned that giving the 2d ARVN Division the support they needed and helping them as much as I could, relieved some of the fighting that the troops in the Americal Division had been performing. At the end of this chapter is a letter from the 2d

ARVN Division Commander on this subject, thanking me for the support that made his Division the best in Vietnam (Inclusion #4).

Aircraft Commander (AC) Wanted to Install an Armored Seat Where I Sat

Shortly after I took command, my aircraft commander brought an aircraft maintenance technician to my aircraft and recommended that they install an armored seat where I sat. He said that they had found as many as three bullets lodged in the aircraft after a one day flight with General Gettys, but General Gettys would not agree to install an armored seat. I told them that while I was in the rear area I had seen some armored seats installed, and I was sure that they would come out quickly in a crash. The technician was a very persuasive person; he convinced me that he could install an armored seat that would be as strong as the seats used by the pilots. I agreed to have the seat installed. It was done that evening after I returned from a full day in the field. (When my helicopter crashed, March 17, 1970, the report states that the armored seat helped to save my life.)

Aircraft Availability

The Americal Division had more aircraft than a regular infantry division. The aircraft consisted of the 16th Aviation Group, the 123rd Aviation Battalion, and the 14th Combat Aviation Battalion. The 14th CAB was the largest aviation battalion in Vietnam with about 1,600 personnel and 129 aircraft. All of these aircraft also gave support to the 2nd ARVN Division. I soon learned, however, that we always had a shortage of aircraft. In fact, we were flying only about 50% of our aircraft when we should have been flying 85%. I immediately began to look into this problem. The aircraft commanders told me that the problem was that they could not get spare parts as soon as they needed them. The spare parts were available in the Saigon area, but we could not get delivery when we needed it. I went to see the 101st Airborne Division Commander to see if they were able to do better. They were flying about 85% of their aircraft because they had a dedicated plane to pick up and deliver their parts.

I came back to my headquarters and discussed the problem with my Air Force Liaison Officer. He told me that we could get dedicated space on the regular supply aircraft but that it would take three to six months to build a case for such dedicated space. I told him that we needed the space now so that we could get our aircraft in the air. I asked him to get me the name and telephone number of the Commander of the supply aircraft so that I could discuss the problem with him. He countered with the offer to attempt to get some dedicated space through his own contacts. Within 24 hours, he had procured X number of tons of dedicated space for our spare parts with the understanding that it could be increased each week if we could justify that we needed more space. We added a few hundred pounds every week for the next three weeks. Within a month we were flying about 85% of our aircraft instead of 50%. We then had enough aircraft to meet our needs most of the time, plus give better support to the 2d ARVN Division.

June 1969: Heavy Fighting

Communist sappers continued to harass Americal firebases during June, and infantrymen repelled a heavy attack on Landing Zone East, 11 miles west of Tam Ky in early June, killing 55 NVA and seven Viet Cong. During four days of fierce fighting throughout the division starting June 8, Americal forces killed 249 NVA and 87 VC, while capturing 89 assorted enemy weapons. By the second week in June, U.S. forces had accounted for more than 130 NVA and 40 VC killed in the Lamar Plain area alone.

July 1969: Operation Russell Beach

On July 21, 1969, the Americal Division concluded Operation Russell Beach on the Batangan Peninsula, 20 miles south of Chu Lai. The massive pacification effort was concluded with the resettlement of more than 1,200 refugees on the peninsula after it had been cleared of enemy bunkers and sanctuaries. But the overall pacification effort in the area continued as an intensive drive to upgrade small hamlets and villages north of Quang Ngai City.

July 21, 1969: Neil Armstrong and Buzz Aldrin Land on the Moon

I remember well when Neil Armstrong, Buzz Aldrin, and Michael Collins blasted off for a landing on the moon on July 21, 1969. We were able to see some of it on our TV in Vietnam. Neil Armstrong and

Buzz Aldrin were on the moon, while Michael Collins flew around the moon to pick them up later. I knew Michael Collins very well. We had lockers close to each other in the Pentagon Officers Athletic Club (POAC) for years, both before and after his trip to the moon. We had many conversations but never discussed his trip to the moon. I also knew his brother, Brigadier General James Collins.

August 1969: Continued Heavy Fighting

The Hiep Duc Refugee Center and two Americal Firebases, Landing Zone Center and Landing Zone West, were believed to be prime targets for the 2d NVA Division. In early August, elements of the 4th Battalion, 31st Infantry, beat off a ground attack at Landing Zone West, killing 59 enemy soldiers.

On August 18, 1969, infantrymen of the 196th Brigade began a battle that killed more than 312 NVA soldiers in 72 hours of fighting in the blistering heat on the Que Son valley floor. Three days later, 103 more enemy soldiers were killed by artillery and air strikes as the battle of the Hiep Duc and Que Son valleys erupted. Their enemy was the well entrenched 2d NVA Division.

Despite enemy heavy automatic weapons fire, Americal Division helicopters continued to fly along the valley airspace, bringing supplies and reinforcements to the men of the 196th Brigade. On the morning of August 19, a helicopter was shot down over Hill 102 inside NVA occupied territory.

Thousands of artillery rounds pounded the NVA bunker complexes during those last days of August. Scores of tactical air strikes echoed through the Hiep Duc and Que Son valleys. Slowly the enemy began to withdraw to the North toward the rugged Nui Chom ridgeline. The American forces pursued determinedly. By August 29, 1969, the major sources of enemy resistance in the Hiep Duc vicinity had been irreparably crushed.

In September 1969, salt became the topic of discussion to the south of Chu Lai as elements of the 198th Brigade's 5th Battalion, 46th Infantry, uncovered more than 292 tons. It was extracted from its Communist storehouses and distributed throughout the area by the

Government of South Vietnam.

August – September 1969: Americal Division Had Some Very Tough Fighting

As you can see from the above, the Americal Division had some tough fighting during this time. In late September 1969, General William B. Rosson, the Deputy Commander in Chief, Military Assistance Command, Vietnam (MACV), spent a day with me in the field. He later wrote the following letter to a friend and sent me a copy. Only a part of the letter is shown.

"29 September 1969

Dear ----------

Only last week I spent a full day with Lloyd Ramsey in the northern reaches of the country. He is doing the thoroughgoing job you would expect of him – indeed, the Americal Division has experienced probably the toughest campaigning of any of our major units during the past couple of months. I'll relay your regards to him when we next get together.

Sincerely,"

Many times during this heavy fighting, I would hover over a fire base, or where the troops were fighting in the field, get in contact with the commander on the ground, and try to give him support, i.e. artillery or air support. I would keep one radio in contact with the Brigade commander to ensure that he agreed with what I was doing. We also picked up lightly wounded soldiers and took them to the hospital. Many times we would pick up Vietnamese civilians who wished to be evacuated to safer areas and turn them over to the Province Chiefs.

Award of the Distinguished Flying Cross (DFC)

As Bill Rosson said in his letter, "…the Americal Division has experienced probably the toughest campaigning of any of our major units during the past couple of months." At the end of this chapter

(Inclusion #5 and #5-2) is the citation for my DFC, dated October 18, 1969, which gives a good description of what we were encountering. The citation covers the period August 18-25, 1969, but this type of fighting went on for weeks.

November 1969: Planned My R&R to Go Home

I planned to take my two weeks of R&R to go home in November 1969. I hated to leave the division in command of one of my assistant division commanders, Brigadier General Edwin Powell, Jr. He was a fine officer, but his specialty was aviation. The fighting was very difficult at this time, and General Powell had no experience with commanding ground troops in combat. The other assistant division commander was Brigadier General John W. Donaldson, who had just been promoted to General Officer, after being my Chief of Staff. I discussed this with Lieutenant General Frank Mildren, C.G. USARV, and asked him if I could get Brigadier General Howard H. Cooksey from his staff to command the division while I took my R&R. Cooksey had been an assistant division commander, Americal Division, before I arrived, had combat command experience, and knew the Americal Division. General Mildren agreed.

November 1969: Rice Denial

Rice denial operations achieved tremendous success. On November 19, 1969, the 3d Battalion, 21st Infantry captured 20,000 pounds of rice. Numerous other large caches of enemy salt and rice were found and were turned over to the government of South Vietnam.

November 1969: Selected Lieutenant Colonel H. Norman Schwarzkopf as a Battalion Commander

In November 1969, my Adjutant General Lieutenant Colonel James A. Ralph, Jr. brought me a short list of names of lieutenant colonels who had been sent into the country for staff assignments and were now recommended for command. In looking at the list, I noted that one, Lieutenant Colonel Norman Schwarzkopf, worked for Major General George L. Mabry, Jr., a very close friend of mine and a Medal of Honor winner in World War II. I also noted that he had been the Aide de Camp to another friend of mine, Major General Charles E. Johnson, who had been the Chief of Staff 3d Infantry Division in World War II while I was the G-3. I knew if a Medal of Honor man would release this man from a staff position to take a command position, he must be pretty good. I also knew that General Johnson was very selective in picking any officer who worked for him. I accepted Lieutenant Colonel Schwarzkopf, and, upon his arrival in December 1969, I assigned him to command a battalion.

My Visit with Glenda at Home

My visit home to see Glenda once again was a wonderful period. We saw all of our families and had some great times together. However, it was very tough to say goodbye once again, not knowing if we would ever see each other again. One never knows what may happen in combat. I was away from the Division for about three weeks in November 1969.

December 24, 1969: Bob Hope Brought His Group to the Americal Division for a Show

On December 24, 1969, Bob Hope brought his group to the Americal Division in Chu Lai, Vietnam. In his group was Neil Armstrong, who had landed on the moon in July 1969. I wondered how the soldiers would accept him because they wanted to see beautiful women and hear comedy from Bob Hope. I was pleasantly surprised when Mr. Hope announced Neil Armstrong and the troops gave him a long standing ovation for his successful trip to the moon. As usual, Bob Hope gave an outstanding show to the almost 3,000 troops we were able to assemble in an area that we felt was fairly safe from enemy shells. We were lucky to have good weather during the show because December weather can be bad.

By the time the show was over, the weather started to get worse. Bob Hope was going to an aircraft carrier from the Americal Division and my helicopters were to take his group to the carrier. Bob and I were talking when his travel manager came to him and said that the weather was so bad that we could not get to the carrier. He recommended to Bob that he return to Saigon and cancel the trip to the aircraft carrier. Bob told his travel manager that we had most of the afternoon to wait for the weather to change and then asked me if I could take care of them for a few hours to see if that would happen. I told him that between my quarters and my mess, we could take care of his group with no problem. We could fix them some food and have drinks for the group. He then asked me if I had someone that could check on the weather. I told him that my aircraft commander would check the weather and keep us informed every 30 minutes or when the weather changed for the good. When the first report came in, the weather was getting worse. Bob's travel manager once again recommended that they return to Saigon. Bob told him that we would wait a while.

Bob was having some trouble with his eyes, and he was also tired. He asked me if there were some place that he could lie down to rest. I took him to my quarters and gave him my bed; he was very pleased. The next weather report gave no improvement. When I went to tell Bob, he was asleep so I did not bother him. I told his travel manager, who wanted to wake Bob and recommend that they return to Saigon. When I would not allow this, he became very upset. On the next report, the weather was improving slightly but not enough to get to the aircraft carrier. The travel manager once again recommended that they return to Saigon.

Bob asked me if we could wait another hour and still make the carrier if the weather cleared. I checked with my aircraft commander and he said that was about as long as they could wait. It was not very long until my aircraft commander came in and told me that the weather was now good enough to take off for the aircraft carrier. We loaded Bob and his group on buses and took them to the choppers for the trip to the aircraft carrier. I was very proud of Bob Hope that afternoon. He wanted to wait as long as he could before canceling a trip to the aircraft carrier to entertain our fighting men. Bob thanked me again and again for taking such good care of his group so that they could get to the carrier and give their show there. Later I received the following message:
    "WE'RE BACK HOME WITH GREAT MEMORIES OF OUR TOUR AND WE HAVE YOU TO THANK FOR YOUR HELP AND YOUR COURTESIES. MAY YOU AND THE MEN OF YOUR COMMAND HAVE A GREAT '70. REGARDS, BOB HOPE."

At the end of this chapter are pictures of Bob Hope and me at the Americal Division (Inclusions #6 through #6-4).

Christmas 1969: The Three Generals to Visit the Troops

Christmas 1969 was not a happy day for me or for the soldiers in the field. I had two assistant Division Commanders, Brigadier Generals Edwin L. Powell, Jr. and John W. Donaldson. I called them in the day before Christmas and told them that I wanted the three of us to wish a Merry Christmas to as many soldiers as we could see. I divided the area into three parts and said that we would leave the headquarters at daylight and return before dark. It turned out to be a much better day than I expected, and the soldiers were happy to see us. Most of all, there was very little fighting in the area that day.

It was getting late in the afternoon and I was visiting my last firebase. The Sergeant that was taking me around told me that I had seen every soldier on that firebase. I asked him if there were some outposts that I had not visited. He said that there was an outpost about 100 feet straight down the side of a high hill but that it was very difficult to get there. There were two soldiers in that outpost. I decided to go see them. It was a treacherous descent down the hill. When we arrived there, the Sergeant called to their dugout and said, "The General is here and wants to wish you a Merry Christmas."

The answer came back, "Tell the General that I am on the phone with the President and come back tomorrow."

The two soldiers were convinced that no general would struggle down that hill to wish them a Merry Christmas. When the Sergeant went into the dugout and brought the two soldiers out, they could not believe that I was there. I told them that I thought their reply was very good and we had a good laugh. We enjoyed a few minutes of Christmas cheer and had a nice conversation about their families. I then departed with their many thanks for understanding their comment and for coming that far to see them. To me that trip alone was worth the entire day. At the end of this chapter (Inclusion #7 through 7-3) is a copy of the 1969 Christmas card for the Americal Division.

I also ordered that every soldier be served a hot meal on Christmas Day if it were possible to get one to their location. Due to the lack of enemy action, I believe that every soldier received a hot meal on Christmas Day. The helicopter pilots flew many missions to get those meals to the soldiers in the field.

December 28, 1969 – January 8, 1970: The Peers Inquiry of the Massacre at My Lai

In early December 1969, I began to receive messages about Lieutenant General William R. Peers coming to Vietnam as part of his inquiry into the massacre at My Lai. The messages told me that I was to house and feed his group, secure the My Lai area for their investigation, and give them helicopter support and any other needed support that I could provide. General Peers and his group arrived on December 28, 1969. General Peers stayed in my quarters with me, and we were able to provide quarters for the others. He and his top attorney, Robert MacCrate, from New York, ate in my mess. I told General Peers that he could use my living room or my porch for his staff conferences and that I would stay out of his way.

Before General Peers and his group arrived, I made plans to secure the area and clear it of land mines. We were able to do this with only one minor injury. I was not entirely satisfied that we had cleared all of the land mines; therefore, I kept a team of experts on the ground with the Peers group when they were in the area. Many times they were removing mines in front of where the group wished to go. No one was injured during the investigation.

My Lai was in Quang Ngai Province, on the northeast coast of South Vietnam. It was a small rural sub-hamlet of about 700 people located in the Tu Cung hamlet of Son My village. Because I knew the previous Division Commander, Major General S.W. Koster, very well, I did not get involved in the investigation, not wishing to take sides. As I understand the situation and from what I have read, on March 16, 1968 Lieutenant William Calley and his 1st Platoon, C Company, under the command of Captain Ernest L. Medina, 1st Battalion, 20th Infantry, 11th Infantry Brigade, came into an area near My Lai (4) by helicopter. (There were four My Lai sub-hamlets. The Army gave them numbers.) As I understand, Lieutenant Calley and his men rounded up all of the civilians in the hamlet. There are reports that Lieutenant Calley was fired upon and that he and his men returned fire. Other reports stated that Lieutenant Calley fired the first shot and his men joined in. Since I stayed clear of the investigation, I do not know what happened, except from what I read later. At any rate, there were over 100 civilians killed in the incident.

The first few days that General Peers was there he wanted to fly over the My Lai area. He wished to cover the entire area, not just the part that had been cleared. He was in an aircraft with Warrant Officer Hugh Thompson, the helicopter pilot who allegedly acted to save some of the Vietnamese. I was in the other helicopter with Robert MacCrate. I had given specific instructions to my pilots not to fly lower than 1500 feet in the area because enemy small arms fire could hit our aircraft below that altitude. Although I had cleared the immediate area where the investigation would take place, there were still enemy pockets around the area.

The only time that any aircraft could go below 1500 feet was to land in the area at a location that I had secured or to fly over the immediate cleared area. It was not long until the other aircraft got below 1500 feet outside of the cleared area. I told my pilot to call the aircraft to obey my orders to stay above 1500 feet. The aircraft immediately returned to 1500 feet, but the pilot said that General Peers wanted to get lower so that he could see better. I told my pilot to tell the other pilot to tell General Peers that I was responsible for his safety and that he would abide by my rules.

When we landed, I immediately went to General Peers and told him that when safety was involved, I was in charge, even though he was in charge of the investigation and outranked me. General Peers agreed and apologized for his actions. General Peers wanted W.O. Hugh Thompson to fly him over the area at a very low level and point out what he had seen on March 16, 1968. When my people came to me with that request, I said that I could not control the area in which he would fly nor could I control his altitude when and if he flew. Therefore, I would not approve of such a flight even if he were qualified to fly the aircraft. I asked if they had checked his qualifications. They had not, so they checked his qualifications and he had not kept up his flying time. That alone turned down the request.

General Peers wished to make the low-level flight with W.O. Thompson in the same aircraft with him. I arranged for one of my pilots to make this flight over the cleared area at a very low altitude. He was well-qualified to fly inside the boundary of the cleared area. General Peers, in his book *The My Lai Inquiry*, page 135, stated the following: *"On January 1, 1970, we made a low level reconnaissance flight over the sites identified by Thompson. He flew as copilot in one helicopter, and I sat behind in the observer seat. Two gunships accompanied us to provide protection, and General Ramsey, in his command helicopter, directed the operation, with Bob MacCrate as a passenger."*

General Peers finished his investigation and left on January 8, 1970. He and Robert MacCrate expressed their appreciation for the support they had received from the Americal Division.

January 1970: Attack

On January 4, 1970, Americal troops of Company B, 4th Battalion, 3rd Infantry, fought off an enemy mortar and sapper attack against their night defensive position. The infantrymen withstood the intense mortar barrage and ground attack and killed 29 of the insurgents.

Fierce action was reported in the 196th area of operation once again on January 13-14, 1970. A task force consisting of 1/1 Cavalry, 1st Battalion, 46th Infantry, overran the positions, resulting in 40 enemy killed and a large quantity of munitions confiscated. 196th Brigade soldiers found themselves in the thick of it the next day as they recorded a total of 62 NVA soldiers killed in action in the "Pineapple Forest" area of Tam Ky.

The first three days of February 1970 saw elements of 1st Battalion, 46th Infantry, in constant contact with the enemy forces south of Tam Ky. During the action the battalion was credited with more than 40 enemy kills. The remaining days of February produced a steady decrease in enemy activity.

1970: Demonstration of a Viet Cong Going Through Triple Concertina Wire

We had a Viet Cong that had defected to our side. He gave us a demonstration of how they could go through triple concertina wire in less than 60 seconds without getting a scratch. This was an eye-opener to most of us. Pictures of his demonstration are at the end of this chapter (Inclusion #8 through #8-3).

1970: Success in Quang Tin Province

I quote from *U.S. Marines in Vietnam, Vietnamization and Redeployment,* 1970-1971, page 146: *"Major General Lloyd B. Ramsey, USA, who commanded the Americal Division until the spring of 1970, discussed the success in Quang Tin Province containing the VC: 'The weakness of the VC was a direct result of the Americal Division, 2d ARVN Division, RF's, PF's, Province Chiefs, Caps, all under the supervision of III MAF and supported by Marine, Navy, and AF air supports. A fine team effort. Also we received outstanding supports from Naval gunfire.'"*

Weather in Vietnam

The weather in Vietnam varied in different areas. In our area, the summer months were very dry with the temperature getting to 110 degrees in the daytime and the humidity 90 to 95 percent. One day I went to Tam Ky to pick up the Province Chief of Quang Tin, who wanted to take me to a village that we had secured. The village was in a valley of some of the mountains. When we arrived there, the thermometer read 127 degrees in the shade. We toured the area, talked to the village chief, who was very pleased with the way things were going, and were ready to return to Tam Ky. Before we loaded, the village chief asked the Province Chief if we could take three of his people back to Tam Ky. The Province Chief asked me if they could come along. I told him that the pilot would make the decision as to whether we could carry that much weight in this heat. The pilot said that he thought he might be able to take two, but he was not sure that he could carry three more people. He said that we could load two; he would then go up 50 to 100 feet and he could tell by then if he could take one, two, or three. We loaded two on the aircraft and the pilot flew up about 100 feet, hovered for a short time, and told me on the radio that he could carry one more person. The village chief was very happy.

In January, February, and March, the temperature would get down to about 65 degrees with the humidity remaining very high. One of the first days that the temperature was down to 65 degrees, I was visiting a firebase, checking some of the fighting positions. They all had dug foxholes for protection, but the men were lying on the ground outside the foxhole. When I asked them why they were not using the foxhole for protection, they said that it was much colder in the foxhole than on top of the ground. This was hard for me to believe so I climbed in the hole and stayed about five minutes. By this time, I could feel the difference.

When I returned to my headquarters, I had my staff research this problem. They came back with the answer that the temperature in the foxhole could be at least five degrees cooler than on top of the ground. With this information, I got special warm clothing for the firebases to use so that the soldiers could keep warm and receive the protection of the foxhole in case of an enemy attack.

Early 1970: Change of Boundary Between the Americal Division and Marines

Based on the fighting that we had done in the Que Son area, I noted that we were having problems with the enemy because of the boundary location. I quote from the book *U.S. Marines in Vietnam, Vietnamization and Redeployment*, 1970-1971, page 46.

"Before the boundary between the 7th Marines and Americal Division was moved south from the foothills of the Que Son to the Ly Ly River, the Marines and Army units encountered many problems controlling enemy movement through the foothills. Major General Lloyd B. Ramsey, who commanded the Americal at the time, recalled why the change was made: 'Because of the problems we were having due to the boundary being in the hills, I made a recommendation to General Nickerson that either I move north and control the mountains and the valley or the Marines move south. Based on what he told me, I believe he was concerned about giving me any more area because I was already overextended – it was just a matter of degree.'"

Picture of a Fire Support Base

At the end of this chapter is a picture of Fire Support Base Center and Fire Support Base Hawk Hill (Inclusion #9). You can see that Firebase Center is on the top of a hill. There is also a picture of Firebase Hawk Hill, which is on a very large hill. It was in a more secure area, but even so they had to have guards around the perimeter day and night.

Trying to Make Villages Safe for the Civilians to Grow Their Crops

The enemy would hide in growths around the villages; many times they would harass the villagers in such a way that they could not work in the fields to grow their crops. General Nickerson had told me that he had cleared some areas for the Marines, and the civilians in the area liked what had been done. I told General Nickerson that I had two areas that I would like to clear to help the civilians. I had coordinated my plan with the Province Chief and the ARVN Division Commander. They also cleared it with the village chiefs. General Nickerson sent the Rome plows down to my area. I asked the 2d ARVN Division Commander, BG Nguyen-Van-Toan, to clear the enemy out of the area, which he did immediately. With the 2d ARVN Division providing security, we then cleared the growth with the Rome plows so that the enemy had fewer places to hide. The villagers felt much safer to work in the fields, knowing the enemy was not hiding in the bushes and would not harass them.

Agent Orange

Agent Orange was a chemical used to defoliate the trees in order that we could see the enemy in the jungle. At the time I was in Vietnam, we were told that it was safe for our troops; therefore, we used it often. I remember many times flying into an area where we had just used Agent Orange, and it would make my eyes water. Later it was proven that Agent Orange caused ill health for many troops months after they had been exposed to it. The type of illness varied, with some ending up with cancer. To the best of my knowledge, I had no ill effects from breathing Agent Orange.

In Addition to Fighting the Enemy, There Were Always Some Important Administrative Problems to Solve; Reenlistment Was a Big One.

USARV constantly pushed units to increase their reenlistment rate. When I took command of the Americal Division, I learned that the reenlistment rate in the Americal Division was below average for the units in Vietnam. Along with many other problems, I started working on this one with my Command Sergeant Major, Sam S. Borrelli. In my opinion Sam was the most outstanding Sergeant Major in the Army. He had a way of working with the enlisted men that made him highly respected by officers, NCO's, and all other men in the Americal Division. It was not long until the Americal Division was at the top of the chart for unit re-enlistment in Vietnam. I was very proud of Sergeant Borrelli and all of the officers and NCO's for accomplishing this task while their primary mission was fighting the war.

Letter from General Arthur E. Brown, Retired

General Arthur E. Brown commanded the 1st Battalion, 52d Infantry during the time that I commanded the Americal Division. Art was one of the most outstanding battalion commanders in the division. He was a soldier's soldier – always looking out for his men. His company commanders admired him greatly. Art held many distinguished positions in the Army, ending his career as the Vice Chief of Staff of the Army, the number two position in the Army. One paragraph from Art's letter reads as follows:

"The days we spent in the Americal Division are permanently engraved in my mind. Those memories are positive largely because of the leadership climate you set throughout the Division. You were a great Division Commander and I am proud to have had the opportunity to serve under you."

Letter from Colonel William Cate, Jr., an Officer in the Americal Division

"Early in my commissioned career, I learned that it wasn't one of my duties to 'rate' my superiors (it was the other way around.), but I have to tell you that I viewed you as a superb Division Commander – with the perfect grasp of the Commander in a combined military/political environment. You earned my sincere admiration. I should have told you this long ago, I suppose. We put so many things off while time keeps marching on."

Letter from Command Sergeant Major Sam S. Borrelli – CSM of the Americal Division

As I have previously written, Command Sergeant Major Sam S. Borrelli was the most outstanding CSM in the Army. He had an ability to work with the enlisted soldiers that made him admired by both NCO's and officers. These are quotes from Sam's letter:

"I strongly believe you would have been promoted to four stars, had your helicopter not crashed, causing your injuries and medical retirement.

"You impressed me with many of your actions concerning the troops. But to command a division of 30,000 men and fly over 100 miles everyday to each firebase to be briefed on activities in the areas and speak to the soldiers, that was outstanding.

"You gave an order on Thanksgiving and Christmas that every soldier would be fed a hot meal, even if they were in the jungle. It was a big order, but it was followed through. This was the talk of the Division.

"When you gave an order you were always level headed and never raised your voice. Your attitude was respected and your orders always carried out. That tells me we had a solid General.

"I talked to an Army Vet a short time back and he mentioned while he was at Fort Benning he had a Colonel that was the best officer he ever met. I asked him if he remembered his name. He said yes, Colonel Lloyd Ramsey. I told him you were now a Major General and commanded the Americal Division in Vietnam. He said, 'Great, he was one damn good officer,' I agree.

"I believe the biggest battle in Vietnam was in the 196th Brigade area. North Vietnam had a division forward and two regiments dug in. The battle was won by the Americal Units under your command. You and I, General, were continually in the battle areas to support the troops.

"Recruiting was a big item in Vietnam, a large trophy was presented to you by a three star General for recruiting the most men to reenlist in combat. It was your Division General, you gave the order and it was done. I enjoyed it.

"General, at all times your appearance was always as a General should be. Despite the heat, humidity, rain, etc. you always presented the appearance of a distinguished and respected General.

"Thank you, General, for allowing me a chopper to visit the troops on my own to talk to them personally. I'd like to think by visiting them, they knew I cared for their welfare too.

"I'll end this by saying you are a Soldier's General. I could write a book about our tour together, General. It's no wonder when I talk about you – often, Fran asked if you could walk on water? After meeting you, she said 'I see what you mean, he's a great man.'

"General, I can't end this without saying: I flew with you everyday except the day the helicopter crashed. I keep wondering if maybe I had been there, I could have done something to prevent the crash. It is on my mind constantly."

INCL. # 1

General Colin L. Powell, USA (Ret)
909 North Washington Street, Suite 767
Alexandria, Virginia 22314

22/12/00

Dear Lloyd,

Thanks for your good wishes.

We were saddened to learn of Glenda's passing. Please accept our sympathy.

Sincerely,

INCL. # 2

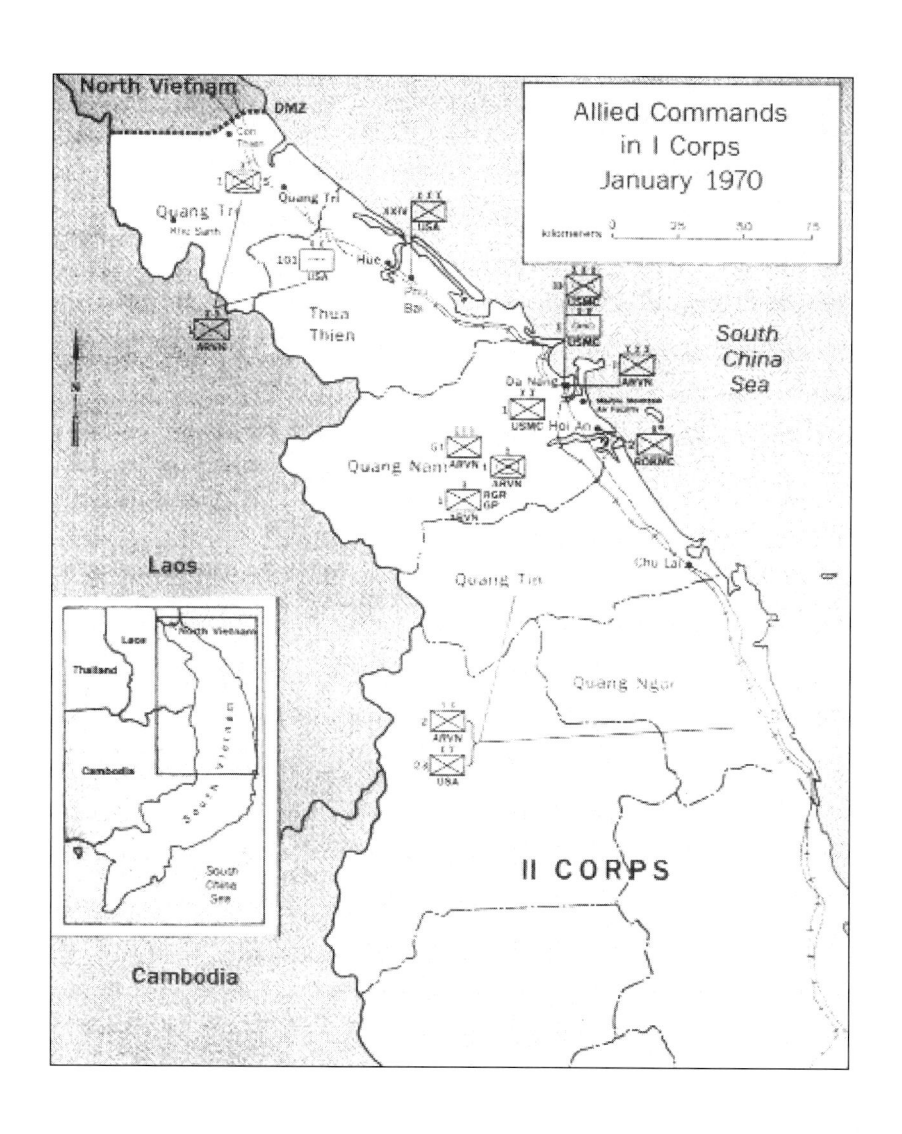

INCL. # 3

29 April 1970.

Major General LLOYD B. RAMSEY
CG, Americal Division.
APO, San Francisco 96374.

Dear General RAMSEY,

I have received your letter and I was really moved after reading it. My regret is that you have got that accident and had to leave before the time set.

During your tenure, our 2nd Infantry Division had been fully supported materially and morally, by you and your staff & men. Thank to that the 2nd Infantry Division has been rated the best division in the Republic of Viet-Nam. And it was due mainly to your sincere cooperation.

I have cooperated with many Advisors and friendly units, but you were the best of our friends who have cooperated the most sincerely and with the highest sense of mutual affection and assistance.

It is reportedly known that you are in convalescence at home; I hope that you will recover quickly and have the nicest time with your family.

Awaiting good news from you, I hope we will meet again some time in the future, to satisfy my heartfelt longing for you.

Very sincerely yours,

BG NGUYEN-VAN-TOAN
CG, 2nd ARVN Inf. Div.

INCL. # 4

CORRECTED COPY

DEPARTMENT OF THE ARMY
Headquarters, United States Army Vietnam
APO San Francisco 96375

GENERAL ORDERS
NUMBER   3881

18 October 1969

AWARD OF THE DISTINGUISHED FLYING CROSS

1. TC 320. The following AWARD is announced.

RAMSEY, LLOYD B 400-54-8204. MAJOR GENERAL United States Army, Headquarters and Headquarters Company, Americal Division, APO 96374
Awarded: Distinguished Flying Cross
Date action: 18 to 25 August 1969
Theater: Republic of Vietnam
Reason: For heroism, while participating in aerial flight, evidenced by voluntary actions above and beyond the call of duty in the Republic of Vietnam: Major General Ramsey distinguished himself by exceptionally valorous actions during the period 18 August to 25 August 1969 while serving as Commanding General of the Americal Division. During that time, elements of the 196th Infantry Brigade were engaged with two regiments of the 2d North Vietnamese Army Division twenty-five miles west of Tam Ky in Hiep Duc Valley. The enemy had established themselves in numerous fortified positions from which they placed effective antiaircraft fire on friendly combat support aircraft and two strategic landing zones in the area. Despite knowing that a large number of friendly aircraft had been damaged by hostile ground fire, General Ramsey unhesitatingly orbited many battlefields in his helicopter during critical phases of contact in order to assess personally the tactical situation and ensure the judicious allocation of division resources. He repeatedly exposed himself to hostile fire and several times landed at potentially dangerous landing zones to coordinate with battalion commanders. His firm leadership and sound judgment contributed greatly to the early termination of the battle and the successful completion of the mission. Major General Ramsey's courage and devotion to duty were in keeping with the highest traditions of the military service and reflect great credit upon himself, his unit, and the United States Army.
Authority: By direction of the President, under the provisions of the Act of Congress, approved 2 July 1926.

INCL. # 5

GENERAL ORDERS NUMBER 3881, dated 18 October 1969, DA, Headquarters, United States Army Vietnam, APO San Francisco 96375 (Cont)

FOR THE COMMANDER:

OFFICIAL: GEORGE L. MABRY, JR.
                                      Major General, US Army
                                      Chief of Staff

John A. O'Brien (signature)

JOHN A. O'BRIEN
Colonel, AGC
Adjutant General

DISTRIBUTION:
  5 - Each unit concerned
  1 - AVHIG
  1 - AVHIO
  1 - AVHAG-A
  1 - AVHAG-AR
 20 - AVHAG-PD
  6 - CINCUSARPAC

SPECIAL DISTRIBUTION:
  2 - TAGO, DA ATTN: AGPE-F
     (for official personnel file)
  1 - Chief, GOB, ODCSPER, DA

INCL. # 5-2

24 December, 1969
I welcome Bob Hope as he
arrives at the Americal Division.

INCL. # 6

I am presenting Bob Hope an Americal Division plaque. See picture, at right, enlarged

INCL. # 6-2

INCL. # 6-3

Bob Hope, me and Lt. Harker.

Some of Bob Hope's group waiting in my mess for the weather to clear.

INCL. # 6-4

𝔗his season's
wish and goal of.

𝔗he
Americal Division

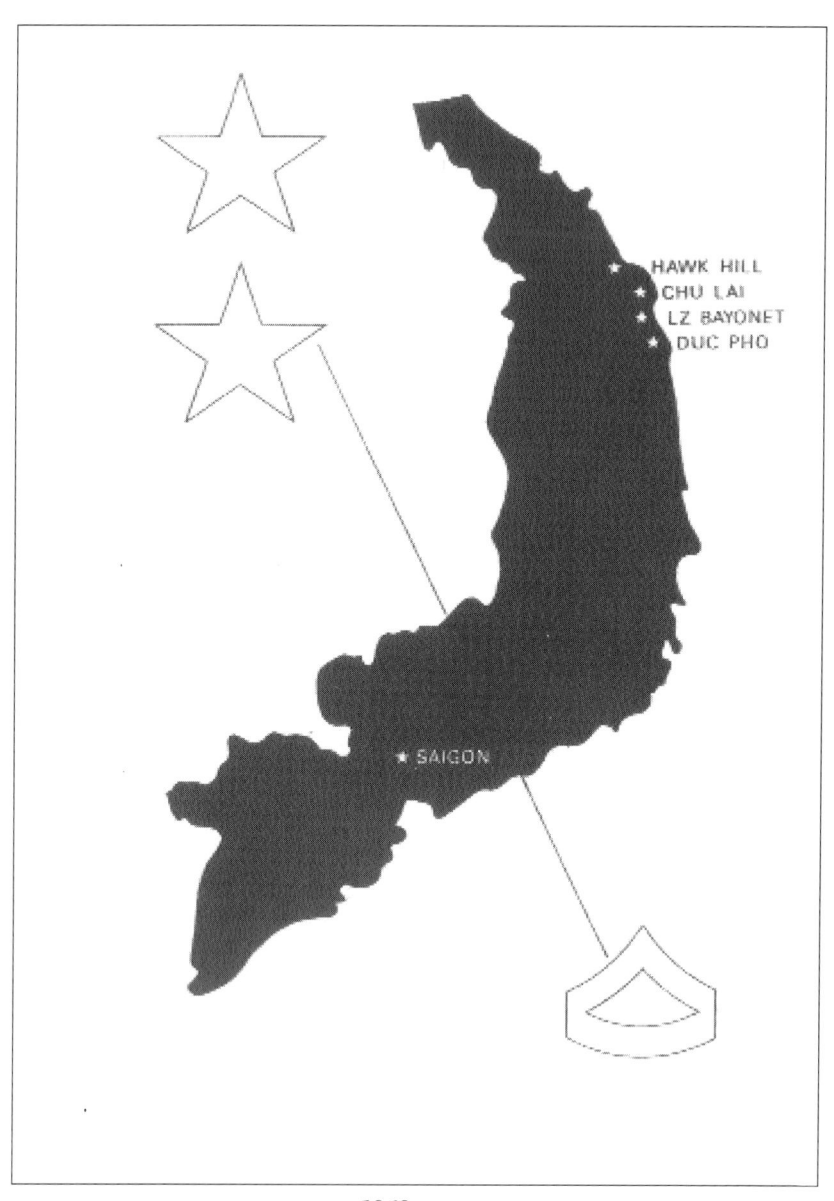

1969
CHRISTMAS CARD
Inside Page

INCL. # 7-2

1969
CHRISTMAS CARD
Inside Page

The next two pages show a Viet Cong, who had defected to our side, giving a demonstration of how they could go through triple concertina wire in less than 60 seconds without getting a scratch.

INCL. # 8

INCL. # 8-2

INCL. # 8-3

*Firebase Center
On top of a hill.*

Firebase Hawk Hill

INCL. # 9

CHAPTER 10

MARCH 17, 1970 – AUGUST 1, 1974 – VIETNAM – WASHINGTON, D.C.

March 17, 1970: Crashed in Helicopter – Missing in Action for 18 Hours

On March 17, 1970, I had spent most of the day in the field, as I usually did. We were planning a new operation, and I needed to get back to my headquarters by 4:00 p.m. for a briefing on the operation. We left Fire Support Base Center and headed to FSB Hawk Hill, where I needed to talk to the Battalion Commander. This was on the way to my headquarters. My pilot was a substitute Aircraft Commander (AC) because my regular pilot, Warrant Officer Carrol V. Lanier, had been grounded by the flight surgeon; he had flown seven days in a row without the proper rest. My pilot always refueled the aircraft at every stop which had fuel because he never knew where I might go next. At this stop, I told the pilot not to refuel the aircraft because I would only be there a very short time, and I needed to get back to my headquarters. Not refueling at this point later proved to have saved our lives.

A picture of my regular crew and my Aide, Captain Thomas J. Ruffing, is at the end of this chapter (Inclusion #1). My Crew Chief Specialist 4th Class Ray Murphy is not in the picture nor is Command Sergeant Major Sam S. Borrelli. Sergeant Borrelli flew with me many days of the week. On many of my flights I would have other passengers who needed to know the area. On this flight, I had Lieutenant Colonel Robert J. Thomas from Anaconda, Montana, who had been in Vietnam for three days and was going to take over a battalion, and Captain John P. Tucker from Lima, Ohio, who worked in the G-3 section and needed to know about the area.

As I explain the operations that went on in the division after my crash, I will mention call signs that are used in the report of the accident by Rattler 3.

    Saber 6 – Major General Lloyd B. Ramsey, C.G. Americal
        Division

Skater 67 – Major General Lloyd B. Ramsey's Helicopter

Rattler 6 – Major Tommie P. James, C.O. 71st Assault Helicopter Company

Rattler 3 – Captain Johnnie B. Hitt, Operations Officer, 71st AHC

King 6 – HC-130 aircraft, 3rd Aerospace Rescue and Recovery Group (ARRGP)

King 4 – Dispatched a HH-53E Jolley Green to pick up victims of the crash.

As we departed Fire Support Base Hawk Hill, the crew chief Ray Murphy, who sat behind me, reached over and connected my radio so that I could hear the crew's conversation. I quote from a report Rescue Saber 6:

"Chu Lai weather, this is Skater 67. What is current weather in Chu Lai?"

"This Chu Lai weather, currently 1500 feet overcast with one mile visibility outside of the clouds, Over."...

"Chu Lai, Skater 67 is a UH-1 climbing to 3000 feet request GCA."

"Skater 67, say position."

"This is 67, off Hawk Hill, heading 090 degrees."

"Roger 67, turn right for identification." Pause..."Skater 67, this Chu Lai approach, stop turn. Radar contact west of Hawk Hill. Turn to heading 090. If you want to expedite, I can let you down over the water and you should break out at 1500 feet."

"This is Skater 67, roger, we will take that procedure, over."

"This is Chu Lai, maintain 090 heading and I will take you out another 2 miles so you will be 5 miles out over the water."

"Skater 67, roger." ...

"Skater 67, descend to 1500 feet. Call me when you are VFR."

"Skater 67, roger."

The AC noted the time at 1556 and began his descent. General Ramsey, along with all other passengers that ride in a helicopter when they are flying in the clouds, noted how much the outside looked like the inside of a milk bottle. It was all white and seemed to be motionless."...

"Suddenly, out the front windscreen, the CG first saw light, then green, then trees. All this happened in moments. At the same time Chief Warrant Two Stephen C. Pike (Skater 67) yelled, "Trees!", he decelerated the helicopter by swiftly pulling the cyclic back into his gut...too late! The tail rotor caught the trees and the helicopter mushroomed into the jungle canopy, separating the tail rotor and then the complete tail boom as the forward force carried the disintegrating chopper into the side of the mountain...One of the two rotor blades struck the upside of the mountain while the blades were traveling toward the tail of the aircraft. The sudden stop of the rotor blade, traveling at 324 revolutions per minute, ripped the transmission out of its support and flung it into the living space of the passenger compartment, bringing the engine with it. This mass of heavy components killed Specialist Murphy as he sat in his crew chief seat. The flying hunk of metals tore through the back of the passenger seat and crashed forward. The mass continued its forward motion from the outside in killing LTC Thomas as it crushed him into the command and control console. The armored seat had saved General Ramsey's life, but it could not prevent the resulting serious injuries. He was knocked unconscious during the crash and would remain so almost throughout his rescue."

My comment: There were two other things that saved my life: 1. When we stopped at Hawk Hill Firebase, I told the pilot not to refuel the aircraft, which they always did where fuel was available because they never knew where I might go next. Having very little fuel in the aircraft may have saved the aircraft from burning. 2. The most important thing was that the good Lord was looking out for me.

"Deathly quiet followed. The breaking of plexiglass, the tearing of sheet metal, and the continuous whining of the turbine engine were no more. Wreckage, crew members, and passengers were scattered everywhere. Dazed and hurt, the survivors struggled to assess what had happened and, more importantly, the current situation. Enemy territory...did they hear us crash? Would they come for us? Who was alive? Who could fight? What did we have to fight with? Captain John P. Tucker felt for his .45 caliber pistol, an action more out of habit than intention. Little did he realize that out of two M-60 machine guns, which were mounted as door guns, four M-16 rifles, and various hand guns, his .45 was the only weapon recovered."

My comment: We had crashed in the jungle about seven miles west of Chu Lai and southwest of Hawk Hill. The question arises, how did we get seven miles inland when the pilot stated that he was headed 090 degrees (East) and Chu Lai had Skater 67 to make a right turn, found him west of Hawk Hill, and directed him to "turn to heading 090..."?

"This is Chu Lai, maintain 090 heading and I will take you out another 2 miles so you will be 5 miles out over the water."...

"Skater 67, descend to 1500 feet call me when you are VFR."

When we descended to 1500, we were about seven miles inland and the mountains and trees were 1500 feet high.

Quoting from another report of the crash, Rescue of a Downed General, 1st Battalion, 6th Infantry, U.S. Army, Vietnam: *"The aircraft crashed after 1600 hours...Apparently both the pilot and the radar operator thought the aircraft was northeast of Chu Lai. Instead, it was on a course that took it directly into the highest ridge of mountains, approximately seven miles west of the sprawling base..."*

"At approximately 1630, TACP Tam Ky, Vietnam, had monitored a distress call.

'Skater 67 approximately five miles northeast of LZ Pineapple/IFR and come up to some mountain.'

A survival radio carried by one of the crew members ultimately had enabled them to establish contact. Heroic efforts were undertaken in hazardous conditions by Major Tommie P. James, 71st Assault Helicopter Company, to reach the survivors."

My comment: Major James, C.O. 71st Assault Helicopter Company, Rattler 6, performed in an outstanding manner, flying his helicopter in extremely bad weather, trying to find us. Rattler 6 made contact with Skater 67 on the emergency radio and tried to home in on the radio signal, but the weather and mountains would prevent him from getting to the crash site, even though he knew approximately where the site was located.

"The ground rescue team was composed of soldiers from Co. C, 1st Battalion, 6th Infantry under a Capt. Trujillo. They were airlifted by CH-47 Chinook from LZ Fat City to a high, large grassy area below the hillsides to be searched. Although known as the 'golf course' for its appearance from the air, the LZ was deceiving. The drop-off point was covered with razor-sharp elephant grass standing over six feet tall. Once on the ground, the soldiers began their difficult trek to the crash."

Quoting from Rescue of Saber 6: *"By this time, the Joint Rescue Command and Control (JRCC) element, responsible for search and rescue operations throughout Southeast Asia, from the 3d Aerospace Rescue and Recovery Group (ARRGP) (USAF) had been alerted. One of the Group's HC-130 aircraft was on station and close enough to monitor the emergency transmissions. At least one and usually two of the HC-130 aircraft were in the air at all times and went by the call sign 'King'. King 6 was the call sign on this particular day. In addition, one USAF Forward Air Controller (FAC) was on station and went by call sign Jake. Jake was under the command and control of King 6."*

Night of March 17, 1970

"The intense activity did not stop during the night of March 17, the division operations center buzzed throughout the night executing the plan they had developed for March 18. The 71st AHC also planned for the next day. In coordination with Battalion, missions were assigned to each crew and the aircraft were assigned. Rattler maintenance assigned the snake doctor UF-1H to Rattler 6 for the next day's mission. The aviation Battalion commander would fly with Major James. Everyone in the company wanted the mission to go without hitch. Check and double check was the theme for the night."

"Through the 198th Brigade, the 1st of the 6th Infantry Battalion had been given the mission that day to move and secure the crash site. Lt Col H. Norman Schwarzkopf (who most people know as General Schwarzkopf of Desert Storm fame) commanded the 1/6th Infantry. A company from the 1/6th had been breaking bush since early evening. They would move all night one inch, one foot at a time through the thick jungle and bad weather with no food or rest."

My comment: I was unconscious all of this time. I am told that during the night a tiger came into the area. Captain Tucker had the only weapon, but they were afraid to fire it because the enemy might hear the shot and come after us. As the tiger kept getting closer, however, the group decided that since there were two dead and others wounded, they had better try to shoot the tiger or he would come in and attack the group. Captain Tucker started firing, but he did not kill the tiger; however, the firing scared him off.

Morning March 18, 1970

"On the morning of the 18th, division presented the final briefing in Chu Lai. Major James attended with the 14th Battalion Commander. Division directed Major James and the Battalion Commander to coordinate the day's rescue operations and act as command and control for the air landing of troops if needed in the vicinity of the downed aircraft.

"Major James flew directly from the Snake Pit to pick up LTC Schwarzkopf and his battalion surgeon, Captain (Doctor) Luis A. Oliver. It was important to have the commander of the 1/6th Battalion on board since they owned the troops moving toward the crash, plus those that were to be airlifted. The weather was no better than it was the day before, about 1000 feet - overcast. This low ceiling made it impossible to air land troops near Skater 67 so it was essential for James to continue the rescue efforts as a single helicopter.

"As Major James turned up the small north-south valley east of LZ Pineapple, Skater 67 came on the radio for the first time in about four hours and confirmed an aircraft was approaching his location. James hovered just above the trees at an indicated altitude of 1000 feet. He carefully maneuvered the helicopter to a position about 50 meters to the west of where they had started up the hill the day before. Skater 67 stated the chopper was very close. James started up the hill

very slowly. The fog and clouds were still hampering their ability to visually search for the crash site and, more importantly, was making it very difficult to hover.

"*James had hovered up the mountain for 15 minutes. Then..., 'Rattler 6, this is Skater 67, I see you, turn LEFT!!' 'Rattler 6 roger.' James cautiously turned the nose of the aircraft to the left, using gentle pressure on the left anti-torque pedal. He continued to hover at a crawl rate. The weather was deteriorating. James slowly decelerated the aircraft with a light aft cyclic pull. The crashed helicopter was visible about 50 feet in front of the aircraft nose. It was lying upside down with no blades, no tail rotor, no tail boom, and very few identifiable features. Skater 67 was standing about 15 feet from the crashed aircraft on a large rock. He asked James not to come any closer. The fuselage of the crashed aircraft was very unstable and he was afraid rotor wash from James' aircraft would cause it to roll downhill. James complied.*

"*It was impossible to land near the crash site due to heavy brush and trees. There were severely wounded soldiers on the ground; medical attention was a priority. James hovered to a spot he thought he could hold. LTC Schwarzkopf and the crew chief secured a rope to the floor of the UH-1H and tied the other end around Captain Oliver (the surgeon). He was gently lowered out of the cargo door, down through the dense canopy to the jungle floor.*"

My comment: Years later, then Colonel Schwarzkopf told me that the doctor took one look at the jungle and said, "Colonel, I am not going down there." LTC Schwarzkopf's response: "Doctor, you are going down there. You would be a lot more help if you went down by the rope."

"*The crash was only about 20 to 30 feet away from his location. The crew chief and gunner had to direct his every step using hand and arm signals because of the heavy undergrowth. Even this short distance took the doctor 10 minutes to navigate. Oliver called for stretchers to be dropped shortly after reaching the wreckage.*"

Quote from *Rescue of a Downed General*: "*After struggling all night upward through dense foliage and steep terrain, the soldiers finally reached the vicinity of the crash site. The vegetation was so thick that they had to hack and chop their way through the under-*

growth. When they were in the vicinity of their destination, they had to fire their weapons into the air so they could be heard by the survivors in order to be guided the final distance. At first light, they were located just across a deep ravine from the crash. Although only a short distance away, the final few meters took longer than expected."

Quote from *Rescue of Saber 6*: "The only possible landing point to pick up survivors was on the wreckage itself. James briefed King 4, who was the search and rescue for March 18, that it would be necessary to make an instrument takeoff after pick up and get a radar vector to Chu Lai hospital. King 4 acknowledged and coordinated the plan with all concerned. The crew chief advised James that the weather was breaking up in the valley just as he started forward to land. James informed King 4 and requested a Jolly Green to make the pickup. King 4 dispatched a Jolly Green but they could not find the location. James immediately turned and flew to the valley floor where he rendezvoused with the Jolly Green and led him to the crash site. They anxiously waited. The weather was still not good enough for the large Jolly Green to maneuver to a pickup point. In a short time the weather lifted enough to get the Jolly Green over the crash site. The rescue operation was nearing completion. Air Force Sergeant Jules Smith and Sergeant Stephen Sano were lowered to assist Captain Oliver. With their expertise on the ground the rescue operation was completed.

"One-by-one, the survivors were hoisted to the Jolly Green. General Ramsey woke in a daze for the first time since the crash with wind and rain in his face. He quickly sank back into unconsciousness and did not wake again until he was in the hospital and the medics were cutting his clothes off.

"James and his illustrious crew returned to the snake pit heroes. To Tommie P. James and his crew it was just another mission in the land of the Rattlers... 'Rattler operation this is Rattler 6, we're home, please close out my flight plan, over.' 'This is Rattler 3, wilco, welcome home, out!'"

My comment: My sincere thanks to Major James (Rattler 6), Rattler 3, King 6, King 4, the Jolly Green, and all the troops on the ground that struggled so hard to get to us, and the many, many others that worked so hard to find us after we crashed and were lost in the jungle for 18 hours. At the end of this chapter (Inclusion #2 through #2-5) are pictures of the crash.

The Media Knew of My Crash but Agreed to Hold the Story for a Time

Shortly after we crashed, the media learned that I was missing in action. The Public Information Officer, MACV, worked with the media and they agreed to hold the story for 24 hours or until I was found, whichever came first. Since I had been the Deputy Chief of Information, Department of the Army, many of the media knew me and they were interested in my family's well-being.

March 17, 1970 (time difference, US-Vietnam): The Army Notified Glenda

Glenda and Judi were living in a townhouse in McLean, Virginia. Between 6:30 and 7:00 a.m. on March 17, 1970, the doorbell rang, and Glenda got out of bed and started down the stairs to see who was there. The front door had glass in the top of the door and she could see uniforms. She called to Judi and said, "Judi, the military is here. Something has happened to Daddy." Judi jumped out of bed and ran down the stairs, almost in a panic. They were expecting to hear that I had been killed.

The Chaplain and the other officer had a very difficult time trying to convince them that I had only been injured. After things settled down, Glenda called Lloyd Ann and notified her of my accident before she heard it on the radio or TV. She then tried to call Larry, who was at Southwest Missouri State College, Springfield, Missouri. He had already left his room, and she could not get word to him. Later in the morning, Larry heard on the radio that I had crashed in the jungle; he immediately called his mother. To learn of my accident this way was very distressing for Larry.

The Army went to great length to properly notify Glenda of my crash, but I thought that they did it very poorly. I had served in the Pentagon for nine years and had many General Officer friends that were serving in the Pentagon. I think that it would have been much better if they had designated someone who knew Glenda to call her and tell her that I had been in a helicopter accident but was not seriously hurt. They could have had the Chaplain waiting and they could have told Glenda that he would be there with more information very soon. After I had spent a few days in the 27th Surgical Hospital, the hospital commander, Colonel (Doctor) George W. Ford, from Roanoke, Virginia, whom I had gotten to know well, put a call through to Glenda so that I could tell her that I was okay. It was a short conversation, but it was great to talk to her under these conditions.

Years later, Dr. Ford told me that the doctors taking care of me in the operating room came to him and said that my left arm was so badly damaged that they suggested it be amputated. Dr. Ford told them that he knew me very well and that he did not believe I was able to understand many things yet. He asked them if it would hurt anything to wait a few days until he was sure that I would understand. They said that they would put my arm in traction and wait. Miraculously, my arm began to heal in a way they never expected. Thanks to Dr. Ford, better known to me as Wally, I still have an arm that is useful, even though it does pain me quite often. Pain is much better than no arm, and I can live with pain.

Visitors

I had many visitors while I was in the hospital. General Abrams, CINC, MACV, came to see me first. Lieutenant General Melvin Zais, U.S. Army, who had taken over command from the Marines, was there at the same time. General Rosson, Deputy CINC, MACV, came very soon. I was very proud of myself that day because I was able to walk out to the chopper to meet Bill Rosson, a friend of many years. I received many other visitors, too numerous to mention.

March 22, 1970: Change of Command Ceremony

On March 22, 1970, General Abrams was going to have a change of command ceremony. The new commander would be Major General A. E. Milloy, who had commanded the 1st Infantry Division. General Abrams was concerned if I could participate. I sent word to General Abrams that I could participate by having two Sergeants standing beside me in case I got weak. At that ceremony, I received the Oak Leaf Cluster to the Distinguished Service Medal from General Abrams, who made some very fine remarks about me commanding the Americal Division. I then received four decorations from the South Vietnamese, presented to me by Lieutenant General Hoan Xuan Lam, the Vietnamese Commander of I Corps. A picture of the change of command ceremony is at the end of this chapter (Inclusion #3). You will note that my left arm is in a cast and a sling. Once again, I was proud of myself for being able to participate in the ceremony, just five days after lying in the jungle unconscious for 18 hours.

Early April 1970: I Was Sent to Walter Reed Army Medical Center in the United States

In early April 1970, the doctors decided that I was strong enough to travel to the United States. To ensure that I would be properly cared for, they sent a doctor with me. Our first stop was overnight in Japan. Early the next day, we headed for Alaska, where we landed to refuel. From there we headed to Andrews Air Force Base, just outside of Washington, D.C. The Commanding General of the Walter Reed Medical Center sent his aide to meet me. Also, Glenda and Judi were there, and it was wonderful to see them once again. The aide drove our car to Walter Reed, and Glenda, Judi, and I rode in the sedan.

The Chief, Orthopedic Service, Colonel (Doctor) George I. Baker was waiting to examine me. The doctor who had accompanied me had brought x-rays and medical reports from Vietnam. Doctor Baker looked them over carefully, gave me a thorough going over, and then gave me a choice. I could stay in the hospital for further evaluation, which he did not believe was needed since he had all the x-rays and medical reports from Vietnam, or I could go home and he would make an appointment for me to come back. There would be one problem if I went home – I would have to sleep sitting up so that my arm would hang in the sling. I elected to go home, and it was wonderful to be there once again. Glenda fixed me a bed in the guestroom and arranged pillows so that I could sleep sitting up so that my arm would hang in the sling. I did as well as could be expected, I guess, but I had difficulty sleeping – not because I was sitting up, but since the crash I had difficulty sleeping.

I went back to see Dr. Baker in a few days. He gave me a ball and told me to squeeze it in my hand so that I would not lose all my muscle strength in my arm. In about three days, I called Dr. Baker and told him my cast was very tight. He told me to come out and he would check it. He agreed that it was tight, so he took that cast off and put on a new one. In four or five days, I called the doctor again and told him the cast was very tight. Once again, he agreed and took the old cast off and put on a new one. Another four or five days went by and once again the cast became tight. I called Doctor Baker once again and for the third time he agreed that the cast was tight and he put on a new one. After he put this one on, he explained that he had fussed at many of his patients for not exercising enough with the ball in the hand. Then he said that he was not fussing at me, but maybe I should not exercise, squeezing the ball, as much as I had been. However, he said that he would much rather change the cast than to fuss at me for not exercising enough. I continued to improve rapidly.

Received Orders to Fort Polk, Louisiana

Before I left Vietnam, and even before my crash, I had received orders that my next assignment would be Fort Polk, Louisiana. After I returned to the United States, I learned that I was selected to be the Commanding General of Fort Polk because the Army had plans to close the post, and because I had been in Public Information I should be good at dealing with the public under such conditions. Between Vietnam and recuperating at home, I arranged for Sergeant Parks, my driver, to go to Fort Polk, sent some of my furniture to Polk, and sent many change of address cards. I talked to the proper staff officers in the Department of the Army about their closing plans. I made a trip to CONARC, the headquarters in charge of the closing, to learn as much as I could about their plans.

About June 1, 1970: Called to the Chief of Staff's Office

About June 1, 1970, I received a call that the Chief of Staff would like to see me. This was the first time since I had crashed that anyone in an official capacity in the Department of the Army had contacted me. I must say that I was disappointed that no one in the Pentagon seemed to care about my condition. I reported to the Chief of Staff at the appointed hour and received a very cold reception, as if I had done something wrong. The Chief did ask me how I was getting along but never gave me the opportunity to answer the question, even though my arm was in a sling. Without any explanation, he told me that he was assigning me as the Provost Marshal General of the Army. He further stated that the last two PMG's had misused the Criminal Investigation

Division (CID), so he had moved the CID out of the PMG's office and was going to leave it there. This sounded as if he did not trust me either.

I tried to explain to him all the preparations that I had made to go to Fort Polk, but he was not interested. I then told him that at Fort Polk I would have government quarters, an aide, two house boys, and my own doctors to take care of my injured arm and my injured back. He said that I was needed as the Provost Marshal General more than I was needed at Fort Polk. I then asked him if I could get government quarters in the Washington area because of my injuries. His very abrupt reply was that the TPMG was not authorized quarters. With the rude treatment that I received from the Chief of Staff and after going through hell in Vietnam, I felt like offering my resignation then and there, but I decided that I should think about this before I went too far.

July 14, 1970: Reported to Duty as The Provost Marshal General of the Army

On July 14, 1970, I reported to my office in the Forrestal Building on Independence Avenue, Washington, D.C., as The Provost Marshal General of the Army. A picture of the ceremony is at the end of this chapter (Inclusion #4). Glenda and Judi are looking on. General Bruce Palmer, VCSA, wrote the following note on the picture: "With high admiration for a great soldier and combat leader. I wish you good luck and continued success on your important new assignment." I very quickly learned that there was lots of work to be done even though I did not have the CID. I was responsible for law enforcement throughout the Army, less criminal investigations. I was responsible for the U.S. Army Disciplinary Barracks (Penitentiary) at Fort Leavenworth, Kansas. I was also responsible for the Retraining Brigade, Fort Riley, Kansas. That is where we retrained soldiers who were sentenced to confinement but who did not receive a discharge. We would eliminate about 50% of those during the retraining as being unfit to serve in the Army, which saved the Army millions of dollars.

Separating the CID and TPMG caused many problems for me for the next four years. The morale in the Military Police, both CID and MP's, was very low because of this split. The commander of the CID Agency had a lot of charisma. He had civilian friends both in the

Secretary of the Army's Office and in the Office of the Secretary of Defense, and he used these contacts for his benefit. He had two serious faults: (1) I was told by some of his subordinates that in order to gain power he collected certain information on Generals and very senior Colonels to pass on to his civilian friends but would never pass this information to military personnel; and (2) he was inclined to bend the truth in such a way that it would hurt me and other Provost Marshals everywhere.

August 20, 1970: Glenda's Father Passed Away

On August 20, 1970, Glenda's father, Mason Emmet Burton, known to our children as Pappap, passed away. We were in McLean, Virginia, and Glenda was called by phone that he was in serious condition; she immediately headed to Somerset, Kentucky, by air, but did not get there before her father passed away.

Early 1971: CID Information

Early in 1971, I learned that the Chief of CID was going to have OSD direct the Army to "…develop a CID agency which has vertical control of all CID's world-wide…" I informed my boss of this but I do not believe that he accepted it. On March 16, 1971, OSD prepared a Memorandum, Subject: "Integrity of Nonappropriated Fund Activities." The last paragraph of that memo states: "…the Army is requested to develop a CID agency which has vertical control of all CIDs world-wide…" A copy of the DOD Memorandum is at the end of this chapter (Inclusions #5 and #5-2). This was accomplished on September 17, 1971, making the CID a major command. This caused my office more problems in the law enforcement field.

June 1972: Trip to Europe

In June 1972, I made a trip to Europe to check on military police activities there. I paid Glenda's way so that she would have a chance to see some of Europe. On Friday evening, June 9, 1972, we were spending the night in a hotel in Garmish, Germany, where we were planning to have a nice weekend vacation. I received a call from a senior officer in the Pentagon saying that the Secretary of the Army would like to see me in his office on Monday morning. He knew that I was in Germany and said that he would leave it up to me as to whether I should return or not. Once I learned the subject, a very sensitive matter in CID, I told the officer to tell the Secretary that I would be there. I met with the Secretary of the Army on Monday, June 12, 1972. Evidently, I presented my case very well because the Secretary accepted my position versus what had been presented to him regarding the CID.

MP Morale

With the split of CID and the MP's, trying to keep morale up and law enforcement going as it should was a large task. My staff and I did a few things that I believe helped the situation. I will only list a few:

(1) My staff and I proposed that the MP's have a badge just like policemen wear, in addition to the arm band. The Army designed the badge and the MP's accepted it enthusiastically.

(2) I proposed to CONARC and to the MP School that the MP's receive more combat and combat support type training. This training made the MP's better soldiers and they were accepted more by the other soldiers.

(3) I arranged to get better sedans for the Military Police, both CID and MP's.

(4) My staff and I organized the Military Police Investigator to cover small crimes that the CID no longer handled. All reports from these investigations were sent to the CID for its file.

Having been on the Army staff for three previous tours, a total of nine years, I knew where to go and whom to see to get things done. One day I had one of my civilians with me when I wanted to get something done. We accomplished our mission. On the way back to the Forrestal Building, he commented somewhat as follows: "General, I have been on staff at The Provost Marshal General for about 25 years. I am amazed at what you can accomplish with the Army staff, where previous PMG's that I worked with did not know how to work with the Army staff." I was very pleased to hear such a compliment.

One project that I started was the accountability of AWOL (absent without leave) soldiers. One of the duties assigned to military police was to pick up as many soldiers who were AWOL as they could find. Having been a commander in the field, I could not believe that the Army had so many AWOL's. I made arrangements to discuss this problem with the Adjutant General of the Army, Major General Verne Bowers, a good friend. He, too, felt the report of AWOL's was high. We decided to form a committee of officers from the AG and the PMG to study this problem.

One of their findings was very interesting. The number of AWOL's reported was correct, but it gave the impression that that was the number of soldiers AWOL. As an example, if a soldier went AWOL one day and returned to duty and then went AWOL again, he was counted as two AWOL's, when he should have been counted as one AWOL on two different occasions. The committee found a few soldiers who were AWOL as many as four times and were counted as four AWOL's; they should have been counted as one AWOL on four different occasions. They also found that many soldiers returning from leave had missed a train, bus, or plane and had arrived a few hours late; they were also counted as AWOL. Based on the findings of the committee, the AG put out new instructions on how to count AWOL's. It was not long until the number of AWOL's was reduced by more than one-third, which made the Army look much better.

I remained as TPMG until an Army reorganization in May 1974 when the Office of TPMG was terminated.

June 17, 1972: President Nixon and Watergate

I remember well on June 17, 1972 when someone broke into the Democratic Party's headquarters at Watergate. (The scandal took its name from the Watergate complex of apartments and office buildings in Washington, D.C.) The police arrested five men for the break-in. Three of the five were James W. McCord, Jr., the security coordinator of the Committee for the Re-election of the President; G. Gordon Liddy, another aide; and E. Howard Hunt, Jr., a White House consultant. On April 30, 1973, President Nixon stated that he had no part either in planning the Watergate break-in or in covering it up. In May a special prosecutor was appointed to handle the case. He was later fired and another special prosecutor was appointed. Also in May, the Senate Select Committee on Presidential Campaign Activities began hearings on Watergate. In July 1974, the President suffered another major setback when the House Judiciary Committee recommended that he be impeached. President Nixon resigned on August 9, 1974.

September 5, 1972: Germany – 11 Israeli Olympians Were Killed by Terrorists

I remember well on September 5, 1972 when terrorists moved into the Olympic Village in Germany and killed 11 athletes from Israel.

June 30, 1973: U.S. Government Ended the Military Draft

I also remember well when the U.S. Government ended the military draft on June 30, 1973. We were still fighting the war in Vietnam, and I wondered if we could maintain our strength in combat without the draft. The good, patriotic Americans proved that we could.

1970 – 1974: My Back Problems Kept Getting Worse from My Helicopter Accident in Vietnam

All during my tour as TPMG my back pains grew worse. I would call Dr. George I. Baker, and he would always see me. He knew that I had some crushed vertebrae, but he kept taking more x-rays. After many visits, Dr. Baker discovered that I had crushed five vertebrae in my back. He said that it was not unusual for all crushed vertebrae not to show up immediately after an accident. He had already given me special exercises to strengthen my back muscles and to help reduce the pain. I was also on pain medication (Valium), which helped considerably.

February 1974: Had a Complete Physical Examination

In February 1974, I took my annual physical examination. After Dr. Baker received all of the reports, I went to see him. He and I had become friends by this time so he knew that he could talk frankly. He said that he had kept me on active duty in the hope that I would improve my physical condition to be qualified to remain on active duty until mandatory retirement. He then said that my physical condition had not improved; in fact, it had gone down. Therefore, I could no longer remain on active duty as a General Officer. He then went on to say that he was going to send in the paperwork for me to be retired on physical disability.

February 1974: Selected to be Chairman of the Organizing Board, McLean Savings and Loan

At a social function in McLean, Virginia, in February 1974, I met Frank Eubank. We had a long conversation, and he told me that he was organizing a McLean Savings and Loan. He seemed to show some interest in me and asked about my future. I told him that it appeared I would retire in the summer on physical disability. A few days later, Frank called me and asked if I would be interested in being the Chairman of the Organizing Board of McLean Savings and Loan. I told him that I appreciated the offer, but I would have to check with the Judge Advocate General (JAG) of the Army to see if this was proper while I was on active duty. When I checked with the JAG, he said that since I was about to retire and since this was an organizing board there would be no conflict of interest. I called Frank and told him that I would accept the position.

Late May 1974: Department of Defense (DOD) Turned Down My Physical Disability Retirement

In late May 1974, Dr. Baker called and told me that the Department of Defense (DOD) had informed the Army that they would not approve my retirement on physical disability. I understood the reason I was turned down was that an Air Force General (four stars) had just retired and was recommended for disability, even though he had been on flight status up to the day of his retirement. DOD told the Army that no General Officer would be approved for disability retirement unless it was recommended by a board of officers. Dr. Baker said that I should be retired on physical disability and that I would have to appear before the Army Physical Examination Board. To do this, I would have to demand a formal board because I did not concur with the findings of the informal board. I did this on June 12, 1974. I would be represented by Captain Gerald A. Schroeder, Judge Advocate General's Corps. My witness would be Colonel George I. Baker, Chief Orthopedic Service, Walter Reed Army Medical Center.

June 24, 1974: Excerpts from Physical Examination Board Proceedings

The board met at 10:00 a.m. on June 24, 1974. Dr. Baker had told me many times that I had five crushed vertebrae. However, he said that the one in my lower back was very difficult to read, so he was going to tell the board that I had four crushed vertebrae. He did not want the board to think that he was trying to exaggerate my condition. Some of his testimony follows:

"In 1970 he had basically two groups of injuries. One was an injury to his back; the other at that time, which was far more important, was the injury to his left arm. This involved a segmental fracture. This is one that has several fragments of the long bone. In other words, there were two major fracture sites as well as damage to the – one of the nerves of the arm, the radial nerve which is the nerve that extends the fingers and brings the wrist up as well as controls some of the movements of the thumb. The fracture was by far the more important of the injuries to the arm at that time. We were concerned as to whether or not this would heal. In July when he was returned to duty it was very questionable and we were suspecting that a bone graft might be necessary. I had discussed the General's problem with the then Surgeon General, General Jennings, who had called me in response to a query he stated he'd received from the Army Staff. I apprised General Jennings of the medical facts and requested that consideration be given to his assignment so that he would be followed preferably by me since I knew his case but I was concerned about the need for further treatment. I think as a result of that conversation that he was assigned in the Washington area rather than to some other position. If memory serves, he was under consideration at that time I was told for a position as a post commander in Fort Polk..."

(This is the first time I had ever heard that my doctor wanted to keep me in the Washington area. I cannot understand why he or the Chief of Staff did not tell me that I was being kept in the Washington area for my own benefit.)

"Unfortunately what has happened with General Ramsey is that his pain has increased; it has required medication; it has resulted in difficulty sleeping; it has caused him to avoid prolonged sitting,

prolonged assumption of any particular position. There have been changes noticed on X-ray. There has been progressive wedging of at least four vertebrae as well as a curvature in the lateral plain which I refer to as a scoliosis in the narrative summary; so all of my predications were wrong..."

"This has been a slow downhill course and one that I did not expect four years ago. I felt that his back was the lesser of the problems but now it has become the greater..."

"Well, it was an earlier visit this year, I believe it was February, following a fall when he injured his left arm again, and although I could find nothing wrong with his arm as far as the x-ray was concerned, we did talk briefly about his other problems, his back specifically, and I knew that he was due for an annual physical within the next several weeks and I advised him that when the time came we would take a good hard look at his back and arm and see what the situation was. The other thing that affected my decision was the knowledge that his assignment as Provost Marshal General was to be terminated by a reorganization of the Army Staff and I felt that I would be asked some questions as to what would be his possibility of serving in another capacity as a General Officer, so I wanted to go into it in depth and I advised him to be sure that he saw me during his annual physical..."

"Well, I think that what I meant was a disability retirement or retirement for medical reasons and not retirement for mandatory purposes which I believe he has at least two years to go before mandatory retirement..."

"Yes, I think that General Ramsey has an extremely high threshold for pain. He's a very stoic individual and during our very intimate relationship with respect to his hospitalization and subsequent contact as doctor-patient, I feel that he has the type of personality that will attempt to override these pain considerations and discomfort but now he's gotten to the point where this is very significant and this is part of the basis for my concern at this time..."

"...I don't feel that you can always exactly correlate symptoms with the degree of compression, particularly in the thoracic spine, because, as I mentioned, there is a great deal of splinting of the area due to the presence of ribs. A 10 percent compression of three vertebrae puts it beyond the mild to the moderate category in my mind, so we have five, six, and seven which are 10 percent compressed. We have T-11 lower down which has 15 percent compression. Now this is an actual decrease in height in the anterior margin as compared to the posterior margin so that this gives a slope to the top and bottom of the vertebral bodies, resulting in an increase in the curvature of the thoracic spine. Now, the other thing that is of importance in this is that there is a progressive scoliosis...so together these things make me say that this gets into the moderate category and since it has been progressive over four years, I'm of the opinion that he may require surgical fusion of this to control his symptoms..."

"The board finds the member, Major General Lloyd B. Ramsey, physically unfit to perform the duties of his office and rank by reason of physical disabilities which are rated at 50 percent. The disabilities are as indicated on DA Form 199. The board recommends that the member, Major General Ramsey, be permanently retired..."

Copies of the Army "Permanent Disability Retirement" letter and DA Form 199 are at the end of this chapter (Inclusions #6 and #6-2). A copy of the Veterans Administration letter, claim for disability, which rates my disability at 60%, is at Inclusion #7.

My comment: Dr. Baker treated me for 14 years. During my next appointment with Dr. Baker, after the PEB hearings on June 24, he told me that the medical profession had done everything that could be done for my back. He complimented me highly by saying that the medical profession could take credit for 50% of my recovery; my attitude and exercises could take credit for the remainder.

He then told me that my physical condition would continue "down hill." He stated that there was no way to stop the downward progression. He said that by taking the proper exercises I could slow the downward progression but that I could not stop it. He predicted that in 15 years, 20 at the most, I would have to have some of my vertebrae fused or have a rod inserted into my back. He went on to say that in the worst case I might even be in a wheelchair.

I am writing this on March 17, 2004 – 34 years to the day that I crashed and almost 30 years after Dr. Baker made the above statement.

After such a bad accident and my being 86 years of age on May 29, 2004, I admit that I have pain in my arm and back, but I am able to live with it. I am lucky to be here and to be able to do the things that I do, such as swim and play golf. I do have difficulty walking more than 150-200 yards because I get a pain in my left hip. My doctor says the pain is caused from arthritis in my back, which is settling in my hip.

June – July 1974: Promotion Board

After my office was terminated in May 1974, I was put on a promotion board. Between the promotion board and my getting ready for the Physical Evaluation Board, I kept fairly busy but I did have some free time.

Late July 1974: Call Regarding Retirement

In late July 1974, I received a phone call from the General Officers Branch regarding retirement. I was told that the Army did not have the money to give every Major General in the Washington area a retirement ceremony and a reception; however, there was to be a retirement ceremony on July 31, 1974 for everyone retiring on that date in the Washington area. When I asked who would be there, I was told that they expected eight to ten Sergeants and two or three field grade officers. Since this was not a retirement ceremony in my honor, I elected not to attend. I was then told that the Chief of Staff would like to bid me farewell on that date in his office. I met with the Vice Chief of Staff on that date, had a very nice visit with him, and was presented with my second Distinguished Service Medal. My wife had not been invited to be there. To me this was not a very good ending of a 34-year career in which I had been wounded five times in World War II as a battalion commander, had crashed in a helicopter in Vietnam while commanding an Infantry Division, and had been missing in action for 18 hours.

I know of one other Major General who commanded a Division in combat and retired in the Washington area but who did not receive a retirement ceremony or a reception. To me this does not speak well for the Army, which I admired and always will admire. There are not many Major Generals who have the opportunity to command a Division in combat, and most of those have over 30 years of service when they retire. Except for this incident regarding my retirement, and when the

Army kept me in the Washington area after my helicopter accident in Vietnam without telling me why and not providing me with quarters when I had some serious injuries, the Army took excellent care of me and gave me some of the finest assignments in the Army. I hold no ill feelings. It was a great life, and I am proud to have served my country in the United States Army.

Decorations

At the end of this chapter (Inclusion #8) is a list of the decorations that I earned during my career.

At Inclusion #9 is a picture of the following:
Plaque – Who's Who in America
My decorations
Map, Germany – Boundary changes between the United States and Soviet zones of occupation
Agreement between the United States of America and the Union of Soviet Socialist Republics
Certificate: Hall of Distinguished Alumni, University of Kentucky
Pictures of the 3d Infantry Division Memorial honoring their war dead, Arlington National Cemetery

Quick Review of My Life

After I retired on August 1, 1974, I looked back on my life and often wondered if and how my life would have been different if three incidents had not occurred:

1. If I had not injured my leg playing football during my senior year in high school, which prevented me from playing at my peak, would I have made All-State Quarterback instead of being an honorable mention, and would I have been offered an athletic scholarship to the University of Kentucky instead of being a walk-on?

2. If I had not broken my neck during spring football practice of my freshman year, at which time I was playing first string quarterback, would I have been the varsity quarterback and, perhaps, been elected

captain of the team? I had been elected captain of the freshman team and these same players would be there.

3. If I had not had the helicopter crash in March 1970 while commanding the Americal Division, where I severely injured my left arm, crushed five vertebrae in my back, and had to give up command of the Division, would I have been promoted if I had stayed healthy and continued to command?

I think that these are good questions for me and me alone to ponder. I have no complaints with my life and am very proud of what I did accomplish during my lifetime.

1970–1974 Reverend Billy Graham

I spent 13 years with the Army in the Pentagon on four different tours. Once every year the army would invite Reverend Billy Graham to speak to the officers, enlisted men and civilians that were available. He was an outstanding Christian and made wonderful presentations. I would always attend his presentations if I were in town. From 1970–1974 I was a Maj. Gen. and would be invited to the luncheon for him after his presentation. On two different occasions I had the honor of sitting next to Billy Graham and enjoyed some very interesting conversations with him.

Our landing pad and Headquarters, Americal Division

We Fly Daily
SP4 Dalane A. Mitchell
SP4 Roger H. Adams
Maj. Gen. Lloyd Ramsey
Capt. Thomas J. Ruffing
WO2 Carrol V. Lanier
WO2 James D. Bullard

INCL. # 1

INCL. # 2

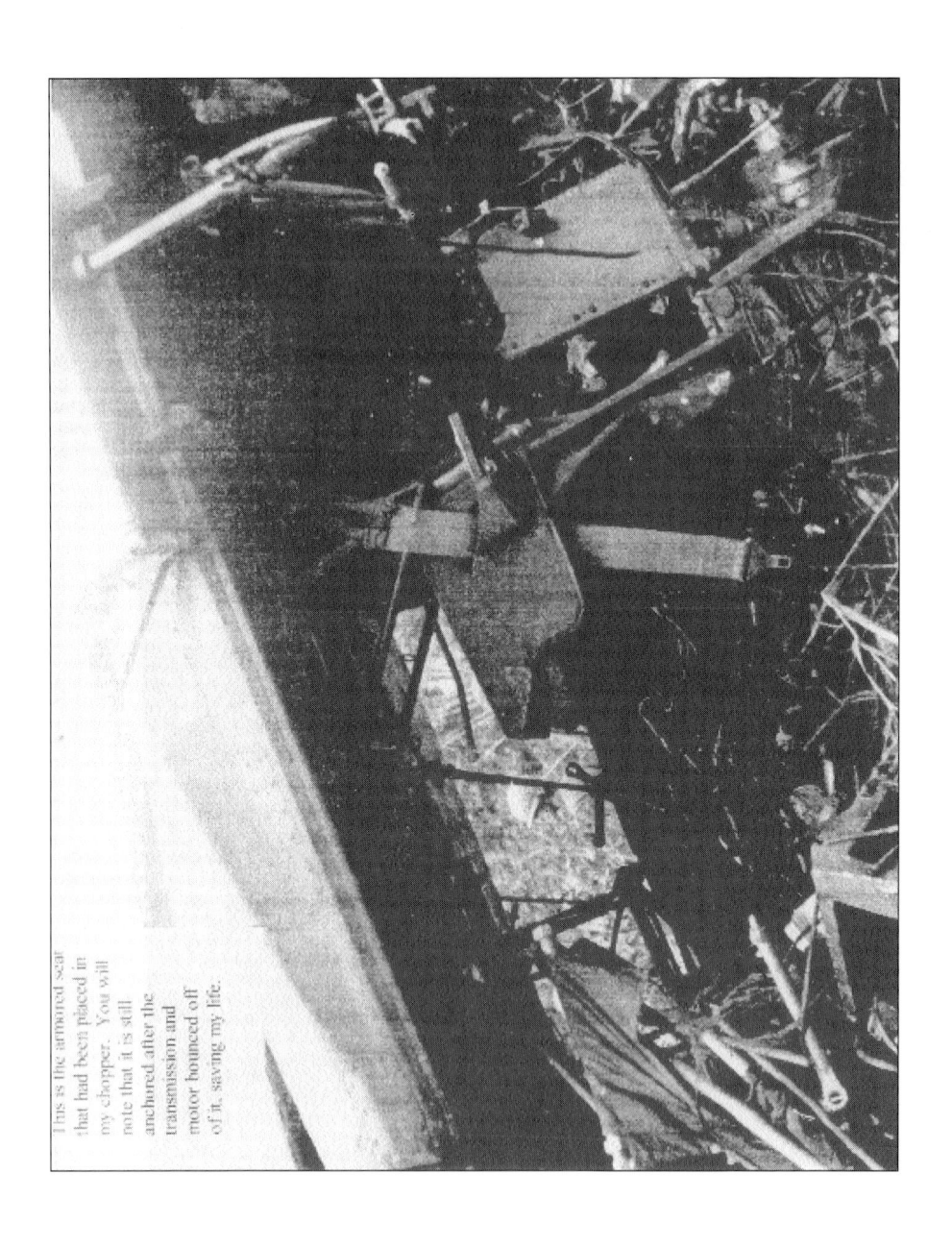

This is the armored seat that had been placed in my chopper. You will note that it is still anchored after the transmission and motor bounced off of it, saving my life.

INCL. # 2-2

INCL. # 2-3

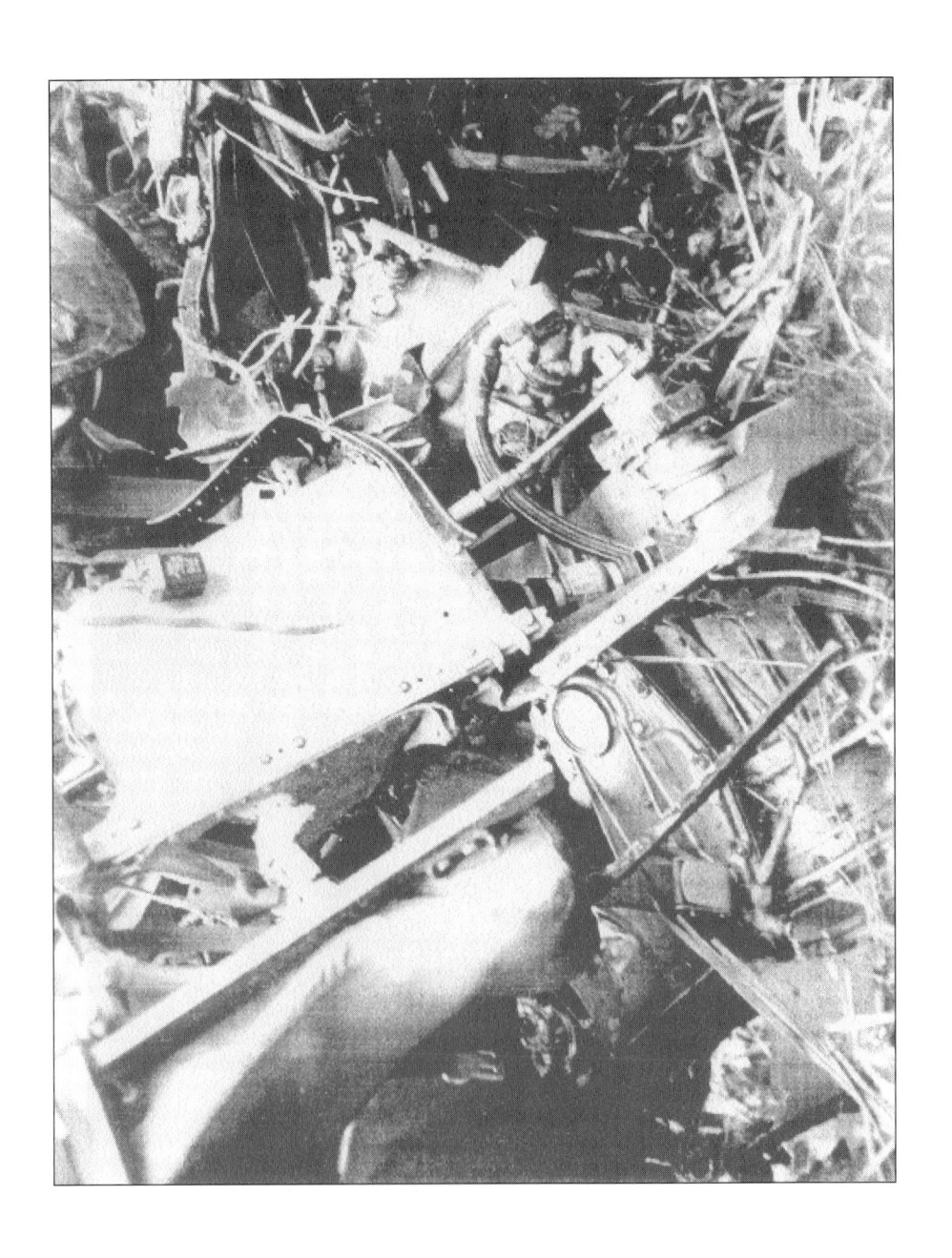

INCL. # 2-4

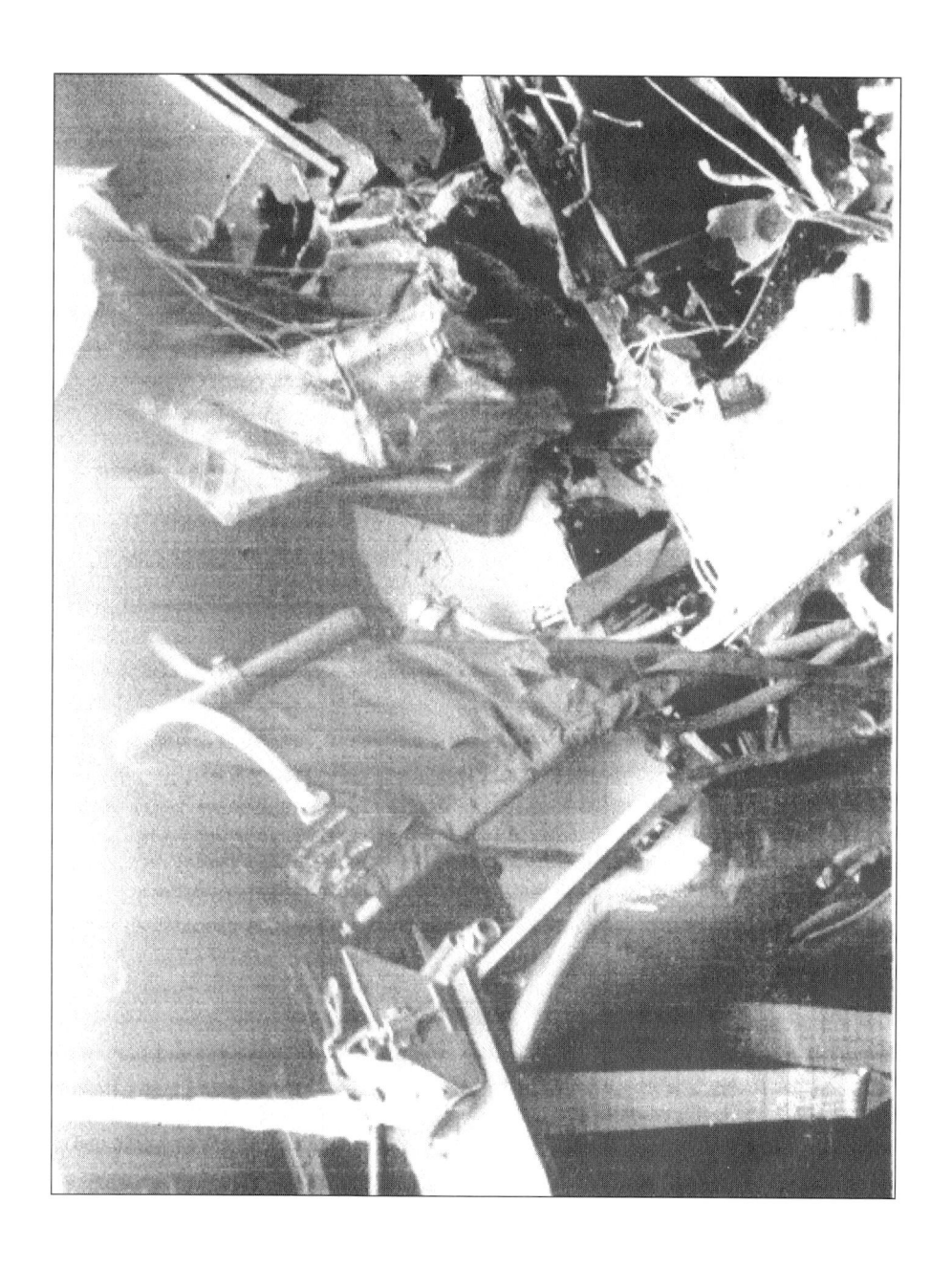

INCL. # 2-5

MG Milloy Takes Command

On March 22, following the injury of General Ramsey, Major General A.E. Milloy assumed command of the Americal Division.

Major General Milloy, a distinguished combat veteran of three wars and a master parachutist, assumed command of the Americal following seven months as the commanding general of the 1st Infantry Division.

Brigadier General Roy L. Attebery became the Assistant Division Commander (Support) on the last day of March.

MG. A.E. Milloy
March, 1970

INCL. # 3

To: MG Lloyd B. Kenney

With high admiration for a great soldier and combat leader. I wish you good luck and continued success in your important new assignment.

Frank R. Linguini
General U.S. Army
Vice Chief of Staff

INCL. # 4

(MAR 16, 1971)
MAR 16 1971

MEMORANDUM FOR Secretaries of the Military Departments
Directors of the Defense Agencies

SUBJECT: Integrity of Nonappropriated Fund Activities

I continue to be deeply concerned that all appropriate actions are taken to assure that the full benefits of nonappropriated fund activities flow only to the military and civilian personnel to whom the funds belong.

By memorandum of August 12, 1969, I requested priority reviews of officer and noncommissioned officer club procedures. You responded with appropriate improvements in management controls over these club operations. I understand that additional improvement actions relating to the management of other nonappropriated fund activities are under way. These actions variously include such matters as the organization, assignment of responsibilities, management and control aspects.

While these actions are important steps in the right direction, I am convinced that an immediate and complete evaluation of the integrity control aspects of all types of nonappropriated funds is essential. Therefore, to the extent that additional studies are necessary, I desire that you take immediate action to have reviews made of the control features of all classes of nonappropriated funds under your management responsibility.

These reviews should include exchange and motion picture service operations. However, in view of the special nature of these systems, it may be advisable to review them separately. Your central internal audit organizations can help in conducting the surveys of the control systems of these activities. This would be consistent with recent DoD instructions which added the requirement that the central audit organizations evaluate periodically the adequacy of audit systems of these activities.

INCL. # 5

However they are performed, the emphasis in all these reviews should be on the detection of weaknesses in operating practices and controls which could impair the integrity of fund assets. Wherever weaknesses are identified, immediate corrective action should be undertaken. Among such actions, I suggest that you consider the establishment of permanent, small, expert investigative teams to make unannounced inspections of such activities on a spot-check basis.

Because the above action relates primarily only to the integrity aspects of operations, I want to review other management and organization aspects of the entire nonappropriated fund structure, possibly using knowledgeable independent consultants. This review would evaluate the improvements initiated by the components and recommend any additional modifications considered desirable.

In order to aid me in planning and timing of this broad study, I would appreciate a report within thirty days covering your individual reviews planned or in process and their timing. Further, if during the course of the studies, conditions are revealed which are particularly significant or which could reflect unfavorably on the Department, I would like you to advise me at once.

Further, it is requested that the following two specific areas of concern be accomplished as soon as possible:

    (1) I desire that the Department of the Air Force, working closely with the other Services and cognizant OSD and Defense Agencies, develop a comprehensive nonappropriated fund activity debarment system effective world-wide and for all services, which reaches individuals as well as firms.

    (2) The Secretary of the Army is requested to develop a CID agency which has vertical control of all CIDs world-wide, similar to the organizational setup of the OSI of the Air Force.

INCL. # 5-2

U.S. ARMY MILITARY PERSONNEL CENTER
200 STOVALL STREET
ALEXANDRIA, VIRGINIA 22332

REPLY TO
ATTENTION OF:

DAPC-PAS-RS Ramsey, Lloyd B.　　　　　　　　　　　　　　23 July 1974
400-54-8204 (24 June 74)

LETTER ORDERS NUMBER D7-348

SUBJECT: Permanent Disability Retirement

Major General Lloyd B. Ramsey, USA
Chief of Staff Holding Detachment
Department of the Army
Washington, D. C. 20310

TC 372. The above named individual having been determined to be PERMANENTLY unfit for duty by reason of disability incurred while entitled to receive basic pay, is RETIRED FROM ACTIVE SERVICE, relieved from assignment and duty, and placed on the RETIRED LIST, as indicated.

ADMINISTRATIVE ACCOUNTING DATA
Ret List: USA
Auth (Ret): Title 10, USC, Section 1201
Auth (Ret gr): Title 10, USC, Section 1372
Auth pl of ret: Fort Myer, Virginia
PCS MDC: 7B05
Eff date: 31 July 1974

FOR THE INDIVIDUAL
Date placed on retired list: 1 August 1974
Permanent grade: Major General
Retired grade: Major General
Percentage of Disability: 50
Special Instructions (APPENDIX B, AR 310-10): 83

BY ORDER OF THE SECRETARY OF THE ARMY:

H. G. MOORE
Major General, USA
Commanding

INCL. # 6

MEDICAL EVALUATION BOARD PROCEEDINGS

MEMBER

1. NAME (Last, First, Middle Initial) MEMBER		2. GRADE	3. ACTIVE SVC	YEARS	MONTHS
RAMSEY, LLOYD B.		MG		OVER 20 YRS	
4. SOCIAL SECURITY ACCOUNT NUMBER	5. PMOS	6. BRANCH AND COMPONENT			
400 54 8204	0002	RA			

7. THE PEB CONSISTING OF THE INDIVIDUALS INDICATED IN EXHIBIT B CONVENED ON **24 June 1974** AT (Location including ZIP Code) **WALTER REED ARMY MEDICAL CENTER, Washington, D. C. 20012**

8. THE BOARD CONSIDERED THE MEMBER'S CONDITION DESCRIBED IN THE RECORDS. EACH DISABILITY IS LISTED BELOW in descending order of significance.

VA CODE	DISABILITY DESCRIPTION	c	d	e	f	g
5202	Malunion, left humerus (minor), secondary to closed segmental fracture in aircraft accident, 17 Mar 70, with moderate deformity, pain, limitation of motion. (Medical Board Diagnosis 2, Clinical Record, Formal Board)	No	Yes	Yes		20
8514	Radial neuropathy, left, minor, incomplete, mild. (Medical Board Diagnosis 3, Clinical Record, Formal Board)	No	Yes	Yes		20
5285-5291	Traumatic arthritis, thoracic spine, residual of multiple compression fractures, manifested by pain, decreased range of motion, and demonstrable deformity of several thoracic vertebrae. (Medical Board Diagnosis 1, Clinical Record, Formal Board) (See Item 16)	No	Yes	Yes		10+10

9. THE BOARD FINDS THE MEMBER IS PHYSICALLY [ ] FIT [X] UNFIT AND RECOMMENDS A COMBINED RATING OF **50%** AND THAT THE MEMBER BE **Permanently retired from the service.**

10. IF RETIRED BECAUSE OF DISABILITY THE BOARD MAKES THE RECOMMENDED FINDING THAT THE MEMBER'S RETIREMENT [X] IS [ ] IS NOT BASED ON DISABILITY RESULTING FROM INJURY OR DISEASE RECEIVED IN LINE OF DUTY AS A DIRECT RESULT OF ARMED CONFLICT OR CAUSED BY AN INSTRUMENTALITY OF WAR AND INCURRED IN LINE OF DUTY DURING A PERIOD OF WAR AS DEFINED BY LAW.

11. EXHIBITS (Identify each)
A. Medical Board Proceedings
B. Appointing orders
C. **Personnel Statement**
D. DA Form 66
E. **Notif of Formal PEB**
F. Rebuttal Statement
G. Member's Exhibit
 1. Memorandum for CG, USAPDA, 19 Jun 74
H. Health & Treatment Records

12. TYPED NAME, GRADE, BRANCH OF PRESIDENT | SIGNATURE | DATE 9 JUL 1974

DA FORM 199

VETERANS ADMINISTRATION
VETERANS BENEFITS OFFICE
2033 M Street N. W.
Washington D. C. 20421

Date: September 26, 1974
In Reply Refer To: 1C-400548204
372-211A

Mr. Lloyd B. Ramsey
6451 Dryden Drive
McLean, Virginia 22101

Your claim for disability compensation has been considered on the basis of all the evidence, including reports received from the Service Department. The evidence establishes service connection for the following conditions evaluated as shown:

Condition	Percent of Disability
Neuropathy, left radial nerve with malunion, left humerus secondary to fracture with deformity, pain and limitation to motion	40%
Traumatic arthritis, thoracic spine, residual of compression fracture with deformity of thoracic vertebrae; and osteoarthritis, both knees	30%

Because you may not receive full payment of service retired pay and VA compensation at the same time, we have no choice but to disallow your claim. However, you may waive a portion of your retired pay and elect to receive VA compensation instead, in the amount(s) and from the date(s) shown below:

Degree of Disability	Monthly Payment	Commencing Date
60%	$233.00	8-1-74

You may make the waiver by completing and returning the enclosed VA Form 21-651 within one year from the date of this letter. Before you decide, please read the instructions and information on the back of this letter.

If you elect VA compensation (as your greater benefit), we will deduct the amount of retired pay you have already received beginning with the commencing date shown above. If your retired pay is greater than VA compensation and you waive that portion equal to the payment shown, your VA compensation payment will begin on the date of reduction of your retired pay.

If you believe our decision is incorrect, please see the enclosure which explains your procedural and appeal rights.

Encl. VA Forms 21-651
VA Form 1-4107

(Over)

FL 21-526
APR 1974(RS)

Show veteran's full name, VA file number, and social security number on all correspondence.

INCL. # 7

MAJ. GEN. LLOYD B. RAMSEY
U.S. ARMY RETIRED

DECORATIONS – BADGES - CITATION
As Worn on Uniform

		Decorations
1st Row	Distinguished Service Medal - with Oak Leaf Cluster	2
	Silver Star – with 2 Oak Leaf Clusters	3
	Legion of Merit – with Oak Leaf Cluster	2
	Distinguished flying Cross	1
	Bronze Star Medal – with V (Valor) & 3 Oak Leaf Clusters	4
	Purple Heart – with 4 Oak Leaf Clusters	5
	Air Medal –16 Oak Leaf Clusters (3 Silver & 1 Bronze)	17
	Army Commendation Medal – with Oak Leaf Cluster	2
2d Row	American Defense Service Medal	1
	American Campaign Medal	1
	European-African-Middle Eastern Campaign Medal with arrow head (amphibious landing) & 10 campaign stars	1
	World War II Victory Medal	1
	Army of Occupation Medal (Germany)	1
	National Defense Service Medal	1
	Vietnam Service Medal – with 4 campaign stars	1
3d Row	Foreign Decorations	
	Member British Empire (MBE)	1
	Croix de Guerre, a l'ordre du Corps d' Armee (France)	1
	Vietnamese National Order, 5th Class	1
	Vietnamese Armed Forces Honor Medal	1
	Vietnamese Gallantry Cross – with Palm	1
	Vietnamese Campaign Medal	1
	Total	49
Other	Combat Infantryman Badge	1
	Presidential Unit Citation	1
	Glider Badge	1
	General Staff Identification Badge	1

INCL. # 8

From right to left:

1. Plaque--Marquis, Who's Who in America
2. Decorations, see Incl. #8
3. Map, part of Germany--Boundary Changes Between United States and Soviet Zones of Occupation.
4. Agreement between the United States of America and The Union of Soviet Socialist Republics
5. Certificate: Hall of Distinguished Alumni University of Kentucky
6. Pictures of the 3d Infantry Division Memorial, Honoring their War Dead--Arlington National Cemetary

INCL. # 9

CHAPTER 11

RETIREMENT

AUGUST 1974 – NOVEMBER 2000

1974 – 1988: McLean Savings and Loan

From February to August 1974, while I was still on active duty, Frank Eubank and I met at least weekly to make plans for the S & L and to choose the organizing board. The board consisted of the following individuals:

Major General Lloyd B. Ramsey,
    Chairman of the Organizing Board
Richard E. Blair, Attorney
Vincent F. Callahan, Jr., Virginia House of Delegates
Charles P. Cocke, CPA
Roxy V. Crack, Detective Lieutenant
    (later resigned from the Board)
Frank Eubank, Planner and Developer
Julius Fogel, Physician
Robert E. Goldstein, Attorney and Investor
John E. Harrison, Attorney
Charles W. Johnson, Assistant Parliamentarian, U.S. House of
    Representatives (later resigned from the Board)
Marshall C. McClean, Stockbroker
Evelyn P. Metzger, Publisher
Alvin F. Robinson, Physician
James E. Travis, Sales Representative
    (later resigned from the Board)
Preston L. Walker, Electrical Contractor

The original management:
John E. Harn, II, Banker	Executive Vice President
R. Robert Rushe	Mortgage Lending
Timothy B. Matz	Secretary
Joanne M. Bryant	Assistant Secretary and Assistant Treasurer

May 1977: McLean Savings and Loan Activated

The organizing board met often. We were in contact with both State and Federal officials trying to receive permission to open the Savings and Loan. There was a great amount of administrative work that had to be done. This work was done by Frank Eubank, our attorneys, John Harrison and Richard Blair, and our CPA, Charles Cocke. All members of the Board had to sell stock, and they did it very well. The board was kept fully informed and gave its approval on subjects that had to come before it. As the Chairman of the Organizing Board, I was always involved. The board was an outstanding group of people. Everyone participated in the discussions. After working for over three years to have a Savings and Loan, we received approval to open McLean Savings and Loan in April 1977. We opened our doors in May 1977. At the first meeting of the Board, after we officially opened, I was elected Chairman of the Board.

McLean Savings and Loan (MSL) did extremely well from the beginning. As we grew, some members of the board recommended that we organize a subsidiary so that we could broaden our base; McLean Financial Corporation (MFC) was organized. After receiving proper approvals for MFC, we were able to expand our base. In a letter to me years later, our MSL attorney, John E. Harrison, wrote the following:

"...MLS, mostly as a result of the business produced by MFC, was by far the most successful and profitable S&L East of the Mississippi River...Unfortunately into this picture of happiness and profitability more than a little rain must fall. Principally as a result of problems in Maryland and Florida, the FSLIC substantially changed the rules for the operation of mortgage subsidiaries by insured S&Ls. These new rules forced profound change in the way MSL financed the operations of MFC..."

We had made approximately $70 million in loans in Texas. All of these loans were properly insured. However, about $35 million of these loans went bad. When the insurance company tried to get out of covering the bad loans, McLean Savings and Loan brought suit against the company. By this time, the FSLIC became concerned about our situation. They said that we had to consider that all $70 million of the loans were bad. We worked very closely with the FSLIC, and it appeared that everything was going well. Then in July 1988, without any warning, the FLIC moved in and took over the Savings and Loan. The FSLIC paid another organization a very large sum of money to take charge of the MSL. The government and the new organization continued the suit against the insurance company that MLS had started and, as we expected, won the suit. The other $35 million in loans turned out to be good. Another comment by John Harrison, *"...As a result of buying MSL, NVR was able to shelter about $100M in development income from its development business with the MSL tax losses caused by the huge reserve for losses that the FSLIC had made the S&L record on its books. So NVR saved about $48M in taxes it would have paid to the government..."*

In this case there were a number of articles both in magazines and newspapers that stated that the FSLIC made some big mistakes by continually changing the rules and by the way that it took over MSL. One good thing that came out of all of this is that no depositor lost any money. The stockholders lost their stock, but at least they were paid very good dividends over a period of years.

1978: Northern Virginia Community Foundation

Northern Virginia Community Foundation was organized in 1978 to raise money for various activities. I was asked to become a charter member of the board. I stayed on the board for about 20 years. We made great strides, and, by the time I left, our financial situation was outstanding.

1979: Significant Sig in the Sigma Chi Fraternity

In 1979, I became a Significant Sig in the Sigma Chi fraternity, which is quite an honor. I was presented the award at a function in the Senate Office Building, Washington, D.C. by Grand Consul Jim Bash. Only two of us received the Significant Sig award that day. At the end of the chapter (Inclusion #1) is a picture of me with Significant Sig's Senator Barry Goldwater, Allan Hunter, and Grand Consul Jim Bash.

March 30, 1981: President Reagan Was Shot

I remember well when President Reagan was shot by John W. Hinckley, Jr., on March 30, 1981. Public Affairs Officer James Brady was with the President and was seriously wounded. Jim was a Sigma Chi, and I had gotten to know him fairly well.

About 1981: Inducted into the Sons of the American Revolution

About 1981 I was inducted into the Sons of the American Revolution in the Washington, D.C. chapter. My mother, Mimi, was a member of the Daughters of the American Revolution. Her ancestor was Joseph M. McAlister, 1754-1833. He fought with the 7th Virginia Regiment in the battle of Cowpens, South Carolina. An interesting story has been told on McAlister. After he moved back to Pulaski County, Kentucky, he came to Somerset one day to shop. While there he bought a bottle of whiskey, which he drank. It was a very rainy day. When he left for home, he had to cross Buck Creek. Because of the rain, the creek was very deep and swift. A friend of his was there and told McAlister that he should not cross the creek because of the current. McAlister said that he had fought in many battles, including the battle of Cowpens, and a little water was not going to stop him from crossing the creek. He started across, but the current was so swift that it swept his horse away and the horse drowned. Fortunately, McAlister got across and made it home. I was able to get into the Sons of the American Revolution using the same ancestor. My Virginia number is 4211, and my NSSAR is 121301.

1984: The Army Distaff Foundation

In 1984, I was asked to become a member of the board of the Army Distaff Foundation in Washington, D.C. I was on the board for about three years. The Army Distaff was the first home built for widows of military personnel. This project went so well that later the other services started a system where retired officers and their wives could live. The Army Distaff Hall eventually changed to accept couples. Most of these facilities have assisted living and a nursing home.

September 8, 1984: Appointed Chairman of a Committee to Build a 3d Infantry Division Memorial

At the annual reunion of the Society of the 3d Infantry Division, September 8, 1984, Colonel Lyle W. Bernard, a very active 3d Infantry Division member, discussed the need for a 3d Infantry Division Memorial in the Washington, D.C. area, preferably in the Arlington National

Cemetery. He told the group that two committees had been formed in previous years to accomplish such a task but both had failed. He was convinced that he could form a committee that could get the job done. Based on Colonel Bernard's comments, the Society passed a resolution tasking Outpost 7, Washington, D.C. to erect such a memorial.

Colonel Bernard formed a committee as follows:
> Major General Lloyd B. Ramsey, USA Retired
> Brigadier General Hallett D. Edson, USA Retired
> Brigadier General Eugene Phillips, USA Retired
> Colonel Lyle W. Bernard, USA Retired
> Colonel Walter E. Tardy, USA Retired
> Colonel Angus B. MacLean, USA Retired
> Captain Carl Swickerath, USA Retired
> CSM Leonard J. Werth, USA Retired
> Technical Sergeant, Terry J. Dalton

Colonel Bernard asked me to be the chairman of the committee but stated that he would do most of the work. All agreed for me to be the chairman. The first thing that the committee did was to outline our work as follows:

1. Design the Memorial
2. Get permission to erect the Memorial in Arlington National Cemetery
3. Raise funds to erect the Memorial
4. Location of the Memorial
5. Dedication ceremony
6. Reception.

1984 – 1990: Six Years of Effort

1. Design the Memorial. Everyone on the committee gave their input to the design of the memorial. After many sessions, we came to the conclusion that the memorial should be a monument 10-12 feet tall with "THIRD INFANTRY DIVISION" on the front and with the 3d Infantry Division patch. Below this we agreed on the following: "In MEMORY of OUR WAR DEAD." We agreed that we needed to have some history of the Division on a plaque to be placed in front of the memorial. We finally found an architect, Francis D. Lethbridge, who would charge

us a very small fee and volunteer most of his services. He put the final touches to our plan and worked with a contractor to install the memorial. It would be 11 ½ feet tall and the plaque would be placed 40 feet in front of the memorial. The plaque would cover a short history of the Division, which I would prepare; the number of campaigns in World War I, World War II, and Korea; and the number of killed, wounded, and missing in those wars. Carl Swickerath, working closely with the Army, would compile the data.

2. Permission to erect the Memorial in Arlington National Cemetery. I wrote the Secretary of the Army asking for permission to erect a 3d Infantry Division Memorial in Arlington National Cemetery. I received an answer that stated he did not have the authority to grant such a request; such authority would have to come from Congress. Brigadier General Phillips, from Georgia, said that he had some good contacts in Congress and that he would take on the project of getting permission from Congress. General Phillips did an outstanding job to get a public law passed in Congress, dated September 29, 1988, that gave the 3d Infantry Division permission to erect a memorial in Arlington National Cemetery.

3. Raising funds. Colonel Bernard wrote many letters for my signature to Society of the 3d Infantry Division Outposts, individuals and organizations. Money was slow coming in; however, once we completed the design and received permission from Congress to place the Memorial in Arlington National Cemetery, we started receiving more support. Unfortunately, during this six years of effort, Colonel Bernard passed away, and Brigadier General Edson became ill and could not help. Colonel Tardy was our Treasurer and he continued the raising of funds project. To accomplish the tasks assigned to the committee, we had to raise about $90,000.00, which we did.

4. Location of the Memorial. Where would we place the memorial in Arlington National Cemetery? I discussed this with the Superintendent of Arlington National Cemetery, R. J. Constanza. He told me that the Vice Chief of Staff of the Army was his boss and suggested that I attempt to get his support. The Vice Chief of Staff was General Arthur E. Brown, who had been one of the finest battalion commanders under my command in the Americal Division. Art commanded the 1st Battalion, 52d Infantry. I made an appointment to see him and he gave me complete

support. The Superintendent offered the Division many locations to select from; the one that appeared to be the ideal was just off a walkway between the Administration building and President Kennedy's grave. Approximately four million people a year would pass that location.

The Fine Arts Commission turned that location down because the Memorial would be a tall monument among the normal size headstones. The executive secretary of the Fine Arts Commission called me about the commission not approving that location and said that the commission had suggested a site across the street from the Memorial Amphitheater. The Superintendent had said that would be a very fine location for the memorial, but he was sure that the Fine Arts Commission would not approve it.

I made arrangements for some of my committee, the Superintendent, and myself to meet with the Executive Secretary of the Commission so that he could point out the area that the Commission was suggesting. We were all amazed that the commission had suggested such a beautiful location. He told us that we would still have to make our presentation to the Commission. Don Lethbridge and I worked hard on our presentation to ensure that we would be successful. When we appeared before the commission, the Executive Secretary called Don Lethbridge as the first witness. Before Don made a comment, the Chairman stated that the Commission had gone to the site that morning and was ready to approve the location but would be glad to hear our presentation. Don immediately stated that he had no comment; we would accept the Commission's decision.

5. Dedication Ceremony. The Committee decided that the dedication should be held on August 15, 1990, the date we landed in southern France in 1944, 46 years earlier. We asked General William B. Rosson, who had been with the Division during World War II, to be our principal speaker. Colonel Angus B. MacLean offered to chair the dedication and reception committee. Angus did an outstanding job as chairman to ensure that everything was properly coordinated. The day of the dedication was very hot and most people looked for shade. More than 400 3d Infantry Division Veterans and their families came to the dedication and the reception. Richard Maniscalco, a Marine, liked the 3d Infantry Division Society and had attended many of our functions; we made him an honorary member of the Society. When he heard about the dedication

and learned that we wanted a tape of the dedication, he offered to attempt to get his government agency to make a videotape of the event. I had to write a letter to support his request. Maniscalco was successful in his request. The tape covers the landing in southern France, pictures of other actions, award ceremonies, and other histories of the Division before it goes into the dedication. It then covers interviews with 3d Division veterans. It is an outstanding tape. At the end of this chapter (Inclusion #2 through #2-4) are pictures of the memorial and its location near the Amphitheater.

6. Reception. After the dedication, a reception was held at the Fort Myers Officers Club and all attendees were invited. The reception was very successful and all 3d Infantry Division veterans and their families enjoyed the occasion. They also paid many compliments to the committee for the beautiful memorial and the outstanding dedication ceremony.

January 28, 1986: Challenger Exploded Killing All on Board

I remember well on January 28, 1986 when NASA launched the Challenger spaceship. In 73 seconds it reached 8.9 miles in the sky and exploded. I was watching this on television and wondered, as everyone else did, if anyone could possibly live through such an explosion. All seven on board were killed. At the end of this chapter (Inclusion #3) is a picture of the explosion as shown in U.S. News & World Report.

January 10, 1988: My Mother Passed Away

On January 10, 1988, my mother, Mimi, passed away. Mimi was still living in her home in Somerset, Kentucky. She had not been very well for the past year. Mimi would have been 96 years old on April 21, 1988. All three boys and their wives (Bill and Eula, Jim and Mary Elizabeth, and myself and Glenda) were present. It was a sad occasion, but Mimi had lived a wonderful life.

October 2, 1989: Glenda's Mother Passed Away

On October 2, 1989, Glenda's mother, Mamma, as she was known by her grandchildren, passed away. Mamma had been living in a nursing home in Lawrenceburg, Kentucky for over a year. She would have been 94 years old on October 17, 1989. All three of her children and their spouses were present (Glenda and myself, Edna Mason and Starling, and Sonny and Marcia). That was a sad occasion, but Mamma had not been very well for the last few weeks. She had lived a great life.

November 9, 1989: The Berlin Wall Fell

I remember well on June 12, 1987 when President Reagan, making a speech at the Brandenburg Gate, West Berlin, made the statement, "Mr. Gorbachev, tear down that wall." The Russians finally gave in and the wall started coming down on November 9, 1989. This was the beginning of the end of the Cold War, which had been going on since the end of World War II.

1990 – 1991: The Persian Gulf Crisis

On August 2, 1990, Saddam Hussein, Iraq, ordered his troops to invade Kuwait. That same day the UN Security Council demanded Iraq's withdrawal from Kuwait. On August 8, Iraq announced the annexation of Kuwait. On November 29, the UN Security Council authorized the use of "all necessary means" to remove Iraq from Kuwait after January 15, 1991.

On January 17, 1991, the Coalition Forces began bombing Iraqi targets. On February 24, 1991, Coalition Forces began a major ground attack. Kuwait's capital, Kuwait City, was liberated on February 27. On February 28, the Coalition attacks against Iraq ended. Iraq accepted the terms of a formal cease-fire agreement on April 6, 1991. The UN Security Council officially declared an end to the war on April 11.

One of the interesting things about the Persian Gulf Crisis, called Operation Desert Storm, was that two principal officers involved were under my command in the Americal Division in Vietnam in 1969-1970. They were General Colin Powell, Chairman of the Joint Chiefs of Staff, and General H. Norman Schwarzkopf, commander of the Coalition Forces. General Powell gave some outstanding briefings to the press in Washington, D.C., as did General Schwarzkopf in the war zone.

February 22, 1991: Our 50th Wedding Anniversary

On February 22, 1991, Glenda and I were in Florida for our annual Florida trip, and that was also our 50th wedding anniversary. Before we left McLean, Virginia, we had made plans for our 50th wedding anniversary party to be held at the Fort Myers Officers Club on March 22. Our children helped us make the plans. To our great surprise, on February 22, we received the most beautiful vase of 50 golden roses from our wonderful children, Lloyd Ann, Larry, and Judi. Those roses lasted until we departed in early March.

At the March 22 party at the Fort Myers Officers Club, Larry, as the spokesman for the children, made some very nice remarks about his mother and father. Then all three presented Glenda and me with a large framed picture of our five grandchildren and a certificate to spend a weekend at the Greenbrier Resort in West Virginia. Glenda and I enjoyed our visit to Greenbrier very much. We used the swimming pool, had massages, played golf on the 18-hole putting green at least twice a day, and took some long walks through some beautiful surroundings. The food was outstanding, and we enjoyed the tea each day. On Sunday, there was a beautiful brunch at the golf course clubhouse. Glenda and I invited the children to join us for that event. Lloyd Ann and Kyle could not come because it was so far from Bowling Green, Kentucky. Larry and Pam and Judi and David joined us, and we had a wonderful brunch, plus we enjoyed many other things around Greenbrier. That is one anniversary that Glenda and I would never forget. At the end of this chapter (Inclusion #4) is a picture of Glenda and me eating some of our anniversary cake at the Fort Myers party.

September 30, 1991: My Brother Bill Passed Away

My oldest brother, William H., Jr. (Bill), passed away on September 30, 1991. Bill had Alzheimer's for the last few years and did not really know what was going on most of the time. Bill was a fine brother and he always told me how proud he was of my accomplishments. His wife, Eula, had passed away on March 14, 1988. Bill had Alzheimer's then, and it was very sad that he did not understand what had happened.

June 17-19, 1994: Ramsey and Burton Reunions

I made arrangements to have a Ramsey reunion on June 17-18, 1994 in or around Somerset, Kentucky. Bill Ramsey, III and Joanne Ramsey Jasper offered their houseboats on Lake Cumberland at Conley Bottom, near Somerset, Kentucky. Each day we would all go to the houseboats, where we had great fun. We would swim, water ski, go out in small boats, and cruise the lake. Everyone brought food so we ate well. At the end of this chapter (Inclusion #5) is a picture of those at the lake.

I also made arrangements to have a Burton reunion on June 19, 1994, following the Ramsey reunion. Sonny and Marcia Burton offered their home in Frankfort, Kentucky. Sonny and Marcia had many things for us to do, and they fed us very well. At the end of this chapter (Inclusion #6) is a picture of those present.

June 29, 1994: Shot My Age in Golf

After I retired in 1974, I started playing golf at the Fort Belvoir, Virginia golf course. We had a regular foursome, and we played about three times a week – weather permitting. Playing this often, I improved my game. On June 29, 1994, I shot my age of 76, and I continued to shoot my age at least once a year until I was 81.

October 29, 1994: Inducted into "The Wall of Fame," University of Kentucky

In 1994, the ROTC Department, University of Kentucky, established "The Wall of Fame." On October 29, 1994, they inducted the first six persons into "The Wall of Fame," and I was one of the six inducted. I considered it a great honor to be selected the first year when they had so many people from which to select.

April 19, 1995: Domestic Terrorism

I remember well on April 19, 1995 when the Alfred P. Murray Federal Building, Oklahoma City, Oklahoma, was destroyed by an enormous explosion. One hundred sixty-eight people were killed, including 19 children who were in a daycare center. It was later determined that this was domestic terrorism, and the perpetrators were Timothy J.

McVeigh and Terry L. Nichols. Both were found guilty, and McVeigh was sentenced to death.

July 18-19, 1997: Ramsey Reunion

The Ramsey reunion in June 1994 went over so well that I was asked to arrange another reunion in the summer of 1997. Bill and Joanne offered their houseboats once again, and we had another great reunion. At the end of this chapter (Inclusion #7) is a picture of those present. At Inclusion #8 is a picture of my immediate family. I tried to arrange another reunion for the Burtons, but it did not work out.

April 20, 1999: Columbine High School Massacre

I remember on April 20, 1999 when two students, Eric Harris, 18, and Dylan Kiebold, 17, massacred a teacher and twelve classmates and wounded 23 other students at Columbine High School, Littleton, Colorado. Harris and Kiebold committed suicide. Two Denver area men who helped the killers obtain an assault pistol pleaded guilty to criminal charges. Philip Duran, 26, was sentenced to 4 ½ years, and Mark Manes received a six-year term.

June 1999: My Third Hole in One

In June 1999 I made my third hole-in-one in golf at the Fort Belvoir, Virginia golf course. My first hole-in-one was at a golf course in Burnside, Kentucky, seven miles from my hometown of Somerset, Kentucky. My second hole-in-one was at the Fort Belvoir golf course but was on a different hole than my third one.

June 20, 1999: Judi's Card to Glenda

The children always wrote very sweet cards to Mother and me on Mother's Day, Father's Day, birthdays, and other days when cards were sent. I kept a number of them, but there were too many to put in this memoir. I selected this card from Judi to her mother as a typical card from the children. A copy of the card is at the end of this chapter (Inclusion #9 and #9-2).

May 29, 2000: My Birthday

Glenda always gave me a very nice birthday with a lovely card. On May 29, 2000 she wrote me the sweetest card that any husband could ever receive. When I read it now, it brings tears to my eyes. The card reads as follows:

Dear Feller,
Not a usual birthday card but I wanted to put in my own words how much I do love you, these words are from my heart. You are the world to me and as the years go by I depend on you for everything, and you have been so wonderful to me. I could not ask for more. I'm just so sorry that our last years have to be so hectic with aches, pills and doctors.
Sorry our family can't be here to help celebrate your birthday. Again, I want to say I love you so very, very much, with all my heart.
Glenda

July 1, 2000: Warren Hecker Passed Away

In 1975, I started playing golf at the Fort Belvoir, Virginia golf course. Colonel Frank Petruzel, who had been a company commander of mine in World War II, invited me to play with him and two others. One of the players was Warren Hecker. Warren was a very friendly person and had lots of wit. We got a regular foursome together and played three times a week – weather permitting. For 25 years, I played golf with Warren. The other two golfers would change after a few years.

In October 1999, we were playing, and Warren was very quiet, which was most unusual. At the end of nine holes, he told me that he did not feel well and was leaving to go to the doctor. They suspected cancer but it took until December before they really knew his condition. It was a very serious cancer, and they gave him no more than ten months to live. It was a shock to all of us to see a man who had been so energetic, with so much wit, and walking 18 holes of golf in early October 1999, find out that he had less than ten months to live. When Warren passed away on July 1, 2000, I lost a very close friend of 25 years. Losing a friend that fast makes you think that the same thing could happen to you.

Spring and Summer 2000: Planning to Move to a Retirement Community

For the past year, Glenda and I had been discussing movement into a retirement home because of Glenda's physical condition and because I could not take care of a house and yard many more years. We had made a deposit in a Fairfax retirement home near Fort Belvoir, Virginia, but that was too far away from our children. Since Judi lived in Salem, Virginia, and Larry lived in Floyd County, about 35 miles away, we decided to look at retirement areas in Roanoke and Salem, Virginia. We visited most every retirement community in the area. Richfield Retirement Community in Salem had a three-bedroom cottage that was available and that seemed to fit our needs more than any of the others. We signed for the cottage with the hope of moving there in September 2000.

We had to sell our house and make plans to move. When we started to look for a real estate agent, I found that USAA had a very good deal. However, one of the people that lived on our street, Cecelia Lofton, was a real estate agent and she said that she could do better than USAA. She had an excellent reputation so we signed with her. She was very helpful and told us what we needed to do to the house to get it ready for sale. About mid-July, we had the house ready.

After much discussion, we settled on a price, in hopes that it would sell soon. We turned the house over to Cecelia on a Wednesday with the plan to have an open house on Sunday. By Friday, she had already received two bids, both over the asking price. On Sunday, she received three more bids – all over the asking price. On Monday, we agreed to sell the house. Cecelia is quite the saleswoman, and Glenda and I were thrilled with the results.

August – September 2000: Our Move to Salem, Virginia

Glenda and I started making arrangements with movers to move us to Salem, Virginia. Many things, too numerous to mention, had to be done, and we did them. We arranged for our belongings to be loaded so that they would arrive at our cottage on September 18, 2000. Since Judi lived in Salem, we spent the night of September 17 with her so that we would be ready for the movers to arrive on September 18.

September 18 was a very busy day. The movers did an outstanding job of placing the furniture, and they unpacked the boxes that we requested. Larry and Judi were a lot of help to us. We did not have enough storage for all of our things, so the remainder was taken to Judi's basement by the movers. Glenda and I stayed in our new home on the night of September 18.

September 27 – October 20, 2000: Glenda's Illness

On September 27, 2000, Glenda became very ill. I called 911, and an ambulance was sent to take her to Lewis Gale Hospital, where she stayed until September 29. On October 3, she felt bad again, and I took her back to the doctor, Dr. R. Sharma, who had treated her while she was in the hospital. He said she had a light case of pneumonia and gave her medicine for that. In a few days, she was feeling much better. Lloyd Ann and Kyle were visiting by then.

We needed some things for the house so we went to Lowe's. While there, Glenda needed to go to the ladies' room. Lloyd Ann went with her and was waiting for her when she heard a fall. Glenda had fallen and hurt her left arm. Lowe's called an ambulance to take her to the hospital, where a doctor said that she had broken her left arm. He thought she should have an operation on the arm to correct the break. The next day we saw her doctor again, and he brought in another doctor to look at her arm. He agreed that she should have an operation to correct the broken arm, but he said that he could not do the operation until she got over the pneumonia. Glenda felt good for a few days. We took a picture of the family sitting on the couch in the living room, which is at the end of this chapter (Inclusion #10). This is the last picture taken of Glenda.

On October 10, Glenda felt bad so I arranged for her to see her doctor again. Telling us that the pneumonia had gotten worse, he increased her medicine and told her to come back on October 13. On that day, he admitted her to the hospital. On October 17, the doctor discovered that her lungs were collecting fluid. They pumped the fluid out of her lungs, which was very painful. Glenda was upset with all of us for letting a doctor perform such a painful procedure. She stated that she had rights and that she did not want to go through such a procedure again. Glenda's heart doctor came by to check on her quite often. He thought highly of Glenda and was very nice to her.

The following day, October 18, the doctor said she was getting more fluid in her lungs. Lloyd Ann, Larry, and Judi were with me when the doctor came back and asked all of us to step outside where we could talk. The doctor then told us that Glenda had very little chance to survive. This news was a shock to all of us. He stated that if we wished to take her home he would release her. The four of us were in tears, but we decided that it would be much better to take Glenda home where she could pass away with some dignity.

We took her home about 3:00 p.m. on October 18, 2000, and immediately called Good Samaritan Hospice for assistance. They came very quickly, first a social worker and later a nurse. On October 19, the nurse checked on Glenda at least two times. On October 20, the nurse came by in the morning and again about 4:45 in the afternoon. Glenda passed away at 5:00 p.m. in her own bed, with all of us at her bedside. This was a very sad occasion for all of us.

I lost my beautiful wife, my constant companion since my retirement on August 1, 1974, my most loyal supporter, and the best-dressed lady anyone has ever seen. Glenda always dressed to perfection and habitually received many compliments about how well she looked. I have lost many friends in combat, but that in no way prepared me to accept this loss. No one will ever know how bad it is to lose the one that you loved the most until it happens to them. God bless Glenda and thanks to the good Lord for the wonderful life that he gave us together and for the three wonderful children that we raised. Glenda's obituary is at the end of this chapter (Inclusion #11).

We held a visitation for Glenda at the Oakey Funeral Home in Salem on October 23 from 7:00 to 9:00 p.m. A copy of "In Remembrance" is at Inclusion #12.

Glenda was buried at Arlington National Cemetery, Arlington, Virginia, on November 1, 2000. We were amazed at the number of friends and relatives at the chapel, the burial site, and at the reception we gave following the burial. At the funeral in the old chapel at Fort Myers, Virginia, Judi wanted to tell our friends and relatives about her mother. This had to be a very difficult task on her part, but Judi made an outstanding presentation. Abby wished to do the same thing for her grandmother. She, too, made a wonderful presentation. I was extremely proud of both of them, and I am sure that Glenda was watching with pride.

A copy of their remarks are at Inclusion #13.

Grandchildren:

Glenda and I had five grandchildren and three great-grandchildren.

Lloyd Ann's family:
    Keith R. Wallace, born 31 July 1969
    Brian D. Wallace, born 21 March 1972

Judi's family:
    Jessamine R. Derr, born 27 November 1978
    Abigail B. Derr, born 18 June 1980
    Mackenzie Lee Derr, born 25 June 1983

Larry's family: no children

Great-Grandchildren:

Keith's family:
    Franklyn K. R. Wallace, born 27 December 1994
    Matthew C. Wallace, born 24 March 1998

Brian's family:
    Clayton A. Wallace, born 23 August 2004

Glenda did not live to see Clay

Letters and Cards Regarding Glenda

I received many letters and cards from friends and relatives everywhere. I am going to quote some of their comments, but I will not put the names of the persons who made the comments.

"I always thought Glenda was such a beautiful woman and she did not change with age."

"Glenda was a beautiful person and we will miss her."

"She, and a few other strong, vital, but still very feminine women, have always been among my favorite heroes. Other than the movie, Steel

Magnolias, I do not believe I have ever seen this type of real, mostly southern, women even remotely displayed in the media. Although I met her only a few times, Glenda radiated this quality. She gave of herself and was obviously loved because of that."

"Glenda truly was a rose, and shared her sweet fragrance and beauty with all who knew her."

"Mrs. Ramsey was admired and held in great respect by all of us who knew her and were among her longtime friends."

"Glenda was a lovely lady with a sweet smile always."

"Glenda was a rare and fine person whom I am privileged to have known. I will miss her and treasure her memory."

"It was so easy for us to see why you loved Glenda so much. She was such a gracious, lovely lady. We will never forget what a very special lady she was and what joy and pleasure it was to be with her."

"Glenda truly was a rose and shared her sweet fragrance and beauty with all who knew her. Our hearts ache with yours at her passing beyond to the other side."

"Glenda was so gracious and lovely."

"From the few occasions that we were together I could see that she was a warm and engaging person and a devoted wife to you."

"Glenda would be very proud of you and your family for the service in Virginia. Such warm and heartfelt feelings for a warm, caring, classy woman. I hope when I finally do get married I will have a marriage as strong and loving as yours. I always saw you like two honeymooners."

"Aunt Glenda was such a special lady. She was my favorite."

"I received several phone calls today from our Outpost 7 members expressing the view that the funeral arrangements for Glenda and the reception were outstanding in every respect."

"I always thought of Glenda as a lovely lady and special longtime friend."

"She was a great lady and a true dear friend of mine. She will be *greatly missed by all of us."*

"She was such a lovely, gracious person. Mom and Dad thought so much of you both. Please know that our thoughts and prayers are with you and your family and that those many happy years with such a beautiful, lovely, gentle woman will eventually begin to comfort you."

"In the brief time we had together, I could tell you all are a special family who loved Mrs. Ramsey very much."

"Your love and attention caring towards Mrs. Ramsey were so apparent and I appreciate the privilege of meeting such a strong family."

"She was such a lovely person and we enjoyed the times we spent with you all so much. She was the epitome of a lady."

"She was a very special lady, and we were fortunate to know her."

"Glenda was a strong woman – think of all the times she's said goodbye to you, Feller – never knowing whether she would ever see you again – it was harder for her to stay home and do the mundane things and keep the home together than it was for you to go fight a war – you got press good but she never did."

"Glenda was such a beautiful Christian lady."

"She was such a beautiful and gracious lady and I admired her charm and grace tremendously. Both individually and as a couple you both have meant so very much to both me and my parents."

"Aunt Glenda was so special to all of us and we too will miss her dearly. I know that she has gone to a special place, and we will always treasure our fond memories of her."

"Glenda was such a very special person in every way, and those of us who know her will always remember her wonderful qualities and her love."

"I have thought a lot about Mrs. Ramsey and what a wonderful person she was."

"I always admired her quiet demeanor and those beautiful eyes."

End of My Memoir

Although I am ending my memoir with Glenda's death, her burial and follow-on comments, I would like to add two items beyond November 2000 that I believe my relatives and friends should know.

September 20, 2001: My Brother James B. (Jim) Passed Away

My brother James B. (Jim) passed away on September 20, 2001. He was living in Somerset, Kentucky. Jim was also a fine brother. He was very proud of the things that I had done, and he always told me how proud he was of my accomplishments.

May 26, 2004: Bad News for Me

In April 2004, while I was seeing a doctor at a VA hospital for insomnia, the doctor stated that she noticed my right hand trembled slightly and asked me if I had noticed the tremor. I told her that I had not. She said that she would make an appointment for me to see a neurology doctor to see if I had Parkinson's disease. I saw Dr. Jean Vike on May 26, 2004. Some of her report follows:

"PAST MEDICAL HISTORY: Sick sinus syndrome, has pacemaker since 2001, macular degeneration, hypertension, DJD knees, hips, low back. History of left arm fracture. History of closed head trauma with prolonged unconsciousness (helicopter crash in Vietnam), and chronic insomnia since the time of head trauma. No history of anxiety or depression. He was never treated with neuroleptics. Leg cramps at night responding well to quinine."

"IMPRESSION:
1. Parkinson's disease. However, in view of the history of significant head trauma, I believe that it is more likely than not that he is suffering from post traumatic parkinsonism, which became more obvious as with aging he lost his CNS reserves.
2. Insomnia: In view of the timing of onset (recovery from head trauma) and the absence of anxiety or other sleep pathology, I suspect that more likely than not the insomnia is the result of traumatic injury to the reticular formation of other diencephalic structures involved in the sleep wake cycle."

At D.C. Sig luncheon, in front from left: Reps. Beryl Anthony & Clair Burgener; Exec. Secretary Bill Bringham; Bill Hecht; Rep. Mike McCormack; in back from left, D.C. Alum President George Hooper; Reps. Henry Hyde, Ike Skelton & Mark Andrews; Grand Consul Bash; Sen. Barry Goldwater; Reps. John Wydler & Jim Abdnor; & Sen. Jake Garn.

Significant Sig Goldwater, left, admires awards of new Significant Sigs Allan Hunter, second from left, & Lloyd Ramsey, right, with Grand Consul Jim Bush.

☐ TWO-THIRDS of the 21 Sigs in the current U.S. Congress participated as the Washington, D.C. Alumni Chapter caucused for its traditional spring luncheon for Capitol Hill brothers, March 28.

Sig Congressmen present were Significant Sig & U.S. Senator Barry M. Goldwater, Arizona '32 (R.-Ariz.); Senator Jake Garn, Utah '54 (R.-Utah); and Representatives Mark Andrews North Dakota State '47 (R.-N.D.); John Wydler, Brown '46 (R.-N.Y.); Jim Abdnor, Nebraska '45 (R.-S.D.); Clair Burgener, San Diego '50 (R.-Cal.); Bob Eckhardt, Texas '35 (D.-Tex.); Henry Hyde, Duke '46 (R.-Ill.); Mike McCormack, Washington State '48 (D.-Wash.); Henson Moore, L.S.U. '62 (R.-La.); 'Bud' Shuster, Pitt '54 (R.-Pa.); Beryl Anthony, Arkansas '60 (D.-Ark.); Ike Skelton, Missouri '53 (D.-Mo.); and Tony Hall, Denison '64 (D.-Ohio).

Grand Consul Jim Bash spoke to the assembled Sigs on the State of the Fraternity, and presented Significant Sig Awards to two successful brothers — Maj. Gen. Lloyd B. Ramsey, Kentucky '40, past Provost Marshall General of the U.S. Army; and Allan Oakley Hunter, Calif. State-Fresno '37, Board Chairman of the Federal Mortgage Association and a former Congressman.

Undergraduates from chapters at George Washington, Maryland, Florida State and William and Mary, along with many alumni, also met and talked with the Grand Officers present, who included:

Grand Consul Bash; Past Grand Consul Bolon B. Turner, Board of Grand Trustees Chairman Malcolm M. Christian; Grand Trustee Fred DeMarr; Eastern Province Grand Praetor E.C. "Wayo" Yegen; Virginia Province Grand Praetor "Mac" McCarthy; Foundation Board of Governors member Roy M. Teel; and Executive Secretary William T. Bringham. ■

INCL. # 1

Third Infantry Division
Memorial
Arlington National Cemetary

IN MEMORY OF OUR WAR DEAD

Dedicated
15 August 1990

INCL. # 2

Principal Speaker

Three diagonal white stripes also
    denoting three noble purposes:
First and foremost, to pay
    tribute to the war dead;
Second, to honor those who have
    served in the Marne Division
    itself—the revered Division
    of which we have been a part,
    and a part of which resides
    within each of us.
        General William B. Rosson
        U.S. Army, Retired

Dedication

As President of the Society of the Third Infantry Division and on behalf of all the veterans of the Third Infantry Division I hereby dedicate this memorial to 11,119 soldiers of the Third Infantry Division that were Killed in Action in World War I, World War II and Korea, and to 1,537 soldiers missing in action during those same wars. May God bless their loved ones.
        Dale L. McGraw

Third Infantry Division Memorial in relation to the Arlington Memorial Amphitheater

INCL. # 2-2

The Memorial Committe
Appointed 8 September 1984

*Fund Raising, Design, Legislation,
Government Agencies Approval,
Installation, Dedication*

Maj. Gen Lloyd B. Ramsey, USA Retired, Chairman
Brig. Gen. Hallett D. Edson, USA Retired, Deceased
Brig. Gen. Eugene Phillips, USA Retired
Col. Lyle W. Bernard, USA Retired, Deceased
Col. Walter E. Tardy, USA Retired
Col. Angus B. MacLean, USA Retired
Capt. Carl Swickerath, USA Retired
CSM. Leonard J. Werth, USA Retired
Tech. Sgt. Terry J. Dalton

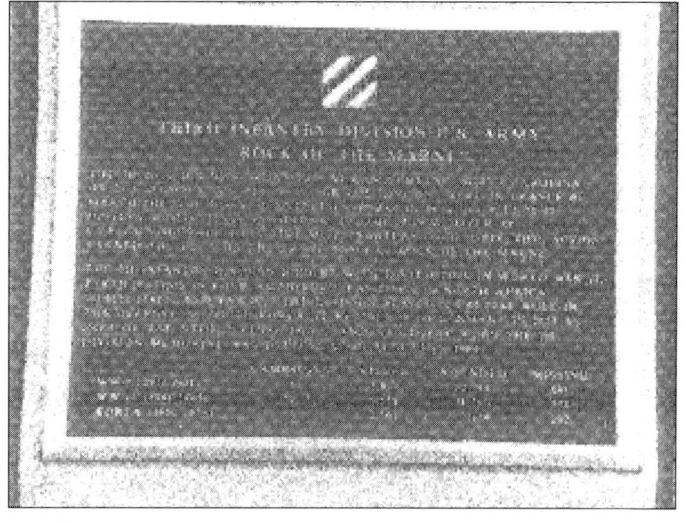

Third Infantry Division Plaque with history, campaigns, killed, wounded and missing in action.

INCL. # 2-3

THIRD INFANTRY DIVISION

"ROCK OF THE MARNE"

THE 3D DIVISION WAS ORGANIZED AT CAMP GREENE, NORTH CAROLINA, ON 23 NOVEMBER 1917. ALL UNITS OF THE DIVISION WERE IN FRANCE BY MARCH 1918. THE DIVISION ENTERED COMBAT IN MAY. ON JULY 15 IT DISTINGUISHED ITSELF IN DEFENSE OF THE MARNE RIVER AT CHATEAU-THIERRY, FORTY-FIVE MILES NORTHEAST OF PARIS. THIS ACTION EARNED THE DIVISION THE PROUD MOTO, "ROCK OF THE MARNE."

THE 3D INFANTRY FOUGHT WITH DISTINCTION IN WORLD WAR II, PRATICIPATING IN FOUR AMPHIBIOUS LANDINGS IN NORTH AFRICA, SICILY, ITALY AND FRANCE. THE DIVISION PLAYED A CRUCIAL ROLE IN THE DEFENSE OF SOUTH KOREA. IT RETURNED TO GERMANY IN 1957 AS PART OF THE NATO DEFENSE FORCE AND WAS THERE WHEN THE 3D DIVISION MEMORIAL WAS DEDICATED ON AUGUST 15, 1990.

	CAMPAIGNS	KILLED	WOUNDED	MISSING
WW-I (1917-1918)	6	3,401	12,764	691
WW-II (1941-1945)	10	5,558	18,766	554
KOREA (1950-1953)	8	2,160	7,939	292

INCL. # 2-4

Jan. 28, 1986. *The explosion that wiped out the Challenger, five career astronauts, an engineer and a teacher who had come aboard*

INCL. # 3

INCL. # 4

The Ramsey Reunion
On the houseboats of Bill Ramsey and Joanne Ramsey Jasper
Lake Cumberland, Conley Bottom, Ky.
17-18 June 1994

Seated: Cindy Ramsey, Cathy _____, Chris Ramsey, Bill Ramsey, Bruce Jasper, Katie Jasper, Linda Jasper, Abby Derr, Cathy Coldiron, Jessa Derr, Amanda Wilson, Maggie Derr

Standing: Feller Ramsey, David Ramsey, Larry Ramsey, Kyle Wallace, David Derr, Lloyd Ann Wallace, Glenda Ramsey, Brian Wallace, Keith Wallace, Phyllis Ramsey, Susan Wilson, Judi Derr, Jim Ramsey, Mary E. Ramsey, Pam Cadmus, Loyd Jasper, Joanne Jasper (holding Puddin), Jimmy Ramsey, Barbara Ramsey, Bill Jasper, Julie Jasper.

Not in picture–At Dinner 17 June 1994: Greg Ramsey, Karen Coldiron, Shelly Girdler, Doug Girdler.

Not in picture, left early: Chris Coldiron, David Coldiron.

Did not attend: Richard Wilson, Cherry Garcia, Steve Garcia, Jessica Garcia, _____ Garcia, Matthew Jasper

INCL. # 5

The Burton Reunion
At the home of Morris and Marcia Burton
Frankfort, Ky.
19 June 1994

1st Row: Alex Sturm, Jamie Sturm, Brice Burton, Paige Burton, Abby Derr, Laura or Janie Gregory, Christy Gregory, Maggie Derr, Anna Gregory.

2nd Row: Beth Sturm, Jill Burton, Thomas Gregory, Janie or Laura Gregory, Sandra Burton.

Third Row: Larry Sturm, Sally Mason Moore, Mason Moore, Pam Cadmus, Judi Derr, Glenda Ramsey, Edna M. Gregory, Jessa Derr, Lloyd Ann Wallace, Marcia Burton.

Standing: Feller Ramsey, Bill Moore, Greg Burton, Stoney Gregory, Larry Ramsey, Josh Gregory, Trey Moore, David Derr, Kyle Wallace, Brian Wallace, Morris Burton, Starling Gregory, Keith Wallace, David Gregory, Mary Gregory

Not in Picture: Brady Sturm (Was taking a nap)

INCL. # 6

The Ramsey Reunion
On the houseboats of Bill Ramsey and Joanne Ramsey Jasper
Lake Cumberland, Conley Bottom, Ky.
18-19 July 1997

Seated: Abby Derr, Katie Jasper, Amanda Wilson, Maggie Derr, Bill Ramsey, Matthew Jasper, Chris Ramsey, Logan Ramsey, Kathy Ramsey.

Standing: Jennifer Wallace, Keith Wallace, Frankie Wallace, Brian Wallace, Kyle Wallace, Lloyd Ann Wallace, Jessa Derr, David Coldiron, Judi Derr, Loyd Jasper, Larry Ramsey, Pamela Cadmus, Bruce Jasper, Linda Jasper, David Derr, Glenda Ramsey, Bill Jasper, Phyllis Ramsey, Shelly Tomlinson, Scott Tomlinson, Jimmie Ramsey, Susan Wilson, Joanne Jasper, Cathy Coldiron, Mikki ____, Mary E. Ramsey, Jim Ramsey, Barbara Ramsey, Feller Ramsey.

Not in picture, left early: Greg Ramsey, Sarah ____, Chris Coldiron, Karen Coldiron, Elizabeth Coldiron, Daniel Coldiron.

INCL. # 7

Abigail B. Derr, Kyle D. Wallace, Lloyd Ann Wallace, David E. Derr, Jessamine R. Derr, Judi R. Derr, Keith R. Wallace, Jennifer R. Wallace, Franklyn Keith R. Wallace, Mackenzie Lee Derr, Brian D. Wallace, Pamela B. Cadmus, Larry B. Ramsey, Glenda B. Ramsey, Lloyd B. Ramsey.

19 July 1997
Landmark Inn
Somerset, Ky.

We had attended a Ramsey reunion on Lake Cumberland on Joanne Jasper and Bill Ramsey's houseboats. There were over 40 of the Ramsey family present.

INCL. # 8

INCL. # 9

You and Dad really are the greatest. I know you feel so bad alot of the time but you always manage to smile and keep your sense of humor. You've been a real trooper through all your problems. I never would have been so confident and self-assured if it weren't for you and Daddy. You've been beside me each when I let you down. I adore you and can't thank you enough for being such a great mom!

XX
all my love,
Jack

INCL. # 9-2

7 October 2000
Judi—Lloyd Ann–Larry–Glenda–Feller
3624 Bowling Drive, Salem, Virginia

INCL. # 10

Lexington Herald-Leader
Monday, October 23, 2000

RAMSEY

Glenda Burton Ramsey, 83, died peacefully, Friday, October 20, 2000 surrounded by her family at her home in Salem, VA where she had moved in mid-September after having lived in McLean, VA for the past thirty years. Born June 20, 1917, she was a native of Sommerset, KY. She was a graduate of the University of Kentucky, and taught school for two years before marrying Lloyd Brinkley Ramsey in 1941. As the wife of an Army officer, she created homes for her family in NC, GA, KS, Japan, MO, PA and VA and raised the children without her husband during WWII and the Korean and Vietnam conflicts. She is survived by husband, Major General Lloyd B. Ramsey, Salem; two daughters, a son and their spouses, Lloyd Ann and Kyle Wallace, Bowling Green, KY; Larry Ramsey and Pamela Cadmus, Terry's Fork, VA; Judi and David Derr, Salem, VA; five grandchildren, Keith R. Wallace, KY, Dr. Brian D. Wallace, IN, Jessamine R. Derr, VA, Abigail B. Derr, SC and Mackenzie L. Derr, VA; two great grandchildren, Franklyn K. Wallace, and Matthew C. Wallace; a sister, Mrs. Starling (Edna Mason) Gregory, Lexington; and a brother, Morris Burton, Frankfort. The family will receive friends at John M. Oakey & Son Funeral Home, Salem, 7-9 p.m. today. Mrs. Ramsey will be interred at Arlington National Cemetery. Please send donations to the American Heart Assoc., 4504 Starkey Rd., Roanoake, VA, 24018 or Good Samaritan Hospice, 3825 Electric Rd., S.W., Suite A, Roanoake, VA 24018.

INCL. # 11

In Remembrance

SALEM FUNERAL HOME

In Memory Of
GLENDA BURTON RAMSEY

Date of Birth
June 20, 1917
SOMERSET, KENTUCKY

Date of Death
October 20, 2000
SALEM, VIRGINIA

Place and Time of Service
11:00 AM Wednesday November 1, 2000
FT. MYER CHAPEL
ARLINGTON, VIRGINIA

Interment
Wednesday November 1, 2000
ARLINGTON NATIONAL CEMETERY
ARLINGTON, VIRGINIA

Arrangements By
John M. Oakey & Son
Salem, Va.

Family
SURVIVORS:
HUSBAND:
Major General Lloyd B. Ramsey
TWO DAUGHTERS, ONE SON AND SPOUSES:
Lloyd Ann and Kyle Wallace
Larry Ramsey and Pamela Cadmus
Judi and David Derr
FIVE GRANDCHILDREN:
Keith R. Wallace
Dr. Brian D. Wallace
Jessamine R. Derr
Abigail B. Derr
Mackenzie L. Derr
TWO GREAT-GRANDCHILDREN:
Franklyn K. Wallace
Matthew C. Wallace
SISTER:
Mrs. Starling (Edna Mason) Gregory
BROTHER:
Morris Burton

INCL. # 12

I just want to say welcome and how wonderful it is to see all our family and good friends. For all our family from Kentucky they know her heart and home were always in Kentucky and how proud she was to tell anyone she was from Kentucky. Whenever I talk to anyone who knew my mother, they would always describe her the same way, sweet, loving, kind, gentle, and always the best dressed lady around.

My mother was so proud of my father, not for just being the general, but for being the very good man that he is. A great husband, wonderful father, grandfather, and a good friend. My mother and dad were in love for 60 years and what a great gift that was for us. Aunt Edna Mason, my mother's sister was so adored and my mother admired and loved her very much. She always referred to her as just Sis. Uncle Sonny or Morris, my mother's brother, how proud she was of him, how much she loved him and he could always make her laugh and giggle. She always looked forward to his special birthday cards. For all the grandchildren, all I can say is how you each brought her such joy and how she worried about you growing up in today's world. For Lloyd Ann, Larry, and myself, how lucky we were to have her for our mother. She was the best.

Judi

For me, my grandmother was the most kind, generous, and loving woman. From her sweet voice, to her soft hands, to her wonderful warm embraces, she was the perfect grandmother. Her five grandchildren, Keith, Brian, Jessa, Maggie, and myself were blessed, enriched and honored by her. Each one of us has our own personal moments of her that will always be in our hearts. All special occasions and special times will seem a little empty without her. I know how proud she was to be blessed with great-grandchildren from Keith and Jennifer but was saddened that she only saw a small part of their lives. Grandmommy was so very proud to see Brian make it to be Dr. Brian, but she said how really sad she was that she would never see Brian, Jessa, Maggie, or me get married. My little sister pointed out that she would be the only one Grandmommy did not get to see her graduate from high school. There will be those certain moments that will never be the same for any of us but we will have to remember that her spirit will always be with us. My last request that I asked my grandmother was not to worry just please be the angel watching over us.

Abby

INCL. # 13

ACKNOWLEDGMENTS

Anzio Beachhead, 22 January – 25 May 1944, (The Battery Press, Nashville, Tennessee).

Commonwealth Journal, (Somerset, Kentucky).

Cosmas, Graham A. and Lieutenant Colonel Terrence P. Murray, USMC, U.S. *Marines in Vietnam: Vietnamization and Redeployment, 1970-1971*.

Encyclopedia Britannica.

Fisher, Earnest F., Jr., *United States Army in World War II: The Mediterranean Theater of Operation, Cassino to the Alps*.

Homespun, "Scrapbook," (Somerset High School Press, Somerset, Kentucky).

Kentuckian 1940, University of Kentucky, (Lexington, Kentucky).

Kroesen, General Federich J., U.S. Army Retired, *The Cottonbaler*, Volume XI, No. 2, Spring 2001.

Lexington Herald-Leader, Lexington, Kentucky.

Pratt, Lieutenant Colonel Sherman W., U.S. Army Retired, *Autobahn to Berchtesgaden*.

Taggart, Donald G., editor, *History of the Third Infantry Division in World War II*.

Valenti, Isadore, *Combat Medic*.

White, Nathan William, *From Fedala to Berchtesgaden: A History of the Seventh United States Infantry in World War II*.

INDEX

A

A la Baraque, 148
Abby, 352, 373
Abrams, General Creighton, 243, 307
Abrams, General CINC, MACV, 307
ACSFOR (Assistant Chief of Staff for Force Development, 242
Adams, SP4 Roger H., 322
Adjutant General of the Army, 313
Advanced Management Program, 240
Advisory Group Korea, 235
Agent Orange, 277
Aide de Camp, 268
Air Force General, 315
Air Force Liaison Officer, 264
Aircraft Commander, 298
Aisne Defensive, 178
Aisne-Marne offensive, 178
Alabama, 57
Alaska, 178, 308
Albania, 118
Aldrin, Buzz, 265, 266
Alexander, General H. R. L. G., 3, 111, 113, 114, 115, 122
Alexander's, General headquarters, 119
Alfred P. Murray Federal Building, 347
Algiers, North Africa, 109, 112, 115, 117, 119
Allied Expeditionary Force, 141
Allied Forces Headquarters, 112, 113, 188
Allied Landings, 185
Allies, 118
All-State Quarterback, 320
Alphabet, 29
Aluminum Company of France, 241
Americal Division (23d Infantry Division), 262
Americal Division and Marines, 276
Americal Division, 3, 262, 263, 264, 265, 267, 268, 269, 270, 274, 275, 277, 278, 279, 287, 288, 291, 307, 321, 322, 342, 345
Americal Firebases, 266
American Legion Cup, Man of War Post, 70
American Universities and Colleges, 66, 87, 88
American zone, 181, 182, 183
Anaconda, Montana, 298
Anderson, Lt. Gen. Kenneth, 112
Andrews Air Force Base, 308
Ann Taylor, 213
Anzio Beachhead, 135, 139, 168, 375

Anzio, Italy, 132, 133, 135, 139, 141, 185
aquaplane, 43
Arizona, 40
Arlington Memorial Amphitheater, 359
Arlington National Cemetery, 341, 342, 352, 358
Arlington, Virginia, 352
Armed Forces Journal, 258
Armstrong, Neil, 265, 269
Army Advisor to the National Defense College, 235
Army Distaff Foundation, 340
Army Ground Forces, 189
Army Physical Examination Board, 315
Army War College, 210, 219, 221, 222, 223, 236
Army, 70, 276, 321
Army, the Pentagon, Washington,
ARVN Division Commander, 264, 277
Askalepov (Askalipov), Guard Major General Vasili S., 183, 184, 185, 200, 208, 209
Assistant Chief of Staff for Force Development (ACSFOR), 261
Athas, Captain William, 134, 135, 136
Atlantic Ocean, 34
Augusta, Georgia, 118
Autobahn to Berchtesgaden, 375
Award of the Distinguished Flying Cross, 285
Award of the Silver Star, 144
AWOL (absent without leave), 313

B

Bad Hershfeld, Germany, 180
Bad Wildungen, Germany, 180
Bagnoli, France, 141
Baker, 48
Baker, Colonel (Doctor) George I., 308, 309, 314, 315, 316, 318
Baker, Leslie, 46
Balfour Province Award, 72, 101
Bari, Italy, 120
Barnett, Aunt Mary Stella, 107
Barnett Family Reunion, 20
Barnett, Frank, 27
Barnett, J. W. (Wor Wor), 11, 20
Barnett, Mama, 12, 40
Barnett, Mary Ella (Mimi), 9
Barnett, Mrs. N. L., 40
Barnett, Napolean L., 9, 11, 40
Barnett, Papa, 12

Barnett, Robert (Bob), 40, 106, 107
Barnett, Uncle Frank, 15, 16
Barnett, Uncle Hampie, 38
Bash, Grand Consul Jim, 339
Batangan Peninsula, 265
Battalion Command Post, 140
Battalion Commander, 298, 319
Battalion Surgeon, 143
Battery Press, The, 375
Battle of Cowpens, 340
Battle of New Orleans, 178
Battle Patrol, 7th Infantry, 149
Bay State Milling Company, 241
Baynham, Jane, 66, 83
Beard, Doctor Eugene, 11
Beatty, Major George, 211
Bee Hive, 214
Behrendt, Captain, 163
Bell, Cadet Major J. O., 81
Benelli, Abel, 46
Benson, Colonel Hank, 226
Berchtesgaden, 160, 161, 162, 163, 164
Berlin Wall, 345
Bernard, Colonel Lyle W., 340, 341, 342
Besancon, France, 145, 148
BG Nguyen-Van Toan, 277, 284
Biesheim, 157
Blair, Richard E., 337, 338
Blandford, Colonel William, 190, 210
Blue Battalion (3d Battalion), 147, 148
Blue Bird swimming pool, 29
Bode, Cadet Cap't J. C., 81
Bolling, Major General, A. B., 216, 218, 219, 229
Borrelli, Command Sgt. Maj. Sam S., 278, 279, 298
Boston, Bill, 68, 93
Boston, Massachusetts, 13, 26
Bourn, Dick, 46, 47
Bowers, Verne, 313
Bowle, Colonel Hamilton H., 229
Bowling Green, Kentucky, 346
Bradley, General, 3, 116, 210
Brady, James, 339, 340
Brandenburg Gate, 345
Bremmerhaven, 180
Brian, 353, 373
Brian, Dr., 373
Briar Jumpers, 37
Brigade of British, 109
Brigade of the 101st Airborne Division, 272
Brinkley, Aunt Jennie, 11
British Eighth Army, 120

British zone, 181
Brown, Doctor, 60, 61
Brown, Fannie, 33
Brown, General Arthur E., 278, 342
Brown, Jimmy, 68, 93, 94
Bruner, Colonel G. E., 186
Bryant, Joanne M., 337
Buck Creek, 340
Buck, 12, 23
Bullard, WO2 James D., 322
Burda, Captain Michael (Mike), 181, 182, 183, 185, 209
Burma Shave signs, 73, 74
Burnside, Kentucky, 31, 348
Burton Reunion, 347, 365
Burton, Brice, 365
Burton, Edna Mason, 104, 125
Burton, Greg, 365
Burton, Jill, 365
Burton, Marcia, 345, 347, 365
Burton, Mason Emmet, 125, 311
Burton, Minnie May, 125
Burton, Morris W. (Sonny), 125, 365, 373
Burton, Mr., 151
Burton, Mrs., 151
Burton, Paige, 365
Burton, Sandra, 365
Burton, Sonny, 108, 212, 345, 347
Butcher, Commander, 116
Butler, Cadet Sgt., 81
Buzzby, 168

C

C. K. C. (all conference team), 48
C. K. C. Champions, 1935, 46, 57
Cadet Colonel of the Corps of Cadets, 65
Cadmus, Pamela B. (Pam), 364, 365, 366, 367
Calabia, Italy, 120
California, 40
Callahan, Vincent F. Jr., 337
Calley, Lieutenant William, 272
Camp Atterbury, Indiana, 189
Camp Herbert Tareyton, Le Havre, France, 187
Camp Home Run APO 895, 188
Camp Kilmer, New Brunswick, New Jersey, 188
Caney Fork Creek, 12
Carlisle Barracks, Pennsylvania, 221, 222
Carter, Cap't G. P., 81
Castillieri, Captain, 163
Cate, Colonel William Jr., 278
Cavalaire-sur-Mer, 144
Centennial "K" Medallion, 245
Central Kentucky Conference (CKC), 37, 46, 48, 57

Centre College, 13, 14, 26
CH-47 Chinook, 302
Chairman of the Board, 338
Challenger, 344
Chamberlin, John, 46
Champagne Marne, 178
Chapel Hill Victory, 188
Chaplain, 306
Chapultepec, 178
Chattanooga, Tennessee, 104
Cherbourg-Havre, 141, 172
Chief of Chaplains, 234
Chief of Staff, 3d Infantry Division, 269
Chief of Staff of Third Army, 249
Chief, 32
Choi, General, 236
Chu Lai Hospital, 305
Chu Lai, Vietnam, 262, 265, 266, 269, 299, 301, 303
Churchill, Prime Minister Winston, 3, 113, 114, 115, 116, 117, 118, 143
Churubusco, 178
Cincinnati, Ohio, 11, 19
Cisterna di Littoria, 134
Cisterna, 140
Citizens National Bank, 107
Clark, General, 128
Clark, Major General, 115
Clever, Private First Class Paul D., 147
Co. C. 1st Battalion, 6th Infantry, 302
Cocke, Charles P., 337, 338
Colby, Carl, 91
Cold War, 345
Coldiron, Cathy, 364, 366
Coldiron, Chris, 364, 366
Coldiron, Daniel, 366
Coldiron, David, 364, 366
Coldiron, Elizabeth, 366
Coldiron, Karen, 364, 366
Colle Monaco, 140
Collins, Brigadier General James, 266
Collins, Michael, 265, 265
Collosius, Colonel, 163
Colmar Pocket, 132, 152, 155
Columbine High School, 348
Combat Medic, 5, 153, 157, 375
Combs, Cadet Sgt., 81
Command and General Staff College, 214, 215
Command of the 3d Battalion, 7th Infantry and Promotion to Lt.Colonel, 141
Command of the Army Forces Far East, 226
Command Post, 149
Commander in Chief, 226

Commanding General, Americal Division, 262
Commonwealth Journal, 375
Company A, 135, 136
Company B, 135, 136
Company B, 4th Battalion, 3rd Infantry, 274
Company K, 137, 147, 148, 149
Company L, 135, 148, 149
Company M, 147
CONARC (Continental Army Command), 234, 309, 312
Congress, 21
Congressional Medal of Honor, 147
Conley Bottom, Kentucky, 347, 364, 366
Conner, Lieut. Garlin M., 153, 155
Connor (Conner), Lieut. Garlin M., 154, 157
Connor, Sergeant James P., 144
Constanza, R. J., 342
Conway, Lt. Colonel Theodore J., 113
Cooksey, Brigadier General Howard H., 268
Corpus Christi, Texas, 178
Cosmas, Graham A., 375
Cotton Baler Regiment, 133, 134
Cotton Baler Troops, 134, 163, 178
Counicras, 178
Counter Intelligence Corps, 218
Courtney, Cadet Sgt., 81
Cowpens, South Carolina, 340
Crack, Roxy V., 337
Creelsboro, Kentucky, 18
Croix de Guerre, 178
Cruse, 49
Cuba, 242
Cumberland Falls, Kentucky, 11
Cumberland River, 18, 30, 31, 33, 41
"Curly," 17
Curtis, Cadet Sgt., 81
Curtis, Houston, 91

D

DA Form 199, 318
Dad, 12, 13, 15, 16, 17, 18, 19, 20, 21, 26, 29, 30, 31, 32, 35, 38, 41, 42, 58, 107, 127, 139, 151, 236, 306
Dallas, Texas, 243
Dalton, Technical Sergeant Terry J., 341, 360
Danville, Kentucky, 13
Daughters of the American Revolution, 340
David, Edwin, 91
Davis, Harold, 46
D-Day, Northern France, 141, 172
Defensive Aisne-Marne Offensive, 178
Demilitarized Zone, 220
Democratic Party, 313
Denny-Murrell- Ramsey Funeral Home, 35

Department of Defense (DOD), 315
Department of the Army, 242, 285, 309
Depression, Great 19, 21
Deputy Chief of Information, 248
Deputy CINC, MACV, 307
Deputy Commanding General, 1st Logistical Command, 244, 261
Deputy Secretary of the Joint Staff, 225, 228
Der Berhof Obersalzberg, 160
Derr, Abby, 364, 365, 366
Derr, Abigail B., 353, 367
Derr, David E., 346, 364, 365, 366, 367
Derr, Jessa, 364, 365, 366, 373
Derr, Jessamine R., 353, 367
Derr, Judi R., 364, 365, 366, 367
Derr, Mackenzie Lee, 353, 367
Derr, Maggie, 364, 365, 366, 373
Desert Storm, 303
Detroit, 13
Dexheimer, Paul, 19
Di Ichi Hotel, 223
Dill, Field Marshall Sir John, 117
Dirksen, Senator Everett M., 239
Distinguished Alumni, 257
Distinguished Service Medal, 307, 319
"Dogface Soldier", 139, 169
Donaldson, Brigadier General John W., 268, 271, 368
Donnelly, PMS & T ROTC Lieutenant Col., 65, 68, 69, 70, 95
Doyle, Jim, 91
Drummy, Cadet Lt. Colonel W. J., 81
Dugan, George, Converse Athletic Prize, 53
Duncan, Colonel, 159, 160, 161
Duran, Philip, 348
Dwan, Major Jack, 186

E

East Berlin, Germany, 219
Eastern Kentucky State Teachers College, 58
Eden, Anthony, 115
Edson, Brigadier General Hallett D., 341, 360
Eighth Army Headquarters, 114
Eighth British Army, 113, 116, 120
Eisenhower, General Dwight D., 3, 112, 113, 116, 117, 118, 119, 141, 164, 171, 188, 172, 210, 238, 240
Eisenhower, President, 238
electronic computer, 230
Ellis, Mildred, 39, 51
Ellison, Aunt Vic Barnett, 11
Encyclopedia Britannica, 165, 166, 375
England, 58
Eubank, Frank, 315, 337, 338

Eula, 344, 346
Europe, 163, 311
Explorer I, 235

F

Falls Church, Virginia, 216, 221
Far East Command Headquarters (FEC Hqs.), 223
Fayetteville, North Carolina, 107, 127
Fecht River, 153
Feller, 127, 170, 349, 355, 370
Fields, Bob, 253
Fields, Sergeant Robert C., 234, 241
Fields, Velma, 253
Fine Arts Commission, 343
Fire Support Base Center and Fire Support Base Hawk Hill, 276, 297, 298
Fire Support Base Hawk Hill, 299, 300
First Baptist Church, Somerset, 40, 104,
First Battalion Headquarters Company, 134
First Battalion, 133
First British Army, 113
First Christian Church, Somerset, 38
first computer, 217
Fisher, Earnest F., Jr., 375
Fisher, Lee Davis, 38
Flemington, New Jersey, 34
FLIC, 339
Florida War, 178
Florida, 250, 338, 346
Floyd County, 350
Flynn, Major, 158
Fogel, Julius, 337
Foley, Edward H., 251
Ford, Colonel (Doctor) George W. (Wally), 307
Ford, Congressman Gerald (Gerry), 3, 240
Forker, Major, 163
Fort Belvior, Virginia, 347, 348, 349, 350
Fort Benning, Georgia, 104, 150, 180, 186, 187, 189, 190, 191, 210, 212, 228, 232, 234, 249, 279
Fort Bragg, N. C., 101, 103, 105, 106, 186, 249
Fort DeRussy, 262
Fort Holibird, Maryland, 218
Fort Hood, Texas, 240
Fort Jackson, South Carolina, 249
Fort Knox, Kentucky, 64, 69, 103,190
Fort Leavenworth, Kansas, 210, 214, 310
Fort Leonard Wood, Missouri, 232, 244, 245, 246, 247
Fort Lewis, Washington, 178
Fort McPherson, Georgia, 232, 245, 248, 249

Fort Myers Officers Club, 344, 346
Fort Myers, Virginia, 248, 352
Fort Polk, Louisiana, 245, 309, 310, 316
Fort Riley, Kansas, 310
Fort Rucker, Alabama, 249
Fort Sheridan, Illinois, 240
Fort Thomas, Kentucky, 103
Fran, 280
France, 142, 143, 187, 241
Frank's Service Station, 27
Franke, Anna, 181
Franke, Wilhelm, 181
Frankfort, Kentucky, 347, 365
From Fedala to Berchtesgaden: A History of the Seventh United States Infantry, 375
FSLIC, 339

G

G-1(Personnel Officer), 263
G-3, 269
Gaines, Cadet Sgt., 81
Garcia, _____, 364
Garcia, Cherry, 364
Garcia, Jessica, 364
Garcia, Steve, 364
Gardner, Vola, 46
Garmish, Germany, 311
Gary, Indiana, 40
Gay, Brigadier General Hobart, 118, 119
General Officer, 306, 315
General Officers Branch, 319
General Services Administration, National Archives and Records Service, 203
General, 312
Georgetown College, 62
German railway guns, 174
German Regiment, 150
Germany Political Map, 192
Germany, 312, 314
Germany, Asbach, Neuseesen, Sickenberg, Vatterode, Weidenbach, Werleshausen, 182
Gettys, Major General Charles, 262, 264
Gibraltar, 109, 110, 166
Gilmore, Doctor, 152
Girdler, Doug, 364
Girdler, Shelly, 364
Glenda, 5, 62, 73, 104, 105, 106, 107, 310, 311 344, 345, 346, 349, 350, 351, 352, 353, 354, 356, 370
Glenn, John, 241
Goldstein, Robert E., 337
Goldwater, Senator Barry, 339

Good Samaritan Hospice, 352
Good Samaritan Hospital, 38, 60
Goodyear, 241
Gorbachev, 345
Gragg, Mrs. Viola, 14, 15
Graham, Reverend Billy, 321
Grant, Dave, 247
Grant, Heidi, 247
Grant, Kenny, 247
Great Crusade, 171
Greenbrier Resort, 346
Greene, Fred, 46
Gregory, Anna, 365
Gregory, Christy, 365
Gregory, David, 365
Gregory, Edna M., 365
Gregory, Janie, 365
Gregory, Josh, 365
Gregory, Laura, 365
Gregory, Mary, 365
Gregory, Starling S., 32, 104, 125, 365
Gregory, Stoney, 365
Gregory, Thomas, 365
Guard Major General, 200
Gulf gas, 27
Gulf Refining Company, 12, 35

H

Hague, Lou R., 241, 253
Hague, Re, 253
Hall of Distinguished Alumni, 245, 248, 257
Ham, Elmer, 11
Ham, Jennie Vic Barnett, 11
Hamilton, Jack, 46
Hammamett, Tunisia, 114
Harding – Cox election, 14
Harker, Lieutenant, 290
Harn, John E., II, 337
Harrell, Colonel Ben, 150, 210
Harrell, Lieutenant General Ben, 242, 243
Harris, Eric, 348
Harrison, John E., 337, 338, 339
Harrodsburg, Kentucky, 78
Harvard vs. Centre College, 13, 26
Harvard, 13, 14, 26, 240
Hauptmann, Bruno Richard, 34
Hawaii, 261, 262
Hawk Hill Firebase, 300
Hawk Hill, 301
Hay, Major, 163
Hayes, Thelma, 54
Headquarters of the 34th Infantry Division, 109
Headquarters Special Troops, U.S. Army

Training Center, Ft. Leonard Wood, Missouri, 255
Headquarters Third Division U.S. Army, Headquarters, U.S. Army, Vietnam, (USARV), 261
Heaton, Bernell, 46, 48
Hecker, Warren, 349
Heinkebein, Sherman, 58, 59
Heintges, Colonel John A., 153, 159, 160, 161, 163, 180
Heintges, Lt. Col. John A., 153
Heiser, Major General Joseph, 261
Hershey, General, 239
Hickey, Cadet Sgt., 81
Hicks, 49
Hiep Duc, Refugee Center, 266
high school awards, 39
high school band, 33
high school, 29
Hill, D.L., 104
Hillenmeyer, Henry, 63, 78, 91
Hinckley, John W., Jr., 339
Hiroshima, 165
History of the Third Infantry Division in World War II, 375
History of the Third Infantry Division, 164
Hitt, Captain Johnnie B., 299
hole in one (third), 348
Homespun "Scrapbook", 34
Homespun, 375
Hope, Bob, 269, 270, 287, 288, 290
Hotel San Vittoria, 137
House Judiciary Committee, 314
Houssen, 155
Howze, Colonel Hamilton H., 216, 217, 229
Howze, Mary, 217
Hull, General John E., 226
Hunt, E. Howard Jr., 313
Hunter, 49
Hunter, Allan, 339
Hunter, Brother, 40, 41

I

I AM THE INFANTRY, 220
I Corps, 308
IBM, 241
ice card, 24
III MAF (III Marine Amphibious Force), 262
Inaugural Committee, 251, 252
Indian gas, 27
Indiana, University of, 13, 39
Infantry Officers Communications Course, 104
Infantry School Troop Command, 232, 234
Integrity of Nonappropriated Fund Activities, 311
Iraq, 345
Ireland, 108
Iron Curtain, 219
Israel, 314
Italy surrenders, 120
Izenour, Colonel Frank, 136, 138
Izenour, Lt. Colonel Frank M., 133

J

Jackson, John B., 241
Jackson, Putsie & John, 253
James, Major Tommie P., 299, 301, 302, 303, 304, 305
Japan, 165, 223, 224, 237, 308
Jasper, Bill, 348, 364, 366
Jasper, Bruce, 364, 366
Jasper, Joanne Ramsey, 347, 348, 364, 366, 367
Jasper, Julie, 364
Jasper, Katie, 364, 366
Jasper, Linda, 364, 366
Jasper, Lloyd, 364, 366
Jasper, Matthew, 364, 366
Jennifer, 373
Jennings, General, 316
Jessa, 373
JO JO, 32, 44
Johnson, Charles W., 337
Johnson, Col. GSC Charles E., 180, 181, 182, 183, 184, 185, 186, 189, 201, 206, 268, 212,
Johnson, General, 269
Johnson, Lyndon Baines (L. B.), 238, 251
Johnson, Major Gen. Charles E., 206, 268,
Johnson, Senator Lyndon B., 3, 238, 240
Joint Rescue Command and Control (JRCC), 302
Jolly Green, 299, 305
Joyce, Private First Class James P., 146
Judge Advocate General (JAG), 315
Judi, 310, 346, 348, 350, 351, 352, 353, 369, 370, 373

K

Kalkhof, 181, 203, 209
Kasserine Pass, Battle, 110, 112
Kasserine, 111, 134
Kautz, Faun, 253
Kautz, Norman (Norm) J., 241, 253
KAZAN, 30, 31, 32
KDKA, 14
Keeler, Corporal Harvey R., 138, 156, 166
Keith, 353, 373

Kennedy, John Fitzgerald, 251
Kennedy, President John F., 240, 242, 343
Kennedy, Senator Jack, 3, 238, 240
Kenny, 247
Kentuckian, 375
Kentucky Hotel, 117
Kentucky Law School, University of, 38
Kentucky, University of, 3, 38, 57, 58, 61, 62, 73, 76, 91, 97, 103, 245, 248, 249, 320, 347, 375
Kentucky, University of, Football Team, 76
Kesselring, Field Marshal Albert, 163
Key, Francis Scott, 21
Kiebold, Dylan, 348
King 4, 305
King 6, 305
King George VI, 3, 115, 128
King, Lieut. Colonel Dick A., 187, 188
King, Martin Luther Jr., 242, 249, 254
Kirwin, Ab, 62, 63, 79
Kirwin, Coach, 64
Kiser, Ed, 46
Koelle, Major, 163
Korea, 216, 220, 223, 235, 238
Koster, Major Gen. S. W., 272
Kret, Captain, 157
Kroesen, General Frederich J., 131, 375
Kuwait City, 345
Kuwait, 345
Kyle, 346, 351

L

Laika, 235
Lake City, Florida, 104
Lake Cumberland (Kentucky), 347, 364, 366
Lam, Lieutenant General Hoan Xuan, 307
Lamar Plain, 265
Lambda Lambda, Chapter of Sigma Chi, 38, 101
Lamp and Cross – Senior Honorary for Men, 66, 86
Lancaster, Kentucky, 39
Landing Zone Center, 266
Landing Zone West, 266
Landmark Inn, 367
Lanier, WO2 Carrol V., 298, 322
Larry, 346, 350, 351, 352, 353, 370, 373
Lawrence, Cadet Sgt., 81
Lawrenceburg, Kentucky, 345
Le Havre, France, 188
Leavell, Ullin W., 72, 100
LeClerc, Maj. General, 161, 162
Legion of Merit, 250
Legislative Liaison, 238, 240, 242

Legislative Liaison, Department of the Army, the Pentagon, Washington, D.C., 238, 242
Lemnitzer, Brigadier General Lyman L., 113, 120, 121, 122, 226, 228
Lethbridge, Francis D. (Don), 341, 343
Letter of Communication, 229
Lewis Gale Hospital, 351
Lewis, Jack, 91
Lexington *Herald-Leader*, 375
Lexington, Kentucky, 33, 38, 58, 61, 63, 117, 375
Liddy, G. Gordon, 313
Liggan, J. Calvin, 5
Lima, Ohio, 298
Lincoln Memorial, 242, 254
Lindbergh, Captain Charles, A., 16, 34
Lipscomb, Major General Thomas H., 246
Littleton, Colorado, 348
livery stable, 27
Lloyd Ann, 30, 117, 150, 151, 189, 190, 346, 351, 352, 353, 370, 373
Lofton, Cecelia, 350
London, England, 108
Longsworth, Ralph, 30
Longwood, Florida, 36
Lorraine Motel, 249
Los Angeles, 40
Louisville, Kentucky, 62
Lowhorn, J.E., 15
Ly Ly River, 276
LZ Fat City, 302
LZ Pineapple, 303

M

Mabry, Major Gen. George L. Jr., 268, 286
MacArthur, General Douglas, 165
MacCrate, Robert (Bob), 272, 273, 274
MacLean, Colonel Angus B., USA Retired, 341, 343, 360
MACV, 306
Maggie, 373
Magruder, Lieutenant General Carter B., 226, 227, 237
Maison Blanc, 109
Mam Maw, 212
Mamma, 151, 344
Manes, Mark, 348
Maniscalco, Richard, 343, 344
Manual High School, 59, 62
Marcia, 345
Marine Division Commander, 262
Marines in Vietnam: Vietnamization and Redeployment, 1970-1971, 375

Marines, 276, 277
Marne Division, 359
Marquis' *Who's Who in America,* 164
Marshall Plan, 213
Marshall, General George C., 213
Mary Elizabeth, 344
Maryland, 338
Mason, (Aunt) Edna, 345, 373
Mason, Starling, 345
Massey, Minnie, 25
Matt, 11
Matz, Timothy B., 337
Maxwell, Robert D., 146, 147
McAlister, Joseph M., 340
McCall, Cyril F., 146
McClean, Marshall C., 337
McClure, Albert, 46
McCord, James W., Jr., 313
McGarr, Col. Lionel C., 153, 180
McGraw, Dale L., 359
McLean Savings and Loan, 315, 337, 338
McLean, Virginia, 238, 306, 311, 315, 346
McMillin, Bo, 13
McVeigh, Timothy J., 347
McVey, Dr. Frank L., President, University of Kentucky, 71
Medal of Honor, 144, 155, 248, 269
Medina, Captain Ernest L., 272
Mediterranean Sea, 109, 115
Member of the British Empire, 122
Memorial Committee, 360
Memorial Day Ceremony, 185
Memphis, Tennessee, 249
Messina, Sicily, 120
Metzger, Evelyn P., 337
Meurthe Stunt, 153
Meuse-Argonne Offensive, 178
Mexico City, 178
Middle East, 112
Mike, 185
_____, Mikki, 366
Mildren, Army Commander Lieutenant General Frank, 261, 268
Military Armistice Commission, 220
Military Assistance Command, Vietnam (MACV), 267
Military Field Day and ROTC Graduation Exercises, 70, 97, 98, 99
Miller Loop, 190
Miller, Robert, 161
Milloy, Maj. General A. E., 307, 328, 170, 236, 340, 344
Mimi, 9, 11, 12, 13, 15, 19, 20, 26, 31, 35, 38, 40, 107, 127, 139, 151, 168,
Mitchell, SP4 Dalane A., 322
Model T Ford, 31, 36
Montelimar, France, 145, 174, 175
Montgomery, General (Sir Bernard), 3, 113, 114, 116, 118, 120
Moore, (Sally) Mason, 365
Moore, Bill, 365
Moore, Major General H. G., 332
Moore, Trey, 365
Morel, Paul, 241, 253
Morel, Paul, Mrs., 253
Mosely, Frank, 57, 68, 79
Murphy, 49
Murphy, Cecil, 46
Murphy, Ray, 299
Murphy, Specialist 4th Class, 298, 300
Murray, Lieutenant Colonel Terrence P., 375
Muskogee, Oklahoma, 178
My Lai, 272, 273
My Lai Inquiry, 274
Myers, Gene, 79

N

Nagasaki, 165
Naive, Delia Barnett, 40
Naples, Italy, 137, 141, 142
Nashville, Tennessee, 375
National Audubon Society, President, 39
National D-Day Museum, 172
Navy, 143
New Haven, Connecticut, 189
New Orleans, Louisiana, 178
New York Port of Embarkation, 188
New York, 16, 272
New Yorker Hotel, 151
NFL, 13
Nice-Cannes, France, 185
Nichols, Terry L., 348
Nickerson, General, 262, 263, 276, 277
Nickerson, Lieutenant General Herman (U.S. Marine Corps.), 262
Ninnie, Aunt (Jennie Vic), 11
Ninth Infantry Division, 103
Nixon, Pat, 238
Nixon, President, 313, 314
Nixon, Richard, 238, 239
Nixon, Vice President Richard, 3, 240
Noel, 49
Noel, Lytt, 46
Nok, Major General Choi Kwang, 235, 236
North Africa, 108, 110, 112, 114, 115
North Korea, 220
North Vietnam, 279

Northern Virginia Community Foundation, 339
Northwest African Tactical Air Force, 114
Nui Chom, 266

O

O'Brien, John A., 286
O'Daniel, General, 149, 150, 160, 161, 162, 180, 211, 212
O'Daniel, Major Gen. "Iron Mike", 149, 186, 210
O'Mohundro, Colonel, 136, 137
Oak Leaf Cluster, 307
Oakey, John M. & Son, Funeral Home, 352, 372
Obersalzburg, 163, 176, 177
Oklahoma City, Oklahoma, 347
Oliver, Captain Luis A. (Doctor), 303, 304, 305
Olympic Village, 314
Omicron Delta Kappa, 67, 89, 90
Operation Desert Storm, 345
Operation Russell Beach, 265
Orlando, Florida, 36
Oswald, Lee Harvey, 243
Outpost 7, 354

P

Pa, 12
Pacific Ocean, 165
Palermo, 118
Palmer, General Bruce, 310
Pam, 346
Pappap, 151, 212, 311
Paris, France, 16, 238
Parkinson's disease, 356
Parks, Sergeant Douglas, 244, 245, 309
Parmley, Hershell, 54
Partridge, Major General R. C., 219
Paschenko, Guard Lt. Col., 184, 201
Patton, General George S., 3, 113, 116, 118, 120
Patton's, General, Seventh Army, 120
Pearl Harbor Day, 106
Pearl Harbor, Hawaii, 106, 165
Peers, General, 272, 273, 274
Peers, Lieutenant General William R., 272
Pennsylvania University, 38, 39
Pentagon Officers Athletic Club (POAC), 266
Pentagon, 210, 216, 232, 238, 248, 261, 306, 312, 321
Perishing Heights, 223
Perkins, Sergeant, 70
Permanent Disability Retirement, 318

Pershing Rifles drill team, 65
Persian Gulf Crisis, 345
Peterson, Aunt Estelle, 40
Peterson, Uncle Olaf, 19
Petruzel, Captain Frank, 137, 138, 168
Petruzel, Colonel Frank, 349
Phelps, Betty, 54
Philadelphia, 13
Philippines, 178
Phillips, Brigadier General Eugene, U.S. Ret., 341, 342, 360
Pike, Warrant Two Stephen C., 300
"Pineapple Forest", 274
Pittsburgh, Pennsylvania, 14
Points, 187
Ponte Rotto, 135, 136
Pop Warner's All-American team, 13
Potter, M.E., 69, 95
Powell, Brigadier Gen. Edwin Jr., 268, 271
Powell, General Colin L. USA (RET), 282, 345
Powell, Major Colin, 3, 263
Pozzuoli, France, 142
Pratt, Lieut. Col. Sherman W., U. S. Ret., 158, 159, 375
Prescott, Donald E., 5
Promotion to Captain, 107
Promotion to Lieutenant Colonel, 141
Promotion to Major, 107
Province Balfour Award, 72
Provinces of Quang Ngai, Quang Tin, part of Quang Nam, 263
Provisional Military Assistance Advisory Group Korea, 235
Provost Marshal General (of the Army), 245, 309, 310, 312, 317
Provost Marshal General, 312
Pulaski County, Kentucky, 340
Purdom, Chris, 39, 52

Q

Quang Ngai City, 265
Quang Ngai Province, 272
Quang Tin Province, 275
Que Son, 266, 276

R

R & R, 268
R. R. Donnelly Publishing Company, 241
R.O.T.C Graduation Exercises, 97, 98, 99
Ralph, Adjutant General Lieutenant Colonel James A. Jr., 268
Ramsey house, 23
Ramsey Reunion, 347, 348, 364, 366, 367

Ramsey, 49
Ramsey, Aunt Della, 18
Ramsey, Barbara, 364, 366
Ramsey, Bill, 11, 364, 366, 367
Ramsey, Bill (Jr.), 12, 17, 151, 263, 344, 348, 366
Ramsey, Bill III, 347
Ramsey, Brigadier General Lloyd B., 255
Ramsey, Cadet Colonel Lloyd Brinkley, 70, 71, 81, 83
Ramsey, Captain Lloyd, 91
Ramsey, Chris, 364, 366
Ramsey, Cindy, 364
Ramsey, Col. and Mrs. Lloyd B., 252
Ramsey, Col. GSC Lloyd B., 184, 201
Ramsey, Colonel, 154, 156, 279
Ramsey, David, 364
Ramsey, Dick, 14
Ramsey, Eula, 344, 346
Ramsey, Feller, 9, 15, 19, 20, 43, 93, 127, 364, 365, 366
Ramsey, Gen. Lloyd, 322
Ramsey, General, 3, 4, 47, 247, 274, 284, 300, 305, 316, 317, 328
Ramsey, Glenda & Feller, 253
Ramsey, Glenda B. (Burton), 117, 212, 213, 214, 215, 222, 223, 224, 228, 237, 238, 240, 244, 247, 248, 249, 250, 306, 307, 308, 310, 311, 344, 345, 346, 349, 367, 371
Ramsey, Glenda, 364, 365, 366
Ramsey, Grandma, 14
Ramsey, Grandpa, 14, 18
Ramsey, Greg, 364, 366
Ramsey, James, B. (Jim), 356
Ramsey, Jim, 12, 17, 18, 19, 20, 40, 59, 60, 151, 344, 364, 366,
Ramsey, Jimmy (Jimmie), 364, 366
Ramsey, Judi, 30, 214, 215, 224, 237, 238, 244, 248, 250, 306, 308, 310, 346, 348, 350
Ramsey, Judy Carol, 214
Ramsey, Kathy, 366
Ramsey, Larry B. (Burton), 213, 215, 224, 364, 365, 366, 367
Ramsey, Lieut. Lloyd B., 101, 229
Ramsey, Lieutenant Colonel Lloyd B., 144, 146, 147, 179, 184, 201, 229
Ramsey, Lloyd (B.), 9, 45, 46, 47, 48, 49, 52, 53, 54, 63, 69, 76, 78, 79, 80, 84, 85, 86, 87, 89, 90, 91, 92, 93, 94, 95, 96, 100, 144, 153, 155, 157, 158, 159, 211, 217, 241, 267, 285, 328, 332, 333, 334, 335, 367
Ramsey, Lloyd Ann, 117, 224, 238, 306, 346
Ramsey, Logan, 366
Ramsey, Maj. Gen. Lloyd B., 3, 207, 275, 276, 284, 298, 299, 322, 329
Ramsey, Maj. Lloyd B. 3d Battalion Commander, 179
Ramsey, Maj. Lloyd B., 135, 140
Ramsey, Major General Lloyd B., 318, 332, 335, 337, 341
Ramsey, Major General Lloyd B., U.S. Retired, 360
Ramsey, Major Lloyd, 128
Ramsey, Mary E. (Ella) (Barnett), 9, 125, 364, 366
Ramsey, Mr. and Mrs. W. H., 101
Ramsey, Mrs., 247, 355
Ramsey, Pam, 346
Ramsey, Phyllis, 364, 366
Ramsey, Ray, 18
Ramsey, Second Lt. Lloyd Brinkley, 123
Ramsey, William Harold (Bill), 9, 125
Randall, Carl, 46
Rattler, 3, 6, 302, 304, 305
Ray, James Earl, 249
Reagan, President, 339, 345
Red Battalion, 133, 134
Red Beach, 143
Red, 13
Reed, Walter, 308
Regimental Executive Officer, 179
Reid, Clyda, 29
Reid, Ray, 29
Reid, Walter, 91
Rescue of a Downed General, 304
Rescue of Saber 6, 305
retirement, 337
Rhee, President, 237
Rhine River, 152
Rhinhardshousen, Germany, 180
Rhodes Scholar, 58
Rhone Canal, 157
Rhone River, 145
Richardson, Maj. Gen., 113
Richfield Retirement Community, 350
Richmond, Kentucky, 58
Riddell, Gene, 91
Rio Grande, 178
Ritter, Charles, 46, 48
Roanoke, Virginia, 307, 350
"Rock of the Marne", 361
Robards, Cadet Sgt., 81
Roberts, Frank B., 63, 78, 91

Roberts, James "Red," 13
Robinson, Alvin F., 337
Rock of the Marne, 361
Rockcastle County, Kentucky, 19
Rodriguez, William, 138, 139
Rogers, Lt. Col. Glenn F., 153
Rome, 142, 185, 277
Roosevelt, President, 21, 38
Rose Bowl, 40
Rossen, Bill, 267, 307
Rossen, General, 307
Rosson, (Rossen) General William B., 184, 307
Rosson, General William B., 222, 267, 343
Rosson, General William B., U.S. Army Retired, 359
Rosson, Lieut. Colonel, William B., 180, 183, 184
Rotary Club Trophy, 70
Rotary Club, 16
ROTC Cadet Corps., 3
ROTC, 63, 64, 68, 70, 71
Rouse, Cadet Lt. Colonel L. T., 81
Ruby, Earl, 14
Ruffing, Capt. Thomas J., 322
Rupert, Joe, 79
Rushe, R. Robert, 337
Russell Building, 238
Russell County, Kentucky, 18
Russell, Senator Richard, 239, 243
Russia, 242
Russian zone, 181, 182, 183

S

Saalach River, 159, 160, 161
Saber 6, 302
Saddam Hussein, 345
Saigon, Vietnam, 261, 264, 269, 270
Salem, Virginia, 350, 352, 370
Salerno, 120
Salisbury, North Carolina, 106
Salzburg, Austria, 159, 163, 164, 180
San Francisco, 286
San Juan Heights, 178
Sano, Sergeant Stephen, 305
_____, Sarah, 366
Saunders, Mrs. Amelia, 14
Savings and Loan, 339
Scabbard and Blade, National Honorary Military Organization, 65, 66, 82
Scarlet Fever, 22
Schmidt, Major Gen. William R., 186
Schoeningh, Sonderfuehrer, 163
Schroeder, Captain Gerald A., 315
Schwarzkopf, Colonel Norman H., 268, 269, 303, 304
Schwarzkopf, General Norman H., 303, 345
Schwarzkopf, Norman, 3
Scott, Cadet Lt. Colonel R. T., 81
Scott, James 91
Scudder, Major Irvine, 70
Sears and Roebuck catalogue, 6
Seattle, Washington, 223
Second Battalion, 134
Second Distinguished Service Medal, 319
Secretaries of the Military Departments, Directors of the Defense Agencies, 330
Secretary of the Army, 39, 243, 312
Secretary of the Joint Staff, 226, 227, 237
Seeman, Major General Lyle E., 244, 246
Seeman, Mrs. Lyle, 244
Senate Office Building, 238, 239
Senate Select Committee on Presidential Campaign Activities, 314
Senior Army Liaison Officer, 238, 242
Senior Army Officer, 238
Sergeant Fields, 234
Sergeant, 271
Seventh Army, 116, 119, 120
Seventh Infantry (troops), 145, 149
Seventh Infantry History, 133, 152
Sexton, Brigadier General W. T., 180, 200, 201
Sexton, General, 182, 183, 184
Sexton, Major General William Thaddeus, 205
Sharma, Dr. R., 351
Sharp, Colonel Frederick D., 219
Shepard, Joe, 59, 62
Sherman, Colonel, 133, 135, 136
Sherman, Emily, 253
Sherman, Jerry, 253
Sherman, Oliver M. Jr., 241
Sherman, William Tecumseh, 131
Shively, Bernie, 61, 79
Shropshire, James S., 91
Shropshire, Jim, 58
Shropshire, Larry, 67, 92
Sicily Invasion, 115
Sicily, 114, 116, 118, 119
Siegfeld Follies, 38, 152
Sigma Chi Fraternity, 58, 59, 65, 72, 80, 100
Sigma Chi, 339, 340
Sigma Chi, Lambda Lambda Chapter, 38
Silver Platter, 217
Sis, 11
Skater 67, 299, 300, 301, 303, 304

Slate Branch, 31
Smith, Air Force Sergeant Jules, 305
Snake Pit, 303
Snorter bill, 117
Soblensky, Private James P., 146
Social Security Act, 38
Society of the Third Infantry Division, 359
Somerset High School Briar Jumpers, 47
Somerset High School Press, 34, 375
Somerset High School, 11, 13, 37, 38, 40
Somerset Vocational School, 11
Somerset, Kentucky, 9, 10, 11, 13, 19, 25, 27, 29, 35, 39, 40, 63, 69, 108, 117, 151, 189, 190, 191, 214, 216, 221, 223, 235, 250, 311, 344, 347, 348, 356, 367, 375
Sonny (Burton), 108, 212, 345
Sons of the American Revolution, 340
Sorrento, Italy, 136
Souk Ahras, Algeria, 110
South Fork River, 31
South Korea, 220
South Vietnam, 263
South Vietnamese, 307
Southeast Asia, 302
Southern France, 143
Southern Railroad, 11
Southwest Missouri State College, 306
Spickard, Cadet Lt. Colonel T. W., 81
Springer, Private First Class Wilbur D., 147
Springfield, Missouri, 147, 306
Sputnik I, 235
St. Tropez, 185
Stahr, Elvis, 38, 39, 58
Stanford Pike, 10, 12, 23
Star Spangled Banner (National Anthem), 21
Starling, 345
Steel Magnolias, 353
STEP (Special Training and Enlistment Program), 243
Stephenson, Letelle, 91
Strasbourg, France, 152
Student Legislature, 66, 85
Student Union Board, 66, 84
Sturm, Alex, 365
Sturm, Beth, 365
Sturm, Brady, 365
Sturm, Jamie, 365
Sturm, Larry, 365
Sueko, 225, 226
Sumien, Louis, 166
Supreme Headquarters Allied Expeditionary Force, 171
Sweeny, Cadet Major R. T., 81
Swickerath, Captain Carl, (U.S. Retired), 341, 342, 360,
swimming team, 77, 78
Syladek, Captain Frank J., 156

T

Taggart, Donald G., 375
Tam Ky, Vietnam, 265, 274, 275, 301
Tarasov, Guard Colonel, 184, 201
Tardy, Colonel Walter E., U. S. Retired, 341, 342, 360
Taylor, Ann, 213
Taylor, Demra, 40
Taylor, General Maxwell D., 226
Tedder, British Air Marshal, 164
Tennessee, University of, 62, 63
Texas, 338
The Cottonbaler, 131, 163, 178, 375
The Courier-Journal, 14
"The Occupation of Germany", 180
The Seventh Infantry History, From Fedala to Berchtesgaden, 133, 145, 148, 152
Third Army Headquarters, 245, 249, 234
Third Army Promotion, 258
Third Infantry Division Memorial, Arlington National Cemetery, 358
Third Infantry Division, 200, 201, 341, 359, 361
Thomas, Colonel Robert J., 298
Thomas, Harry, 46
Thomas, LTC, 300
Thompson, Warrant Officer Hugh, 273, 274
Throckmorton, Lieutenant General John L., 249, 250
Throckmorton, Mrs. (John), 250
Toffey, Jr., Lt. Colonel John J., 137
Tokyo Bay, 165
Tokyo, Japan, 223, 224, 228
Tomlinson, Scott, 366
Tomlinson, Shelly, 366
Toshiko, 226
TPMG, 310, 313
Training for Invasion of Southern France, 142
Travis, James E., 337
Treaties and Other International Acts Series 3081, 199
Trimble, Willard, 46
Trujillo, Captain, 302
Truman, President, 165
Truscott, General Lucian K., 142
Truscott, Maj. General, 133

"Truscott Trot," 142
Tu Cung hamlet of Son My village, 272
Tucker, Captain John P., 298, 301, 303
Tucker, John P., 48, 298
Tunis, 128
Tunisia, 114
Tunisian campaign, 113, 114
Tyler, Captain O. Z., 106
Tyler, Mrs. O. Z., 106

U

U. S. Government, 314
U. S. II Corps., 113
U. S. Marines in Vietnam, Vietnamization and Redeployment, 275, 276
U.S. News & World Report, 344
U.S. Army Center for Military History, 181
U.S. Army Disciplinary Barracks, 310
U.S. Riviera Recreation Area, 186
UN Security Counsel, 345
Union of Soviet Socialist Republics, 183, 209
United Nations Command (UNC), 223, 228, 237
United Nations, 171
United States Army in World War II, 375
United States Army, 3, 320
United States of America, 209
United States Senate, 238, 242
United States Zone, 185
United States, 308, 309
Urich, Pfc. Nick, 176, 177
USA Today, 217
USAA, 350
USAF Forward Air Controller (FAC), 302
USS Arizona, 106
USS Leadstown, 109, 110
USS Missouri, 165
USS Stone, 109

V

Vagney, France, 150
Valenti, Isadore, 5, 153, 155, 157, 158, 375
Vancouver Barracks, 178
Vanguard I, 235
Vera Cruz, 178
Vesely, Colonel, 69
Veterans Administration letter, 318
Veterans Administration, 334
Vice President (Pro Consul) of Sigma Chi Fraternity, 65
victrola, 21
Viet Cong, 274, 294
Viet-Nam, 284
Vietnam, 3, 4, 245, 250, 261, 264, 265, 272, 275, 277, 278, 279, 298, 308, 309, 310, 314, 319, 320, 345, 356
Vietnamese Commander, I Corps, 308
Vietnamese, 273
Vike, Dr. Jean, 356
Villiere's Plantation, Louisiana, 178
Vinson, Carl, 243
Vinson, Chairman, 244
Virginia, 354
Von Orloff, Major, 163
von Scharfenberg, 185
von Scharfenberg, Mr. and Mrs. W., 181
von Scharfenberg, Veleska, 182
von Scharffenberg, Mr. and Mrs. D, 203, 209
Von Weber, First Lieut., 163
Vosges Mountains, 152
Vy-Les-Lures, France, 148, 149

W

Waddle, Bob Bruce, 47
Waddle, Dick, 46
Waddle, E., 49
Waddle, Milford, 36
Waddle, N., 49
Waddle, R. B., 46
Waikiki Beach, 262
Waitsboro, Kentucky, 31
Walker, Preston L., 337
Wall of Fame, 347
Wallace, Brain D., 353, 367
Wallace, Brian, 364, 365, 366, 373
Wallace, Clayton A., 353
Wallace, Frankie, 366
Wallace, Franklyn Keith (K.) R., 353, 367
Wallace, Jennifer (R.), 366, 367, 373
Wallace, Keith R., 353, 367
Wallace, Keith, 364, 365, 366, 373
Wallace, Kyle (D.), 364, 365, 366, 367
Wallace, Lloyd Ann, 364, 365, 366, 367
Wallace, Matthew C., 353
Walter Reed Army Medical Center, 308
Walter, Pvt. Bennet A., 176, 177
Wanfried, Saxony, Germany, 181, 183
Ware, Brigadier General Keith, 248
Washington Heights, 225
Washington, 310, 316, 319, 320
Washington, D. C., 39, 68, 108, 216, 238, 245, 248, 254, 308, 310, 313, 339, 340, 341
Watergate, 313, 314
Werth, CSM Leonard J., U. S. Retired, 341, 360
West Berlin, Germany, 219, 345
West Point, 222

West Virginia University, 38
West Virginia, 346
Whall, Colonel Winston, 262
White, Nathan William (W.), 161, 375
Who's Who Among Students in American Universities and Colleges, 66, 87, 88
Wickersham, Major Dan, 186
William H., Jr. (Bill), 346
Williams, Colonel J.B., 69
Williams, Dick, 13
Williams, Virginia Elliot, 69, 70
Williamson, Maj. Gen. E. W., 4
Wilson, Amanda, 364, 366
Wilson, Richard, 364
Wilson, Susan, 364, 366
Wine, James J., 66, 72
Wine, President (Consul) James J., 65, 72
Woodlawn Park, 59
Wor Wor, 11, 20
World Book Encyclopedia, 14
World War II, 4, 39, 103, 164, 165, 262, 268, 319
Wymond, Gilbert, 91

Y
Yale University, 189, 210
Yates, Captain Ralph J., 148

Z
Zais, Lieutenant General Melvin, 307
Zolling, Colonel, 163

UNITS

101st Airborne Division Commander, 264
101st Airborne Division, 164
10th Infantry, 103
123rd Aviation Battalion, 264
141 Force Headquarters, 114, 115
14th Battalion Commander, 303
14th Combat Aviation Battalion, 264
14th Infantry Battle Group, 232
15 Army Group, 122
15th Army Group Headquarters, 114, 119
15th Infantry, 136
16th Aviation Battalion, 264
18th Army Group, 113,
196th Brigade, 131, 266, 274, 279
196th Brigade's 5th Battalion, 46th Infantry, 266
198th Brigade, 303
1st (First) Battalion, 133, 134, 135, 136,
1st Battalion, 20th Infantry, 11th Infantry
1st Battalion, 52nd Infantry, 278, 342
1st Battalion, 6th Infantry, 301
1st Battalion, 7th Infantry, Anzio, 133
1st Infantry Division, 111, 307
1st Platoon, C Company, 272
25th Panzer Division, 135
27th Surgical Hospital, 307
29th Infantry Battle Group, 232
29th Infantry, 228, 232
2d ARVN Division, 263, 265, 277
2d Battalion of O'Mohundro's 7th 2d NVA Division, 266
2nd Infantry Division, 284
30th Infantry Regiment, 150
30th Infantry, 180, 183
31st Anniversary Luncheon, 204
39th Infantry, 103, 108, 109
39th Infantry, 9th Infantry Division, 186
3d Aerospace Rescue and Recovery Group (ARRGP) (USAF), 302
3d Battalion, 140, 141, 142, 145, 148
3d Battalion, 21st Infantry, 268
3d Battalion, 7th Infantry, 145, 152
3d Division, 344
3d Infantry Division Memorial, 340, 342, 343
3d Infantry Division, 222, 262, 340, 343, 344
3rd Battalion, 109, 135, 136, 137, 140, 143, 144
3rd Battalion, 39th Infantry, 109, 110,
3rd Battalion, 7th Infantry, 135, 136, 143, 144, 176, 177
3rd Infantry Division Memorial Committee, 66
3rd Infantry Division, 121, 122, 131, 132, 180, 181
4th Battalion, 31st Infantry, 266
506th Parachute Regiment, 164
6th Infantry Battalion, 303
71st Assault Helicopter Company, 301
7th Infantry Battle Patrol, 143
7th Infantry Headquarters, 136
7th Infantry Regiment, 164, 178
7th Infantry, 135, 136, 139, 141, 143, 178
7th Marines and Americal Division, 276
7th Virginia Regiment, 340
82nd Airborne Division, 186